## To Renew Books

### PHONE (510) 253-2233 OR 254-0200 X361

# Clinical Handbook of
# Sleep Disorders in Children

# CHILD THERAPY SERIES

## A SERIES OF BOOKS EDITED BY
## CHARLES SCHAEFER

Cognitive-Behavioral Play Therapy
*Susan M. Knell*

Play Therapy in Action: A Casebook for Practitioners
*Terry Kottman and Charles Schaefer, Eds.*

Family Play Therapy
*Lois Carey and Charles Schaefer, Eds.*

The Quotable Play Therapist
*Charles Schaefer and Heidi Kaduson, Eds.*

Childhood Encopresis and Enuresis
*Charles Schaefer*

The Therapeutic Powers of Play
*Charles Schaefer, Ed.*

Play Therapy Techniques
*Donna Cangelosi and Charles Schaefer, Eds.*

Children in Residential Care: Critical Issues in Treatment
*Charles Schaefer and Arthur Swanson, Eds.*

Therapeutic Use of Child's Play
*Charles Schaefer, Ed.*

Clinical Handbook of Sleep Disorders in Children
*Charles Schaefer, Ed.*

Clinical Handbook of Anxiety Disorders in Children and Adolescents
*Andrew R. Eisen, Christopher A. Kearney, and Charles Schaefer, Eds.*

Practitioner's Guide to Treating Fear and Anxiety in Children and
Adolescents: A Cognitive-Behavioral Approach
*Andrew R. Eisen and Christopher A. Kearney*

# Clinical Handbook of
# Sleep Disorders in Children

*Edited by*
Charles E. Schaefer, Ph.D.

**JASON ARONSON INC.**
*Northvale, New Jersey*
*London*

Production Editor: Ruth E. Brody

This book was set in 10 point Goudy by TechType of Upper Saddle River, New Jersey, and printed by Haddon Craftsmen of Scranton, Pennsylvania.

**Library of Congress Cataloging-in-Publication Data**

Clinical handbook of sleep disorders in children / edited by Charles E. Schaefer.
    p.  cm. — (Child therapy series)
    Includes bibliographical references and index.
    ISBN 1-56821-324-7
    1. Sleep disorders in children. I. Schaefer, Charles E.
II. Series.
    [DNLM: 1. Sleep Disorders—in infancy & childhood. 2. Sleep
Disorders—therapy. 3. Psychotherapy—in infancy & childhood.   WM
188 C6417 1995]
RJ506.S55C55  1995
618.92'8498—dc20
DNLM/DLC
for Library of Congress             94'19702

Manufactured in the United States of America. Jason Aronson Inc. offers books and cassettes. For information and catalog write to Jason Aronson Inc., 230 Livingston Street, Northvale, New Jersey 07647.

# Contents

Contributors     vii

Preface     xi

1   Introduction to Sleep and Its Disorders     1
*Jamie Whyte and Charles Schaefer*

2   Sleep and Sudden Infant Death Syndrome     15
*Anne Christake Cornwell*

3   Infant Night Waking     49
*Sheila A. Spasaro and Charles E. Schaefer*

4   The Treatment of Nighttime Fears:
A Cognitive-Developmental Approach     69
*Kevin C. Mooney and Michael Sobocinski*

5   A Developmental Approach to Sleep Problems
in Toddlers     103
*Joyce Hopkins, Crystal Isaacs, and Paula Pitterle*

6   Night Terrors                                                      125
    Bryan Lask


7   Sleepwalking in Children and Adolescents                           135
    Kaan R. Özbayrak and Richard M. Berlin


8   Treating Nightmares in Children                                    149
    Gordon Halliday


9   Childhood Insomnia                                                 177
    Mark J. Chambers


10  Nocturnal Bruxism in Children                                      203
    Kenneth R. Lofland, Jeffrey E. Cassisi, and
    Ronald S. Drabman


11  Childhood Enuresis                                                 223
    Deborah R. Barclay and Arthur C. Houts


12  Managing the Child with Obstructive Sleep Apnea                    253
    Sandra Palasti and William P. Potsic


13  Narcolepsy in Children                                             267
    Vincent P. Gibbons and Suresh Kotagal


14  The Relationship of Sleep Disturbances to Childhood
    Panic Disorder                                                     285
    E. Jane Garland


15  Treatment of Multiple Sleep Disorders in Children                  311
    V. Mark Durand, Jodi Mindell, Ellen Mapstone,
    and Peter Gernert-Dott


Index                                                                  335

# Contributors

**Deborah R. Barclay, Ph.D.**
Postdoctoral Fellow, St. Jude Children's Research Hospital, Memphis, Tennessee.

**Richard M. Berlin, M.D.**
Director, Sleep Disorders Program, Berkshire Medical Center, and Associate Professor of Psychiatry, University of Massachusetts Medical School at Berkshire Medical Center, Pittsfield, Massachusetts.

**Jeffrey E. Cassisi, Ph.D.**
Assistant Professor, Illinois Institute of Technology, Chicago, Illinois.

**Mark J. Chambers, Ph.D.**
Clinical Director, The Sleep Clinic of Nevada, Las Vegas, Nevada.

**Anne Christake Cornwell, Ph.D.**
Associate Professor of Pediatrics, Albert Einstein College of Medicine and Director, SIDS Project.

**Ronald S. Drabman, Ph.D., A.B.P.P.**
Professor, The University of Mississippi Medical Center, Jackson, Mississippi.

## V. Mark Durand, Ph.D.

Associate Professor of Psychology, University at Albany, State University of New York, Albany, New York.

## E. Jane Garland, M.D. F.R.C.P.(C)

Clinical Assistant Professor, University of British Columbia, Director, Child and Adolescent Mood Disorder Clinic, University Hospital - UBC Site.

## Peter Gernert-Dott

Doctoral Fellow in Psychology, The University at Albany, State University of New York.

## Vincent P. Gibbons, M.D.

Assistant Professor, Department of Neurology, St. Louis University Health Sciences Center, St. Louis, Missouri.

## Gordon Halliday, Ph.D.

Psychologist, The Center for Individual and Family Services, Mansfield, Ohio.

## Joyce Hopkins, Ph.D.

Associate Professor of Psychology, Illinois Institute of Technology, Chicago, Illinois.

## Arthur C. Houts, Ph.D.

Professor and Director of Clinical Training, The University of Memphis, Memphis, Tennessee.

## Crystal Isaacs, M.A.

Doctoral fellow, Illinois Institute of Technology, Chicago, Illinois.

## Suresh Kotagal, M.D.

Professor, Department of Neurology, St. Louis University Health Sciences Center, St. Louis, Missouri.

## Bryan Lask, M.D.

Consultant Psychiatrist, The Hospitals for Sick Children, London, England.

## Kenneth R. Lofland, Ph.D.

Clinical Director, Headache Program, The Pain and Rehabilitation Clinic of Chicago, Chicago, Illinois.

**Eileen Mapstone**
Doctoral Fellow in Psychology, The University of Albany, State University of New York.

**Jodi Mindell, Ph.D.**
Psychology Department, St. Joseph's University, Philadelphia, Pennsylvania.

**Kevin C. Mooney, Ph.D.**
Human Relations Center, Valparaiso, Indiana.

**Kaan R. Ozbayrak, M.D.**
Associate Director, Sleep Disorders Program, Berkshire Medical Center, Pittsfield, Massachusetts.

**Sandra Palasti, M.D.**
Lecturer, Pediatric Otolaryngology and Human Communication, The Children's Hospital of Philadelphia, Department of Otorhinolaryngology: Head and Neck Surgery, University of Pennsylvania School of Medicine.

**Paula Pitterle**
Doctoral Fellow, Illinois Institute of Technology, Chicago, Illinois.

**William P. Potsic, M.D.**
Director of Pediatric Otolaryngology and Human Communication, The Children's Hospital of Philadelphia; Professor of Otorhinolaryngology: Head and Neck Surgery, University of Pennsylvania School of Medicine.

**Charles E. Schaefer, Ph.D.**
Professor of Psychology, Director, Better Sleep Center, Fairleigh Dickinson University, Teaneck, New Jersey.

**Michael Sobocinski, Ph.D.**
The Denver Children's Home, Denver, Colorado.

**Sheila A. Spasaro**
Doctoral Fellow, Clinical Psychology, Fairleigh Dickinson University, Teaneck, New Jersey.

**Jamie Whyte, M.D.**
Associate Director, Sleep Pathology Lab, Columbia Presbyterian Medical Center, New York, New York.

# Preface

Sleep disturbances are among the most commonly reported behavior problems in young children and children seen in mental health clinics. Disturbed sleep in children is a cause of serious concern for two main reasons. First, a strong association has been found between nighttime problems and daytime behavior difficulties for the child, and second, a disruptive sleep pattern in the child places enormous stress on the family.

Since childhood sleep problems tend to persist for many years, the development of successful and practical techniques for treating these problems is essential. In the past thirty years there has been an upsurge of interest and research in the area of childhood sleep disorders. The resulting knowledge has made it possible for professionals to understand the etiology of most of these disorders and intervene with eclectic treatments. Unfortunately, it is difficult for child mental health professionals to keep abreast of the recent developments in the field. Consequently, numerous sleep problems such as an infant night waking, sleep terrors, apnea, and narcolepsy go undiagnosed and untreated in children.

The purpose of this handbook is to bring together in one volume the latest refinements in the diagnosis and treatment of sleep difficulties in children. Rather than focusing on research details, the book seeks to bring practical knowledge to the attention of clinicians who are actively treating children. To this end, the chapters discuss the incidence, clinical presentation, diagnostic features, differential diagnosis, and state-of-the-art treatment techniques for the most common sleep disorders in children. This book should be of interest to professionals (and students) in the fields of psychiatry, psychology, pediatrics, social work, and counseling.

Charles E. Schaefer, Ph. D.

October, 1994

# 1

# Introduction to Sleep and Its Disorders

Jamie Whyte
Charles Schaefer

Disorders of sleep and arousal are common clinical problems throughout childhood. These disorders can have a serious adverse effect on both the child's and family's physical health and/or psychological functioning. Only recently has the importance of normal sleep and arousal in the daily lives of children and adults become recognized by mental health professionals and the general public.

Many of the advances in the diagnosis and treatment of sleep disorders have been due to the establishment of sleep centers across the country. The Association of Sleep Disorders Center (ASDC) was organized in 1976 to set standards for certification of all aspects of a sleep disorders center, including research and practice.

## Physiology of Sleep

Dr. Nathaniel Kleitman and his colleagues (Aserinsky and Kleitman 1953) at the University of Chicago were the first to study eye movements of sleeping subjects and thus discovered two separate sleep states: REM and NREM. REM (rapid eye movement) sleep is linked with dreaming, while NREM (non-rapid eye movement) sleep is a deeper sleep state. NREM is further subdivided into four sleep stages of progressively deeper (nonarousable) sleep, each clearly recognizable by its distinct brain wave pattern.

Stages of sleep and wakefulness can be operationalized by exclusive reference to polysomnographic criteria derived from the electroencephalogram (EEG), electromyogram (EMG), and electrooculogram (EOG). Formal criteria for defining sleep and wakefulness and differentiating among the various sleep stages have been developed by Rechtshaffen and Kales (1968). These criteria form the basis for virtually all research and clinical work with human subjects.

The awake subject has an EEG dominated by high frequency, low amplitude brain waves. When the eyes are closed there is a predominant alpha rhythm (8–12 Hz) in the EEG, most prominent occipitally. In either case, muscle tone is elevated and eye movements are voluntary and sharp.

Stage 1 (NREM) sleep is a transitional state, generally serving as a bridge between wakefulness and sleep. Intervals of stage 1 in excess of 5 minutes' duration are unusual. Stage 1 has characteristics intermediate between sleep and wakefulness and is considered by some not to represent true sleep. The shift from wakefulness to stage 1 is marked by a shift in the EEG to a lower-voltage, mixed frequency pattern and the occurrence of slow, rolling, involuntary eye movements. Muscle tone in stage 1 is slightly reduced compared with wakefulness.

Stage 2 (NREM) sleep is defined by an EEG with a background rhythm of theta waves (4–7 Hz) upon which are superimposed phasic elements termed sleep spindles and K-complexes. Sleep spindles are bursts of EEG activity in the range of 14–16 Hz lasting for 0.5 to 1.5 seconds. In a typical individual they may occur several times each minute. K-complexes are isolated, high amplitude, biphasic waves with an initial negative component. The K-complex often has a tail consisting of a full or incipient sleep spindle. The eyes are quiescent and muscle tone is further reduced.

Stages 3 and 4 (NREM) sleep are characterized by delta waves—a high amplitude, low frequency (0.5–3.0 Hz) EEG—in which the phasic elements of stage 2 are sparse or absent. Stages 3 and 4 differ only in the number of slow waves present and are often considered together under the rubric of *delta sleep*. Stage 3 is present when delta activity occupies 20–50% of an epoch, while stage 4 is present when delta activity exceeds 50%. Eye movements are rare and muscle tone is low.

REM sleep is a paradoxical state that in some ways more closely resembles wakefulness than the non-REM sleep stages. The EEG is of

low voltage and mixed frequency and may contain a characteristic saw-tooth pattern. The brain is highly active during REM sleep, as evidenced by the dreaming that is specific to this stage. Eye movements, the defining feature of this stage, are rapid, conjugate, and sharp. Tone of the skeletal muscles is actively suppressed. This condition is referred to as postural atonia and is presumed to be a mechanism to prevent the occurrence of manifest dream enactment. During REM sleep, autonomic lability is typically noted. Fluctuations in sympathetic and parasympathetic tone occur and may be important in the genesis of cardiac ectopy, arrhythmias, and ischemic events.

During the night, the sleeping individual proceeds through each of these stages, usually starting with stage 1 until stage 4 is reached. The person then starts to ascend into progressively lighter sleep, first with stage 3, then stage 2, and back again to stage 1 NREM sleep. This NREM sleep course is then followed by the first REM or *active* sleep state. The time from the first stage of NREM sleep through the first REM period is termed the first *sleep cycle*. The duration of this cycle is usually 90 minutes for adults, but this ultradian rhythm is only 50 minutes for infants. NREM and REM sleep states proceed to alternate during the night, which results in at least five complete cycles.

## Classification

A diagnostic classification of sleep and arousal disorders was first published in 1979 by the ASDC. This widely accepted nosology contains four broad categories of sleep disorders: disorders of initiating and maintaining sleep (DIMS) such as insomnia, disorders of excessive somnolence (DOES) such as sleep apnea or narcolepsy, disorders of the sleep/wake schedule (SWSD) such as delayed phase syndrome, and dysfunctions associated with sleep stages or partial arousals – parasomnias such as night terrors or sleepwalking. These categories are more or less applicable to children who have reached school age and must comply to society's time schedules. A brief description of some of the over sixty known sleep disorders follows.

### Delayed Sleep Phase Syndrome

The delayed sleep phase syndrome is a sleep/wake pattern in which the times of sleep onset and terminal awakening are later than desired, or demanded by school or work schedules, but in which the quality of sleep is normal and daytime somnolence is absent under conditions of ad libitum sleep. Thus, the typical patient cannot fall asleep before 3:00 A.M. and, when unfettered by outside demands, will sleep until noon. The distinguishing feature of phase delay is the absence of any complaint, save for the onset insomnia, when ad libitum sleep is obtainable. Clinically the presentation is usually less clear as vocational, educational, and social obligations infringe upon an unencumbered sleep/wake cycle. Under such circumstances, difficulty in early morning awakening and daytime somnolence may become major clinical complaints.

Phase delay syndrome has a somewhat uncertain etiology. An organic diathesis has been postulated in the form of a relative unresponsiveness to cues that normally entrain circadian rhythms to the 24-hour day/night cycle. A predisposition to phase delay in the blind, who are deprived of the daily changes in ambient light, supports this view. However, our experience indicates that in sighted individuals behavioral factors are invariably paramount. In adults the condition is referred to as *free lance writer's syndrome*, an epithet which emphasizes the predisposing environmental factors.

In adolescents and young adults an unwillingness or inability to maintain a regular sleep/wake schedule is the proximate cause. Individuals with supranormal sleep needs are at particular risk. Inadequate sleep may promote daytime napping, which hinders nocturnal sleep onset. The onset insomnia causes further sleep deprivation, increased napping, and an extended phase delay. Ultimately, the full phase delay syndrome develops. College students are most susceptible given the irregularity of class schedules and the newly available social freedoms.

Diagnosis of phase delay syndrome on clinical grounds is sometimes possible. Potential exacerbating factors including drug use, psychiatric problems, and psychosocial stressors should always receive careful attention. The role of the sleep specialist in evaluating suspected phase delay syndrome is variable. When the diagnosis is uncertain, testing with polysomnography will often clarify the situation. The testing protocol should designate an early bedtime to document the phase delay in sleep onset. Ad libitum sleep should be permitted in the morning to ensure that sleep deprivation is not a confound, and one or more multiple sleep latency test naps should then be conducted. Under these conditions a long onset to sleep latency, normal nocturnal sleep, and normal latencies on Multiple Sleep Latency Test (MSLT) naps make the diagnosis certain.

Treatment of phase delay in the adolescent is behavioral. A regular sleep/wake schedule that provides adequate total sleep time is the cornerstone of management. Napping should be strongly discouraged. Of course, such a schedule is more easily recommended than accomplished. A strong effort toward motivating the patient should receive high priority. Forging a successful alliance between patient, parents, and therapist may prove decisive in securing a favorable outcome. The adjunctive use of hypnotic medication is rarely necessary or desirable in the treatment of phase delay in the adolescent.

## Sleep Apnea Syndrome

Sleep apnea is the cessation or attenuation of inspiratory airflow in sleep. Apneas are divided into subtypes of obstructive, central, and mixed (combined obstructive and central). Syndromes of central apnea are rare and, except as they may be involved in SIDS (sudden infant death syndrome, discussed elsewhere in this volume), are not of great practical interest. Mixed apneas usually are dominated by an obstructive component and are handled clinically without regard for the central element. It should be noted that not all apnea is pathological; central events in REM and at the transition from wakefulness to sleep are physiologically normal.

The formal definition of sleep apnea syndrome employs a criterion of ten events (apneas or hypoapneas) per hour of sleep. Clinically, this quasi-arbitrary threshold has utility but its limitations should not be overlooked. Factors such as the degree of respiratory straining, the association of dysrhythmic breathing with a particular sleeping position or sleep stage, and the occurrence of sleep-disruptive snoring in the absence of frank apneas and hypoapneas are clinically important. Overreliance on formal criteria poses a particular hazard in children as the daytime sequelae of minor sleep-related breathing abnormalities can be marked in the pediatric population. The ensuing discussion uses the term sleep apnea in the broadest sense, referring to any disorder of sleep-related breathing that is of clinical significance.

The cardinal symptoms of sleep apnea are snoring and daytime somnolence. The snoring is often loud and irregular, with apneic pauses interrupted by sharp inspiratory gasps as the patient awakens and the obstruction is overcome. However, the degree to which the snoring is irregular varies and a report of smooth, sonorous snoring does not rule out apnea. Snoring must be differentiated from wheezing or stridor, which have quite different diagnostic implications.

The daytime somnolence is often unequivocal and manifested by irresistible sleepiness and unintended sleep at inappropriate times. But the presentations of daytime somnolence are Protean and may involve depression, irritability, and personality change. Children who present with behavioral or scholastic problems coupled with loud snoring should generate a high index of suspicion.

In the adult, sleep apnea is multifactorial in etiology. Upper airway morphology, body habitus, age, and gender are among the most important determinants. For the adult with apnea, a precise delineation of cause or causes is rarely undertaken and treatment is mainly contingent upon syndrome severity, the role of sleeping position and sleep stage, and patient preference. In children, conversely, the cause of sleep apnea is nearly always upper airway obstruction due to enlarged tonsils and adenoids. Craniofacial dysmorphias including Treacher-Collins syndrome and Goldenbar syndrome have also been associated with obstructive apnea.

The sleep laboratory is essential to the diagnosis of adults with possible sleep apnea but has a much more circumscribed role in pediatric cases. As enlarged tonsils and adenoids are causative in the vast majority of instances, resection of the offending tissues is generally curative. Detailed characterization of the apnea syndrome that is essential to management of adult apneics, for whom many treatment options exist, is often superfluous. When sleep apnea is suspected in a child for whom tonsillectomy and adenoidectomy are otherwise indicated, polysomnography is unnecessary. Use of the sleep laboratory is only indicated when the diagnosis is uncertain and surgery is not otherwise indicated.

Nonsurgical interventions for pediatric sleep apnea have been used with success, but their utility is limited. CPAP (continuous positive airway pressure) is a modality in which oropharyngeal pressure is increased by forced air delivered through a nasal mask or nasal cannula. The increased pressure serves as a pneumatic splint to maintain patency of the airway. CPAP does not address the underlying pathophysiology and is effective only when used on a continuous, nightly basis. While CPAP is an alternative to surgery, it requires long-term use and poses definite problems with compliance. Except in unusual circumstances, surgery is preferred.

The mandibular advancement oral appliance is another treatment option gaining popularity in the treatment of adults. The appliance is a dental orthotic that advances the mandible and, by reconfiguring the relative positions of upper airway structures, improves luminal patency of the airway. Several types are available but all have the general appearance of a protective mouthpiece worn in athletic competition. The appliance has the advantages of comfort and convenience but is virtually untried in children. It cannot be recommended for routine use in pediatric patients at this time.

## Sleep Research

The use of two objective sleep measures—the polysomnogram and the Multiple Sleep Latency Test (MSLT)—opened the door to scientific study of sleep and its disorders, and is the basis of the clinical practice of sleep disorders medicine.

### Polysomnographic Studies

The polysomnographic study (PSG) is a multichannel electrographic recording of a patient during sleep. The PSG is the principal diagnostic tool of the sleep specialist and is the only means by which many primary sleep disorders can be definitively diagnosed. It may also reveal characteristic changes in sleep architecture—the disposition of the various sleep stages within the night—or other sleep parameters known to occur in neurological, psychiatric, or systemic disorders.

Requisite to the PSG are recording leads needed to accurately define the stages of sleep: the electroencephalogram (EEG), electrooculogram (EOG), and electromyogram (EMG). Additional routine monitoring includes a single lead electrocardiogram (ECG), a measure of respiratory airflow, usually by application of nasal/oral thermistors, and audio/visual recording. The specific EEG montage is dictated by the clinical presentation. One central and one occipital lead represent a technical minimum but montages with up to eight leads are commonly employed. Similarly, ancillary recording devices are added in accord with the presenting complaint. Suspected apnea requires pulse oximetry and a measure of chest and/or abdominal excursion. Recording from the anterior tibialis muscle identifies patients with periodic movements in sleep. The evaluation of male sexual dysfunction is accomplished with strain gauges that measure nocturnal penile tumescence. Clearly, polysomnography is a flexible technique that may be adapted to familiar or novel clinical circumstances.

The polysomnograph is now reduced in size so that home monitoring is technically feasible. A technician travels to the home, wires the patient, and returns the following morning to collect the equipment with electronically stored data. The data are then returned to the laboratory for analysis. The use of home monitoring is controversial. The advantages attendant to conducting the test in a familiar environment are especially pronounced in the pediatric population and the home study is less expensive. Nevertheless, the home study only inconsistently produces satisfactory results and suffers several manifest disadvantages.

Presently, most sleep researchers do not conduct home monitoring and do not advocate its use. The difficulties in acquiring technically adequate data without a technician in attendance are considerable. Also, the availability of videotape monitoring under infrared light renders a laboratory study superior. Finally, the low cost of home monitors has enabled technicians and inexperienced clinicians to enter the field performing and interpreting polysomnographic studies with predictably uneven results. Home study will assume an important role in the evaluation of disordered sleep, but until technical advances are made and techniques are standardized the laboratory study is greatly preferred.

## Multiple Sleep Latency Test

The multiple sleep latency test (MSLT) is a clinical measure of daytime somnolence. The test consists of five nap opportunities offered at about two-hour intervals through the course of a day. In each, the patient is placed in bed with polysomnographic monitoring and asked to attempt to sleep. The mean latency to sleep onset in the naps is considered to represent an underlying physiological drive to sleep and is the measure of the test. Patients who fall asleep, on average, within five minutes are considered to be pathologically sleepy. In addition, the MSLT is used to diagnose narcolepsy, in which pathological somnolence in association with three or more naps containing REM sleep is pathognomonic.

In experienced hands the MSLT may be modified to extract the maximum amount of clinical information. The confounding factor of sleep deprivation, always problematic when a forced awakening ends the polysomnogram, can be eliminated by permitting ad libitum sleep in the morning. This protocol may reduce the number of naps that can be conducted (i.e., patient arising at noon will not receive the full complement of naps) but controlling for sleep loss is often more important.

The MSLT is a valuable clinical tool, but its limitations should be appreciated. False positive results are arguably impossible, save for the exceptional instance of drug use. False negatives clearly do occur though their incidence and clinical significance have received only scant attention in the literature.

In children, the MSLT is only occasionally of benefit. Possible narcolepsy is an exception in that the MSLT is mandatory. The main use is in adolescents with excessive somnolence of uncertain etiology. Here, multiple tests using different protocols may be required for a single patient. In some instances the MSLT is useful in differentiating depression with lethargy from true physiological somnolence. Suspected sleep apnea is rarely an indication.

## Developmental Changes in Sleep

### Sleep in the Infant

Newborns spend approximately 16 to 17 hours a day asleep. Total sleep time then slowly declines to 14 to 15 hours a day by 4 months of age, and 13 to 14 hours a day at 6 to 8 months of age. The duration of single sleep episodes increases from about 3½ hours at 3 weeks of age to approximately 6 hours by 6 months (Coons 1987). These developments reflect neurological maturation and are not related to the start of solid foods. The sleep onset latency of newborns is about 30 minutes at 2 months of age. By 9 months this latency is down to 15 minutes. At sleep onset, the newborn usually goes right into REM sleep. This slowly changes during the first 3 months of life so that at sleep onset the child is in NREM. Also, the total amount of REM sleep decreases markedly over the course of the first six months, from 50% to 30% of total sleep time. The predominance of this active REM sleep in infants seems to serve the purpose of providing stimulation for the maturing brain to develop. At age 5 years, REM sleep time decreases to the adult level of 20% of total sleep.

Brief nocturnal awakenings are more frequent during the first two months of life than at older ages. Newborns are more apt to awaken from active (REM) sleep than from quiet (NREM) sleep. Slow wave

EEG with delta activity is observable at about 8 to 12 weeks of age. At this time, quiet (NREM) sleep becomes differentiated into the four distinct stages.

## Sleep in Children

Sleep disorders, especially those involving initiating and maintaining sleep are among the most common problems parents report in preschool children. Klackenberg (1982) found that 34% of 4- to 5-year-olds still wake regularly at night. The frequency of these wakings then drops off so that less than 15% of 6-year-olds and less than 10% of 8-year-olds experience such wakings.

School-age children (6 to 12 years) spend 8 to 9.5 hours in bed and sleep about 95% of that time. Their sleep patterns resemble those of older individuals. Stage 4 sleep decreases from about 2 hours in the preschool child to 75 to 80 minutes in children this age. This decline is associated with an increase in the amount of stage 2 sleep. Naps are rare in school-age children, who tend to be alert throughout the day.

The onset of REM sleep decreases from about 140 minutes in 6- and 7-year-olds to approximately 124 minutes in 10- and 11-year-olds. The etiology of most sleep disorders in children is not readily known. Current evidence suggests that both biological vulnerabilities and psychological difficulties within the family are associated with poor sleeping.

## Sleep in the Adolescent

Any discussion of sleep in the adolescent must immediately differentiate between sleep as it occurs in the environment and sleep as it occurs in the laboratory. Total sleep time in the laboratory demonstrates a striking constancy between prepubescent children and older adolescents. Groups of subjects in each of these stages average between 9 and 10 hours of sleep; there is no significant change in sleep need despite the physical, psychological, and social upheaval that characterize this period of maturation. REM sleep also is constant in occurrence across this age range, and continues throughout adult life to show only a modest attenuation. The major change in sleep architecture during adolescence is the decline in sleep stages 3 and 4. In combination, these deep stages of non-REM sleep are reduced by 35% for adolescents versus those at prepubescence. The decline in slow wave sleep continues across the life span. Not uncommonly, the senescent adult is completely without stage 3 and 4 sleep.

Although adolescents do not have a reduced need for sleep as they mature, the total amount of sleep they report decreases as they age. Prepubescent children average about 10 hours a night, midadolescents about 8.5 hours a night, and older adolescents (primarily college students) about 7 hours a night. The older adolescents increase their sleep on weekends as they try to compensate for the sleep debt they accumulate during the school week. Most older adolescents in this country report a state of chronic sleep deprivation which undoubtedly produces decrements in their daily functioning, particularly at long, monotonous tasks such as attending lectures and reading.

## Sleep in the Normal Young Adult.

Normal sleep is defined by several criteria, most important of which are (1) total sleep time; (2) sleep continuity; and (3) sleep architecture. Total sleep time in the adult averages 7.5 hours. Unfortunately, this figure has been widely misconstrued to mean that the average adult requires roughly 8 hours of sleep each night to maintain physical and mental well-being. In fact, sleep need is highly idiosyncratic and the range of normal is actually quite wide, generally considered to be 6 to 9 hours. But even these figures are statistical norms rather than strict measures of physiological normalcy. Individuals who require less than two hours of sleep each night have been identified and their sleep needs documented polysomnographically. Similarly, adults who require 10 or more hours of sleep to be fully alert are far from unknown. These groups are termed *short sleepers* and *long sleepers* respectively and they differ from normals only in the amount of sleep that they require. Patients inquiring about sleep need should be informed that sleep is of sufficient quantity when it enables full alertness throughout the day.

Sleep continuity is the extent to which a sleep period is free from arousals and awakenings. Studies of disordered sleep clearly demonstrate that even when total sleep time is adequate to meet the physiological sleep requirement, if that sleep is sufficiently fragmented its usual powers of restoration will be lacking. Parameters of interest in assessing sleep continuity are sleep efficiency and the percentage of stage 1 sleep. Sleep efficiency is the total sleep time divided by total time in bed. A child or young adult should spend nearly all of his time in bed asleep. Thus, sleep efficiencies greater than 90% are normal while a sleep efficiency consistently less than 80% is definitely abnormal. Severe insomnia may produce sleep efficiencies to 50% or lower. A low sleep efficiency indicates that one or more sustained periods of wakefulness have occurred during the night.

Sleep fragmentation refers specifically to the disturbance of sleep by multiple, brief arousals or awakenings. Invariably a brief awakening from REM or non-REM stages 2 to 4 is characterized by a return to deep sleep through one or more epochs of stage 1. As intervals of stage 1 occur almost exclusively in transition between wakefulness and deeper sleep and are rarely sustained, the amount of stage 1 is an accurate if indirect measure of sleep fragmentation. Stage 1 sleep should comprise less than 10% of sleep period time and, in children, amounts greater than 5% may suggest underlying pathology. Stage 1 may comprise 50% or more of sleep period time in patients with severe sleep apnea, while periodic movements in sleep with restless legs syndrome are associated with values between 20% and 40% of sleep period time.

Under usual circumstances, sleep architecture follows a regular pattern. The night begins with a transition from wakefulness to stage 1 sleep that is quickly followed by a descent to stage 2. The latency to stage 2 should be less than 30 minutes. Sleep onset latencies that are consistently longer define a sleep onset insomnia. Following sleep onset, a short interval of stage 2 ensues, during which the EEG progressively slows while increasing in amplitude. Within minutes, stage 3 is reached. High amplitude EEG slowing increasingly dominates the polygraphic record and the next hour or more is primarily filled by stage 4.

Approximately 90 minutes from sleep onset the first REM period occurs. The initial REM period is brief, usually less than 10 minutes in duration. This 90 minute cycle of alternating REM and non-REM sleep is then repeated through the night with two progressive changes. First, the proportion of stage 2 sleep increases during the non-REM phase of the cycle while the proportion of stages 3 and 4 are commensurately decreased. Second, the REM periods increase in length and occupy greater portions of the 90 minute cycle. Thus, normal sleep architecture is distinguished by decreasing amounts of slow wave sleep and increasing amounts of REM as the night progresses. A graphical representation of the relationship between REM and NREM sleep is contained in Figure 1-1.

Abnormal sleep architecture is not so tied to patient complaints as are sleep deprivation or sleep fragmentation, but clinical correlations

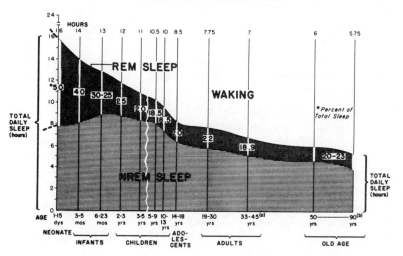

Figure 1-1: Changes with age of total amounts of daily sleep, daily REM sleep, and in percentage of REM sleep. Note sharp diminution of REM sleep in the early years. REM sleep falls from 8 hours at birth to less than 1 hour in old age. The amount of NREM sleep throughout life remains more constant, falling from 8 hours to 5 hours. However, these NREM data do not show the large decreases in stage 4 sleep, which decreases from 1.2 hours in young adulthood to 0 to 0.5 hours in old age. Reprinted from *Sleep Disorders: Diagnosis and Treatment*, by R. L. Williams, I. Karacan, and C. A. Moore. Copyright © 1988 by John Wiley & Sons. Inc. and used by permission.

have been made. Sleep onset REM periods (REM sleep latency of 10 minutes or less) are virtually pathognomonic for narcolepsy. Less markedly abbreviated REM latencies, in the range of 20 to 45 minutes, can be associated with endogenous depression. An even distribution of REM across the night has also been associated with disordered mood. Very high amounts of REM or slow wave sleep may indicate prior deprivation. Patients with newly treated sleep apnea, for example, may approach 50% REM and 50% stages 3 and 4 on a single night. Curiously, stage 2 sleep is not conserved and does not demonstrate rebound.

An analysis of slow wave sleep distribution has less utility than a similar analysis of REM but may offer insight into the regularity of an existing sleep/wake schedule. An unexpected reduction in slow wave amount and amplitude suggests that slow wave-suppressing agents are being ingested.

## References

Aserinsky, E., and Kleitman, N. (1953). Regularly occurring periods of eye motility and concomitant phenomena during sleep. *Science* 18:273–274.

Association of Sleep Disorders Centers (1979). Diagnostic classification of sleep and arousal disorders. *Sleep* 2:1–137.

Coons, S. (1987). Development of sleep and wakefulness during the first 6 months of life. In *Sleep and Sleep Disorders in Children* ed. C. Guilleminault, pp. 17–27. New York: Raven.

Klackenberg, G. (1982). Sleep behavior studied longitudinally: data from 4–16 years on duration, night-waking and bed-sharing. *Acta Paediatrica Scandinavica* 71:501–511.

Rechtschaffen, A., and Kales, A. eds. (1968). *A manual of standardized terminology, techniques, and scoring system for sleep stages of human subjects.* Washington, D.C.: US Government Printing Office (Public Health Service).

Williams, R. L., Karacan, I., and Moore, C. A. (1988). *Sleep Disorders: Diagnosis and Treatment,* New York: Wiley.

# 2

# Sleep and Sudden Infant Death Syndrome

Anne Christake Cornwell

## Sleep Problem

Sudden infant death syndrome (SIDS) is the leading cause of death in infancy after the neonatal period, but its cause is unknown (Shannon and Kelly 1982, Valdes-Dapena 1980). The earlier reference to SIDS as "crib or cot death" had its origin in the unexpected discovery of the dead infant in the crib during the early morning hours following a sleep period.

SIDS is a serious disorder of global dimensions, which is responsible for an estimated 6000 to 7000 deaths of apparently healthy infants each year in the United States alone. It has been the focus of many investigations concerned with discovering the etiologic factor or combination of factors that result in the unexplained death of thousands of babies throughout the world.

The current definition of SIDS is "the sudden death of an infant under 1 year of age, which remains unexplained after a thorough investigation, including performance of a complete autopsy, examination of the death scene, and review of the clinical history" (Willinger et al. 1991). Therefore, SIDS remains a diagnosis of exclusion and is considered a medical mystery.

The incidence of SIDS is 1.5 to 2.0 per 1000 live births in normal full-term infants between 2 weeks and 1 year with a peak incidence between 2 to 4 months old. The rate among poor African-Americans, American Indians, and Alaska natives is higher (5.04/1000, 5.93/1000 and 4.5/1000 live births, respectively) than it is for the Caucasian and Asian populations of the United States. Variations in the SIDS mortality rate have been reported among countries that differ in geographic location and climate (Shannon and Kelly 1982). Ford and colleagues report that the highest SIDS rate in the world (8.00/ 1000 live births) among Maori Indians, who are considered the most disadvantaged socioeconomically.

Sociodemographic data reveal a higher rate in males (61% of SIDS victims), in preterm and low birthweight infants, and in those from a lower socioeconomic background. Infants of teenage, unwed, poor mothers with a history of little or no prenatal care and multiple pregnancies are particularly at risk. Smoking and/or prenatal exposure to narcotics are additional factors that significantly increase the risk of SIDS. The National Institute of Child Health and Human Development epidemiological study of risk factors for SIDS reported that 25.6% of the mothers of SIDS babies had used illicit drugs (1988). One of the most consistent epidemiological findings is that SIDS occurs predominantly during the winter months in all parts of the world where infant mortality data and SIDS rates are documented (Ford and Pearce 1989, Shannon and Kelly 1982).

Paradoxically, in SIDS victims there is an absence of disease or disorder prior to dying. Although SIDS is frequently associated with a recent mild cold, such as an upper respiratory infection (URI), this is not regarded medically as life threatening.

SIDS strikes unexpectedly, without any sound or stridor, usually some time in the early morning when a baby is asleep. (Cornwell 1985). The high incidence of mortality during the night when a baby is presumed to be asleep provides strong evidence that SIDS is a sleep-related dysfunction (Steinschneider 1972) whose organization and maturational basis is of clinical and scientific significance.

Not only is sleep a complex behavior that is neuroanatomically interlocked with respiration, but its pattern of rhythmic control changes during development as the integrative activity of the central nervous system (CNS) matures and new functional relationships are established. The study of this development is important because disturbances in these systems may cause respiratory dysrhythmia during sleep and, in some instances, cause death (Moss 1989).

Previous conceptions had regarded sleep, as opposed to waking, as a unitary, passive state that restored the organism's metabolic functions and provided rest from daytime activity. The differentiation of sleep into different states that are precisely definable and can be quantitatively measured was one of the key findings that contributed to the understanding of the organization of sleep patterns. This work, based on the initial observation of eye movements and behavioral changes during sleep by Aserinsky and Kleitman (1953), led to the identification of two kinds of sleep states, namely, active or rapid eye movement (REM) and quiet or non-rapid eye movement (NREM), which in adults alternate rhythmically every 90 minutes throughout the night. In infants, the periodicity of the REM–NREM sleep cycle is approximately forty-five minutes. As development proceeds, a circadian rhythm is established in which sleep occurs at night in uninterrupted prolonged periods.

A series of classical experiments by Jouvet (1969) reported that sleep has a regularly oscillating cycle of behavioral and brain activity with two separate phases, each with its own distinctive electroencephalographic (EEG) pattern and physiological parameters. REM (active) sleep is characterized by a low-amplitude, fast, desynchronized EEG (similar to the waking state), absence of muscle tone, rapid eye movements, which in humans are associated with periods of dreaming, grimaces, behavioral twitches, and irregular cardiorespiratory activity. NREM (quiet) sleep is differentiated from REM sleep by a high-amplitude, slow, synchronized EEG, active muscle tone, the absence of rapid eye movements, behavioral quiescence, and regular cardiorespiratory activity. The implications of these and other findings were that sleep is controlled by a biological clock with its own periodicity and serves a continuously shifting set of functions.

### Assessment and Differential Diagnosis

SIDS occurs in apparently normal infants who show no symptoms of a clinical disorder or illness prior to death. Frequently, such babies had been examined by their pediatrician within hours before dying and found to be in good health (Guntheroth 1989). In many cases an upper respiratory infection (URI) was diagnosed, but this is common in babies of that age and ordinarily is not associated with any risk to their life. SIDS is neither predictable nor preventable in an asymptomatic infant. Therefore, the infant's clinical course is not followed closely by a pediatrician and the circumstances surrounding the fatal cardiorespiratory collapse are unknown since no danger is suspected.

There is another group of babies, however, who are considered to be at high risk for SIDS following a sudden, prolonged sleep apnea attack with bradycardia (slow heart rate), cyanosis or pallor, and limpness that required immediate resuscitation to save the baby's life. This unique population of infants suffers a Sudden A-Ventilatory Event (S.A.V.E.), previously known as "near miss" or aborted SIDS, and subsequently named Apparent Life Threatening Events or ALTE, (National Institutes of Health Consensus 1986). SIDS and S.A.V.E. infants share several epidemiologic and demographic characteristics, justifying referring to S.A.V.E. infants as "the living equivalent of the SIDS baby" (Valdes-Dapena 1980). These characteristics include: seasonality (higher incidence in the wintertime), age (peak occurrence from 2 to 4 months), frequent presence of an upper respiratory infection (URI), apparently normal health, and low socioeconomic status (Cornwell 1987). However, thus far no specific etiological link has been established between the two disorders.

Infants at risk of SIDS have been studied over a period of years to identify the possible physiological disturbances of the cardiorespiratory and sleep systems in SIDS and to provide a model for understanding its etiology (Cornwell 1985, Guilleminault and Korobkin 1979).

Such infants were reported to have an increased frequency of brief respiratory pauses (Steinschneider 1972), excessive periodic breathing (Kelly and Shannon 1979), diminished ventilatory sensitivity to hypercarbia or hypoxia (Shannon and Kelly 1977), an impaired arousal responsiveness to hypercarbia or hypoxia (Coons and Guilleminault 1985, Hunt 1981) and prolonged sleep apnea (Cornwell 1985, Cornwell et al. 1978, Guilleminault et al. 1975).

Another avenue of inquiry pursued the identification of other risk conditions that could prolong and exacerbate an apnea in vulnerable infants. One of these is the disturbance of sleep routine alone or in combination with sleep loss, which could be a contributing factor to risk or act as trigger mechanisms for SIDS. Since mild cold symptoms (URI) frequently accompanied by sleep disturbances have been reported in more than 50% of SIDS victims and in "near miss" cases

(Cornwell 1979, Cornwell et al. 1978, Guntheroth 1989), sleep loss in combination with a URI may be a high risk factor for SIDS or for respiratory disturbances during sleep. The data of McGinty and Harper (1974) suggested a relationship between sleep apnea and sleep loss. They found that 10-day-old sleep-deprived kittens showed an increase in respiratory arrest (apnea) during sleep. The apnea gradually became prolonged, cerebral ischemia developed, and some animals succumbed a few hours later. Sleep deprivation has also been shown to affect respiratory events in normal healthy 1- to 6-month-old infants (Canet et al. 1989) and in high risk for SIDS infants (Cornwell and Laxminarayan 1988).

Moreover, disturbances of sleep patterns caused by frequent awakenings or sleep loss might produce internal desynchronization of body rhythms (Kripke 1976). This instability could affect the respiratory control system of infants susceptible to SIDS during a critical stage in development.

An investigation of the hypothesis that a disruption of the sleep/wake cycle in vulnerable infants deregulates their respiratory control system and results in an increase in apnea was carried out in 1- to 6-month-old high risk for SIDS infants and controls matched for age, sex, birthweight, and socioeconomic status (Cornwell et al. 1986, Cornwell and Laxminarayan 1988). The data indicate that there are significant differences between risk and control babies as a function of sleep deprivation. The interaction of sleep state and sleep deprivation is associated with an increase in the number and frequency of apneas in REM sleep and with a longer duration of apnea in NREM sleep. These findings suggest that a disturbance of the rhythmic forty-five-minute REM–NREM sleep cycle in these sleep-deprived high risk babies may compromise an infant's respiratory regulation throughout the entire sleep period. Control infants, on the other hand, were not affected by sleep deprivation, but by sleep state, which showed an increase in number and frequency of apnea during REM sleep, typically associated with greater autonomic instability.

The pathogenetic factor(s) that precipitate the initial prolonged apneic episode may reflect a transient functional or neurochemical defect of the CNS (central nervous system), particularly brainstem regions involved in respiratory regulation, which may be affected by one or more physiological or environmental events that place such infants at risk (Naeye 1980, Valdes-Dapena 1980).

Infants born preterm are also considered to be at high risk for

SIDS. The recurrent sleep apnea that is characteristic of preterm infants during early infancy may result from the underdevelopment of the brain, the selective death of certain cells, and the damage of networks as a consequence of respiratory difficulties (Weitzman and Graziani 1974), all of which could lead to further CNS abnormalities. Many of the social factors associated with premature delivery can predispose an infant to SIDS (Naeye 1980) including inadequate pre- and perinatal care, exposure to narcotics in utero, and poor heating conditions, especially during the cold winter months. These can compound the physiological risk factors such as low birthweight, a possible noradrenaline deficiency, and a brainstem abnormality that may be responsible for disturbed respiratory control.

## Theoretical Issues

Scientists have proposed several hypotheses to explain the mystery of SIDS (Cornwell 1979, Dawes 1968, Downing and Lee 1975, Naeye 1973, Schwartz 1976, Steinschneider 1972, Tonkin 1975, Valdes- Dapena 1980, Weitzman and Graziani 1974), but its etiology continues to elude medical science. Current evidence suggests that SIDS is multifactorial.

The possibility that developmental factors related to sleep could potentially influence events leading to SIDS became the focus of attention in the last two decades when it was determined that most deaths attributed to SIDS occurred when the baby was asleep or presumed to be sleeping.

The hypothesis of Weitzman and Graziani (1974) implicated the control of respiration and sleep in the pathogenesis of SIDS. It was based on the supposition that in vulnerable infants who have a subtle brainstem defect of respiratory control, a prolonged apnea can endanger the gas exchange needs of the baby and result in cardiorespiratory failure.

Dawes (1968), based on a series of animal studies, postulated that a chemosensitive reflex may cause death in infants who aspirate water or formula into their upper respiratory tract. Downing and Lee (1975) hypothesized that infants who succumb to SIDS may have a reduced respiratory drive in which anemia may play a critical role, since the red blood cell concentration reaches a minimum at 3 to 4 months when the incidence of SIDS peaks and affects more babies from lower socioeconomic groups. The evidence of Lardy and colleagues (1975) that SIDS victims have a much lower concentration of a glucose-synthesizing enzyme suggested the hypothesis that impaired glucose synthesis from amino acids could contribute to a rapid and fatal drop in the concentration of glucose in the blood, particularly when combined with fewer feedings at night and the factor of cold stress.

One of the most prevalent theories implicates a disturbed respiratory pattern characterized by recurrent apnea and hypoxia (low oxygen level). This theory was developed on the basis of the pathological findings of Naeye (1973, 1974, 1980) showing hypertrophy and hyperplasia of the small pulmonary arteries (indicative of chronic hypoxemia) in infants who died of SIDS. Although the possibility that these pathological anomalies may cause apnea and eventually death cannot be ruled out, Naeye believes they are the result of chronic prolonged apnea with a consequent oxygen deficiency to respiratory and sleep neurons that are anatomically linked in the brainstem.

Hunt and Brouillette (1987) cite a brainstem abnormality in neuroregulation of respiratory control as the underlying cause of the final pulmonary failure in SIDS. The abundance of astroglial cells in the lateral reticular formation, the center of respiratory control, in SIDS victims supports this theory.

The brainstem dysfunction hypothesis may have a substantial relationship to a developmental abnormality in the sympathetic nervous system (Haddad et al. 1981, Hoppenbrouwers et al. 1976), which results in a defect in cardiorespiratory variability (Shannon and Kelly 1982).

Another hypothesis that postulates that the pathophysiology of SIDS involves a neurochemical mechanism is supported by extensive experimental and clinical findings (Cornwell 1979). Specifically, an abnormality of the catecholamine system in vulnerable infants who have a deficiency of noradrenaline (NA) results in severe hypothermia and eventually cardiorespiratory failure. This hypothesis accounts for the major epidemiologic and pathological data that have been proposed thus far and provides a crucial step in understanding the etiology of SIDS. (See Figure 2-1.)

Noradrenaline has two speculative roles in the etiology of SIDS, one as a mediator of thermogenesis, and another as a regulator of sleep. NA mediates chemical or nonshivering thermogenesis, which is the primary mechanism of heat production during the first year of life. Brown adipose tissue, with its abundance of mitochondria, serves as the medium for this process. At the age of approximately 4 months the

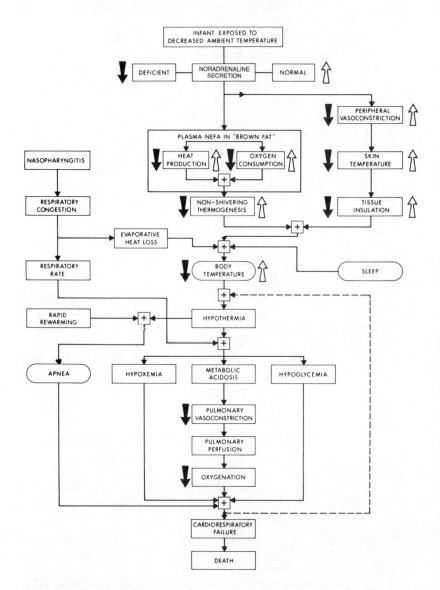

Figure 2-1: A schematic diagram of the critical events leading to severe hypothermia, cardiorespiratory failure, and SIDS in infants with a deficiency in the catecholamine noradrenaline. (Cornwell 1979. Copyright © 1979 by Gordon and Breach Science Publishers and used by permission.)

increased production of adrenaline by the adrenal gland is responsible for the conversion to shivering thermogenesis, the typical adult pattern. The gradual disappearance of brown fat stores correlates well with the time of this conversion, which is complete by the age of 1 year (Stern 1977).

Vulnerable infants who have a deficiency in the neurotransmitter NA are at greater risk during the winter months when NA is responsible for an infant's response to cold. A defect in thermoregulation could lead to severe hypothermia, hypoglycemia, metabolic acidosis and a decrease in arterial p02. These factors may result in a deterioration of cardiorespiratory function to which the infant succumbs without a sound or struggle.

Another consistent finding in SIDS is that these infants die in the early morning hours during a sleep period. Sleep, therefore, is an important physiological event that may be etiologically significant in SIDS. In infants the onset of sleep is in REM, a state in which they spend 50% of their sleep time. In later infancy a change occurs from sleep onset REM to NREM. This correlates well with the conversion from nonshivering to shivering thermogenesis that begins at the age of 4 to 5 months and corresponds to the peak incidence of SIDS. Thus, a deficiency of NA may be a key etiologic factor (Cornwell 1985).

Several investigators have speculated that the mechanism of death in SIDS may be cardiac arrhythmia. Fraser and Froggatt (1966) reported that electrocardiographic tracings of infants who subsequently died of SIDS demonstrated a prolonged Q-T interval (the time interval between the Q and T portion of a Q, R, S, T, waveform in an electrocardiographic tracing), which is associated with an increased vulnerability to ventricular arrhythmias that may be fatal. Maron and colleagues (1976) investigated the potential role of the prolonged Q-T interval in a group of parents of SIDS victims. Their examination of electrographic tracings indicated that an inherent cardiac conduction abnormality or an abnormality in autonomic innervation of the heart may be a predisposing factor in sudden death, but they failed to identify a direct link to SIDS. A cardiac mechanism involving the prolonged Q-T syndrome was suggested by Schwartz (1976) who proposed that a decrease in cardiac stability and a developmental imbalance of the autonomic nervous system renders babies more vulnerable to chance events.

Botulism is a systemic illness that was suspected of being responsible for some cases of SIDS (Arnon et al. 1978, Arnon and Chin 1979). The bacteria *Clostridium botulinum* can germinate in an infant's intestine where the powerful toxin that is produced can cause sudden death in its most extreme form. However, in the vast majority of cases autopsy examinations have failed to attribute the death to infant botulism.

Recent evidence has implicated the prone sleeping position as a possible risk factor in SIDS. This led the American Academy of Pediatrics (AAP) Task Force on Infant Sleep Positions and SIDS to recommend placing healthy infants on their back or side during sleep (1992). The AAP asserts, however, that preterm infants with respiratory or upper airway distress or those who are diagnosed as having gastroesophageal reflux with frequent vomiting should adopt the prone sleeping position.

Most studies that investigated this problem have reported a decline in SIDS among infants sleeping in the supine position (de Jonge and Engelberts 1989, Dwyer et al. 1991, Faroqi et al. 1991). A higher incidence of SIDS is reported in infants sleeping face down, compared to those who sleep on their back or side, particularly when this is coupled with soft bedding material, swaddling in a blanket, and sleeping overdressed in an overheated room (Fleming et al. 1990). The risk increases when an infant who has a nasal congestion or other infection is placed in the prone position while asleep. The rebreathing of carbon dioxide has been identified as a possible contributory factor.

Other problems singled out by Engelberts et al. (1991) regarding their data collected in the Netherlands are the possible misclassification of their cases over time since only 50 to 60% were autopsied, the increased rate of babies born preterm, maternal smoking, and overheating. Additional research is needed to elucidate the particular events that lead to SIDS since infants who sleep in the supine position are also vulnerable, for as yet unknown reasons.

Orr's investigation of the effect of position and sleep state on the rate and duration of central and obstructive apnea in infants with a history of sleep apnea found no difference in these variables during REM or NREM sleep (Orr et al. 1985).

The hypothesis that some infants require help in learning how to breathe and may be vulnerable to SIDS was proposed by Lipsitt (1982). According to McKenna (1991) a co-sleeping environment between infant and parent may contribute to the development of a sleep pattern that is most beneficial for optimal infant growth and may also reduce the risk of the sudden infant death syndrome.

## Summary of Empirical Research

One of the first studies that singled out the importance of sleep in the pathogenesis of SIDS found evidence of high rates of short duration sleep apnea, frequently in conjunction with URI, in "near miss" infants who later died of SIDS (Steinschneider 1972). The brief apneas that occurred during both REM and NREM sleep, but more often in REM, led to the hypothesis that a prolonged apneic episode during sleep is part of the final common pathway of this disorder.

The work of Naeye (1973, 1974) on the pathological alterations in SIDS victims provided support for the hypothesis that an abnormality in the CNS is responsible for a failure in respiratory control during sleep (Weitzman and Graziani 1974). The subtle physiological defects in the lungs and brain of SIDS victims indicative of chronic, recurrent hypoxemia prior to death that Naeye found were not present in infants who did not suffer oxygen deficiencies. He identified several markers supporting the view that SIDS is not caused by a single traumatic hypoxic episode resulting in death, but by repetitive sleep-related apneic events. The most significant pathological changes were hypertrophy and hyperplasia of the small pulmonary arteries, prolonged retention of periadrenal brown fat, abnormalities of neural astroglial cells in the brainstem, extramedullary hematopoiesis (synthesis of red blood cells in organs other than the bone marrow), and a smaller than normal carotid body (Naeye 1980). In an independent study, the work of Valdes-Dapena (1977) confirmed the main pathological findings reported by Naeye.

A distinctive feature of infants unexpectedly found dead during sleep was evidence of intrathoracic petichiae (small hemorrhages) that were rarely present in infants dying of other causes, such as suffocation or asphyxia (Werne and Garrow 1953). Beckwith (1988) reported that intrathoracic petichiae are characteristic of most SIDS cases, but remains skeptical that such pathological changes prove that chronic hypoxia plays a role in typical SIDS cases (National Institutes of Health Consensus 1986). In his view it is not clear from existing evidence whether SIDS is primarily due to respiratory or cardiac factors.

A corollary of the hypothesis of respiratory failure in SIDS led to studies of sleep apnea in another group of infants originally known as "near miss" (or aborted) SIDS. Research focused a great deal of attention on the association between central breathing control and sleep as a possible causative factor in the mechanism of SIDS. The onset of such an episode is sudden and unexpected and occurs in normal fullterm infants whose age parallels the age at which SIDS occurs, typically within the first six months of life. The frequency of these episodes is significantly greater during the cold winter months, a pattern similar to SIDS (Cornwell 1989). The etiology of this disorder is equally unknown.

These infants were unexpectedly found, apparently lifeless, by their parent (or caretaker). They were cyanotic or very pale and not breathing, usually while asleep. This sudden respiratory arrest (apnea) was of sufficient severity to require immediate resuscitation or vigorous stimulation, but subsequent physical examination did not reveal any identifiable cause or disease that could explain the sudden loss of respiratory control. A thorough pediatric examination and extensive medical tests fail to reveal any abnormality or disease to which the severe cyanotic/apneic attack could be attributed, with the exception of a minor cold (URI) that is not considered life threatening. The supposition was that infants who survive a prolonged apneic attack could provide a vital link to the mystery of SIDS. (See Figure 2–2.)

Many of these infants have been monitored extensively subsequent to their recovery of normal respiration and color. Differences in the methodological approach of these studies, however, have compounded the problem of interpretation. Variations in recording methods have made it difficult to ascertain whether the data were the result of the acute life-threatening event, due to developmental changes characteristic of a given age or to a combination of these factors. Sleep/wake parameters were scored based on behavioral criteria alone (Dittrichova 1966), by polygraphic criteria (Emde and Walker 1976, Haddad et al. 1981), or by a combination of polysomnographic and behavioral variables (Cornwell, 1989, 1990, 1991, 1992, 1993, 1994, Cornwell et al. 1978, 1982, 1986, Dreyfus-Brisac 1979, Guilleminault et al. 1975, 1981, Harper et al. 1978, 1981, Hoppenbrouwers et al. 1976, 1988, Kahn and Blum, 1982, Monod et al. 1986, Samson-Dollfus 1988).

Another factor adding to the variability is recording length, which in some instances was restricted to one to two interfeeding periods (Emde and Walker 1976, Leistner et al. 1980, Navelet et al. 1979, Navelet et al. 1984) while others employed all-night or twenty-four hour recordings (Challamel et al. 1981, Dreyfus-Brisac 1979, Guilleminault et al. 1975, 1981, Harper et al. 1981, Hoppenbrouwers et al. 1976, 1988, Kahn et al. 1988, Monod et al. 1986).

With the exception of the studies of Cornwell (1993) and Corn-

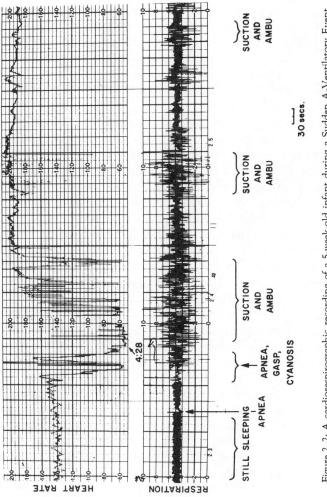

Figure 2-2: A cardiorespirographic recording of a 5-week-old infant during a Sudden A-Ventilatory Event (S.A.V.E.) with severe bradycardia that occurred while the infant was asleep. A physician who observed and documented the event administered vigorous resuscitation to save the infant's life. (Cornwell et al. 1982. Copyright © 1982 by Gordon and Breach Science Publishers and used by permission.)

27

well and colleagues (1978, 1982) there have been no other investigations in which sleep/wake cycles recorded with polysomnography were
followed for continuous periods up to seventy-two hours and subsequently repeated in the same risk and matched control infants at
monthly intervals. Polysomnography refers to multiple channel recordings of various physiologic parameters, including sleep, for scoring sleep
stages according to standardized sleep scoring criteria (Anders et al.
1971, Anders and Zangen 1972).

Brief respiratory pauses occur in all healthy infants typically
during REM sleep as isolated events or in repeated intervals that are
characteristic of periodic breathing (Hoppenbrouwers 1989, Hoppenbrouwers et al. 1976). Both preterm and full-term infants with a history
of an acute apnea/cyanotic attack demonstrate impaired ventilatory
responses to carbon dioxide, which can predispose these infants to
life-threatening apnea (Shannon et al. 1977).

Impaired cardiorespiratory control in infants who succumbed to
SIDS has suggested that autonomic centers may be altered during
particular sleep states. These changes include: an increase in the
number and/or duration of sleep-related apneas (Kahn et al. 1989),
higher heart rate and/or heart rate variability (Kelly et al. 1986,
Schechtman et al. 1989), and abnormal heart rate and blood pressure
response to postural change (Fox and Matthews 1989). Based on daytime nap recordings, Haddad and colleagues (1981) reported that shorter R-R intervals in "near miss" than control infants during REM than
NREM sleep correlated with a higher rate of SIDS. (See Figure 2–3.)

The localization of the postulated deficit to brain structures
involved in autonomic function led to a number of studies that
revealed a persistence of dendritic spines in a region of the brainstem
where catecholaminergic neurons are located (Quattrochi et al. 1980,
1985, Takashima and Becker 1985, Takashima et al. 1991). These data
support a hypothesis of delayed maturation of adrenergic neurons in
SIDS victims.

A further link to the postulated autonomic disturbance in SIDS
was provided in an immunohistochemical study of catecholamine
synthesizing enzymes (Kopp et al. 1993). An absence of adrenergic
neurons in nucleus tractus solitarius of the lower brainstem in SIDS
cases suggested a maturational delay of that brain structure possibly
due to anoxia.

Corroborative evidence for a hypothesis of developmental delay
is provided in a recent study of changes in sleep/wake states in high risk

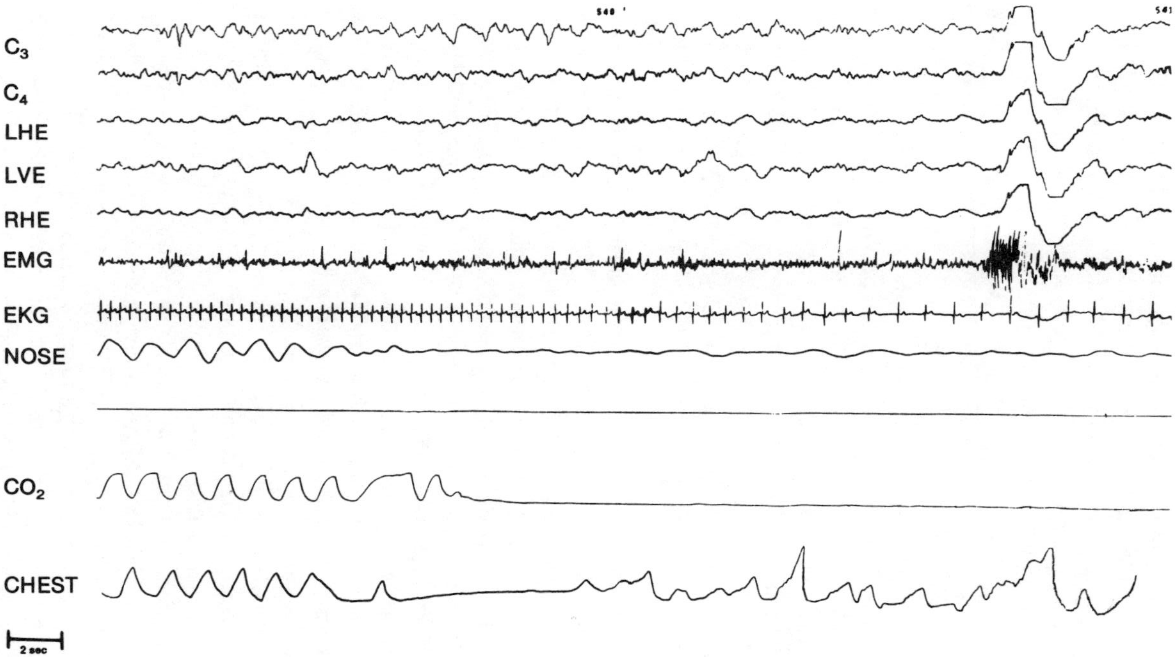

Figure 2–3. Central apnea followed by obstructive apnea with marked bradycardia during sleep in a high risk for SIDS infant. (Cornwell et al. 1982. Copyright © 1982 by Gordon and Breach Science Publishers and used by permission.)

29

for SIDS infants compared to rigorously matched controls during the peak age for SIDS, that is, 2 to 4 months old (Cornwell 1992, 1993). Electrophysiological changes in REM, NREM, and Transitional sleep and wakefulness were analyzed at three stages of maturation to compare the development of sleep/wake patterns in males and females. The data based on continuous twenty-four to seventy-two-hour in-hospital recordings show that high risk male infants fail to demonstrate an increase in wakefulness with age and reveal a lag in the maturation of REM sleep compared to male and female control and to high risk female infants during the critical age for SIDS. The greater susceptibility of male infants to SIDS emphasizes the importance of this new finding which was based on unique long-term recordings.

An immature sleep/wake organization that occurs differentially in male high risk for SIDS infants suggests that a CNS functional disorder is present selectively in male infants as a precursor to SIDS. Another finding that suggests a CNS immaturity, specifically of the sleep system, reveals a persistence of Sleep Onset REM Periods (SOREMPS) after prolonged wakefulness in 1- to 6-month old S.A.V.E. infants. Matched controls made the normal transition to sleep onset NREM (Cornwell and Laxminarayan 1993). SOREMPS are a cardinal diagnostic criterion of the sleep disorder narcolepsy (see Chapter 13 in this volume). These results raise the possibility that in vulnerable infants sleep disturbances can contribute to a prolongation of SOREMPS and greater autonomic instability. Disturbances of circadian (about twenty-four hours) and ultradian (under twenty-four hours) regulation can lead to abnormalities of sleep organization and development in vulnerable infants with a history of sleep apnea and sleep deprivation.

Since a majority of SIDS deaths occur in 2- 4-month-old infants, an age when the CNS is undergoing rapid neuronal development, an investigation was carried out to determine whether changes in the CNS were correlated with catecholamine metabolism in its target organs (Ozand and Tildon 1983). Their study of the activity of catecholamine enzymes in brain specimens of SIDS victims found a decrease of dopamine hydroxylase activity and an increase in tyrosine hydroxylase activity in certain brain regions (hypothalamus, putamen, and caudate nucleus), providing evidence for a biochemical marker in such infants.

Recurrent sleep apnea, which is typically present in high risk infants, may result from the underdevelopment of the brain, especially of the brainstem region at the time of birth (Henderson-Smart et al.

1983). The later stages of development of any part of the brain, the formation of synapses, the selective death of certain cells, and the stabilization of networks may be damaged by the hypoxemia resulting from respiratory difficulties (Weitzman and Graziani 1974). This could lead to further central nervous system abnormalities.

An association of SIDS with a delay in the maturation of hematopoiesis was explored by Guilian and his colleagues, who examined the levels of fetal hemoglobin (HbF) in fifty-nine SIDS and forty control cases (Giulian et al. 1987). Since elevations of HbF could be associated with a compromised delivery of oxygen to sensitive tissues, this test could be used prospectively as a useful marker for SIDS to identify infants at risk. The finding of significantly higher levels of HbF in SIDS cases than in controls offers corroborative data for Naeye's (1974) anatomic evidence of chronic hypoxemia. However, a subsequent report using intact hemoglobin for studying this issue failed to show significant differences between a SIDS and control population (Kline et al. 1989).

The possible relationship of immunization for diphtheria-tetanus-pertussis (DPT) and the risk of SIDS was investigated in a major NICHD epidemiological cooperative study (Peterson et al. 1987). Using a large multicenter, population-based case control method they reported that immunization is not a significant factor in the occurrence of SIDS. Two other reports, one from England (Taylor and Emery 1982) and another from Norway (Solberg 1985) also failed to find an association between DPT immunization and SIDS. Although fewer SIDS victims than control infants had been immunized, reflecting general health care practices, immunization was often accompanied by a period of fussiness and sleep loss that could contribute to a higher risk of SIDS. However, in infants with a history of prolonged apnea, recent DPT immunization was not associated with an increase in sleep apnea. (Keens et al. 1985).

Chacon and Tildon (1981) found significantly higher levels of T3 (tri-iodothyronine) in SIDS infants compared to normal controls and to infants who had died of other causes. They postulated that this finding may account for the faster heart rate (Haddad et al. 1981), lower beat-to-beat variability (Harper et al. 1978), and shorter Q-T intervals (Schwartz 1976) in S.A.V.E. infants who had experienced a life-threatening event or in subsequent SIDS victims.

In the course of searching for an answer to the SIDS dilemma, what started out as a promising link to the mystery of SIDS has generated new issues concerning the pathophysiology of respiratory, cardiac, sleep, and behavioral mechanisms in infants with a history of life-threatening apnea. Trying to understand the physiological basis of sudden unexplained apnea in normal, apparently healthy babies also poses great difficulties, including the possible etiologic link to SIDS, but no etiologic relation has been definitively established.

Nevertheless, certain striking similarities between these two clinical disorders, SIDS and S.A.V.E., do exist, namely: (1) both are disorders of infancy with an unknown etiology, (2) both are characterized by a cluster of comparable high-risk factors, (3) no single factor alone is known to be an etiologic agent or part of a trigger mechanism, and (4) in both, there is a possible interrelationship between sleep state and cardiorespiratory failure during a vulnerable chronological age.

Some of the differences that may provide certain clues regarding the cause of these disorders include the peak age, which is 2 to 4 months in SIDS cases, whereas in S.A.V.E. babies it is 1 to 2 months (Cornwell 1987). Another significant factor may be a disturbance in biological rhythm, since SIDS typically strikes during the night and early morning, whereas life-threatening events occur most often in daylight or early evening hours. This question is of utmost importance to parents, physicians, and scientists because data from such studies could offer valuable clues to SIDS.

The search for an answer to the SIDS dilemma, however, has yielded neither a working hypothesis that provides a clear-cut direction for future research, nor a cohesive body of data.

## Treatment Approach Based upon an Integration of Theory, Research, and Practice

An apparently healthy infant who suddenly experiences life-threatening apnea that requires immediate intervention to regain normal cardiorespiratory rhythm, represents a pediatric emergency. Usually the collapse occurs in the home and the only witnesses are the parents or caregiver who attempt to resuscitate the lifeless infant. Such infants are considered to be at high risk for SIDS. Preterm infants with a history of apnea and asymptomatic infants, such as siblings of SIDS babies, are also at risk, but since no reliable predictive tests are available to assess the probability of an acute life-threatening episode, each case must be evaluated and managed on an individual basis.

Recurrent, life-threatening episodes of apnea in infants involve complex problems of diagnosis and management. The need to evaluate high-risk babies using scientifically based, medically sound principles prompted the development of a uniform set of guidelines (Guilleminault and Korobkin 1979) that became the basis for infant screening procedures. These procedures are: a thorough pediatric examination, including history, physical examination, and neurological examination; laboratory tests; chest X-ray; electroencephalogram (EEG); and other subspecialty consultations, as required. A pneumogram recording of heart rate and respiration during sleep also became part of the standard screening procedure to evaluate the need for monitoring, although the validity of pneumograms has come under question (Cornwell 1985, Kahn and Blum 1982).

In the majority of cases a cardiorespiratory home monitor is prescribed by a physician, usually in a hospital-based center with multidisciplinary facilities for infant care and family support. The recommendation is made by a team of medical and home health care experts who give special consideration to the multiplicity of issues concerning the health and well-being of the infant, on the one hand, and the capability of the parents to undertake the responsibility of caring for an infant on a home monitor, on the other. Prior to the infant's discharge, the parents require instruction by a nurse trained in cardiopulmonary resuscitation, in the use of the standard impedance type of monitor, and in follow-up care. The psychological support of infants at risk for SIDS and their families represents an important aspect of their care and recovery (Cornwell 1987).

The duration of the monitoring period varies depending on the severity and frequency of subsequent prolonged sleep apneas requiring intervention and on the type of resuscitation that is required, such as bag and mask, mouth-to-mouth, vigorous stimulation, and so forth. Each apnea and/or bradycardia (heart rate below 60 beats/min.) that is recorded on a pneumogram is signaled by an alarm to alert the parents. The type of intervention is documented on a daily log, which is then reviewed by the physician during monthly follow-up visits to assess whether the infant continues to be at risk or if monitoring can be terminated. The decision to discontinue monitoring is based on an evaluation of the infant's clinical condition and on the criterion of at least two to three months without significant episodes of apnea/ bradycardia or periodic breathing.

The average length of time on a monitor for infants identified as being at high risk for SIDS is seven months (Kahn and Blum 1982,

Kelly et al. 1978). One or more incidents of apnea (sometimes with bradycardia) that required parental intervention to recover normal breathing were cited in these studies. In both of these studies the use of home monitors was regarded as life saving with a survival rate for infants in one home monitoring program of 93.4% (Kelly et al. 1978). In this study, resuscitation was unsuccessful in four cases. They concluded that "infants who have experienced near miss SIDS are at great risk of recurrent apnea, hypoxia and sudden death. Most deaths can be prevented by supervised home monitoring of respiration and appropriate intervention by parents trained in resuscitation" (p. 514).

After monitoring 500 infants at risk for SIDS, Kahn and Blum (1982) came to the conclusion that if they are identified in time, "some infants may be protected against SIDS through home monitoring" (p. 94). The cause of these repeated apneas of infancy that require monitoring is unknown and the possibility that it is related to SIDS cannot be ruled out.

Home monitoring of these infants, however, is a controversial issue because claims that monitors can protect infants from SIDS led to concerns by the professional and public community over the efficacy of home monitoring for babies regarded as being at statistically higher risk for SIDS.

One of the limitations of cardiac/apnea monitors is that, heretofore, they were restricted to recording only central apnea, but obstructive or mixed apneas were not recorded by impedance pneumonography. Our studies (Cornwell et al. 1978, 1982), were the first to single out the importance of using both cardiac and respiratory signals since an obstructive apnea that is often accompanied by bradycardia can be a pernicious event that places the infant at greater risk for life-threatening prolonged apneas, which could lead to SIDS. Kahn and colleagues (1988) reported that the duration and incidence of central (diaphragmatic), obstructive (upper airway), and mixed (central followed by obstructive) apneas was greater in infants who subsequently died of SIDS than in controls. This finding, however, was not documented using pneumogram recordings at home (Southall 1983). The weakness of the technique of cassette tape pneumograms is that it is limited to recording central apneas, but neither obstructive nor mixed apneas can be identified. It is also not possible to record sleep variables to determine the specific state in which apneas occur.

The importance of recording the sleep state of the infant must be stressed, because other conditions, such as seizures and gastroesophageal reflex, occur more commonly during wakefulness and both are treatable conditions (Guntheroth 1989).

As Kahn and colleagues (1989) pointed out, "detractors of home monitoring argue that SIDS may not be preventable despite home monitoring, that monitoring devices are expensive, that home monitoring could induce significant psychological trauma, and that injuries related to misuse of components of home monitors have occurred" p. 81. Deaths have been reported on monitors (Kelly et al. 1978, Monod et al. 1986, Oren et al. 1986). Some occurred because of malfunction of the equipment, inappropriate type of monitor or alarm system, failure to hear the alarm, inadequate response, or non-utilization of the monitoring devices. Occasional reports indicate that some children could not be resuscitated despite parental responses.

Documented monitoring represents the latest development in home monitoring techniques. These monitors permit the recording of additional variables, such as pulse oximetry and nasal air flow, which can provide data of respiratory activity both before and after an event that triggers an alarm (Hunt 1992; Reiterer and Fox 1992; Weese-Mayer and Silvestri 1992). The date and time of day for each event are documented, allowing a comparison with the caretaker's log, an assessment of parental compliance, and documentation of the criteria for discontinuing the use of the monitors (Weese-Mayer and Silvestri 1992). Reiterer and Fox (1992) believe that multichannel recordings might help identify those infants at risk for SIDS.

The use of methylxanthine medication (theophylline) in infants with sleep apnea and in siblings of SIDS babies has also been prescribed and found to reduce the symptoms on the pneumogram (Hunt et al. 1983).

## Case Presentation

One of the most devastating experiences parents can live through is the sudden loss of an apparently healthy baby to SIDS. Normally, the birth of a baby is anticipated and welcomed as a joyous event. Parents and family members eagerly follow the baby's growth with expectations of seeing their baby boy or girl develop normally.

Every night many parents across the country go to bed secure in the knowledge that their baby is resting safely in the crib only to discover their infant lifeless in the morning. When SIDS strikes, the happy morning tending and feeding hour becomes a scene of anguish and grief as the horrified parents try to grasp what has happened to their child.

These families rush to get help in a state of shock, confusion, and disbelief. They may be overwhelmed and desperately cling to the hope that somehow their baby can be saved. There was no illness, trauma, or injury to make the death understandable. Why did their healthy infant die? Some parents react with numb silence or violent hysteria at the inexplicable calamity that befell them. In this tragic event, both the dead infant and the surviving family members are the victim.

The pain of the anguished cry is difficult to grasp. Szybist (1988), the mother of a 3-month-old boy who had been in good health and unexpectedly died of SIDS, recalls "a vivid memory . . . of picking up your still little body, your face disfigured from the pooling of blood, and stiff from the postmortem changes. What I found that early morning was not your living smiles of the day before. I don't recall just now how long it took me to replace your living smiles from the picture of the face of death . . ." (p. 34).

Although there is precedent in medicine for diseases whose etiology and treatment are unknown, SIDS is unique in engendering a terrifying, catastrophic reaction because it strikes lethally without any warning or alarm at a seemingly healthy baby. Subsequently there is no identifiable cause or disorder to explain the event. A mother who lost her baby more than nineteen years ago, said that "a day does not go by without my thinking about my baby" (personal communication). All of the hopes and expectations nurtured by the parents for their baby become immersed in sorrow, guilt, self-recrimination, endless grief, and, often, despair. SIDS has only recently emerged from the "dark ages" when parents were sometimes incarcerated in jail because of suspected child abuse or ostracized by neighbors and friends for presumed neglect (Guntheroth 1989).

"It is still difficult to explain to anyone how the grief process malfunctions when someone you love, especially your defenseless child, dies of 'something' that has no name and very limited scientific credibility, if any at all" (Szybist 1988, p. 34).

Since SIDS has never been observed, it is believed to occur under mysterious circumstances. Babies who are discovered not breathing, however, can be successfully resuscitated by a parent or caregiver who is present within seconds of the event, although there is no way of proving that such an acute life-threatening attack would have become a SIDS case. A controversy ensued regarding this issue in part because the diagnosis of such a "near miss" episode came under suspicion since it was almost always obtained from parents who were in a state of emotional stress and the report lacked objective description by a medically trained person. Opposition to home monitoring was an additional factor contributing to the dispute.

The first documented observations of a "near miss" event by a physician occurred during a recording of a 5-week-old infant's heart rate and respiration in a pediatric hospital unit (Cornwell et al. 1982). A trained pediatric nurse noted that the infant had been quietly asleep before the prolonged apnea, limpness, and cyanosis were observed. The previous two-hour sleep period was characterized by many short (ten to twelve second) apneas that were followed by spontaneous breathing. The physician who resuscitated the infant with the use of a mask and manual ventilator stated that the infant would have been a SIDS case if immediate intervention had not been provided. This case provided clear-cut documented evidence that parental descriptions of comparable "near miss" episodes can be regarded as reliable reports of the infant's condition.

Immediately after this attack, a complete forty-eight hour polysomnographic recording of cardiorespiratory, sleep, and behavioral variables was made to determine whether this infant would continue to be at risk for recurrent sleep apneas or if the cardiorespiratory system would stabilize and return to normal. The data showed a high frequency of apneas during REM and NREM sleep (often accompanied by marked bradycardia) (Cornwell et al. 1982). The relationship between age and sleep apnea was of further interest since subsequent monthly twenty-four- to forty-eight hour in-hospital recordings did not show a decrease in the number of sleep apneas until the age of 5 months. Moreover, the developmental course that was monitored until the age of 1 year revealed no signs of neurological or respiratory disease in this baby. Although long term follow-up was not carried out, the parents communicated to the project director that when the child reached school age she was diagnosed as having a language delay and learning difficulties, but no formal study of this problem was pursued.

Parents of S.A.V.E. babies live in constant fear of a recurrence of the initial traumatic episode which, if repeated, could be fatal unless they are successful in intervening immediately. Lack of specific medical information regarding the cause and predictability of this disorder contributes to their anxiety about the survival of their child.

## Summary

SIDS is the largest cause of postneonatal death in infants, yet its cause remains unknown. SIDS occurs in all parts of the world without regard for ethnicity, geographic location, or religion. Although the affluent are not spared, the socioeconomically disadvantaged are more commonly afflicted. Despite considerable progress in elucidating many of the events associated with SIDS, it continues to be a medical mystery.

The cause of SIDS has been attributed to many factors and several hypotheses have been postulated to explain this syndrome. A hypothesis that accounts for most pathological and epidemiological data related to SIDS implicates a neurochemical mechanism. These data led to the formulation that a disturbance in thermoregulatory control can lead to cardiorespiratory failure in infants who become severely hypothermic due to a deficiency of the catecholamine noradrenaline.

Sleep apnea in infants who recover from a potentially life-threatening, sudden, unexplained apnea that required immediate intervention to prevent probable death has been the focus of research on the mechanism of the pathophysiology of SIDS.

Infants who suffer such a prolonged sleep apnea attack, siblings of SIDS infants, and babies born preterm pose an ongoing need for medical evaluation and management to safeguard their health care. This is available in individualized centers that are specialized in providing the monitoring devices and necessary support system for carrying out such a program.

The ultimate goal of SIDS research is to prevent SIDS. To do so, research must focus on the identification of infants at risk and on the underlying mechanisms and causes of this syndrome.

The present review emphasizes the complexity of the maturation of the infant twenty-four-hour REM, NREM, and waking cycle. Sleep disturbances that may deregulate respiratory control mechanisms in vulnerable infants may be part of the mechanism of SIDS.

## References

American Academy of Pediatrics Task Force on Infant Positioning and SIDS (1992). *Pediatrics* 89:1120–1126.

Anders, T. F., Emde, R. and Parmelee, A. A. (1971). A standardized terminology, techniques and criteria for scoring states of sleep and wakefulness in infants. Los Angeles: UCLA Brain Information Service.

Anders, T. F., and Zangen, M. (1972). Sleep state scoring in human infants. Psychophysiology 9:653–654.

Arnon, S. S., and Chin, J. (1979). The clinical spectrum of infant botulism. Reviews of Infectious Diseases 1:614–621.

Arnon, S. S., Midura, T. F., Damus, K., et al. (1978). Diphtheria-tetanus toxoids-pertussis vaccination and sudden infant deaths in Tennessee. Journal of Pediatrics 1:1273–1277.

Aserinsky, E., and Kleitman, N. (1953). Regularly occurring periods of eye motility and concomitant phenomena during sleep. Science 118:273–274.

Beckwith, J. B. (1988) Intrathoracic petichial hemorrhages: a clue to the mechanism of death in Sudden Infant Death Syndrome. Annals, New York Academy of Sciences 533:37–47.

Canet, E., Gaultier, C., D'Alleset, A. M., and Dehan, M. (1989). Effects of sleep deprivation on respiratory events during sleep in healthy infants. Journal of Applied Physiology 66:1158–1163.

Chacon, M. A., and Tildon, J. T. (1981). Elevated values of tri-iodothyronine in victims of sudden infant death syndrome. Journal of Pediatrics 99:758–760.

Challamel, M. J., Revol, M., Leszcynski, M. C., and Debilly, G. (1981). Organization nychthemerale des etats de vigilance chez le nourrisson normal et le nourrisson dit "rechappe d' un syndrome de mort subite." Revue Electroencephalographique et Neurophysiologique 11:28–36.

Coons, S., and Guilleminault, C. (1985). Motility and arousal in near-miss sudden infant death syndrome. Journal of Pediatrics 107:728.

Cornwell, A. C. (1979). S.I.D.S. Sudden Infant Death Syndrome: a testable hypothesis and mechanism. International Journal of Neuroscience 10:31–44.

_____ (1985). Advances in infant sleep apnea, "near miss" and SIDS research. Proceedings IEEE/Engineering in Medicine and Biology Society Annual International Conference 5:1077–1083.

_____ (1987). Risk factors for SIDS and "Near Miss" in relation to sleep/wake states. Proceedings IEEE/Engineering in Medicine and Biology Society Annual International Conference 9:2072–2073.

_____ (1987). "Near Miss" SIDS at risk babies and their families: a psychological support project. Salud Mental 10:22–25.

_____ (1989). Influence of seasonality and sleep deprivation on apnea of infancy. *Apnea of Infancy 7th Annual Conference*. Annenberg, CA.

_____ (1990). Sleep/waking variability in Sudden A-Ventilatory Event (S.A.V.E.) at high risk for SIDS infants and controls. *Proceedings IEEE/Engineering in Medicine and Biology Society International Conference* 12:2033.

_____ (1991). Sleep/wake biological rhythm disturbance in high risk for SIDS infants. *Sleep Research* 20A:508.

_____ (1992). A maturational delay in the sleep/wake pattern of male high risk for SIDS infants. *Proceedings IEEE/Engineering in Medicine and Biology Society 14th Annual International Conference* 14:2613–2614.

_____ (1993). Sex differences in the maturation of sleep/wake patterns in high risk for SIDS infants. *Neuropediatrics* 24:8–14.

_____ (in press). Sleep disturbances and SIDS. *Proceedings First International SIDS Conference*, Florence, Italy, 1994.

Cornwell, A. C., and Laxminarayan, S. (1988). Biological rhythms of apnea in relation to sleep deprivation in S.A.V.E. (Sudden A-Ventilatory Event) and control infants. *Proceedings IEEE/Engineering in Medicine and Biology Society Annual International Conference* 10:1803–1804.

_____ (1993). A sleep disturbance in high risk for SIDS infants. *Journal of Sleep Research* 2:110–114.

Cornwell, A. C., Weitzman, E. D., and Kravath, R. E. (1982). Respiratory and cardiac events observed and recorded during and following a "near miss" for SIDS episode. *International Journal of Neuroscience* 16:231–239.

Cornwell, A. C., Weitzman, E. D., and Marmarou, A. (1978). Ambulatory and in-hospital recording of sleep state and cardiorespiratory parameters in "near miss" for SIDS and control infants. *Biotelemetry* 5:112–122.

Dawes, G. S. (1968). *Foetal and Neonatal Physiology*. Chicago: NY Medical.

de Jonge, G. A., and Engelberts, A. C. (1989). Cot deaths and sleeping position. *Lancet* 336:1149–1150.

Dittrichova, J. (1966). Development of sleep in infancy. *Journal of Applied Physiology* 21:1143–1146.

Downing, S. E., and Lee, S. E. (1975). Laryngeal chemosensitivity: a possible mechanism for sudden infant death. *Pediatrics* 55:640–649.

Dreyfus-Brisac, C. (1979). Ontogenesis of brain bioelectrical activity and sleep organization in neonates and infants. *Human Growth* 3:157–182.

Dwyer, T., Ponsonby, A. L. B., Newman, N. M., and Gibbons, L. E. (1991). Prospective cohort study of prone sleeping position and sudden infant death syndrome. *Lancet* 337:1244–1277.

Emde, R. N., and Walker, S. (1976). Longitudinal study of infant sleep: results of 14 subjects studied at monthly intervals. *Psychophysiology* 13:456–461.

Engelberts, A. C., de Jonge, G. A., and Kostense, D. J. (1991). An analysis of trends in the incidence of sudden infant death syndrome in the Netherlands 1969–89. *Journal of Paediatric and Child Health* 27:329–333.

Farooqi, S., Perry, I. J., and Beevers, D. G. (1991). Ethnic differences in sleeping position and in risk of cot death. *Lancet* 338:1455.

Fleming, P. J, Gilbert, R. Azaz, Y., et al. (1990). Interaction between bedding and sleeping position in the Sudden Infant Death Syndrome: a population-based case control study. *British Medical Journal* 301:85–89.

Ford, R. P. K., McCormick, H. E., and Pearce, G. R. (1990). Cot deaths in Canterbury: the pattern over twenty years. *New Zealand Medical Journal* 103:588.

Ford, R. P. K., and Pearce, G. R. (1989). Infant mortality in New Zealand: an analysis of the causes of death and the relative importance of cot death (Sudden Infant Death Syndrome). *New Zealand Population Review* 16:4–33.

Fox, G. P. P., and Matthews, T. G. (1989). Autonomic dysfunction at different ambient temperatures in infants at risk of Sudden Infant Death Syndrome. *Lancet* 336:1065–1067.

Fraser, G. R., and Froggatt, P. (1966). Unexpected cot deaths. *Lancet* 2:56–57.

Giulian, G. G., Enid, B. A., Gilbert, E. F., and Moss, R. L. (1987). Elevated fetal hemoglobin levels in SIDS. *New England Journal of Medicine* 316:1122–1126.

Guilleminault, C., Ariagno, R., Korobkin, R., et al. (1981). Sleep parameters and respiratory variables in "near miss" sudden infant death syndrome infants. *Pediatrics* 68:354–360.

Guilleminault, C., and Korobkin, R. (1979). Sudden Infant Death: Near miss events and sleep research: some recommendations to improve comparability of results among investigators. *Sleep* 1:423–433.

Guilleminault, C., Peraita, R., Souquet, M., and Dement, W. (1975). Apneas during sleep in infants: possible relationship with Sudden Infant Death Syndrome. *Science* 190:677–679.

Guntheroth, W. G. (1989). *Crib Death: The Sudden Infant Death Syndrome.* New York: Futura.

Haddad, G. G., Walsh, E. M., Leistner, H. L., et al. (1981). Abnormal maturation of sleep states in infants with aborted sudden infant death syndrome. *Pediatric Research* 15:1055–1057.

Harper, R. M., Leake, T., Hoppenbrouwers, T., et al. (1978). Polygraphic studies of normal infants and infants at risk for the sudden infant death syndrome: heart rate variability as a function of state. *Pediatric Research* 12:778–785.

Henderson-Smart, D. J., Pettigrew, A. G., and Campbell, D. J. (1983). Clinical apnea and brainstem neural function in preterm infants. *New England Journal of Medicine* 308:129–131.

Hoffman, H. J., Damus, K., Hillman, L., and Krongrad, E. (1988). Risk factors for SIDS: results of the National Institute of Child Health and Human Development SIDS Cooperative Epidemiologic Study. *Annals New York Academy of Sciences* 533:13–30.

Hoffman, H. J., Hunter, J. C., Damus, K., et al. (1987). Diphtheria-tetanus-pertussis immunization and SIDS: results of the National Institute of Child Health and Human Development Cooperative Epidemiologic Study of SIDS risk factors. *Pediatrics* 79:598.

Hoppenbrouwers, T. (1989). Sudden Infant Death Syndrome (SIDS) and sleep. *Proceedings IEEE/Engineering in Medicine and Biology Society Annual International Conference* 11:453–454.

Hoppenbrouwers, T., Hodgman, J. E., Harper, R. M., et al. (1976). Incidence of apnea in infants at high and low risk for sudden infant death syndrome (SIDS). *Pediatric Research* 10:425–433.

Hoppenbrouwers, T., Hodgman, J. E., Arakawa, K., et al. (1988). Sleep apnea as part of a sequence of events: a comparison of three months old infants at low and increased risk for SIDS. *Neuropaediatrie* 9:320–337.

Hunt, C. E. (1981). Abnormal hypercarbic and hypoxic sleep arousal responses in near miss SIDS infants (sudden infant death syndrome). *Pediatric Research* 15:1462.

_____ (1992). The cardiorespiratory control hypothesis for sudden infant death syndrome. *Clinical Perinatology* 19:757–771.

Hunt, C. E., and Brouillette, R. T. (1987). Sudden Infant Death Syndrome: 1987 perspective. *Journal of Pediatrics* 110:669–678.

Hunt, C. E., Brouillette, R. T., and Hanson, D. (1983). Theophylline improves pneumogram abnormalities in infants at risk for SIDS. *Journal of Pediatrics* 103:969.

Jouvet, M. (1969). Biogenic amines and the states of sleep. *Science* 163:32–40.

Kahn, A., and Blum, D. (1982). Home monitoring of infants considered at risk for the Sudden Infant Death Syndrome. *European Journal of Pediatrics* 139:94–100.

Kahn, A., Blum, D., Rebuffat, E., et al. (1988). Polysomnographic studies of infants who subsequently died of sudden infant death syndrome. *Pediatrics* 82:721–726.

Kahn, A., Rebuffat, E., Sottiaux, M., and Blum, D. 1989). Problems in the management of infants with an Apparent Life Threatening Event. In *The Sudden Infant Death Syndrome: Cardiac and respiratory mechanisms and interventions.* Annals, New York Academy of Sciences, pp. 78–88.

Kahn, A., Van de Merckt, C., Magres, P., et al. (1987). Transepidermal water loss during sleep in infants at risk for sudden death. *Lancet* 2:140–141.

Keens, T. G., Ward, S. L., Gates, E. P. et al. (1985). Ventilatory pattern following diphtheria-tetanus-pertussis immunization in infants at risk for SIDS. *American Journal of Diseases in Children* 139:991–996.

Kelly, D., Golub, H., Carley, D., and Shannon, D. C. (1986). Pneumograms of infants who subsequently died of SIDS. *Journal of Pediatrics* 109:249–257.

Kelly, D., and Shannon, D. C. (1979). Periodic breathing in infants with near miss SIDS. *Pediatrics* 63:355–359.

Kline, C. A., Ellerbrooke, R. C., Goldstein, D. E., et al. (1989). Measurement of fetal hemoglobin (HbF) in sudden infant death syndrome (SIDS) and controls using radial immunodiffusion (RID) and high pressure liquid chromatography (HPLC). *Pediatric Research* 25:270A.

Kopp, N., Chigr, F., Demoroy, L., et al. (1993). Absence of adrenergic neurons in nucleus tractus solitarius in Sudden Infant Death Syndrome. *Neuropediatrics* 24:25–29.

Kripke, D. (1976). Biological rhythm disturbances might cause narcolepsy. In *Advances in Sleep Research*, vol. 3, ed. C. Guilleminault, W. Dement, and P. Passouant, pp. 475–483. New York: Spectrum.

Lardy, H. A., Bentle, L. A., Wagner, M. J., et al. (1975). *National Institutes of Health SIDS Conference.*

Leistner, H. L., Haddad, G. G., Epstein, R. A., et al. (1980). Heart rate and heart rate variability during sleep in aborted sudden infant death syndrome. *Journal of Pediatrics* 97:51–55.

Lipsitt, L. (1982). Infant learning. *Review of Human Development*. New York: John Wiley & Sons.

Maron, B. J., Clark, C. E., Goldstein, R. E., and Epstein, S. E. (1976). Potential role of Q-T interval prolongation in sudden infant death syndrome. *Circulation* 54:423.

McGinty, D. J., and Harper, R. M. (1974). Sleep physiology and SIDS: animal and human studies. In *SIDS, 1974*, ed. R. R. Robinson. Canada: Canadian Foundation for the Study of Infant Deaths.

McKenna, J. J. (1991). Mothers and infants sleeping apart and together: implications for SIDS. *Proceedings IEEE/Engineering in Medicine and Biology Society Annual International Conference* 13:897–898.

Monod, N., Plouin, P., Sternberg, B., et al. (1986). Are polygraphic and cardiopneumographic respiratory patterns useful tools for predicting the risk for sudden infant death syndrome? *Biology of the Neonate* 50:147–153.

Moss, I. R. (1989). Ontogeny of respiratory patterns in relation to sleep/wake states in fetal and early postnatal life. *Proceedings IEEE/Engineering in Medicine and Biology Society Annual International Conference* 11:323–324.

Naeye, R. L. (1973). Pulmonary arterial abnormalities in the sudden infant death syndrome. *New England Journal of Medicine* 289:1167–1170.

———— (1974). Hypoxemia and the sudden infant death syndrome. *Science* 186:837–838.

———— (1980). Sudden infant death. *Scientific American* 242:56–62.

National Institutes of Health Consensus Development Conference on Infantile Apnea and Home Monitoring (Sept. 29 to Oct. 1, 1986) Consensus statement (1987). *Pediatrics* 79:292–299.

Navelet, Y., Benoit, J., Lacombe, G., and Bouard, G. (1979). Respiration and night sleep in children at risk for sudden and unexpected death. *Revue Electroencephalographique et Neurophysiologique Clinique* 9:258–265.

Navelet, Y., Payan, C. Guilhaum, A., and Benoit, J. (1984). Nocturnal sleep organization in infants at risk for SIDS. *Pediatric Research* 18:654.

Oren, J., Kelly, D., and Shannon, D. C. (1986). Identification of a high-risk group for Sudden Infant Death Syndrome among infants who were resuscitated for sleep apnea. *Pediatrics* 77:495.

Orr, W. C., Stahl, M. L., Duke, J., et al. (1985). Effect of sleep state and position on the incidence of obstructive and central apnea in infants. *Pediatrics* 75:832–835.

Ozand, P. T., and Tildon, J. T. (1983). Alterations of catecholamine enzymes in several brain regions of victims of sudden infant death syndrome. *Life Sciences* 32:1765–1770.

Peterson, D. R., van Bell, G., and Hasselmeyer, E. G. (1987). Diphtheria-tetanus-pertussis immunization and sudden infant death: results of the National Institute of Child Health and Human Development cooperative epidemiological study of sudden infant death syndrome risk factors. *Pediatrics* 79:598–611.

Quattrochi, J. J., Baba, N., Liss, L., and Adrion, W. (1980). Sudden Infant Death Syndrome (SIDS): a preliminary study of reticular dendritic spines in 95 infants. *Brain Research* 181:245–249.

Quattrochi, J. L., McBride, P. T., and Yates, A. J. (1985). Brainstem immaturity in SIDS: a quantitative rapid Golgi study of dendritic spines in 95 infants. *Brain Research* 325:39–48.

Reiterer F., and Fox, W. (1992). Multichannel polysomnographic recording for evaluation of infant apnea. *Clinical Perinatology* 19:871–889.

Roffwarq, H. P., Muzio, J. N., and Dement, W. C. (1966). Ontogenetic development of the human sleep-dream cycle. *Science* 152:604–619.

Samson-Dollfus, D. (1988). Sleep organization in children at risk for sudden infant death syndrome. *Sleep* 11:277–285.

Schechtman, V. L., Harper, R. M., Kluge, K. A., et al. (1989). Heart rate variation in normal infants and victims of the sudden infant death syndrome. *Early Human Development* 19:167–181.

Schwartz, P. J. (1976). Cardiac sympathetic innervation and the sudden infant death syndrome. *American Journal of Medicine* 60:167–172.

Shannon, D. C., and Kelly, D. (1977). Impaired regulation of ventilation in infants at risk for sudden infant death syndrome. *Science* 197:367.

———— (1982). Medical Progress: SIDS and Near SIDS *New England Journal of Medicine* 306 (I):959–965, (II):1022–1028.

Shannon, D. C., Kelly, D., and O'Connell, K. (1977). Abnormal regulation of ventilation in infants at risk for sudden infant death syndrome. *New England Journal of Medicine* 297:747–750.

Solberg, L. K. (1985). DTP immunization, visit to child health center and sudden infant death syndrome (SIDS). *Report to the Oslo Health Council*. Norway.

Southall, D. P. (1983). Home monitoring and its role in the sudden infant death syndrome. *Pediatrics* 72:133–138.

Southall, D. P., Richards, J. M., Rhoden, K. J., et al. (1982). Prolonged apnea and cardiac arrhythmias in infants discharged from neonatal intensive care units: failure to predict an increased risk for sudden infant death syndrome. *Pediatrics* 70:844–851.

Steinschneider, A. (1972). Prolonged apnea and the sudden infant death syndrome. Clinical and laboratory observations. *Pediatrics* 50:646–654.

Stern, L. (1977). Thermoregulation in the newborn infant: physiologic and clinical observations. *Journal of Pediatrics* 30:3–14.

Szybist, C. M. (1988). Sudden Infant Death Syndrome Revisited. *Developmental and Behavioral Pediatrics* 99:33–37.

Takashima, S., and Becker, L. E. (1985). Developmental abnormalities of medullary "respiratory centers" in Sudden Infant Death Syndrome *Experimental Neurology* 90:580–587.

Takashima, S., Mito, T., and Becker, L. E. (1991). Delayed dendritic development of catecholaminergic neurons in the ventrolateral medulla of children who died of Sudden Infant Death Syndrome. *Neuropediatrics* 22:97–99.

Taylor, E. M., and Emery, J. L. (1982). Immunization and cot deaths. *Lancet* 2:271.

Tonkin, S. (1975). Sudden infant death syndrome: hypothesis of causation. *Pediatrics* 55:650–661.

Valdes-Dapena, M. A. (1977). Sudden unexplained infant death, 1970 through 1975. *Pathology Annals* 12:117–145.

_____ (1980). A review of the medical literature, 1974–1979. *Pediatrics* 66:597–613.

Weese-Mayer, D. E., and Silvestri, J. M. (1992). Documented monitoring: an alarming turn of events. *Clinical Perinatology* 19:891–906.

Weitzman, E. D., and Graziani, L. (1974). Sleep and the Sudden Infant Death Syndrome. In *Advances in Sleep Research*, pp. 327–341. New York: Spectrum.

Werne, J. J., and Garrow, I. (1953). Sudden apparently unexplained death during infancy. I. Pathologic findings in infants found dead. *American Journal of Pathology* 29:633.

Willinger, M., James, L. S., and Catz, C. (1991). Defining the Sudden Infant Death Syndrome (SIDS): deliberations of an expert panel convened by the National Institute of Child Health and Development. *Pediatric Pathology* 11:677–684.

# 3

# Infant Night Waking

Sheila A. Spasaro
Charles E. Schaefer

Karen and Bill were thrilled at the birth of their daughter, Julie, eight months ago. Since that time, however, they have experienced numerous nights disturbed by their baby's frequent arousals, bouts of crying, and their own attempts to soothe her back to sleep. They find that both their work performance and their social life have suffered and, most distressing to them, they never seem to have the energy to enjoy each other as they did in the past. All of this has left Karen and Bill exhausted, irritable, and desperate for advice that will help them to solve their child's sleep problem.

Karen and Bill are not alone. Parents visiting the Center for Psychological Services at Fairleigh Dickinson University frequently describe their infant's night waking and delayed sleep onset as significant problems of child rearing. Often these parents have failed to establish a fixed bedtime or wake up time for their child. They complain of the negative side effects that their infant's inconsistent sleep schedule and night waking have on the entire family, including chronic weariness, stress, reduced productivity, irritability, depression, and marital discord. They share a common need for useful strategies and management techniques that will assist them in dealing more effectively with their child's sleep disturbance.

Infant Sleep Patterns

Night waking is a common occurrence in the first year of life. Infants monitored by polygraphic recordings were found to awaken fifteen to seventeen times per night at 1 to 2 months of age, a number which decreased significantly to eight incidents per night by the time the babies had reached 6 months of age (Hoppenbrouwers et al. 1988). Occurrences of night waking are both normal and frequent and are generally not considered to be a matter of concern to parents unless the infant requires care-giver intervention in order to return to sleep. Anders (1979) found that 44% of 2-month-old infants and 78% of 9-month-old infants slept without removal from their cribs between the hours of midnight and 5 A.M., but time-lapse video recordings showed that, in fact, only 15% of the 2-month-old and 33% of the 9-month-old infants actually slept without awakening during that period. Sleeping through the night, then, does not mean sleeping without awakening, but satisfying the conventional definition of "settling," that is, sleeping without crying or fussing between the hours of midnight and 5 A.M. (Moore and Ucko 1957).

The organization of the sleep-wake cycle is a major developmental achievement of the first year of life. A convergence of evidence indicates that the sleep pattern matures over time. The ratio of active or REM (rapid eye movement) to quiet or non-REM sleep is an indicator of the level of maturation of the sleep cycle. Several infant sleep studies have shown that the amount of time spent in active sleep (AS) decreases with age while the amount of time spent in quiet sleep (QS) increases with age in both full-term and pre-term infants (Anders 1979, Emde and Walker 1976, Holditch-Davis 1990, Hoppenbrouwers et al. 1988). A concurrent maturational development is the reduction in the number of arousals and an increase in the intervals between awakenings. The amount of time spent awake increases from eight to eleven hours over the first year of life, and the duration of individual sleep episodes at night also increases (Hoppenbrouwers et al. 1988). There is a natural tendency on the part of infants to lengthen nighttime sleep and to shorten sleep periods during the day (Moore and Ucko 1957, Scher 1991), a schedule that provides a more favorable match with parental sleep patterns. Nevertheless, parents like Karen and Bill frequently complain that their infant's night waking is a source of distress to the family. Psychologists and medical practitioners are often called upon by parents to deliver advice that will enable them to better manage their child's sleep habits.

## Causes of Infant Sleep Disturbance

Moore and Ucko (1957) found that 50% of infants had settled, or slept through the night, at 3 months of age, and that this percentage had increased to 83% by 6 months. About 50% of those who had settled reverted to night waking later in the first year. Other researchers have described similar findings. The infant's night waking is linked to his ability to fall back asleep without parental intervention after he awakens, as he frequently does, during the night. A recent study (Anders et al. 1992) provides evidence that problematic night waking may be, in most cases, a learned behavior. The study looked at the sleep habits of twenty-one full term infants and found that their ability to soothe themselves back to sleep after spontaneous awakenings during the night was associated with the parent–infant interactions and the method of inducing initial sleep onset at bedtime. Specifically, infants who were put to bed asleep at 3 months of age were more likely to signal for caretaker intervention when they awakened in the middle of the night. Their age cohorts, on the other hand, who were placed in bed while awake and allowed to fall asleep without assistance, were more likely to fall asleep on their own after waking during the night. Other researchers (Adair et al. 1991) found that frequency of infant awakenings was significantly higher when parents were present at initial sleep onset than when they were absent, even when factors such as maternal feelings of isolation, infant temperament, use of sleep aids, breast-feeding, presence of siblings, and maternal demographics were controlled. Clearly, some infants who awaken during sleep require parental presence to return to sleep because of a learned association between this condition and the initial sleep onset. Furthermore, research with healthy 6-month-old infants (Keener et al. 1988) found signalers and self-soothers to be comparable in the maturational aspects of sleep, that is, to have similar ratios of AS to QS. It is reasonable to infer, therefore, that night waking in a number of infants is, primarily, environmental in origin.

In determining that the source of a particular baby's problematic night waking is, indeed, learned, it is important to rule out other possible etiologies. Some babies awaken and cry because of physical discomfort. Schaefer and Petronko (1987) point out that medical problems could be the source of the disturbance. Certainly colic, middle ear or urinary tract infection, congestion, dermatitis, pain, and hunger should be considered as possible sources of distress. Allergy to cow's milk protein has been associated with insomnia in infants (Kahn et al. 1987) and may cause abdominal or musculoskeletal pain, respiratory distress, itching skin, or metabolic imbalance (Kahn et al. 1985). Side effects caused by various medications, such as antihistamines, antibiotics, and stimulants, used to treat other ailments, may contribute to a child's sleeplessness. Occasionally, parents may spike a child's bottle with alcohol in a desperate attempt to initiate sleep onset, only to cause middle-of-the-night wakefulness. Clearly, when such causes of infant insomnia are found, appropriate interventions should be initiated to relieve the problem. It is possible, however, that the infant may have come to expect parental comforting during sleepless periods, and so the sleep problem may persist even after the initial source is removed.

## The Infant–Parent Interaction

Sleep behavior in infants is the result of an interaction among parent, child, and environmental variables. In evaluating and advising parents about their child's sleep habits, clinicians should consider issues of infant temperament, parental reactions, and the family's cultural background. Parental assessments of their infant's temperament have been shown to be associated with the infant's behavior in laboratory settings (Healy 1989, Stifter and Fox 1990) and with parental reports of infant sleep disturbance (Van Tassel 1985). One interpretation of these data is that parental perceptions of the soothability of their baby are probably accurate. If the parents see their child as difficult to soothe, they may react by providing an increased level of attention and comforting for the child, who comes to expect such treatment. Evidence suggests that children judged to have "difficult" temperaments are significantly more likely to be night wakers than "easy" children (Schaefer 1990a, Weissbluth 1981). In addition, difficult children were shown to sleep about two hours less per night and one hour less per day than children with easy temperaments (Schaefer 1990a). Parents of these more difficult, night-waking infants may respond by providing extra care and comfort at sleep time. Such children may be more likely to be rocked, held, bottle-fed, or nursed to sleep. In time, a habit develops and the child becomes dependent on the parent in order to initiate sleep, a pattern which is repeated in spontaneous nighttime awakenings.

Cultural factors may influence a parent's perception of infant night waking and so affect parental response to the behavior. The practice of co-sleeping for example, in which parents and children share a family bed, is associated with sleep disturbance in white but not black families, where co-sleeping is an acceptable subcultural norm (Medoff and Schaefer 1993). It is likely that co-sleeping in many white, but not black, families is a response to sleep disturbances. While the practice of "reactive" co-sleeping may initially increase sleep time (McKenna et al. 1993), the practice is more likely to temporarily suppress, but not solve, a sleep problem (Medoff and Schaefer 1993). Expectations about child rearing are clearly implicated in parental tolerance and response to night waking. In studying maternal responses to the night waking of 218 healthy Korean infants, Lee (1992) found that these mothers saw infant night waking as a normal developmental event, and responded to it by patting, holding, feeding, and changing their babies. These mothers were unlikely to use Western methods such as medication or behavioral techniques in dealing with their infants. In Finland, how-ever, mothers who reported a need for help with their infant criers perceived their babies' cries as more powerful, summoning, and com-plaining than mothers who did not report a need for assistance. The help-seeking mothers also expressed feelings of failure, exasperation, and anger at themselves (Michelsson et al. 1990). A study done in the United Kingdom reported ethnic differences among maternal reports of sleep problems in their 8-month-old infants (Zuckerman et al. 1987). It would seem that health care providers should be sensitive to differ-ences in expectations and attitudes about infant sleep behavior that may be the result of cultural diversity. Western norms may themselves be somewhat contradictory in their aims. For example, time-lapse video recordings demonstrated that 3-week-old infants were capable of falling asleep on their own but were routinely soothed and rocked to sleep by their caretakers. Ironically, Western cultural norms also dictate that most infants sleep independently, that is, in their own rooms, and that they soon achieve the milestone of sleeping through the night (Anders et al. 1992).

## Pharmacotherapy

When an infant's sleep behavior becomes troublesome, parents often seek guidance from a health care professional. The advice they receive varies in its usefulness and acceptability to the family. Medical intervention may involve the use of pharmacotherapy for the sleep disorder although the use of sedatives and hypnotics merely suppresses the problem temporarily and does not represent a cure for the sleep disturbance. In addition, parents are often reluctant to use this form of treatment in their very young children. Safety issues are particularly pertinent in treating young children with medication because of the immaturity of metabolic functioning and the fact that the blood-brain barrier is not completely formed before the age of 2. Extra caution is necessary in dose titration as side effects and toxicities are particularly dangerous in the very young. In addition, optimal dosage may be difficult to achieve because of wide interindividual variability among children (Campbell et al. 1985).

Given the special problems involved in medicating infants, it would seem that pharmacotherapy should be a treatment of last resort or at least that it should be required to demonstrate a unique advantage over other available therapies for the treatment of sleep disorders. An early study (Russo et al. 1976) found diphenhydramine reduced latency of sleep onset and number of awakenings in children but did not increase the total amount of sleep time over the placebo group. Richman (1985) looked at the effect of using the sedative trimeprazine tartrate for a brief period to treat twenty-two children with severe waking problems. Results indicated only limited therapeutic efficacy in these children that disappeared by the 6-month follow-up, so that even this moderate clinical usefulness was temporary in nature. The study failed to produce any evidence that trimeprazine tartrate was helpful in breaking the habit of waking. France and colleagues (1991) compared the results of using extinction (i.e., discontinuance of parental response to infant waking) alone, extinction plus trimeprazine tartrate, or extinction plus placebo in sleep-disordered infants. All subjects reduced their sleep disturbance to low levels. The only difference was that the sedative group reduced its waking and crying abruptly while the other groups achieved the same results more gradually. It should be noted, however, that this more rapid change did not reduce levels of parental anxiety in the sedative group over the two control groups so that the practice of temporarily suppressing infant sleep disturbance with medication in order to relieve parental anxiety may be a futile one. In addition, there was a slight rebound when the trimeprazine was withdrawn that did not occur in the other two groups. The results do not indicate clear superiority for the use of trimeprazine.

Phenothiazines are central nervous system (CNS) depressants that are occasionally used for their sedative action. Kahn and Blum (1982) demonstrated an association between the use of phenothiazines and sudden infant death syndrome (SIDS) and suggest that the depressive effect of the drug on the CNS continues long after the child is sleeping and may disturb the infant's natural ability to awaken, thereby enhancing the possibility of hypoxia. Clearly, there is a need for a treatment of infant sleep disturbance other than the use of medication. Behavioral approaches are gaining popularity because they have been found to be both safe and effective.

## Behavioral Interventions

Sleep behavior, like any behavior, is a product of the interaction between the individual, in this case the infant, and the individual's environment, largely defined here by parental reactions. The infant brings both physiological and psychological characteristics to the interaction. Temperament and the maturity of the sleep-wake cycle may predispose an infant to a particular sleep pattern, but the caregiver's reaction to that pattern will largely be responsible for whether or not the child develops sleep behavior that is problematic to the family. For example, from an early age, infants form an association between feeding and sleeping. Infants awaken when hungry and may be allowed by parents to fall asleep while feeding. Problems occur when an infant is bottle- or breast-fed to the point of sleep. In this case, the association between feeding and sleeping is maintained and reinforced. The bottle, the breast, and even the mother become part of a sleep onset ritual on which the infant comes to depend. It becomes a pattern that the infant expects to repeat in middle-of-the-night awakenings.

Since sleep problems are learned through associations and consequences, they can be unlearned by changing the contingencies. This is done through stimulus control and withdrawal of reinforcement for undesirable behaviors. Currently, three effective behavioral techniques are generally offered as interventions for infant sleep disturbance. They are extinction, gradual extinction, and scheduled awakenings. Often parents have tried a variety of management techniques before seeking professional assistance. In some cases, the inconsistency of parental attempts has created an intermittent schedule of reinforcement and has led to infant behavior that is particularly resistant to extinction. This raises the issue of parental compliance in any behavior management program directed at their children. Parents must be made aware of the necessity for 100 percent consistency in their efforts. A parent who is inconsistent raises the possibility of intermittent reinforcement and probable treatment failure. The therapist should discuss treatment options with the parents and settle on the one with which the parent is most comfortable. Extinction, gradual extinction, and scheduled awakenings are all viable treatments for infant sleep disorders. Successful treatment depends on compliance, which, in turn, is facilitated by adequate parental education about the techniques and support by the therapist throughout treatment.

## Extinction

Common mistakes made by parents of sleep disturbed infants include providing parental attention for the child's disturbances at awakening, failing to institute consistent sleep schedules, and promoting the association of daytime and nighttime activities like sleeping and feeding. Parents who foster an association between their presence and initial sleep onset and who respond on demand to their infant's cries upon awakening by rocking, patting, feeding, and cuddling are encouraging a nighttime dependence in the baby that can maintain his crying. The only way to discourage such dependence is to break the association between the pleasurable experience of being soothed and fed by caretakers and the onset of sleep. Numerous researchers have shown that establishment of bedtime routines, like regular bed and wake up times, and the removal of parental attention for night waking, including not feeding or cuddling the child on these occasions, result in marked improvement of the infant's sleep problem that is maintained at follow-up (Schaefer 1987, 1990b, Seymour et al. 1989).

A recent study by France and Hudson (1990) evaluated the effects of stimulus control and extinction on night waking in seven sleep disordered infants. A standard extinction program was carried out in which parents placed their children in bed, while awake, at a pre-established bedtime and did not respond to the infant's signaling unless illness or danger was suspected. When checking the infant's condition was deemed to be necessary, it was done quickly and with a minimum of noise and light. Results showed that, at the end of the intervention, all subjects had improved over their baseline levels on both the frequency and duration of their nighttime awakenings. These improvements were maintained at 3-month and 2-year follow-ups. It should be noted that, in this study, subjects initially exhibited increases in their levels of nighttime awakenings when parents decreased their attention to the disturbances. Post-extinction response burst, that is, an increase in the level of a target behavior when reinforcement is initially withdrawn, is a well-known phenomenon in behavioral management programs. Such bursts of activity are temporary and are quickly followed, as they were in this study, by a rapid decrease in the target behavior. Parents should be made aware of the potential for increased crying that may occur when a treatment program is instituted. They should be encouraged to persist in the treatment method and to avoid the potentially negative side effect of strengthening the target behavior through inconsistent responses that create a schedule of intermittent reinforcement. Such encouragement can be given through regular contact with the therapist, either face-to-face or by telephone, during which the therapist reinforces the parents' efforts with her support.

Another useful technique is to provide the parents with sleep diaries in which to record the infant's sleep behavior such as time of sleep onset, frequency and duration of signaling, parental interventions, and time of awakening. Such records provide information to be discussed with the parents during therapy sessions and a way to monitor treatment progress. They also provide parents with tangible evidence that behavioral change is actually occurring in their infant. Such evidence may supply encouragement to parents who are feeling anxious as a result of their infant's crying during the extinction process. Nevertheless, even with supportive management techniques, there will be some parents who find "cold turkey" extinction to be an unacceptable procedure for their children. Fortunately, effective alternative treatments exist for these families in the form of gradual extinction and scheduled awakenings.

## Gradual Extinction

Gradual extinction is essentially a modification of the extinction technique in which the reinforcer, that is, parental attention to night waking, is not withdrawn abruptly, but systematically, over a period of time. This treatment represents an option to parents who cannot tolerate the aversiveness of ignoring their baby's cries. In order to implement a program of gradual extinction, baseline measures of parental reinforcement of infant night waking should be taken. The goal of the program becomes one of eliminating the night waking by reducing parental attention from its baseline level to zero over the period of the treatment. This is accomplished in one of two ways. In one technique, parental response to infant crying is immediate but is given for progressively shorter periods of time. In an alternate procedure, parents wait successively longer periods of time before responding to their baby's cries. In both cases, parental attention to night waking is gradually faded from baseline to zero.

Lawton and colleagues (1991) evaluated the effectiveness of gradual extinction as a technique in the management of six infants with frequent night awakenings. Their study used a gradual approach in which parents immediately responded to infant crying but reduced the duration of their attending from baseline to zero over a period of twenty-eight days. Their results showed that gradual extinction was successful in reducing night waking for this group of infants over baseline measures. The technique did not, however, eliminate post-extinction response bursts nor did it entirely abolish parental stress during the treatment period. Although the parents in this study reported high levels of satisfaction with the procedure, half of them indicated that they found the technique to be stressful. The authors point out that gradual extinction is a more complex technique than regular extinction, which, since it does not entirely eliminate parental stress, should probably only be used with parents who resist a more standard extinction procedure.

The alternate technique of gradual extinction employs incremental increases in the amount of time that parents wait before intervening in a child's night waking episode. Durand and Mindell (1990) described the case of a 14-month-old infant whose night waking was successfully treated using this technique. The parents were directed to increase the intervals between their responses to their daughter's nighttime awakenings by increments of five minutes, the longest period being twenty minutes before an intervention. Furthermore, the parents were instructed that their interventions should consist of one parent entering the child's room for a period of fifteen seconds and providing her with reassurance in a neutral tone of voice. The question arises as to why this particular approach to gradual extinction does not, in fact, shape longer and longer crying bouts. Durand and Mindell (1990) suggest that limiting the parental response to neutral reassurance during which the child is never held simply does not provide a potent enough reinforcer to shape increased crying behavior. As with the previous gradual extinction technique, a caveat should be considered.

This procedure is more complex to implement than the standard extinction procedure and probably should only be offered to parents who find outright extinction to be aversive and unacceptable.

## Scheduled Awakenings

Both extinction and gradual extinction are techniques that involve some degree of planned ignoring of the infant's cries. Spontaneous awakening is a treatment technique that may be useful for parents who cannot tolerate their baby's crying and find any extinction procedure to be unacceptable. In order to implement a program of scheduled awakenings, baseline measurements must be taken of the child's spontaneous night waking activity. When the timing of the spontaneous awakenings has been determined, scheduled awakenings can be set for a period of fifteen to sixty minutes prior to the expected ones. During the scheduled awakenings, the baby is fed, consoled, and generally tended. The spontaneous awakenings are effectively precluded and the scheduled ones are gradually reduced and eliminated. Research has shown that scheduled awakening is an effective management technique for infant sleep disturbance (Johnson and Lerner 1985). One study (Rickert and Johnson 1988) compared the effectiveness of the scheduled awakening technique with systematic ignoring, that is, extinction. Both the scheduled awakening and the extinction groups showed decreases in the number of awakenings but the extinction group improved two times as rapidly. Scheduled awakening provides another alternative in the therapist's effort to match an acceptable treatment to a particular family's needs. Because this technique may be somewhat slower in achieving desired results than other behavioral methods, however, therapist support of parental efforts is especially important in order to encourage compliance early in the treatment before the benefits have become apparent.

## The Quick-Check Method

In our work at the Center for Psychological Services at Fairleigh Dickinson University, we have found it helpful to teach parents the Quick-Check Method (Schaefer and Petronko 1987) for dealing with a child's problematic sleep habits. The Quick-Check Method employs basic principles of behavioral modification and has been successful in treating infant sleep disturbance. The following procedure has been effective in helping parents to teach their very young children to initiate sleep and to return to sleep after middle-of-the-night awakening.

1. Establish a fixed bedtime for the infant. It is helpful to choose a time when the infant typically appears to be sleepy. Once the bedtime is set, it is important that parents remain committed to it. Consistency of time of sleep onset serves to establish a sleep-wake rhythm in the baby.

2. Create a bedtime ritual that is relaxing to the child. It might include a warm bath, soothing music, and comforting time spent with the parent. The routine should follow the same sequence each night and should take about twenty minutes to complete.

3. At the end of the bedtime ritual, the parent should be instructed to say good night and leave the bedroom while the child is still awake. It is essential that the child fall asleep on his own. Parents should be reminded not to rock, feed, or pat the infant to sleep. It is precisely this dependence on parental assistance at the time of initial sleep onset that causes the infant to signal in the middle of the night.

The condition of the infant's bedroom should be exactly the same at initial sleep onset as it will be in the middle of the night. The room should be quiet, with a minimum of light, and no parent should be present. If the bedroom environment is the same in the middle of the night when the infant awakens as it was when he fell asleep, the infant will feel comfortable to return to sleep unaided.

4. Parents should be instructed to follow this procedure in response to their infant's cries. If the infant signals by crying when placed in the crib at bedtime or awakens and signals during the night, the parents should be instructed to wait five minutes before responding. When five minutes have passed, the parent may reassure herself by going into the infant's bedroom and quickly checking that the infant is not ill or in any danger. Parents should be reminded that the baby should not be picked up. Instead, the parent may tell the infant in a neutral voice that it is sleep time and quickly leave the room while the infant is still awake.

If the infant continues to cry for twenty minutes after the first check, the procedure may be repeated. Again, the parent should leave the room before the baby has fallen asleep. The checking procedure is repeated at twenty-minute intervals for as long as it takes the infant to tire and eventually fall asleep. If the infant is whimpering softly at the end of the twenty-minute period, the parent should not enter the baby's room. Allowing parents to check on their infants serves two functions. First, it assures the parent that the infant is, in fact, all right; second, it allows the infant to know that he has not been abandoned.

5. Parents should awaken their baby at the pre-established wake up time in the morning. There should be no adjustments in this schedule regardless of the amount of sleep the infant or the parent managed to achieve the previous night. Daytime naps should be taken as scheduled, and waking activities, such as playing and feeding, should be conducted at their usual times.

6. Sleep diaries should be given to parents, and they should be instructed to keep a record of the time of their infant's initial sleep onset, the frequency and duration of their infant's cries, morning arousal time, and time and duration of daytime naps. Such information is useful in evaluating the course of the treatment.

7. In order to encourage parent compliance to the treatment methods, they should be educated about what to expect in the early part of the treatment. Parents should be told to expect that their child will cry loudly for one or two hours on the first night of treatment. On the second night, there will typically be a slight reduction in the amount of crying. The third night should bring a significant decrease in crying which is usually followed on subsequent nights by the infant's sleeping through the night, that is, awakening but soothing himself back to sleep without rousing parents. It is very likely that parents will not have to use the checking procedure after the third night of treatment. Some children, however, will require a week or two before they are able to sleep through the night.

8. Parents should be cautioned against actively listening to their baby's cries. Active listening is defined here as purposely attending to the sounds of the infant's cries. Various noise abatement procedures can be used, including closing doors and using ear plugs to muffle the sound. It is best to remind parents that they should also not listen passively to their child's cries. Passive listening occurs when parents hear their infant's crying although their attention is not intentionally directed toward the sounds. Attention can be directed at other activities like exercise, reading, or watching television to avoid passive listening.

9. It is important to obtain parental commitment to adhere to the treatment program for a minimum of three nights. Parents should be explained the consequences of intermittent reinforcement of their baby's disturbed sleep habits.

10. It is helpful to advise parents to begin the program on a night that is most convenient for them, such as Friday night if they do not have to work on the weekends.

11. The program should be used at nap times as well. Parents should set a fixed nap schedule and apply quick-check methods to their child's crying behavior. It might be best for some parents to begin the program during nap time since they may be better able to tolerate the crying during the day when it does not interrupt their own sleep.

12. Finally, parents should be instructed that crying is not, in itself, harmful to babies and may even provide a mode of tension release.

## Cases Treated with the Quick-Check Method

### Jennifer

Eleven-month-old Jennifer S. had learned to fall asleep with one or both of her parents, Jeff and Susan, standing over her crib. Her bedtime ritual included rocking, patting, and singing and took more than one hour to complete. Jennifer's parents wanted their daughter's ritual ended and sought help to accomplish this goal.

On the first night of treatment, Jennifer was placed in bed at 7:30 P.M. Her parents had been instructed to say good night and leave the room at once, without the customary rocking, patting, and singing. When her parents left, Jennifer immediately began to cry. Jeff went into Jennifer's room for the first quick-check at 7:35 P.M. He checked to see that Jennifer was safe and comfortable and then left the room quickly. Jeff recorded both the crying and the initial quick-check in the sleep diary.

Jennifer continued to cry, and so Susan returned to her daughter's room at 7:55 P.M. Again, a quick-check was made to ascertain that Jennifer was physically safe. Susan left the room one minute after she had entered it and recorded both the 20 minutes of crying and the second quick-check. Two more quick-checks were necessary on the first night, one at 8:15 P.M. and one at 8:35. Jennifer fell asleep at 8:50 P.M. Jeff and Susan recorded four quick-checks and eighty minutes of crying on the first night of treatment.

Although Jennifer continued to cry on subsequent nights, Susan and Jeff persisted in the treatment and recorded their daughter's crying time and their entrances into her room to check on her safety. The sleep diaries were helpful to these parents in overcoming their discouragement during the extinction process and maintaining their compliance. The record made it clear that Jennifer was, indeed, making progress because her total crying time was decreasing. Finally, on the sixth night of treatment, Jennifer was placed in bed at 7:30 and went to sleep without protest.

## Michael

Six-month-old Michael W. had learned to fall asleep while nursing, a practice that Michael's mother, Donna, wanted to end. After consultation with the therapist, Donna decided that it would be easier for her to tolerate Michael's crying at nap time so it was decided that the program would begin then.

Donna put Michael in for his morning nap at 10 A.M. while Michael was still awake. He immediately began to cry. Donna waited five minutes and returned to quickly check on Michael's condition. Michael continued to cry for an additional hour and five minutes, so his mother checked him three more times during that first nap period. Michael did not fall asleep and was removed from the crib at the end of his nap time.

Michael was placed in his crib for his afternoon nap at 3 P.M. This time he screamed as Donna left him. Michael screamed for forty minutes but finally fell asleep. His mother complied with the treatment program by checking on Michael twice during his crying, and awakening him at his normal wake up time of 5 P.M. Michael cried for ten minutes at his morning nap on the second day and for five minutes in the afternoon. On the third day, he cried for seven minutes in the morning and went to sleep without protesting in the afternoon.

## Julie

Karen and Bill C. reported that they began to notice 8-month-old Julie's sleep problem when she was 3 months old. According to Karen, it began with Julie's restless behavior, such as crying and moving while sleeping. Later, Julie developed frequent crying bouts during the night. Typically, the first episode occurred about one hour after being placed in bed when she awakened and cried. This pattern would be repeated again three or four hours later. During these occasions, Julie would stand in her crib and scream. She would often remain awake for one or two hours.

Karen and Bill had tried various responses to Julie's behavior. First they tried replacing her pacifier and patting her while she was still in the crib. Later, they rocked her gently to sleep. They tried leaving a light on in her room. On occasion, they even tried letting their daughter cry. Finally, in desperation, they began bringing Julie into their own bed, a practice they did not wish to continue.

Karen and Bill's pattern of intermittent reinforcement had made Julie's undesirable sleep habits potentially resistant to extinction. This fact was explained to the parents and encouragement and support of their efforts to help Julie learn new behaviors were provided by the therapist. Both parents worked outside the home during the day, and so they established a 9 P.M. bedtime for Julie, which allowed them sufficient time with their daughter in the evening.

On the first night of treatment, Julie was placed in her crib at 9 P.M. Karen and Bill said good night, and their daughter began to cry. Karen performed the first quick-check at 9:05 P.M. Julie continued to cry, so Bill entered her room at 9:25. The checking procedure continued until Julie fell asleep at 10:20 P.M. Julie awakened on that first night at 1:45 A.M. It was Karen's turn to check on her. She entered Julie's room at 1:50. Julie remained awake and crying until 2:30 and required one additional quick-check before falling asleep. At 3:15 A.M., Julie was again awake and crying. Although they were exhausted, Karen and Bill resisted the urge to take their daughter into their bed and continued with the program. They checked Julie at 3:20 A.M. and this time she remained awake until 3:45, again requiring a second check. Julie awakened one final time for the night at 6:20 A.M. This was 30 minutes before the established wake up time of 7 A.M. so a final quick check was made at 6:25. Julie returned to sleep at 6:35 and remained asleep until she was awakened by her parents at 7:00.

On the second night, Julie was placed in bed at 9 P.M. She immediately began to cry. She was checked at 9:05 and continued crying until 10:00, requiring two more checks. Julie slept until 2:15 A.M. She was checked at 2:20 and returned to sleep within the next twenty-minute interval so no further checking was done. This time Julie slept until the designated 7 A.M. wake up time.

On the third and fourth nights, Julie cried when initially placed in her crib. She required one quick-check each night at sleep onset, but there were no middle-of-the-night awakenings. On the fifth night, however, Julie repeated her pattern of both initial sleep refusal and night waking. This time she awakened at 4:05 A.M. and remained awake until 5:30 A.M., requiring five quick-checks. On the sixth night, Julie cried when she was placed in bed and remained awake for one hour. On the seventh night, Julie was placed in her bed at 9 P.M., as usual, and, to her parents' delight, she went immediately to sleep. Julie remained asleep throughout the night. Karen and Bill report that on subsequent nights they have placed Julie in her bed at 9 P.M., and she has gone to sleep without protest. In addition, Julie has consistently remained asleep throughout the night.

## Conclusion

Clearly, infant sleep refusal and middle-of-the-night wakefulness can be significant sources of distress to the families involved. The emphasis in this chapter has been on a behavioral management approach to the treatment of infant sleep disorders. Parents should be included in all decisions regarding the specifics of the approach. Treatment is much more likely to succeed if parental goals and individual tolerances for the baby's sleep habits and crying behaviors are taken into account. The therapist should listen carefully to parental wishes and modify treatment techniques when such adjustments appear necessary to ensure treatment compliance.

Sleep diaries are used as a source of information to both the parents and the therapist. The records are a valuable asset because they allow the therapist to monitor the progress of the treatment, and they provide tangible evidence to the parents that their child is improving. The knowledge that her baby's crying is decreasing may support an exhausted parent's decision to continue with the program.

Finally, then, the success of the intervention depends on the therapist's ability to listen to the parents and to provide them with techniques that will enable them to help their child. If these strategies are offered with adequate education and support, parents can teach their infants to sleep through the night.

References

Adair, R., Bauchner, H., Philipp, B., et al. (1991). Night waking during infancy: role of parental presence at bedtime. *Pediatrics* 87(4):500-504.

Anders, T. F. (1979). Night-waking in infants. *Pediatrics* 63(6):860-864.

Anders, T. F., Halpern, L. F., and Hua, J. (1992). Sleeping through the night: a developmental perspective. *Pediatrics* 90(4):554-560.

Campbell, M., Green, W. H., and Deutsch, S. I. (1985). *Child and Adolescent Psychopharmacology*. Vol. 2. Beverly Hills, CA: Sage.

Durand, V. M., and Mindell, J. A. (1990). Behavioral treatment of multiple childhood sleep disorders: effects on child and family. *Behavior Modification*, 14(1):37-49.

Emde, R. N., and Walker, S. (1976). Longitudinal study of infant sleep: results of 14 subjects studied at monthly intervals. *Psychophysiology*, 13(5):456-461.

France, K., Blampied, N., and Wilkinson, P. (1991). Treatment of infant sleep disturbance by trimeprazine in combination with extinction. *Developmental and Behavioral Pediatrics* 12(5):308-314.

France, K. G., and Hudson, S. M. (1990). Behavioral management of infant sleep disturbance. *Journal of Applied Behavior Analysis* 23(1):91-98.

Healy, B. T. (1989). Autonomic nervous system correlates of temperament. *Infant Behavior and Development* 12:289-304.

Holditch-Davis, D. (1990). The development of sleeping and waking states in high-risk preterm infants. *Infant Behavior and Development* 13:513-531.

Hoppenbrouwers, T., Hodgman, J., Arakawa, K., et al. (1988). Sleep and waking states in infancy. *Sleep* 11(4):387-401.

Johnson, C. M., and Lerner, B. S. (1985). Amelioration of infant sleep disturbances: effects of scheduled awakenings by compliant parents. *Infant Mental Health Journal* 6(1):21-30.

Kahn, A., and Blum, D. (1982). Phenothiazines and sudden infant death syndrome. *Pediatrics* 70(1):75-78.

Kahn, A., Mozin, M. J., Casimir, G., et al. (1985). Insomnia and cow's milk allergy in infants. *Pediatrics* 76(6):880-884.

Kahn, A., Rebuffat, E., Blum, D., et al. (1987). Difficulty in initiating and maintaining sleep associated with cow's milk allergy in infants. *Sleep* 10(2):116-121.

Keener, M. A., Zeanak, C. H., and Anders, T. F. (1988). Infant temperament, sleep organization, and nighttime parental interventions. *Pediatrics* 81(6):762–771.

Lawton, C., France, K., and Blampied, M. (1991). Treatment of infant sleep disturbance by graduated extinction. *Child and Family Behavior Therapy* 13(1):39–55.

Lee, K. (1992). Pattern of night waking and crying of Korean infants from 3 months to 2 years old and its relationship with various factors. *Behavioral Pediatrics* 13(5):326–330.

Medoff D., and Schaefer C. E. (1993). Children sharing the parental bed: a review of the advantages and disadvantages of co-sleeping. *Psychology* 30(1):1–9.

McKenna, J. J., Thoman E. B., Anders, T. F., et al. (1993). Infant–parent co-sleeping in an evolutionary perspective: implications for understanding infant sleep development and the sudden infant death syndrome. *Sleep* 16(3):263–282.

Michelsson K., Rinne, A., and Paajanen, S. (1990). Crying, feeding and sleeping in 1 to 12-month-old infants. *Child: Care, Health and Development* 16:99–111.

Moore, T., and Ucko, L. E. (1957). Night waking in early infancy: part I. *Archives of Diseases in Children* 32:333–342.

Richman, N. (1985). A double-blind drug trial of treatment in young children with waking problems. *Journal of Child Psychology and Psychiatry* 26(4):591–598.

Rickert, V. I., and Johnson, C. M. (1988). Reducing nocturnal awakening and crying episodes in infants and young children: a comparison between scheduled awakenings and systematic ignoring. *Pediatrics* 81(2):203–211.

Russo, R., Gururaj, V., and Allen, J. (1976). The effectiveness of diphenhydramine HCL in paediatric sleep disorders. *Journal of Clinical Pharmacology* 16:284–288.

Schaefer, C. E. (1987). The efficacy of a multimodal treatment program for infant night waking. *Sleep Research* 16:442.

_____ (1990a). Night waking and temperament in early childhood. *Psychological Reports* 67:192–194.

_____ (1990b). Treatment of night wakings in early childhood: maintenance of effects. *Perceptual and Motor Skills* 70:561–562.

Schaefer, C. E., and Petronko, M. R. (1987). *Teach Your Baby to Sleep through the Night*. New York: Penguin.

Scher, A. (1991). A longitudinal study of night waking in the 1st year. *Child: Care, Health and Development* 17:295–302.

Seymour, F. W., Brock, P., During, M., and Poole, G. (1989). Reducing sleep disruptions in young children: evaluation of therapist guided and written information approaches, a brief report. *Journal of Child Psychology and Psychiatry* 30:913–918.

Stifter, C. A., and Fox, N. A. (1990). Infant reactivity: psychological correlates of newborn and 5-month temperament. *Developmental Psychology* 26(4):1–7.

Van Tassel, E. B. (1985). The relative influence of child and environmental characteristics on sleep disturbances in the first and second years of life. *Developmental & Behavioral Pediatrics* 6(2):81–86.

Weissbluth, M. (1981). Sleep disturbance and infant temperament. *Pediatrics* 99:817–819.

Zuckerman, B., Stevenson, J., and Bailey V. (1987). Sleep problems in early childhood: continuities, predictive factors, and behavioral correlates. *Pediatrics* 80(5):644–671.

# 4

# The Treatment of Nighttime Fears:
## A Cognitive-Developmental Approach

Kevin C. Mooney
Michael Sobocinski

### Introduction

Psychological theorists from Freud (1909) and Watson and Rayner (1920) to Bandura (1969) have been concerned with children's "unreasonable fears": those fears which appear out of proportion to a given benign or undefined stimulus (Miller et al. 1974), and not directly contributing to the avoidance of environmental danger or physical pain (Lang 1968). Fears involve outer behavioral expressions, inner subjective feelings, and concomitant physiological changes (Reed et al. 1992). The present chapter deals with one common group of fears: those fears that are associated with nighttime and/or the dark.

The prevalence of nighttime fears or fear of the dark has been examined in normative fear research through the use of interviews, questionnaires, and fear checklists given to children and their parents. Personal interviews have generated the highest reported prevalence of nighttime fears, peaking with Lapouse and Monk's (1959) finding that 30% of a sample of 6- to 8-year-olds, and Bauer's (1976) finding that 67% of his sample of 8-year-olds experienced nighttime fears. Research utilizing checklists, questionnaires, and rating scales has generally found fewer nighttime fears. Using a questionnaire, Mooney (1980) found a peak of about 23% of 9- to 10-year-olds reporting either intense or very intense nighttime fears, while Pratt (1945) and Hagman (1932) both identified peaks of approximately 11% for kindergarten and preschool children. Girls have reported more nighttime fears than boys (Mooney 1980, Pratt 1945), although there is some question here as to whether these differences in the number of reported fears represent differences in the numbers of fears that girls and boys actually *have* (Ferrari 1986). As Ferrari (1986) writes, it is probably safe to conclude "that there is a trend for girls to report a greater number of fears than boys, fears of a somewhat different type, and to demonstrate a greater intensity of fear response" (p. 81). In two studies which collected data about children from both children and parents, parents reported fewer nighttime fears than children (Mooney 1980, Lapouse and Monk 1959).

The task of sifting through the normative research with its different methodologies, respondents, and demand characteristics is difficult. With mild nighttime fears there may be relative peaks of fear at about ages 5 to 6 and again at ages 9 to 11. It appears that the majority of children have mild nighttime fears at some time in their childhood, with most of these children soon overcoming or outgrowing them. About 10 to 20% of children ages preschool to about 11 seem to have intense or particularly disruptive nighttime fears. Past clinical research has shown that for many children and their families, nighttime fears are extremely severe and disruptive (Graziano and Mooney 1980). As is the case with severe childhood fears in general (Reed et al. 1992), it also appears that severe nighttime fears may not normally go away but may instead persist for years (Graziano et al. 1979b, Graziano and Mooney 1980). We are not aware of any empirical literature with adolescents and adults addressing nighttime fears. Whether and how severe nighttime fears might dissipate or change focus in adolescence and adulthood remains unknown.

### Assessment and Differential Diagnosis

There is no single best measure of fear. Fear, normal or abnormal, may most usefully be viewed as referring to the occurrence of subjective/ verbal, behavioral/motor, and physiological/autonomic responses in a series of imperfectly coupled response systems (Lader 1972, Lang 1968). The subjective/verbal experience of fear often involves self-focused attention, hypervigilance, distortions in time, compulsive scanning of the environment, selective encoding of memory, distortions of visual and auditory perception, inability to anticipate probabilities, and verbal restrictions. Difficulties with assessment methods employing subjective/verbal accounts of fear include variations in the content of what is reported according to a child's current motivation, the necessity of assuming that what children think about fears is what they actually report (Morris and Kratochwill 1991), as well as other possible sources of bias and distortion. Retrospective accounts of fear are also subject to attempts to re-construct past events, as well as to the influence of interference on memory.

The primary behavioral/motor response to fear is some kind of avoidance of the feared situation. Measurement of the expressions of such responding can vary due to motivation and demand characteristics that may change over situations (Kelley 1976, Lick and Bootzin 1975), as well as differences in culture, family mores, temperament, and so forth.

Lang (1968, 1977, 1979) has repeatedly and astutely pointed out that no current physiological measure is an unambiguous index of fear or anxiety. Thus, for example, while a person feels very different when afraid as opposed to sad, the autonomic response is similar in both instances (Ekman et al. 1983). Physiological changes reflect the intensity of an individual's often idiosyncratic pattern of arousal, and hence do not provide a reliable index of fear or anxiety.

While various theoretical persuasions may argue as to whether nighttime fears are a response to the dark or are elicited as a result of an internally (symbolic) perceived cue, from a clinician's point of view, nighttime fears per se are relatively straightforward to assess. Perhaps most prominent in the clinical presentation of the child with severe nighttime fears are the behaviors associated with going to bed that are highly emotionally charged and protracted in nature, such as "crying and severe panic, crawling into parents' and siblings' beds, insisting upon bright lights . . . [and] restless nights continually interrupted in the early morning hours by frightened calling-out" (Graziano et al. 1979b, p. 221). Often these fears are highly disruptive, such that there has been a significant lowering of the child's overall level of functioning over an extended period of time, which may include a progressive withdrawal from peer activities outside of the home in an effort to avoid potential embarrassment (Graziano et al. 1979a,b).

A more difficult question revolves around assessing coexisting problems that may be contextually relevant to the treatment for the child's fear and/or other difficulties that may also need intervention. Separation disorders, identity disorders, attention deficit disorders, oppositional disorders, adjustment disorders, post-traumatic disorders, depression, other anxiety spectrum disorders, behavior due to specific family or marital stresses, and other environmental situations and contingencies all share features, or are contextually relevant to night-time fears and need to be examined or screened for by the clinician.

The most commonly identified area of comorbidity relevant to children's fears deals with anxiety and depression. It appears that between one-fourth and one-third of children diagnosed with anxiety disorder also have depressive features, with more depressive features associated in older children and adolescents (Strauss et al. 1988; Hershberg et al. 1982). Parents' ratings of their children also support the association of anxiety and depression (Achenbach 1978, cited in Reed et al. 1992). Caution should be exercised in interpreting these findings in that specific fears are grouped with other anxiety spectrum disorders and, as with the case of many specific fears, a large subset of nighttime fears does not imply the presence of a more general anxiety condition (Graziano and Mooney 1980). From a treatment perspective, a clinician should be on the alert for depressive features when encountering a nighttime fearful child.

As we will discuss later in the chapter, we believe that fears arise from a variety of contexts, some more and some less obviously associated with other forms of psychopathology. Obviously, if a fear is associated with trauma such as physical or sexual abuse and/or chronic parental conflict, treatment should typically address these issues. However, the child's nighttime fear may also have become established as a somewhat separate problem for the child, and it cannot be assumed that by dealing with other treatment issues the fear will automatically extinguish. In such cases, the treatment for the fear should be tailored to take into account these issues.

### Review of Theoretical Issues

#### Single Factor Theories

The etiology of fear has played a major role in psychological theorizing. Watson and Raynor (1920), in their famous study of "little Albert," found that a direct pairing of a loud noise with a rat could condition a fear response in an infant towards rats which then generalized to other furry objects (e.g., a rabbit, a seal skin coat, and, to a lesser extent, a dog). They posited a *classical conditioning* model of fears where neutral stimuli acquired secondary motivating (fearful) properties when paired or associated with noxious stimuli.

Some experimental (Venn and Short 1973) but primarily anecdotal evidence suggests that fears may be acquired *vicariously*. Modeling has been frequently speculated upon as the cause of some fears (cf. Jones and Jones 1928, Bandura and Menlove 1968). In such cases, a child who had previously experienced no fear in a particular situation would watch another person react fearfully in that situation. If, when this child was put in that same situation again and he or she reacted fearfully, a fear would be said to have been acquired through modeling.

Verbal or written information may be another vicarious contributor to fear reactions in children (Lazarus and Abromovitz 1962, Ollendick and Gruen 1972, Rimm et al. 1977). For example, Lazarus and Abromovitz (1962) report a 10-year-old boy's fear of the dark originating when he saw a frightening film and subsequently was told by his grandmother to keep away from all doors and windows at night, as burglars and kidnappers were on the prowl. An 11-year-old boy who had severe night fears, when being questioned about them by the first author, commented that he was afraid of "sulzes" which he said were "big, black, hairy, and dangerous." This fear had apparently begun when a policemen had encountered him and a friend in a vacant lot and warned them to be careful as there had been "assaults" in the area.

Symbolic or temporal *displacement* has also been posited as a cause of children's fears. Freud (1909), for example, explained "little Hans's" fear of horses by positing that anxiety from a real source of fear (in this case a problematic oedipal relationship with his father in which Hans was unconsciously afraid his father was angry at him and intended to harm him) could become displaced to another, otherwise neutral, object or situation (in this case, horses). The previously neutral stimulus comes to represent the real source of the fear. In a similar vein, fears of objects or situations have frequently been reported after a calamitous event or series of events that have little to do, except temporally, with the event itself (Lazarus 1960, Lazarus and Abromovitz 1962).

Anecdotal evidence also supports the notion that fear may be extended or increased through various *environmental contingencies* that provide secondary gain to the child. School phobia is a good example of this, where a child may be rewarded for not attending school by being allowed to stay up later at night and sleep late in the morning, by never having to separate from the attention or affections of a parent, and so forth.

However well each of the factors noted above seems to explain the fears they discussed, other experience and research shows each to be inadequate for even an approximation of a comprehensive model of the development of fear in children. Very early in the field of fear research, it became clear that not all objects were equally likely to be feared. Bergman (as cited in Rachman 1978) could not condition fear reactions to geometrically shaped wooden objects or cloth curtains by pairing their presentation with a loud (noxious) and startling bell. Seligman (1971) and DeSilva and colleagues (1977) expanded on a variety of findings such as this and argued that many prevalent fears are of natural importance to the survival of the species and that these fears are evolutionarily prepared, selective, resistant to extinction, and acquired with minimal experience (cf. Marks 1987). Other, less prevalent, fears, on the other hand, appear to be evolutionarily unprepared or even contra-prepared.

Another line of research has involved the direct acquisition of fears in infants (cf. Scarr and Salapatek 1970, Bowlby 1973). Bowlby (1973) contends that there are certain innate fear-provoking stimuli, such as strangeness, sudden movements, rapid or looming approach, and heights, which have the potential for arousing fear reactions in infants, particularly when they are alone. Jones (1924) also points out that *unexpectedness* is one particularly potent factor in producing fear throughout early childhood.

Hagman, in a classic study in 1932, posited that certain fear "factors" might cause a fear reaction only under certain situations. Looking at factors such as pain, suddenness, preparation, restraint, first time, strangeness, warning, physical contact, sound, sight, and dark, he found certain factors of situations tended to coexist in the original situation when a fear appeared to begin. He stated an obvious conclusion that was largely ignored for the next fifty plus years: "The significance of these relationships lies in the implications indicated for the cause of fear. The existence of these conditions together tends to show that singular causes cannot be postulated as being productive of all fears" (p. 119).

Other researchers have hypothesized that chronic or generalized anxiety or general overactivity of the autonomic nervous system (cf. Kelly et al. 1970, Costello 1971) precipitates a fear or phobia. Others, such as Andrews (1966), have implicated coping styles, basically arguing that a dependent, nonassertive, clinging style of coping might inhibit normal mastery of anxiety and fears by the child.

## The Development of Children's Fears

It appears that the structure or content of childhood fears demonstrates a fairly reliable sequence of developmental changes from early childhood through adolescence, although the specific behavioral manifestations may appear quite different at different ages. While the number of fears that children report declines with age (e.g., King et al. 1989) there is some evidence that fears may once again increase around the ages of 9 to 11 (Macfarlane et al. 1954, Smith 1970, both cited in Reed et al. 1992). The existence and significance of this resurgence in reported fears is difficult to determine with any degree of certainty, and some researchers argue that some of the data upon which this latter increase in fears was based may have been confounded because of cohort effects (Ferrari 1986). Additionally, while there have been general age changes identified in terms of the content of childhood fears, our understanding of how actual fear responses may themselves change across developmental periods, as well as how children themselves experience their fears remains relatively poorly understood by researchers and clinicians alike (Ferrari 1986).

There appears to be an age-related trend evident in the content of children's fears, such that earlier fears tend to be general, vague, and ill-defined, whereas later fears are more realistic and specific in nature (Bauer 1976). The pattern of age-related changes may be understood to reflect in part the development of more complex cognitive and linguistic abilities in children. For the young child whose thinking displays significant limitations in the ability to assume the perspective of another, who may confuse appearance with reality, and who may reason in a precausal manner, the appearance of an object may be seen as sufficient cause for fear, as reported by the kindergartners in Bauer's (1976) study, who claimed that an object elicited fear for reasons such as "his face looks ugly" (p. 72).

Thus, during infancy, fears of loud noises or other excessive or novel stimuli, of falling, of separation from parent(s), or of strange persons predominate (Reed et al. 1992, Rutter and Garmezy 1983). During the preschool years fears of dogs or other large animals, of the dark, of being alone and separated from parents, and of imaginary creatures (Bauer 1976, Poznanski 1973, cited in Reed et al. 1992) assume prominence, while fear of school begins to increase around age 6 with the child's first venture into the school setting (Smith 1970 cited in Reed et al. 1992). During the elementary school years (ages 6 to 12) fears of parental conflict and punishment (Croake and Knox 1973, Ollen-dick 1983, both cited in Reed et al. 1992), of poor school performance and social rejection (Beidel and Turner 1988, Turner et al. 1986, both cited in Reed et al. 1992), and health problems (Reed et al. 1992) assume prominence. Adolescence finds new fears of crime in general, of war and nuclear destruction, sexual issues (including pregnancy and AIDS), and of family concerns (Robinson et al. 1991).

For the purposes of the current chapter, it should be noted that Bauer (1976) found no significant differences in the content of chil-dren's bedtime fears in his study of fifty-four kindergarten through sixth-grade children, relative to the content of those fears identified in response to a question inquiring into what children were most afraid of, or relative to those fears identified in the context of dreaming. This study also identified a non-significant trend towards reporting fewer bedtime fears from kindergarten (53%) to 2nd grade (67%), and finally to 6th grade (35%). Interestingly, Mooney (1985) reports that children who were identified as having high levels of nighttime fears did not differ significantly from children identified as having low levels of nighttime fears with respect to the type of fear that they most com-monly experienced: for both groups, fears related to a loss of personal security were most common. It may be that children normally progress through a developmental sequence in which their understanding of death and personal mortality undergoes predictable changes, and that confrontation of this issue is inevitable (see, e.g., Bauer 1976, for a discussion of the development of children's conceptions of death). There is also evidence that children's bedtime fears may fall into three separate categories or groupings (Mooney et al. 1984): concerns for one's own life, safety or loss, or others' safety and continued presence; *imaginal-numinous* concerns, such as of ghosts, monsters, or dangerous animals; and concerns about characteristics inherent in the night, such as shadows in the room or banging or knocking noises.

## A Cognitive-Developmental Approach

Kegan (1982) has suggested that both affect and cognition be consid-ered as aspects of one overall motion or process of life itself, namely the quest to "make meaning," or the striving to bring coherence to our experiences, which he views as the defining or central aspect of what it means to be human. In this chapter we will place nighttime fears within such a constructivist cognitive-developmental framework, which recognizes the progression of regular, predictable changes in the structure of children's thought when attempting to understand the meaning of a fear for an individual child. At the same time, we also pay close attention to the manner in which the life experiences of the child interact to determine the type and intensity of fear. Thus, it would not suffice simply to frame a 6-year-old's fear of thunderstorms within an early concrete-operational stage of cognitive development. We must also take into account the fact that the home of this child's grandparents was recently destroyed by a hurricane if we are to formulate an accurate and empathic understanding of the child's current experience.

The current treatment approach also incorporates the efforts of Schwartz and Shaver (1987) in the field of prototype emotion theory, which conceptualizes discrete emotions (e.g., fear, sadness, anger) as arising in large measure out of a cognitive appraisal of a situation, object, or event as "good or bad, helpful or harmful, consistent or inconsistent with a person's motives and values" (p. 221). In other words, the interpretation of circumstances and situations serves as a cognitive antecedent to specific emotional responses. Within this framework, fear may be conceptualized as arising out of an appraisal of a situation as a real or potential threat to the goals of the individual, whether these be physical safety and comfort, interpersonal security, or a sense of personal identity. In addition, Schwartz and Shaver (1987) have identified a "set of situational factors (unfamiliar situation, being in the dark, being alone) which increase the person's perceived vulnerability to such threats and impede his or her chances of coping effectively" (p. 209). As such, the emotion of fear implies the simultaneous presence of the individual's sense of self as an essential aspect of the emotional response. In all fear situations, as with other human emotions, the manner in which the person understands the feared person, object, or event is ultimately critical for any attempt at intervention.

Consistent with recent theory that has attempted to extend Piagetian concepts to an understanding of the development of the self, to psychopathology (e.g., Kegan 1982, Noam 1988), and to therapeutic approaches to working with trauma survivors (e.g., Briere 1992), the understanding of childhood fears being proposed here emphasizes the adaptive, constructive nature of behavioral manifestations of fears. The integrative, synthesizing function of the self implies a "central psychological function of self-integration. Such a motivation is behind the continuous attempt of all persons to create a sense of self and identity, a personal and interpersonal continuity over time" (Noam 1988, p. 291). Such a view of childhood fears emphasizes the active struggles of the child client to cope with the threat that is represented in the manifest fear object. As Briere (1992) writes regarding the problematic behavior often exhibited by trauma survivors: "In other words, the behaviors in question are not passive symptoms of some greater disturbance, but instead usually reflect the client's ongoing attempts to do what the therapist would have him or her do: cope and respond to the environment as effectively as possible" (pp. 85–86). From this perspective, we can see that the development of fears in children represents just such an attempt to make sense out of experience, although, because of the threatening nature of the feared object or event and the impact of high levels of affective arousal, the child's cognitive skills are pushed beyond their functional ability to differentiate and integrate his/her experience. Thus, a child's capacity to make subjective sense out of his/her experiences relies on operations, schemas, and structures that are partly conscious but largely unconscious (Fischer and Pipp 1984).

Fish-Murray and colleagues (1987), in their work with children who have been through a traumatic experience, state that "these mental systems are not just elements or aggregates of experience but condensations and transformations of experiences resulting from the child's interaction with his world" (p. 90). They have observed that when emotionally upset, the traumatized child's cognitive organization and flexibility are severely limited. In particular, they found that the child is pulled toward predominantly visual and less developed and interactive structures of thought. This type of visual thinking makes time sequencing difficult and keeps a child centered on his/her own world and stuck in earlier forms of preoperational logic. Descriptions of the quality of thought displayed in children with severe nighttime fears suggest that similar processes may be operative within this group.

An important aspect of this striving for coherence in one's experience is the attribution of causality to events. Shirk (1988), reviewing prominent theories of the role of causal analysis in everyday social interactions, notes that these "processes are not only a means of providing the individual with a predictable view of the world, but also a means of maintaining the exercise of control in that world" (p. 58).

Young preoperational children's causal attributions differ reliably from those of older children and adults along three dimensions (Shirk 1988). The first of these is an internal–external dimension, where it has been found that preoperational children tend to give external causal explanations for events, and only later do they reliably formulate psychological and interpersonal explanations. The second dimension is a proximal–distal dimension, which refers to young children's tendency to focus upon one salient aspect or feature of a situation, which Piaget referred to as centration. The causal explanations offered by young children tend to be temporally centered as well, meaning that they focus on proximal causes for events such as the experience of fear, with little awareness of how past events may exert continuing effects. The third causal dimension is conscious–unconscious. According to Shirk's (1988) analysis of the literature, prior to adolescence unconscious determinants of behavior may not be recognized as lying outside of the "actor's awareness" (p. 78). The recognition of causes of behavior that lie outside of a person's awareness is a complex cognitive process, and unconscious causes of behavior are difficult for children to recognize because of the cognitive skills required to construct them. They also require the recognition that such behavior is overdetermined, that is, that several causes for human behavior may occur simultaneously.

Given the presence of strong cognitive constraints in younger children influencing the nature of their causal explanations one can readily see that children are likely to construct explanations for their experiences that are external, that are temporally contingent, that lie at the level of conscious awareness, and that recognize single as opposed to multiple causes. Taken together, these lines of thought suggest that the early preoperational 2-year-old's display of fear over her father's sudden loss of his beard, and the concrete operational 6-year-old's inability to sleep at night because of the monsters and ghosts that inhabit his bedroom are not only the result of their current level of cognitive development, but also active attempts at fashioning causal attributions for, and coping with, what are perceived to be threats to the coherence of their sense of self. As another example, a child's nighttime fear of burglars or other potentially aggressive, dangerous figures might incorporate several aspects of this tendency to construct causal explanations. It is possible that earlier events from the day, such as an aggressive encounter on the school playground or at home with parents or a sibling, may somehow become "disconnected" causally from the fear that is understood to arise out of the burglars that inhabit the bedroom. For the child who struggles with fears of threatening creatures at night, the attempt to understand the causes of her/his own behavior, feelings, or impulses may lead to the attribution of disturbing thoughts and feelings to an object (the burglars), as opposed to a more cognitively complex explanation that may locate the source of these disturbing experiential components within the person her/himself.

While knowledge of a particular child's general level of cognitive development can help one understand the specific quality of the child's fears, it is important to note that it is an oversimplification to categorize a child as preoperational or concrete operational, if this label is meant to serve as a blanket categorization of the child's current level of cognitive functioning. As recent cognitive-developmental research and theory have pointed out (e.g., Fischer 1980) children display an unevenness across cognitive skill domains, such that specific cognitive capacities might demonstrate a more complex level of development due to environmental support and opportunity for practice. What this means with respect to children's fears is that a child who appears to be functioning at a particular level of cognitive development may demonstrate specific areas where she/he seems younger, such as the 10-year-old who suddenly develops a fear of alien characters from a popular television show. These pockets of earlier cognitive functioning represent a challenge to the child's ability to differentiate and integrate the components of his/her experience, either because of the negative impact of affect upon the operation of newly acquired and not fully consolidated cognitive skills, a lack of sufficient environmental support and practice leading to generalization of previously acquired cognitive skills in other domains, or the complexity of the task (Fischer 1980).

Fischer, in highlighting the importance of environmental support for the acquisition of cognitive skills, has discriminated between an individual's level of optimal and typical performance (Fischer and Kenny 1986, Fischer and Pipp 1984). Basically, the presence of environmental support, such as is found in the opportunity to practice and receive feedback on one's performance, is important in the acquisition of more complex cognitive skills. This principle appears to operate in those therapeutic interventions which allow children to differentiate, integrate, and finally symbolize their fears through the use of storytelling, visual representation through drawing, and visual imagery techniques.

In terms of our understanding of childhood fears, there are

several implications that seem to follow from the above considerations: first, the behavioral responses ("symptoms") to childhood fears should be seen as communicating a perceived threat to the child's sense of coherence to his/her self and/or experiential world, even though the manner in which this message is expressed may make it difficult to interpret the underlying message.

Second, the child's response to this perceived threat represents an attempt to cope with, and thereby control, the threatening person, object, or event. As such, the task that is being presented to the child represents one that is more successfully resolved through the use of more complex cognitive skills, which are currently beyond the child's ability to employ. Third, the presence of high levels of affect, in this case fear, may be seen to interfere with the assimilation of the threat into existing cognitive schema, or, alternatively, with the accommodation of the child's cognitive structures in a manner that more adequately accounts for the reality of the threat (Fischer 1980, Fischer and Pipp 1984). Because of the negative impact of high levels of emotional arousal, the threatening material remains unsymbolized and is not integrated into the child's cognitive structures.

## Summary of Empirical Research

Three clinical analogue studies selected nursery school and kindergarten children to receive treatment for what appeared to be quite mild fear of the dark (Leitenberg and Calahan 1973, Kanfer et al. 1975, Kelley 1976). These studies were well-designed, using control groups, duration of dark tolerance as pre- and post-treatment behavioral measures, and visual "fear thermometers" for subjective reports by, or feedback, to, the subjects.

Leitenberg and Calahan (1973) used a *reinforcement practice* method in which children were instructed to remain in a dark room for increasing periods of time, for five trials per session, two sessions per week, for a maximum of four weeks or until the child reached a criterion of two consecutive five-minute dark tolerance trials. For each successful trial the children were reinforced with praise and prizes. The authors report a significant treatment and control group difference on post-training dark-tolerance tests. However, the mean post-training dark-tolerance time for the experimental group was only about three minutes compared to half a minute for the control group. It is unclear whether a three minute dark-tolerance, however reliable, has any personal or clinical significance.

Kelley (1976) assigned forty fear-of-the-dark children to three desensitization groups, one play placebo control group and one no-treatment control group, and reported no difference between treatment and control conditions or among the three treatment conditions. The most striking finding of this study was the significant effect of a simple demand manipulation; that is, verbal instructions to remain longer in the dark room dramatically increased dark tolerance and was "a far more powerful influence on both behavioral and self-report change scores than three sessions of therapy" (p. 80).

Kanfer and colleagues (1975) used a verbal mediation self-control approach to children's fear reduction. Children 5 and 6 years old rehearsed one of three verbal mediation responses: (1) sentences emphasizing the child's control or competence (e.g., "I am a brave girl (or boy). I can take care of myself."), (2) sentences aimed at reducing the fear stimulus value of the dark (e.g., "The dark is a fun place to be."), or (3) neutral sentences (e.g., "Mary had a little lamb."). In dark-tolerance post-tests the competence group significantly outperformed the others. However, the mean change in dark tolerance for the competence group was less than two minutes.

Other hints of the possible effectiveness of verbal mediation are found in case studies (Ayer 1973, Lazarus and Abramovitz 1962, Merritt 1991) in which children rehearsed highly "competent," (i.e., mastery-oriented) and very imaginative, strategies for coping with fear stimuli. The modeling research by Jakibchuk and Smeriglio (1977) suggests the necessity of a first-person, self-speech narrative to accompany a symbolic modeling film. One possible interpretation of these various hints is that the children's own verbal self-instructions — whether originally received from a film, from specific sentences given them to rehearse, or from fanciful pictorial and verbal images — on how to deal successfully with the fear stimuli may be a central component of the various effective interventions.

Three studies have dealt with more severe levels of nighttime fear (Graziano and Mooney 1980, Graziano et al. 1979b, Kellerman 1980). Kellerman (1980) presented three cases of children, ages 5, 8, and 13, with nighttime fears. He used a multifaceted treatment approach fit specifically to each child that included a reciprocal inhibition component in which the children were taught counter-anxious behaviors (being angry, watching TV, getting a snack), earning monetary rewards for fearless behavior, dealing with reality factors around the nighttime fear (e.g., making sure the house is secure), and parental limitations on reinforcing nighttime fear behavior. Follow-ups at nine to twenty-four months showed maintained improvement.

Graziano and colleagues (1979b), in a multiple-case pilot study, reduced severe childhood fears using verbal self-control strategies. Seven children presented severe, long-term nighttime fears (range = 3 to 6 years duration, mean duration = 4.6 years) that involved serious nightly family disruptions. From descriptions of the children's behavior, it appeared reasonable to expect that a successful intervention would employ a strategy designed to interrupt the motor and cognitive escalation of fear early in those sequences, and also provide and reinforce alternative competent self-speech coping responses early in their nightly fear sequences. It was assumed that the most effective setting in which to practice coping skills would be at bedtime, at home, and that parents would be the most available persons to supervise this practice of coping skills. The pilot study strongly suggested the value of practice in verbal self-control skills to reduce severe nighttime fears.

Graziano and Mooney (1980) experimentally tested the effectiveness of the procedures suggested by the pilot study. The major goal of the study was to test whether simple verbal instructions to parents and children on how to carry out home practice of cognitive and behavioral self-control skills could systematically reduce severe and highly disruptive levels of nighttime fears. The methodology was drawn largely from Leitenberg and Callahan's (1973) "reinforced practice," Kelley's (1976) direct instructions, and Kanfer, Karoly, and Newsman's (1975) self-control through verbal mediation procedures. The use of relaxation with children was based upon earlier work by Graziano and Kean (1968).

Three treatment sessions were conducted over three weeks. Children were instructed to handle their fears by: (1) muscle relaxation, (2) imagining an individualized pleasant scene, and, (3) repeating the following competence-related sentences: "I am brave. I can take care of myself when I am alone. I can take care of myself when I am in the dark." Parents were taught to aid the child in practicing the exercises nightly before bed, and were also instructed in how to institute a token economy for correct practice and nonfearful nighttime behavior throughout the night. After the completion of ten consecutive fearless nights where the child had received all the possible tokens for correct practice and nonfearful behavior, the tokens were exchanged for a party at McDonald's.

The results clearly showed that following the three-week intervention the experimental group had significantly less nighttime fear behavior than the wait-control group. The two groups did not differ on post-treatment measures of school and social adjustment and total number of fears, thereby supporting their prediction that the intervention effects in the short term would largely be specific to the nighttime fear behavior. Because of random assignment of subjects to the experimental and control groups and the findings of no pre-treatment differences between groups on any of the measures, it was concluded that the results support the effectiveness of the treatment "package" in reducing children's nighttime fears. It should be noted that this experiment used multiple behavioral devices—relaxation, imagination, cognitive self-statements, and token reward—and does not indicate which behavioral interventions were effective. It was, however, the first experimental study of children that led to significant improvement in treating severe fear in childhood.

A follow-up over a period of two and one half to three years (Graziano and Mooney 1982) did show continued improvement as well as some apparent generalization of treatment effects. This follow-up tracked thirty-four of the forty participants in the original Graziano and Mooney (1980) study. Maintenance of essentially all of the original treatment gains was reported in thirty-one of the thirty-four children, while only two showed decay toward the pretreatment baselines. Nine of the thirty-four reported the development of new problems since the termination of the intervention, although the parents did not believe that these problems were related to the child's nighttime fears. Perhaps most interesting was the finding that there was some degree of generalization of treatment effects in this sample of children. Although only a minority of the parents (ten of thirty-four) stated that their child had continued to employ the specific fear-reduction self-control methods taught in the original intervention, many more (twenty of thirty-four) felt that the child's "successful experiences of having solved or significantly decreased their long and severe night fears problems seemed to have helped them become generally more 'confident' in facing problems" (p. 599). Overall, the results of this study provided evidence for the maintenance of therapeutic gain across a long-term follow-up.

McMenamy and Katz (1989) conducted a follow-up study with a

small sample (N = 5) of children aged 4 to 5 years, utilizing the procedures outlined by Graziano and Mooney (1980). Although several modifications of the procedures employed in the earlier Graziano and Mooney study were necessitated because of the younger age group, the authors attempted to replicate this protocol as closely as possible. Relaxation training, the use of pleasant imagery, and self-instructional training in anxiety reduction methods were included, as was parent training in the use of positive reinforcement for compliance and change in their child's fearful behavior. Post-treatment measures of fearful behaviors demonstrated a 40% reduction relative to baseline scores, while a six-month follow-up showed maintenance of these treatment gains.

There have been no systematic studies of child or parent personality or parent–child relationships vis-à-vis children's nighttime fears, and, as with anxiety disorders in children, in general, there appear to be many subtypes. Reed and colleagues (1992) state that in anxiety disorders, many of the children are inhibited outside of the home but tyrants in the home. We have anecdotally observed distant fathers, conflicted parental feelings toward nurturance and discipline, and depressed mothers in families of anxious children. However, such anecdotal evidence cannot determine whether these factors are robust, whether they are caused by the nighttime fear behavior, whether they are causal, or whether there is an interactive effect. We have also anecdotally observed that many parents of nighttime fearful children remembered having difficulties at nighttime when they were children. Again, we have no way of determining whether this implies a genetic component, a learning component, or selective memory.

## An Integrative Treatment Approach

We consider the treatment of nighttime fears as being integrally tied to the child's construction of meaning in his/her life, a perspective which draws heavily upon cognitive-developmental principles. In treatment, the first two tasks of the clinician, then, are (1) to attempt to understand, in context, the meaning of the fear experience for the child, and (2) to position oneself vis-à-vis the child and family to assist in a more healthful or more developmentally appropriate reorganization of meaning for the child.

The first task has to do with the assessment of the child's overall life context, in order to assist with differential diagnosis, the formulation of an understanding of the child's attempts to cope with various life events, and treatment planning. For research purposes or in more intense hospital settings, the Schedule for Affective Disorders and Schizophrenia in School Aged Children (K-SADS) (Puig-Antich and Chambers 1978), the Diagnostic Interview for Children and Adolescents (DICA) (Herjanic and Reich 1982) or the Diagnostic Interview Schedule for Children (DIS-C) (Costello et al. 1984) might be useful, but for patients in outpatient settings, these are very time-consuming to employ on a regular basis. In their outpatient practice the present authors utilize a more global parent-rated checklist, such as the Achenbach Child Behavior Checklist (Achenbach 1979) for parents, and separate historical/diagnostic interviews with the child and parent designed to establish the larger systemic context within which the child's fear exists. Relevant information regarding socioeconomic, cultural, and extended family factors, life cycle issues within the nuclear family, individual parental issues relevant to the child's current functioning, parenting practices, school functioning, peer relationships, sibling relationships, the possibility of abuse or other traumatic experiences, and other significant life change or concurrent difficulties is collected during the assessment phase of treatment. The clinician must approach the issue of concurrent difficulties with considerable care and also with an awareness that children may have other difficulties in addition to the reported night fear. The possibility of physical/sexual abuse, or some other traumatic experience (such as hospitalization or other extensive medical treatment) needs to be sensitively and ethically entertained, as children who have experienced trauma exhibit symptoms that include extreme fear and/or anxiety and sleep disturbances (Everstine and Everstine 1989).

We also suggest, if feasible without jeopardizing the therapeutic relationship, the administration of the TAT (Thematic Apperception Test) or CAT (Children's Apperception Test) to the child. These instruments can be useful in suggesting hypotheses regarding generalized anxiety, depressive and other irrational thinking, feelings of aggression, and interpersonal view of others that might not be evident through the use of direct questioning and more objective approaches to assessment.

During this assessment process, the clinician is attempting to position him or herself to be an effective agent of change. Generally this involves establishing a working therapeutic alliance and relationship that involves respect, interest, understanding, commitment to the work of therapy, and hope, belief in positive change (Gelso and Carter 1985, Sexton and Whiston 1994). With nighttime fears, this will certainly involve first empathically gaining as much information as feasible from the child and parents regarding what the fear is like and how they have tried to cope with it. By validating the child's fear and the methods that the child and parent have used to cope with it, not only do the family members feel understood, but also the stage is set for empowering them to cope with the fear. Parental reports of the intensity, frequency, duration, and amount of disruption caused by the fear are used to form a baseline from which change can be assessed.

During the assessment and treatment processes, the child also increases his or her understanding of the fear and of the fear situation. Through art, verbal description, and educating the child about other children's fears (Hyson 1979, Merritt 1991, Robinson et al. 1991, White 1989), the child's ability to cognitively identify and express her or his fear expands. This cognitive expansion and differentiation of the fear itself allows for the integration of the previously unsymbolized material through verbal, pictorial, or, frequently, metaphorical means. The use of metaphor with child clients is often particularly powerful, as metaphor may serve to impart form to children's often incomplete understanding of their experiences, direct the course of behavior in specific situations, and also effect a higher degree of cognitive and affective functioning (Brooks 1981, 1985, Santostefano 1984, 1985). Similarly, in detailing their coping behaviors, the child and family set the stage for later constructing more causally complex, situational and interpersonal explanations of events.

The next step in treatment typically involves reframing the fear experience in a manner that fits into the child's and parents' schema for understanding their behavior. Here, the understanding of the family's and child's values, the idiosyncratic meaning ascribed to the fear, the cognitive-developmental level of the child, family (and especially parental) explanations for and interactions around the fear, and the child's previous experience coping with problems, that was gathered in the initial phase needs to guide the course of treatment. For instance, if the family focuses on the importance of a prior traumatic event in the etiology of the fear, the clinician would need to fit that event into the treatment. At this point in the treatment the child is helped to construct a causal attribution for the nighttime fear that provides for both a sense of coherence and control over the feared stimulus. Metaphor and the use of storytelling are particularly powerful in this aspect of treatment. Consequently, what were initially unconnected thoughts, feelings, and behaviors are now encouraged to be connected in new ways. The child's own role in creating and maintaining his/her fear can be discussed. This newly constructed integration of previously affectively charged and threatening material provides an increased perception of control, and forms the basis for the self-regulation procedures (such as the use of "brave" self-statements) that are used later in the treatment.

For simple but severe nighttime fears, Graziano and Mooney (1982) utilized the explanatory model that all children are afraid of the dark at one time or another and that some children learn effective ways to cope with their fear. The fear treatment for the child was merely to teach him/her skills learned from other children who had had similar nighttime fears and learned to cope with them and become "braver." It was presented to the parents that theirs was a supportive role to help their children cope better and be braver. In particular, they were taught ways to assist the child in coping with the subjective, physiological, and behavioral/motor aspects of fear. Suddenly, parents who were feeling conflicted and guilty over their handling of the fear were empowered with specific tasks that they could perform to support their child. Instead of feeling sorry for, and giving in to, their child, they were able to validate the child's feelings and yet maintain firm and consistent behavioral expectations as necessary for the child's mastery of his/her fears.

At this time, tentative decisions are made regarding the scope of the intervention with the child and family. Is the fear a rather specific phenomenon, or is it related to broader issues of past abuse or a more generalized coping style? Is there dysfunction at a parental or family level that may merit therapeutic attention? If broader issues are raised, the family needs to be presented with the scope of, and limitations on working with, the child's fear and the choice to participate in a more expanded treatment framework that may include family and couples counseling. We generally present this treatment framework in stages, beginning with working on the specific nighttime fear first and then deciding with the family whether more extensive treatment is warranted.

The degree to which generalization of previously-learned cognitive skills to novel situations should be expected to occur can easily be overestimated by the clinician. Without sufficient environmental support (in the form of practice) for the transfer of cognitive skills to other content domains, it is unlikely that children will employ a more sophisticated cognitive understanding in their attempts at coping with their nighttime fears.

At this point in treatment, we still may have a child who, in the feared nighttime situation, through what appears to be a rapid, automatic appraisal process, finds that his/her mental system is overloaded, resulting in the subjective experience of fear and the use of avoidant behavioral coping strategies. Even if the child's cognitive causal view has shifted, the child, at this time in the feared situation, may not have the ability to shift through effective appraisal and coping sets that might be effective in the situation.

In Piagetian terms, in the feared situation the child still cannot effectively assimilate the fearful experience into previously learned mental sets or schemas of thought or action, or explore effective methods to accommodate to the fearful experience. Given the extremely quick, "automatic" nature of many fears, children with nighttime fears often need very direct and explicit help with methods of coping with their fear and more generally with exercising control over their world. In addition to the behavioral support of parents, relaxation, pleasant imagery, and verbal self-statements have often been the treatment of choice, all emphasizing the child's ability to master the situation. Each is tailored to the individual child. For instance, some children find verbal self-statements most helpful in countering their largely visual fears; others find a specific pleasant or mastery image to be particularly effective for them.

## Treatment Principles: The Case of Patrick

The model of treatment for childhood nighttime fears being proposed in this chapter emphasizes the role of four interactive elements in the successful resolution of these fears: (1) the understanding of the manner in which specific fears represent the child's possibly idiosyncratic efforts to bring a sense of coherence and meaning to her/his experience, (2) the understanding of the adaptive, pragmatic nature of those behaviors (i.e., the "symptoms") that the child displays in attempting to exert a sense of personal control over the feared stimulus, (3) the lowering of the current, highly disruptive level of affect that interferes with the child's ability to cope, and (4) the assistance of the child in symbolizing currently unintegrated material. In order to illustrate the interaction of these treatment components in actual clinical practice, a case presentation format will be employed.

Patrick was a 10-year-old boy who was referred for treatment by his parents, who had become concerned over his recent inability to get to sleep at night within a "reasonable amount of time." When his bedtime arrived, Patrick would begin to find little tasks that he needed to accomplish before heading off to bed (such as straightening up his collection of sports trading cards), in an effort at delaying the inevitable rendezvous with his bed. Once in bed Patrick initially complained of not feeling tired, and asked his parents to allow him to stay up until 10 P.M. (his normal bedtime was 9 P.M. on school nights). He had come into his parents' bedroom one night and asked to sleep with them, something that his parents could not remember having occurred for many years. After several nights of this sort of behavior, Patrick's parents succeeded in getting him to state that he was frightened to go to bed, "because the Borg might get me." When asked to explain the basis of his fears, Patrick was unable to elaborate upon this initial statement, other than to say that he feared that they would come into his room and take him away if he were to go to sleep. Apparently, Patrick had developed a fear of alien creatures that had made a recent appearance on "Star Trek: The Next Generation," a popular television show that Patrick had watched for some time without experiencing any significant degree of anxiety.

The therapist, meeting with Patrick and his parents, learned that the family had recently moved several hundred miles to their new home, and that this move had been the first that Patrick had experienced since he was less than 2 years old. He had attended the same school since pre-school, and had recently completed the fourth grade prior to the family's move, which occurred approximately a month before the start of the new school year. His school performance had been satisfactory in his old school, and he had participated in several sports there. Patrick was experiencing some difficulties in making the academic transition into the fifth grade, as evidenced by lower grades than he customarily earned. In addition, his fear of the imaginary alien creatures was beginning to impact his adjustment to his new home in other ways. For example, Patrick had recently turned down several invitations from classmates to attend overnight sleepovers at their homes because of his anticipatory anxiety of being away from home and having to deal with his fears alone. Patrick was the older of two children, and his younger sister, Beth, who was 8 years old, was described by her parents as adjusting very well to the move, and as making numerous friends in the children's new school.

Patrick's father, Jim (35 years old), was a successful professional in the arts, and the family had elected to move to the new city in order to allow him to advance his career by accepting an upper administrative position with a local symphony. Since the move, he had been heavily involved in his new position, and was working sixty-five to seventy hours per week outside of the home. Patrick's mother, Laurie (33 years old), while not currently working outside of the home, had previously taught for a number of years at the middle school level, and was contemplating a return to school in order to pursue an advanced degree in education.

During the course of the initial session with Patrick and his family, the therapist learned that the move had been mostly his father's idea, and that Patrick's mother had been somewhat reluctant to leave behind her own career and friends. It also became clear that the parents had divergent ideas regarding how best to help their son with his fears. Laurie's concern for her son found expression in her attempts to reassure and comfort him, while Jim's stance was more distant and disapproving regarding his son's "unrealistic fears." This distance seemed to be reflected generally in Jim's relationship with Patrick, and there were subtle indications that Jim was somehow disappointed with Patrick, possibly because his son did not share his own interests in the arts, and preferred instead to participate in sports. While Jim wanted Patrick to stay in bed and to remind himself that his fears had no basis in reality, Laurie was more likely to permit Patrick to come into their room late at night, and to spend time sitting on the edge of his bed reassuring him that everything would be fine, until he was finally able to get to sleep.

As was discussed earlier, the family, school, and peer environments of the child provide an important context for the child's attempts to integrate his/her experience.

Patrick's fears of the alien creatures that he had seen in the television episode, while not clearly articulated, nonetheless may be seen to incorporate his perceptions of some event(s) in his life as potentially threatening or dangerous. The "choice" of these aliens was found, through further discussion with Patrick, to be significant for several reasons, not the least of which had to do with the modus operandi of the creatures on the television show. The Borg was a collective entity that conquered other races of beings and assimilated them into the collective, where they lost their individual sense of identity. For a child who had been uprooted from a school and peer community in which he had fashioned his own sense of identity, and who may have been very much in a state of uncertainty regarding his ability to fit in with his new peers, the Borg represented a dramatic object of fear. Additionally, the very premise of the show itself was one that had explorers head off into the great uncharted expanse of the universe in pursuit of the unknown, a parallel with Patrick's own recent move, which was not lost on him as therapy progressed.

A cognitive-developmental approach to understanding Patrick's fears would also draw the clinician's attention to the role of the environment in supporting Patrick's ability to understand and structure his experiences. Here the therapist's assessment of the family dynamics, and especially the manner in which the parents attempted to deal with their son, as well as with the move, became informative. Upon further discussion with Mom and Dad, it became evident that both parents had been uncomfortable discussing their own sense of ambivalence over the move, and had instead attempted to cope with their mixed feelings on their own. As such, Jim seemed to have consciously adopted a sense of enthusiasm and optimism regarding the move, although he later acknowledged that he had experienced some moments of uncertainty and anxiety. He stated that he felt that he had to keep all of that to himself, for fear that the rest of the family might decide that the decision to move had been a mistake.

Laurie's predominant feelings, on the other hand, were doubt and insecurity, as well as some feelings of anger towards her husband for having pushed so forcefully for the move. For Laurie, the difficulty in accepting her own feelings of excitement over the educational opportunities that her new city presented lay in what she perceived to be her husband's unwillingness to acknowledge and validate her sense of having temporarily placed on hold her own career for the opportunity to advance his. Both parents, however, were currently unable to hold up both sides of their own ambivalence surrounding this life change. They had attempted to cope on their own without one another's support or the support of friends or colleagues.

It was found that Patrick had also not been provided with the opportunity simply to express his feelings, without either feeling that he had to defend them to his father, or worry about causing his mother to become overly concerned with him. The complexity of the cognitive skills required to adequately appraise the situation and recognize that both the positive, enthusiastic, and adventurous feelings, as well as the fearful, anxious feelings accompanying such a life change, were beyond Patrick's ability to control at this point in time. Earlier it was mentioned that the behavioral manifestations of the fear response may be seen to represent efforts to cope with a situation that lies beyond the child's current developmental abilities. There existed for Patrick a relative lack of environmental support from his parents, who themselves had not provided him with adequate models for articulating and integrating conflicting emotions, or encouragement and support for attempting to begin this process himself. Given this situation at home, it is not surprising that Patrick himself dealt with these conflicting affective elements of his own experience through the use of less developed cognitive operations than he was capable of in other circumstances (Fisher and Pipp 1984). This was manifested in the displacement of affect upon another object (the Borg), and the condensed (the Borg represented several non-differentiated elements of his own experience) and magical nature of his thinking. Patrick's current level of cognitive operations with respect to the object of his fears seemed to lie largely at an unconscious level.

Additionally, there are elements in his thinking that incorporate the causal attributions that Shirk (1988) has identified as representing young children's attempts at bringing order to their world: Patrick had constructed an explanation for his fears that was external to himself, temporally proximal, and conscious, and avoided the difficulties inherent in a multiply-determined causal explanation. Recalling that Harter (1986) has outlined a developmental progression in children's ability to integrate conflicting emotions regarding a single object, we can see that Patrick appeared to be unable to perform this rather advanced cognitive task, which may reflect the negative impact of his emotional arousal, rather than the lack of the requisite cognitive skills.

Following the initial session, the therapist, in consultation with Patrick and his parents, elected to meet with Patrick in individual and family sessions, and also to work with his parents in conjoint sessions. Part of each meeting was spent with Patrick individually, and the remainder of the session with either his parents or in a family meeting. The therapy lasted a total of eight sessions, which took place over the course of approximately two and a half months.

The initial focus of the individual work was to provide Patrick with the opportunity to gain a sense of personal control over the content of his fears, as well as to lower his level of fear and anxiety through procedures that exposed him to progressively higher levels of fear. In order to assist Patrick in this aspect of therapy, the therapist made the decision to work with him using storytelling, a medium that the therapist thought would gain Patrick enough emotional distance from the threatening material to allow for a reduction in fear, an increased sense of self-efficacy, and the eventual symbolization of the fear-eliciting material. Relaxation training was also incorporated.

Accordingly, Patrick, with the therapist's assistance, began to write the story of a young lieutenant in Star Fleet who started out on his first mission following graduation from the academy, and who learned how to deal with the uncertainties and conflicting emotions that accompanied this journey. Eventually the ship that the young officer was on ran across various forms of alien life, and the chronicles of these encounters began to describe the excitement and challenge that accompanied each new adventure. One day the ship carrying the hero of the story happened to engage the Borg, and slowly Patrick worked at describing the experience of the young officer in terms of his sensations, thoughts, feelings, and behaviors during this particular mission. While the young Star Fleet officer initially experienced a highly disruptive degree of affect, he was eventually able to handle his feelings, through the use of various coping behaviors, including problem solving, the use of positive, "brave" self-statements, and reliance upon friends and colleagues as sources of support and encouragement. Interestingly, as the work on the story continued, Patrick not only came to talk about the challenges facing the young lieutenant, but also began to comment upon parallels with some of his own fears.

The sessions with Jim and Laurie provided the parents with an opportunity to discuss their own ambivalent feelings regarding the move, as well as to agree upon a consistent approach for dealing with Patrick's nighttime behavior, something that the parents had been unable to do previously. With respect to this latter aspect of the parent sessions, the therapist presented the parents with information regarding the usefulness of providing Patrick with a supportive environment where he might begin to verbalize his feelings, and have these feelings acknowledged and validated without having to justify or explain them. Although the work with the parents carefully focused upon Patrick and his current difficulties, both Laurie and Jim acknowledged that it was helpful for both of them to be able to discuss the struggles that they were experiencing, and to gain some support from one another.

Family sessions focused upon having Laurie and Jim explain their agreed-upon plan for helping Patrick at night, which included some time each night during which Patrick and his parents discussed the events of the day. It was hoped that this would provide an opportunity for Patrick to begin to identify and discuss his feelings regarding his adjustment to his new school and peer environment, as well as allow him to observe his parents express their own feelings regarding these issues. Other aspects of the plan included the use of muscle relaxation exercises, Patrick's imagining himself in a pleasant scene, and coping self-statements devised by Patrick and his parents. By the end of the eight sessions, Patrick reported that his level of fear had decreased significantly at night, and, without experiencing any undue distress, he had accepted an invitation to sleep over at a friend's house. Laurie and Jim made the decision to continue in couples counseling with the therapist for several additional sessions in order to continue with the work that they had begun.

The specific combination of interventions that was chosen for use with Patrick reflected an underlying developmental orientation that seeks to help the child successfully integrate his/her fear-eliciting material into a symbolic form. Storytelling is a metaphorical manner of working with Patrick on his fears, providing the therapist with the ability to work with Patrick through a series of stages that progress from an interpretation of characters within the story, to providing interpretative links between the characters and himself, to indirect interpretations about himself, to his finally being able to directly discuss and interpret the personal significance of the material in the story (Harter 1983).

Through the use of this technique, Patrick was able to gain some needed distance from the content of his fear, as well as control the rate at which he approached the feared stimulus. When his levels of fear and anxiety decreased sufficiently, Patrick was able to construct a coherent and personally meaningful narrative, one that eventually allowed him to claim the feelings of the main character in his stories as his own. The end result of this procedure was an increase both in his self-understanding and his sense of control. In this case, as Harter (1983) and Shirk (1988) have pointed out, any attempt by the clinician at an earlier stage in the therapy to interpret the multiple meanings of the Borg for Patrick would most likely have been met with either an inability to grasp the interpretation, or else with open resistance. By having been allowed the time necessary to reduce the level of disruptive affect that he had been experiencing, Patrick was eventually able to employ a more highly developed level of cognitive understanding, one more in keeping with his overall level of cognitive development.

In order to facilitate this process, the therapist sought not only to establish for Patrick a medium (storytelling) through which this integration might occur, but also to intervene at the level of his environment. By providing Patrick's parents with a safe arena for discussing and therefore bringing a greater sense of coherence to their own experiences, a suitable context was created for Patrick's continued efforts to understand what the recent move meant to and for him. This intervention may be understood as primarily developmental in nature, as it provided Patrick with the environmental support necessary to begin the process of symbolizing and eventually integrating the fear material. Patrick's parents themselves supported his efforts at "holding" both sides of the affective ambivalence that accompanied his fear of the alien creatures. By being encouraged to identify and express the conflicting emotions surrounding the recent move, Patrick was able to move toward a more comprehensive and adequate account of this episode. In this newly fashioned narrative, Patrick integrated both the fear and anxiety arising from the uncertainty surrounding the move, and the sense of hopeful possibility that was an inherent aspect of his experience.

## Summary

Nighttime fears are likely a universal experience. For a majority of children, at one time or another, this becomes an acknowledged issue. For somewhere between 10 and 20% of children, it becomes an issue of considerable disruption to them and to their families. Single factor etiological theories of classical conditioning, vicarious learning, displacement, reinforcement and other environmental contingencies, preparedness, physiological responsivity, and other miscellaneous theories have been shown to be inadequate in their explanatory power. An examination of the development of children's fears reveals that a cognitive-developmental approach shows promise both for the understanding and the treatment of children's fears. Children's fears can be conceptualized as inadequate attempts to bring coherence to their experience, hence threatening their sense of self-integration, and resulting in discomfort and disruption of their current functioning. This leads to a treatment approach that involves the identification and differentiation of the fear, expansion of appraisal and coping sets, reframing of causal attributions, and lowering of affective interference so that the child can make sense of and master his/her fear. This approach is linked to specific techniques to ameliorate and cope with children's nighttime fears.

## References

Achenbach, T. M. (1979). The Child Behavior Profile: an empirically based system for assessing children's behavior problems and competencies. *International Journal of Mental Health* 7:24–42.

Andrews, J. (1966). Psychotherapy of phobias. *Psychological Bulletin* 66(6):455–480.

Ayer, W. A. (1973). Use of visual imagery in needle-phobic children. *Journal of Dentistry for Children* 40:125–127.

Bandura, A. (1969). *Principles of Behavior Modification*. New York: Holt, Rinehart, and Winston.

Bandura, A., and Menlove, F. (1968). Factors determining vicarious extinction of avoidance behavior through symbolic modeling. *Journal of Personality and Social Psychology* 8:99–108.

Bauer, D. H. (1976). An exploratory study of developmental changes in children's fears. *Journal of Child Psychology and Psychiatry* 17:69–74.

Bowlby, J. (1973). *Attachment and Loss. Vol. II. Separation*. New York: Basic Books.

Briere, J. N. (1992). *Child Abuse Trauma: Theory and Treatment of the Lasting Effects*. Newbury Park, CA: Sage.

Brooks, R. (1981). Creative characters: a technique in child therapy. *Psychotherapy: Theory, Research and Practice* 18:131–139.

Brooks, R. B. (1985). The beginning of child therapy: of messages and metaphors. *Psychotherapy* 22(4):761-769.

Costello, A. J., Edelbrock, C., Kalas, R., et al. (1984). *Development and testing of the NIMH Diagnostic Interview Schedule for Children (DIS-C) in a clinic population: final report.* Rockville, MD: Center for Epidemiological Studies, NIMH.

Costello, C. (1971). Anxiety and persisting novelty of input from the autonomic nervous system. *Behavior Therapy* 2:321-333.

DeSilva, P., Rachman, S., and Seligman, M. (1977). Prepared phobias and obsessions: therapeutic outcome. *Behavior Research and Therapy* 15:65-77.

Ekman, P., Levenson, R. W., and Friesen, W. V. (1983). Autonomic nervous system activity distinguishes among emotions. *Science* 221:1208-1210.

Everstine, D. S., and Everstine, L. (1989). *Sexual Trauma in Children and Adolescents: Dynamics and Treatment.* New York: Bruner/Mazel.

Ferrari, M. (1986). Fears and phobias in childhood: some clinical and developmental considerations. *Child Psychiatry and Human Development* 17(2):75-87.

Fischer, K. W. (1980). A theory of cognitive development: the control and construction of hierarchies of skills. *Psychological Review* 87(6):477-531.

Fischer, K. W., and Kenny, S. L. (1986). Environmental conditions for discontinuities in the development of abstractions. In *Adult Cognitive Development: Methods and Models,* ed. R. A. Mines, and K. S. Kitchener, pp. 57-75.

Fischer, K. W., and Pipp, S. L. (1984). Development of the structures of unconscious thought. In *The Unconscious Reconsidered,* ed. K. Bowers and D. Meichenbaum pp. 88-148. New York: Wiley.

Fish-Murray, C. C., Koby, E. V., and van der Kolk, B. A. (1987). Evolving ideas: the effect of abuse on children's thought. In *Psychological Trauma,* ed. B. A. van der Kolk, pp. 89-110. Washington, DC: American Psychiatric Press.

Freud, S. (1909). Analysis of a phobia in a five year old boy. *Collected Papers. Vol. 3.* New York: Basic Books, 1959.

Gelso, C. J. and Carter, J. A. (1985). The relationship in counseling and psychotherapy: components, consequences, and theoretical antecedents. *The Counseling Psychologist* 13(2):155-243.

Graziano, A. M., DeGiovanni, I. S., and Garcia, K. A. (1979a). Behavioral treatment of children's fears: a review. *Psychological Bulletin* 86:804–830.

Graziano, A. M., and Kean, J. E. (1968). Programmed relaxation and reciprocal inhibition with psychotic children. *Behavior Research and Therapy* 6:433–437.

Graziano, A. M., and Mooney, K. C. (1980). Family self-control instruction for children's nighttime fear reduction. *Journal of Consulting and Clinical Psychology* 48(2):206–213.

———— (1982). Behavioral treatment of "nightfears" in children: maintenance of improvement at 2 ½- to 3-year follow-up. *Journal of Consulting and Clinical Psychology*, 50(4):598–599.

Graziano, A. M., Mooney, K. C., Huber, C., and Ignasiak, D. (1979b). Self-control instruction for children's fear-reduction. *Journal of Behavior Therapy and Experimental Psychiatry* 10:221–227.

Hagman, E. (1932). A study of fears of children of preschool age. *Journal of Experimental Education* 1:110–130.

Harter, S. (1983). Cognitive-developmental considerations in the conduct of play therapy. In *Handbook of Play Therapy*, eds. C. E. Schaefer and K. J. O'Connor, pp. 95–127. New York: Wiley.

Harter, S. (1986). Cognitive-developmental processes in the integration of concepts about emotions and the self. *Social Cognitions* 4(2):119–151.

Herjanic, B., and Reich, W. (1982). Development of a structured psychiatric interview for children: agreement between child and parent on individual symptoms. *Journal of Abnormal Child Psychology* 10:307–324.

Hershberg, S. G., Carlson, G. A., Cantwell, D. P., and Strober, M. (1982). Anxiety and depressive disorders in psychiatrically disturbed children. *Journal of Clinical Psychiatry* 43:358–361.

Hyson, M. C. (1979). Lobster on the sidewalk: understanding and helping children with fears. *Young Children* July:54–60.

Jakibchuk, Z., and Smeriglio, V. L. (1977). The influence of symbolic modeling on the social behavior of preschool children with low levels of social responsiveness. *Child Development* 47(3):838–841.

Jones, H. E., and Jones, M. C. (1928). A study of fear. *Childhood Education* J: 136–143.

Jones, M. C. (1924). Elimination of children's fears. *Journal of Experimental Psychology* 7:382–390.

Kanfer, F. H., Karoly, P., and Newman, A. (1975). Reduction of children's fear of the dark by competence-related verbal cues. *Journal of Consulting and Clinical Psychology* 43:251–258.

Kegan, R. (1982). *The Evolving Self: Problem and Process in Human Development.* Cambridge: Harvard University Press.

Kellerman, J. (1980). Rapid treatment of nocturnal anxiety in children. *Journal of Behavior Therapy and Experimental Psychiatry* 11:9–11.

Kelley, C. K. (1976). Play desensitization of fear of darkness in preschool children. *Behaviour Research and Therapy* 14:79–81.

Kelly, D., Guirguis, W., Frommer, E., et al. (1970). Treatment of phobic states with anti-depressants: a retrospective study of 246 patients. *British Journal of Psychiatry* 116:387–398.

King, N. J., Iacuone, R., Schuster, S., et al. (1989). Fears of children and adolescents: a cross-sectional Australian study using the Revised-Fear Survey Schedule for Children. *Journal of Child Psychology and Psychiatry and Allied Health Disciplines* 30:775–784.

Lader, M. (1972). The nature of anxiety. *British Journal of Psychiatry* 121:481–491.

Lang, P. (1968). Fear reduction and fear behavior: problems in treating a construct. In *Research in Psychotherapy*, vol. III, ed., J. M. Shlien pp. 90–103. Washington, D. C.: American Psychological Association.

Lang, P. J. (1977). Imagery in therapy: an information processing analysis of fear. *Behavior Therapy* 8:862–886.

_____ (1979). A bio-information theory of emotional imagery. *Psychophysiology* 16:495–511.

Lapouse, R., and Monk, N. (1959). Fears and worries in a representative sample of children. *American Journal of Orthopsychiatry* 29:803–818.

Lazarus, A. (1960). The elimination of children's phobias by deconditioning. In *Behavior Therapy and the Neuroses*, ed. H. J. Eysenck. pp. 114–122. New York: Pergamon.

Lazarus, A. A., and Abramovitz, A. (1962). The use of "emotional imagery" in the treatment of children's phobias. *Journal of Mental Science* 108:191–195.

Leitenberg, H., and Callahan, E. J. (1973). Reinforced practice and reduction of different kinds of fears in adults and children. *Behaviour Research and Therapy* 11:19–30.

Lentz, K. A. (1985). The expressed fears of young children. *Child Psychiatry and Human Development* 16(1):3–13.

Lick, J. and Bootzin, R. (1975). Expectancy factors in the treatment of fear: methodological and theoretical issues. *Psychological Bulletin* 82:917-931.

Marks, I. (1987). The development of normal fears: a review. *Journal of Child Psychology & Psychiatry* 28(5):667-697.

Merritt, J. E. (1991). Reducing a child's nighttime fears. *Elementary School Guidance and Counseling* 25:291-295.

McMenamy, C., and Katz, R. C. (1989). Brief parent-assisted treatment for children's nighttime fears. *Developmental and Behavioral Pediatrics* 10(3):145-148.

Miller, L. C., Barrett, C. L. and Hampe, E. (1974). Phobias of childhood in a prescientific era. In *Child Personality and Psychopathology: Current Topics*, ed. A. Davids, vol. 1, pp. 89-134. New York: Wiley.

Mooney, K. C. (1980). *Children's nighttime fears: parent and child correspondence on normative measures.* Paper presented at the American Psychological Association, Montreal, Canada.

_____ (1985). Children's nighttime fears: ratings of content and coping behaviors. *Cognitive Therapy and Research* 9(3):309-319.

Mooney, K. C., Graziano, A. M., and Katz, J. N. (1984). A factor analytic investigation of children's nighttime fear and coping responses. *Journal of Genetic Psychology* 146(2):205-215.

Morris, R. J., and Kratochwill, T. R., eds. (1991). Childhood fear and phobias. In *The Practice of Child Therapy*. 2nd ed., pp. 76-114. New York: Pergamon.

Noam, G. G. (1988). The theory of biography and transformation: Foundation for clinical-developmental therapy. In *Cognitive Development and Child Psychotherapy*, ed. S. R. Shirk, pp. 273-317. New York: Plenum.

Ollendick, T. H., and Gruen, G. E. (1972). Treatment of a bodily injury phobia with implosive therapy. *Journal of Consulting and Clinical Psychology* 38:389-393.

Pratt, K. C. (1945). The study of the "fears" of rural children. *Journal of Genetic Psychology* 67:179-194.

Puig-Antich, J., and Chambers, W. (1978). *The Schedule for Affective Disorders and Schizophrenia for School-Aged Children.* New York: New York State Psychiatric Institute.

Rachman, S. (1978). *Fear and Courage.* San Francisco: Freeman.

Reed, L. J., Carter, B. D., and Miller, L. C. (1992). Fear and anxiety in children. In *Handbook of Clinical Child Psychology.* eds. C. E. Walker and M. C. Roberts, 2 ed., pp. 237-260. New York: Wiley.

Rimm, D. C., Janda, L. H., Lancaster, D. W., et al. (1977). An exploratory investigation of the origin and maintenance of phobias. *Behaviour Research and Therapy* 15:231–238.

Robinson, E. H., Rotter, J. C., Fey, M. A. and Robinson, S. L. (1991). Children's fears: toward a preventive model. *The School Counselor* 38:187–202.

Rutter, M., and Garmezy, N. (1983). Developmental psychopathology. In *Handbook of Child Psychology*, vol. 4. ed. P. H. Mussen, pp. 775–991. New York: Wiley.

Santostefano, S. (1984). Cognitive control therapy with children: rationale and technique. *Psychotherapy* 21:76–91.

——— (1985). Metaphor: integrating action, fantasy and language in development. *Imagination, Cognition and Personality* 4:127–146.

Scarr, S., and Salapatek, P. (1970). Patterns of fear development during infancy. *Merril-Palmer Quarterly* 16:53–90.

Schwartz, J. C., and Shaver, P. (1987). Emotions and emotion knowledge in interpersonal relations. *Advances in Personal Relationships* 1:197–241.

Seligman, M. (1971). Phobias and preparedness. *Behavior Therapy* 2:307–320.

Sexton, T. L. and Whiston, S. C. (1994). The status of the counseling relationship: an empirical review, theoretical implications, and research directions. *The Counseling Psychologist* 22(1):6–78.

Shirk, S. R. (1988). Causal reasoning and children's comprehension of therapeutic interpretations. In *Cognitive Development and Child Psychotherapy*, pp. 53–89. New York: Plenum.

Strauss, C. C., Last, C. G., Hersen, M., and Kazdin, A. E. (1988). Association between anxiety and depression in children and adolescents with anxiety disorders. *Journal of Abnormal Child Psychology* 16:57–68.

Venn, J. R. and Short, J. G. (1973). Vicarious classical conditioning of emotional responses in nursery school children. *Journal of Personality and Social Psychology* 28(2):249–255.

Watson, J. B., and Rayner, R. (1920). Conditioned emotional reactions. *Journal of Experimental Psychology* 3:1–14.

White, M. (1989). Fear busting and monster taming: an approach to the fears of young children. *Selected Papers*, pp. 107–113. Adelaide, Australia: Dulwich Center.

# 5

# A Developmental Approach to Sleep Problems in Toddlers

Joyce Hopkins
Crystal Isaacs
Paula Pitterle

Mr. and Mrs. S. called an infant/preschool diagnostic and treatment clinic complaining about their 3-year-old daughter Sue's sleep difficulties. They reported that at bedtime (8:00 P.M.), she would come out of her room numerous times, asking for water or complaining that she couldn't sleep unless one of her parents lay down with her. In desperation, one of her parents would comply with her request, even though this was their only time to complete needed tasks. Once her mother or father joined her in bed, Sue would finally fall asleep at around 10:00 P.M. However, she also had frequent night awakenings, usually beginning around 1:00 A.M., shortly after her parents had gone to bed. Once awake, she would go into her parents' room and insist that they either let her sleep with them, or that one of them lie down with her again. These scenes were repeated three to four times per night. By the time her parents came to the clinic, they were exhausted, discouraged, and at the end of their rope. Both parents worked outside the home, and they reported that the lack of sleep was interfering with their job performance.

Although this may be a fairly extreme case, the types of difficulties described are typical for children from 18 months to 3 years. Large-scale epidemiological data about the incidence of sleep problems in toddlers are lacking. However, Crowell and colleagues (1987) reported that sleep disruptions were common in a sample of 100 middle-class toddlers 18 to 36 months old. For example, they found that about 24% of the children had a sleep onset latency of more than thirty minutes. Several behaviors showed developmental changes, rising or declining with age, even within this restricted age range of one-and-a-half years. Night waking was the most frequent problem for the youngest group of toddlers (18 to 23 months), whereas delayed sleep onset was more common in the middle age group (24 to 29 months). Both night waking and delayed sleep onset declined in frequency in the oldest age group (30 to 36 months).

These data highlight the importance of developmental considerations in determining what constitutes a sleep problem during the toddler years. It is important to determine the areas of developmental vulnerability for a particular age group when examining the incidence of sleep disturbances. In addition to appreciating developmental vulnerabilities that are associated with specific sleep problems, it is also important to be aware of developmental changes in normal sleep patterns during the preschool years. It goes without saying that an understanding of normal changes in sleep is a prerequisite to determining what constitutes a problem.

## Sleep Patterns from 18 Months to 5 Years

Normal sleep patterns during the preschool years show two major, but gradual, shifts. One is a reduction in the total amount of sleep time from about 13.5 hours at 18 months to about 11 hours at 5 years of age. The second is a reduction in daytime napping, from one nap of about two hours at 18 months to no regular daytime naps by 5 years of age (Ferber 1985).

Previously, researchers reported a longer latency to the first period of rapid eye movement (REM) sleep, as well as increased stage 4 sleep, in 5-year-olds as compared to 2-year-olds (Feinberg 1969, Roffwarg et al. 1964). However, these investigators did not include the amount of stage 4 sleep during naps in the 2-year-old group. In order to determine if there was an actual increase in stage 4 sleep in older children, Kahn and colleagues (1973) compared the sleep patterns of 2- and 5-year-olds by monitoring naptime as well as nighttime sleep. Results indicated that, indeed, the 5-year-olds had more stage 4 sleep at night than the 2-year-olds. However, there was no difference in the amount of stage 4 sleep between the younger and older subjects when the nap was taken into account. Furthermore, if naptime was included, the percentages of each sleep stage, including stage 4, were very similar for both groups. One difference between the two age groups was in the length of the REM–NREM (non-REM) cycle, indicating that there are increases in the length of this cycle through the first five years of life, with the adult level being attained by 5 years of age (Kahn et al. 1973).

Sleep–wake schedules are another aspect of preschoolers' sleep behaviors that may show developmental changes. Weissbluth (1987) reported that at around 2 years of age, most children go to sleep between 7:00 and 9:00 P.M. and wake up between 6:30 and 8:00 A.M. Seventy percent of children at this age are napping once per day for one to three hours. Between 3 and 5 years of age there is no change in sleep schedule (bedtime 7:00 to 9:00; wake up 6:30 to 8:00), but nap times gradually decrease in duration so that few children are still napping at 5 years.

The switch from sleeping in a crib to sleeping in a bed, which usually takes place between the second and third birthday (Weissbluth 1987), is another important developmental milestone that may play a role in the onset of a sleep problem. That is, the child's newfound freedom in being able to get out of bed on his or her own may lead to power struggles with the parents about staying in bed, which, in turn, may result in sleep onset difficulties.

To summarize, significant normal developmental changes take place in children's sleep behaviors between 18 months and 3 years of age. There is a gradual reduction in the total sleep time, as well as a cessation of daytime sleep. The percentage of each sleep stage appears to be nearly constant from 2 to 5 years of age, although there is a gradual increase in the length of the REM–NREM cycle until age 5, when adult levels are attained. Nighttime sleep schedules do not show much variation, although there may be a tendency for an earlier bedtime when the nap is given up. Finally, there is a shift in sleeping arrangements from the relative confinement of a crib to the autonomy provided by a bed.

These normal changes in sleep patterns may create a potential for the development of sleep difficulties. For example, the 4-year-old, who is sometimes still napping during the day, may develop a transient disturbance in sleep onset latency because he is not tired on days when he is napping. Depending on parental response, this transient difficulty may then develop into a full-fledged sleep problem that persists even after the nap has been completely abandoned. The shift to a bed may lead to the child's wandering into his parents' room when he wakes up in the middle of the night. Again, depending on parental response, this behavior may lead to a chronic problem in returning to sleep during nocturnal arousals.

In addition to changes in sleep and sleep-related behaviors, the period between 18 months and 5 years of age is marked by major developmental shifts in the child's cognitive and socioemotional functioning. Thus, the same type of sleep problem at different chronological ages may be related to very distinct developmental processes and therefore require very different interventions. The 18-month-old toddler is just emerging from the sensory-motor period of development into the preoperational period. A strong attachment to a primary caretaker has developed. However, representational thought and cognitive mediational skills are rudimentary. Separation from the attachment figure at bedtime may increase vulnerability to sleep problems. Thus, delayed sleep onset in an 18-month-old may be due to distress at separation combined with a difficulty in self-soothing (for a complete discussion of this issue, see Chapter 3, this volume).

By 3 years of age, the preschooler has developed an impressive array of cognitive skills, including representational thought and language. Separation issues are no longer so paramount and peer socialization has emerged as another significant aspect of socioemotional development. One of the major socioemotional tasks of this age period is the development of a sense of autonomy, and there is often an escalation in parent–child power struggles beginning in the first half of the second year of life that culminates in the oppositional behavior and temper tantrums of the "terrible two's." Thus, sleep problems in 3-year-olds may be related to issues of control and/or be part of a general pattern of oppositional behavior.

In the case of the 18-month-old toddler, extinction, or gradual extinction, may be the only intervention required to deal with the difficulty in self-soothing. In the 3-year-old, however, positive reinforcement for appropriate bedtime behavior may be required in addition to extinction.

## Sleep Problems: Definition and Incidence

Normative data indicate that both night waking and difficulty falling asleep are very common during the toddler years (Crowell et al. 1987, Jenkins et al. 1980, Johnson 1991, Richman 1981). However, different investigators have used different criteria to define what constitutes a problem, so that incidence data on sleep problems vary widely. For example, Lozoff and colleagues (1985) defined sleep problems as bedtime struggles or night waking occurring three or more times per week. Richman (1981) used multiple criteria including (a) waking three or more times per week and/or (b) waking for more than twenty minutes at a time, or (c) refusing to go to sleep at bedtime for more than thirty minutes, or (d) required parental presence to fall asleep.

Another problem in determining the incidence of sleep problems in toddlers and preschoolers is that various populations have been studied, including children referred to pediatric and psychiatric clinics (Lozoff et al. 1985, Ragins and Schacter 1971), as well as community samples (Johnson 1991, Richman 1981). A community survey of a London borough indicated that 24% of 1- to 2-year-old children woke two to four nights per week, and another 20% woke five to seven nights per week (Richman 1981). Johnson (1991) reported that 33% of the parents of toddlers (ages 24 to 35 months) surveyed in a small midwestern town considered their child to have a problem with waking during the night. The parents who reported that their child had a problem with night waking also indicated that the toddlers woke an average of 1.8 times per night for 5.6 nights per week.

Another complicating factor in determining the incidence of sleep problems in toddlers is that parents vary widely in their degree of tolerance and their beliefs about which sleep behaviors constitute a problem. Crowell and colleagues (1987) reported that, based on questionnaire results, 21% of the 18- to 23-month-old children in their sample had frequent night awakenings, but only 12% of the parents reported that their children had a sleep problem.

To summarize, incidence figures about sleep problems during the toddler years vary from about 20 to 40%, due to differences in definitional criteria and populations studied. There are also differences in the frequency of actual difficulties in settling and night waking compared to the number of problems reported by parents. Nevertheless, it is apparent that both night waking and difficulty settling to sleep are frequent occurrences during the toddler years, and that sleep problems are one of the most common concerns for which parents of toddlers consult their pediatricians (Ferber 1985).

### Predictors and Correlates of Sleep Problems

Surprisingly, given the frequency of sleep problems in toddlers, little attention has been paid to etiological factors. This may be due to a lack of consensus about the nature of sleep problems in young children—that is, whether they are a hallmark of a general psychological disturbance or merely reflect a developmental vulnerability. A recent study (Minde et al. 1993) examined maternal and child characteristics that differentiated between toddlers (ages 12 to 36 months) who were reported to be either good or poor sleepers. Results indicated that the poor sleepers had a higher frequency of perinatal complications, colic, and allergies, compared to the good sleepers. Minde and colleagues, (1993) concluded that in some children poor sleep may be a reflection of a problem in central nervous system regulation since colic, allergies, and a medically compromised neonatal period are signs of behavioral disorganization. Data from other studies examining the relationship between temperament and sleep problems in toddlers provide some support for Minde and colleagues' hypothesis. That is, several investigators (Schaefer 1990, Scher et al. 1992, Weissbluth 1984) have found an association between temperamental difficulties and sleep problems. One of the identifying features of an infant who is considered to be temperamentally difficult is a problem with self-regulation (Thomas and Chess 1977). Therefore, difficulties in self-regulation, which are reflected in temperamental characteristics (easy vs. difficult), may predispose a child to sleep problems.

Another child characteristic which has been shown to play a role in night waking is the ability to self-soothe. Difficulties in self-soothing may reflect either self-regulatory problems, as discussed above, or may be related to parental behavior. In their study of toddlers who were good and poor sleepers, Minde and colleagues (1993) found that the mothers of the poor sleepers often carried their children around at night until they were sound asleep, thereby preventing them from learning to fall asleep on their own. This finding is consistent with data from infant studies that suggest that sleep problems are associated with differences in how parents put their infant to sleep (Anders et al. 1992). That is, results of several studies (Adair et al. 1991, Anders et al. 1992) indicate that the major difference between self-soothers (infants who did not signal their parents during normal nocturnal arousals) and signalers, is that parents of self-soothers allowed them to fall asleep on their own at bedtime, whereas parents of signalers soothed their child to sleep. If this pattern of parental intervention at bedtime continues past infancy, it is likely that the toddler will fail to develop the ability to soothe him- herself to sleep and will persist in signaling the parent during nocturnal arousals. This speculation is supported by Minde and colleagues' (1993) study in which videotaped recordings of toddlers' sleep revealed no differences in the frequency of night awakenings between good and poor sleepers. However, as evidenced by the video-tapes, the good sleepers used various self-soothing maneuvers after an awakening (e.g., thumb sucking or hugging a toy) to soothe themselves back to sleep, whereas the poor sleepers always cried out or called for a parent.

Thus, converging data indicate that there is a relationship among parental behaviors (i.e., soothing the child to sleep), difficulties in self-soothing, and night waking. There is also compelling evidence that difficulties in self-regulation may predispose a child to sleep problems (Minde et al. 1993). Given the reciprocal effects in the parent–child relationship, it is likely that both infant characteristics and parent behaviors mutually influence each other in the development of a sleep problem. Thus, a constitutional characteristic such as a difficulty in self-regulation may both predispose an infant to sleep problems and also affect how the parents handle bedtime. Similarly, the parents' behavior at bedtime may have an effect on the child's learning how to self-soothe, thereby affecting the child's self-regulatory capacities.

Several other factors have been associated with sleep distur-bances in young children. These include environmental stress (Kataria et al. 1987), early disturbances of the waking–sleeping rhythms (Salza-rulo and Chevalier 1983), and maternal psychiatric disorder (Ragins and Schacter 1971, Richman 1985).

It is surprising that little attention has been paid to the role of attachment issues in toddlers' sleep problems since it is obvious that bedtime entails a separation from the attachment figure. According to attachment theory, children have different responses to separation based on the security of their attachment to the primary caregiver (Ainsworth et al. 1978). Children who are insecurely attached may experience increased anxiety about separation at bedtime that might lead to difficulty falling asleep and bedtime struggles.

Benoit and colleagues (1992) examined the relationship between *maternal* security of attachment and sleep problems in toddlers. Results indicated that 100% of the mothers of sleep-disordered toddlers were classified as insecurely attached (as assessed by the Adult Attachment Interview) compared with 57% of the control mothers. It seems logical that attachment issues would be related to how a mother would handle bedtime, which entails a separation from her child. However, it is not clear from this study how the mothers' representations of the attachment relationship affected how they actually handled separations from their toddlers at bedtime. Also this study does not shed light on the relationship between the *child's* security of attachment and sleep problems. It is likely that a child who is anxious about separation would be at risk for developing sleep problems. The relationship between the child's security of attachment and sleep problems is a promising area for future research.

## Intervention

The need for reliable assessment techniques and effective treatment strategies for sleep problems in young children is clearly indicated by the high prevalence rate of these disturbances during the preschool years. Furthermore, recent data (Kataria et al. 1987) indicate that these problems are persistent (84% of a sample of preschoolers with sleep problems had persistence of sleep disturbances after three years). In addition to the effects of decreased sleep on the child, there is evidence that there are negative effects on the parents (Kataria et al. 1987). Therefore assessment and treatment would help to reduce family stress as well as directly benefit the child.

## Assessment

Due to its obvious practicality, parental report is the most common strategy for assessing sleep problems in young children. The usual method consists of a sleep diary in which parents record the child's bedtime, sleep onset latency, number of night awakenings, duration of awakenings, and wake up time in the morning. Richman and colleagues (1985) developed a method for rating each of these parameters from 0 to 4 to derive a Composite Sleep Score. Richman (1985) suggested that children with severe sleep disorders have a Composite Sleep Score of 12 and above.

The reliability of parental report is often questioned. Recently, Minde and colleagues (1993) compared actual video recordings of sleep to maternal sleep diaries for toddlers with and without sleep problems. Results indicated that although the diaries were not completely accurate, there were significant correlations between the diaries and the recordings, particularly in the poor sleepers. However, the mothers tended to underestimate the number of awakenings. These data suggest that the diaries can be reliably used to determine if a sleep problem exists since they provide a conservative estimate of sleep disturbances.

Treatment

Two treatment approaches, pharmacotherapy and behavior therapy, have been investigated. Both treatment modalities have been shown to be effective in alleviating a variety of toddlers' sleep disorders. However, each has specific problems associated with implementation.

*Pharmacotherapy*

Data suggest that as many as 25% of children suffering from sleep disorders are prescribed sedatives before the age of 2 (Ounsted and Hendrick 1977). There are data which indicate that specific medications are effective in temporarily relieving sleep disturbances in children (Besana et al. 1985, Russo et al. 1976). Unfortunately, due to the wide age range of the children studied (e.g., 2 to 12 years), it is difficult to determine the efficacy of these medications in preschool children. Russo and colleagues (1976) demonstrated that diphenhydramine, administered to children between the ages of 2 and 12 years, reduced both time before sleep onset and night awakenings. There was no difference, however, between drug and placebo in the total amount of sleep time.

Besana and colleagues (1985) examined the effectiveness of niaprazine in reducing sleep disturbances in a sample of children hospitalized with a variety of diagnoses. Children receiving niaprazine displayed fewer sleep problems than controls from the first day of treatment and continued to improve in the following days. However, the relevance of these data to a healthy population of toddlers is unclear.

To date, there are only two studies specifically examining the efficacy of medication for the treatment of sleep problems in children below 5 years of age. Richman (1985) found that trimeprazine decreased the number and duration of night awakenings in a group of children between 1 and 2 years of age with sleep problems. However, the gains were short-lived, disappearing by a six-month follow-up.

There are a number of disadvantages to prescribing sedatives to young children. First, there may be safety issues due to immature metabolic functioning. Other disadvantages include difficulties establishing optimal dosage, potential side effects, and parental hesitancy or noncompliance. There is also a problem of rebound once the medication is discontinued (Weitzman 1981). Furthermore, the use of medication does not address aspects of the parent–child interaction that may be contributing to the sleep problem.

A recent study evaluated the effects of combining sedative medication with the behavioral method of extinction, which consisted of not attending to the child once put to bed (France et al. 1991). Results demonstrated that both extinction, and extinction plus placebo, effectively treated infants' and toddlers' sleep disturbances and had lasting positive effects. An advantage of using both medication and extinction was that this strategy led to more rapid results. However, a slight rebound effect occurred when the drug was withdrawn. Also, some parents reported that their infants appeared drowsy during the day after having been given the drug at bedtime. The researchers' rationale for combining the two methods was to decrease parental anxiety and encourage compliance with treatment. However, parents' scores on an anxiety measure administered four times throughout treatment indicated that there were no significant differences between parents whose infants were treated with extinction alone and those whose infants were treated with both medication and extinction.

In summary, various medications produce sedative effects in children which may temporarily alleviate sleep disturbances. However, pharmacotherapy does not promote the learning of new behaviors which are necessary to maintain improvements in sleep. Also, medication does not address characteristics of the parent–child interaction that play an important role in problematic sleep. Thus, it is unlikely that medication alone is an appropriate treatment for sleep disturbances in toddlers. Combining sedatives with behavioral techniques may prove useful if the child's parents are simply unable to comply with the demands of the behavioral intervention. For example, if a parent cannot tolerate the child's crying at bedtime during extinction, medication may decrease the amount of crying, thereby increasing the likelihood that the parent will continue the behavioral intervention. Ultimately, the benefits of medication in treating sleep problems in young children must be carefully weighed against the significant disadvantages of such treatment.

## Behavioral Approaches

Behavioral approaches are targeted at changing specific sleep-related behaviors, including decreasing negative behaviors (e.g., tantrums at bedtime) and increasing appropriate ones (e.g., staying in bed). Unlike medications, they also address the pattern of parent–child interaction which revolves around the sleep behavior.

A variety of behavioral techniques has been shown to be effective in treating toddlers' sleep disturbances (Piazza and Fisher 1991, Richman et al. 1985, Rickert and Johnson 1988). These techniques include extinction, gradual extinction, positive reinforcement, cuing, shaping, scheduled awakenings, and faded bedtime.

Extinction involves the withholding of parental attention in response to night waking. It has been shown to be an effective strategy for infants (France and Hudson 1990, Schaefer 1987). There is one study demonstrating the efficacy of extinction in treating night waking in both toddlers and infants (Rickert and Johnson 1988). However, it is much more difficult to use extinction with toddlers once they are able to get out of bed on their own, since parents must actively intervene to return the child to bed, while paying minimal attention to any protests. Therefore, parents must be carefully instructed and coached in how to avoid eye contact and to minimize responsiveness while gently, but firmly, placing the child back in bed.

Gradual extinction, a variant of extinction in which parents check quickly on the infant at predetermined intervals, also seems to be an effective strategy for reducing night wakening in infants (Ferber 1985, Lawton et al. 1991). It seems likely that it would also be effective with toddlers. However, the same caveat applies here. That is, gradual extinction can only be used with younger toddlers who are still in a crib since the technique depends on the child being unable to leave the bed on his/her own. The choice between extinction and gradual extinction should be determined by parental preference since both procedures seem to be equally effective. Some parents prefer gradual extinction since it does not require them to ignore long bouts of crying. However, other parents feel that their resolve may waver once they enter their child's bedroom, and therefore prefer a "cold turkey" approach.

Scheduled awakening is another strategy designed to overcome parental resistance to allowing the child to cry. Parents are instructed to awaken their child fifteen to thirty minutes prior to the child's normal time of spontaneous awakening, as determined by baseline measurements. During the scheduled awakenings, the parent comforts the child and generally behaves as he/she usually would when awakened by the child. Apparently, the scheduled awakenings lead to a decrease in spontaneous awakenings, presumably by interrupting the usual sleep schedule, thereby making it more susceptible to manipulation. As the spontaneous awakenings gradually diminish, the scheduled awakenings are faded out. There is evidence (Johnson and Lerner 1985) that scheduled awakening is effective in reducing night waking in both infants and toddlers (6 to 30 months old).

In order to determine the relative effectiveness of scheduled awakening versus extinction, Rickert and Johnson (1988) compared these two strategies in a sample of infants and toddlers (6 to 30 months). Results indicated that both techniques were equally effective. However, there are advantages and disadvantages to each strategy that should be carefully weighed in selecting a treatment option. Specifically, extinction leads to more rapid improvement but is intolerable to some parents, for whom scheduled awakening would be a more appropriate strategy. Extinction would be the treatment of choice for toddlers who experience both night waking and difficulty going to sleep, since scheduled awakening does not address the latter problem.

Bedtime fading is an intervention which specifically targets difficulty in settling at bedtime. First, a bedtime is arranged in which there is a high probability that the child will fall asleep within fifteen minutes. This initial bedtime is determined by taking the average time when the child fell asleep during baseline and adding one half hour. For example, if the mean time when the child fell asleep was 10:30, the new bedtime is set at 11:00. The child's bedtime is then faded to a more age-appropriate time by adjusting the bedtime by a predetermined amount of time each night, dependent on whether or not the child fell asleep within a fifteen minute period on the previous night. If the fifteen minute criterion is met, the bedtime is moved up 15 to 30 minutes. If the criterion is not met, the bedtime is moved back 15 to 30 minutes. The fading procedure is continued until a predetermined appropriate bedtime is met. Piazza and Fisher (1991) found that bedtime fading may eliminate other sleep problems which may coexist with difficulty settling at bedtime. However, this technique has been studied only with developmentally disabled children. Further research is needed to determine if it is an effective strategy for children without developmental problems.

Positive reinforcement strategies can be used with older toddlers who have acquired language. Positive reinforcement has the advantage of focusing on the child's appropriate behaviors and, in general, is considered to be the most effective strategy for changing behavior. A number of different bedtime behaviors can be targeted including maintaining an age-appropriate bedtime, staying in bed, and returning to sleep without parental intervention during night awakenings. A specific goal for each behavior is set and the child is reinforced in the morning for meeting the goal. Fading is used to gradually withdraw the program once age-appropriate sleeping habits have been established. Other strategies can be combined with positive reinforcement including: cuing, or setting the stage for sleep with some type of bedtime ritual; extinction; and punishment for inappropriate sleep behaviors (e.g., loss of tokens for screaming at bedtime). Using a combined treatment approach, Richman and colleagues (1985) found that 77% of a sample of children between 1 and 5 years of age showed marked or complete improvement with an average of 4.4 treatment sessions.

## Adjunctive Treatments

Parental compliance is critical to the success of behavioral strategies. However, compliance with a behavioral regimen is often difficult. First, it is extremely stressful for some parents to listen to their child's crying during extinction. Also, parents find it difficult to persistently ignore their child and repeatedly carry him or her back to bed, particularly in the middle of the night when they are tired. Therapist support and reassurance are essential to help parents deal with the stress they may experience during the implementation of the behavioral program. Cognitive restructuring, which involves explaining to parents that they are not doing something bad to their child by letting him or her cry, but rather that they are teaching the child how to self-soothe, is another recommended strategy for dealing with the issue of compliance.

In addition to the stress engendered by the behavioral strategies themselves, specific intra- and interpersonal factors also may affect treatment compliance. Parents may have difficulty implementing behavioral interventions either because of individual or marital issues, or difficulties in the parent–child relationship. For example, parental withdrawal and lack of responsivity, which often accompany depression, would interfere with the ability to set consistent limits at bedtime. Sharing a bed with their child may serve a protective function for couples who are avoiding intimacy. Finally, a pattern of interaction characterized by oppositionality and anger may be enacted in the bedtime routine, with the child refusing to go to bed and the parent responding angrily and inconsistently. Therefore, an assessment of the functioning of the individual family members, the parent–child interaction, and the couple is recommended to determine if any of these factors plays a role in the child's sleep problem. If there are any issues that would likely have an effect on the success of a behavioral intervention, then individual, marital, or family therapy should be an integral part of the treatment plan.

## Case Examples

### Sue

Sue, the 3-year-old described at the beginning of the chapter, had never learned to fall asleep on her own as an infant. One or the other parent held her until she fell asleep. If she woke during the night, they would again rock her back to sleep. This did not cause a problem until Sue was about a year old, when her parents began to feel that she was "old enough to sleep through the night." However, she continued to wake and cry for her parents several times a night even when she was 2. At this point, her parents moved her from her crib to a bed, believing that having a "big girl bed" might help her to stay in bed. Instead, the problem worsened, since Sue now refused to lie down on her own at bedtime, and would repeatedly get out of bed. Also, when she awoke in the middle of the night, she would come into her parents' room and insist on getting into bed with them. Since she was a restless sleeper, this interrupted her parents' sleep, particularly her mother's. Her parents had tried a number of strategies including reasoning, promising her a special treat if she stayed in bed, and sometimes, when they had exhausted their patience, yelling. By the time they called my (JH) office, they were exhausted and discouraged.

A comprehensive evaluation of Sue indicated that she was developing appropriately in all domains, with very advanced verbal skills. Temperamentally, except for her oppositionality at bedtime, she was an easygoing child who did not present any difficulties during the daytime to either her parents or her baby-sitter.

Both parents were stable, well-functioning individuals, who had professional-level jobs. They had been married for five years and reported that they did not have any significant marital conflicts.

Since there did not seem to be any underlying issues that would affect parental compliance, a behavioral approach using extinction, cuing, and positive reinforcement was selected as the treatment of choice.

First the program was explained to Sue's parents and then they were instructed on how to present to Sue what they were going to do. The verbal instructions to be given to Sue were as follows:

We are going to help you learn how to sleep on your own, like a big girl. Tonight, we will read you a bedtime story and kiss you goodnight. Then we will leave the room. Your job is to stay in bed and fall asleep. We will make a star chart and if you fall asleep on your own, in the morning, you will get a star. If you get five stars this week, then you will get a special treat.

The basic principles of extinction were then explained to Sue's parents. The extinction strategy included ignoring any requests after the designated bedtime, as well as removing any potential reinforcers for getting out of bed. Sue's parents were taught how to ignore and also how to gently but firmly pick up their daughter and put her back in her bed each time she got out. They were reminded not to make eye contact or engage in any dialogue, but to simply say, "It's bedtime."

The star chart was used to reinforce Sue for successive approximations of appropriate bedtime and nighttime behavior. First she received stars for falling asleep on her own. Then, as she reached criterion on this behavior, stars were made contingent on staying in bed and not leaving her room during the night.

Both parents agreed that Sue's father would be responsible for waiting near her door at bedtime and during the night to ensure that she would be returned to her bed as quickly as possible whenever she got out.

The first night, Sue seemed excited about "being a big girl" and sleeping in her own bed. Everything went smoothly during the bedtime routine. However, as soon as her lights were turned out at 8:00 P.M., she began to call for her parents, complaining that she couldn't fall asleep on her own. After about twenty minutes of calling with no response, she left her bed. As planned, her father immediately picked her up and put her back in bed. This sequence was repeated twenty times before Sue finally fell asleep on her own at 10:30. She woke up at 1:00, but was prevented from going into her parents' room by her father who picked her up and put her back in bed. This time she was returned to her bed ten times before finally falling back to sleep on her own. She woke up once more at 4:30, but this time fell back asleep after being returned to bed five times.

In the morning, she received her star, since she had fallen asleep on her own. Her parents also praised her and indicated how proud they were of her for falling asleep on her own.

The second night, Sue left her bed five times before falling asleep at 9:00 P.M. She woke only once during the night and had to be returned to bed one time. The third night she remained in her bed at bedtime and did not disturb her parents during the night at all.

At this point the criteria for earning a star were changed so that Sue had to remain in her bed at bedtime and not leave her room during the night in order to receive a star. By the end of the week, she had earned seven stars. For her special treat she chose to bake cookies with her mother.

The star chart was gradually faded out by the third week of treatment. Sue was now falling asleep on her own between 8:00 and 8:30 P.M., and was no longer getting out of bed during the night. Her parents reported that they were feeling significantly better as they were getting a solid eight hours of sleep per night. Her mother reported that her work performance had also improved since she was less fatigued. Both parents were also extremely pleased with the additional time they now had to share in the evenings to "relate as adults," as well as to get needed tasks done.

A six month follow-up indicated that Sue was still falling asleep on her own between 8:00 and 8:30. She did not leave her bed during the night, except for the rare occasion when she was ill.

## Caitie and Kevin: Siblings with Sleep Problems

Caitie, who was 4½ years old, and her brother, Kevin, who was 2 years old, had similar sleep problems. They both fell asleep very late in their parents' bed. Once asleep, they were carried to their own beds, but when they woke during the night they would return to their parents' room and insist on getting back into bed with them.

This pattern started when Caitie was 13 months of age. At that time, she learned how to climb out of her crib when she woke up during the night, and, as her father described, "slip into her parents bed very quietly." Since she did not disturb her parents when she climbed into bed with them, they did not consider this a problem and they allowed her to spend the rest of the night in their bed. Then, as she got older, she began to insist on falling asleep in her parents' bed as well. When her brother Kevin was born it seemed easier for the parents to have both children sleep with them.

However, Kevin, unlike Caitie, was a "restless sleeper," and as he got older (and bigger) his sleep habits began to interfere with his parents' sleep. Also, both children went to bed very late, since their bedtime routine consisted of watching TV with their parents until they turned out the lights. Initially, the late bedtime was not a problem since the children also woke up late in the morning. However, once Caitie started preschool, she had to get up by 8:00 A.M., and she seemed tired during the day (which was not surprising since she was sleeping only about eight hours). Therefore, Mr. and Mrs. C. decided that it was time for the children to develop more developmentally appropriate sleep habits.

Initially, a week of baseline recording was conducted to determine the usual bedtime, as well as the number of hours each child slept if not wakened in the morning. The baseline recordings indicated that both children were falling asleep between 10:30 and 11:00 P.M. in their parents' bed. If the parents did not wake them, they woke spontaneously between 8:30 and 9:00. Kevin was also napping about two hours during the day. Thus, both children were sleeping about ten hours at night if not awakened.

The treatment goals were threefold: (1) to establish a more age-appropriate bedtime, (2) to establish a bedtime routine that included having the children fall asleep in their own bed, and (3) to teach the children to stay in their own bed during night awakenings. For practical reasons, it was decided to treat each child successively, starting with Caitie.

First, after consulting with the parents about the family's schedule, a final bedtime goal of 9:00 was set. To accomplish this, a fading procedure was used, whereby bedtime was initially set thirty minutes earlier than baseline (i.e., 10:00 P.M.). Then if Caitie fell asleep within fifteen minutes of this time, it was moved back the next night another thirty minutes. Secondly, a cuing strategy was used to set the stage for bedtime. A new bedtime routine was developed which included a bath and then a bedtime story read while Caitie was in bed. Finally, both extinction and positive reinforcement were used to eliminate night waking. The extinction procedure involved ignoring any requests after bedtime. Also, one parent remained outside Caitie's door after bedtime, and as described above, picked her up and returned her to her bed whenever she tried to leave to go to her parents' room. The positive reinforcement strategy included the use of a star chart, whereby Caitie received stars for staying in bed. The new bedtime routine was explained to her as follows:

Caitie, we want to help you learn to go to sleep in your own bed and stay in your bed until morning. To help you, we will read you a bedtime story in your bed and then turn out the light. If you fall asleep in your own bed you will get a star in the morning.

Caitie's response to the behavioral program indicated that, developmentally, she was ready to learn more independent sleep habits. The first night, she stayed in bed after the lights were turned out and slept until 8:00 the next morning. Needless to say, her parents were very pleased and praised her effusively. She also received a star. The second night, she got out of bed once, but after being returned to bed, slept until 8:00 the next morning. The third night, her bedtime was moved back another thirty minutes to 9:30. She fell asleep at 10:20, woke once briefly during the night, and then slept until 8:00 A.M.

The next day, her brother Kevin announced, "I want to sleep in my own bed, too!", illustrating the positive effects of peer modeling. Therefore, it was recommended to the parents to begin treatment for Kevin at this point. That night, both children were put to sleep at 9:30 after a bedtime story. Caitie fell asleep by 10:00 without getting out of her bed. Kevin, however, cried and asked to get in his parents' bed. His father remained by his door, effectively preventing him from leaving his room. He eventually fell asleep in his own bed at 10:30. Surprisingly, he slept through the night until 8:00. That morning, both children were praised for having fallen asleep in their own bed, and they both received a star.

The next evening, both children were put to bed at 9:30. Caitie fell asleep without any difficulty, while Kevin remained awake until 10:15. He woke up at 1:00 A.M. and was brought back to bed by his father, who remained at his door until he fell asleep at 1:30. He had one more awakening, at 2:10, but fell back to sleep in ten minutes. Both children were then awakened by their parents at 7:30 (after ten hours of sleep). Bedtime was maintained at 9:30 for the next evening since Kevin had taken longer than fifteen minutes to fall asleep. This time, both children fell asleep quickly and slept through the night, to be woken at 7:30.

On the seventh night, bedtime was moved back thirty minutes to 9:00 P.M. Caitie fell asleep within fifteen minutes, whereas Kevin remained awake for thirty minutes. They both slept through the night and woke up spontaneously at 7:00 A.M.

During the second week of treatment, bedtime was firmly established at 9:00 P.M. Both children were sleeping in their own beds and remaining in their rooms until they woke in the morning between 7:00 and 7:30. The star chart was gradually faded out.

Both children seemed proud of their new ability to sleep in their own beds. Their parents reported that they enjoyed their time together in the evening without the children present, and that having this time enabled them to be "more affectionate and patient with the children during the day."

## Conclusion

Sleep problems, including difficulty settling and sleeping through the night, are very common during the toddler years, and may reflect areas of developmental vulnerability. Nevertheless, the need for intervention is clearly indicated by the fact that these problems tend to be persistent and often lead to increased parental stress.

To date, behavioral interventions have received the most empirical support. Behavioral strategies include extinction, scheduled awakenings, bedtime fading and positive reinforcement. The specific strategy chosen depends on a number of factors including: the type of problem (night waking versus difficulty settling), parental beliefs (e.g., children should not be left to cry), and developmental considerations (e.g., utilization of a star chart requires that the child has developed language).

Pharmacotherapy does not seem to be an effective treatment when used alone. However, there may be specific cases where it would serve as a useful adjunct to behavioral treatment.

A comprehensive treatment approach requires an assessment of individual, marital, or family issues that may be related to the child's sleep problem. Once these are identified, they can be addressed in psychotherapy (individual, couple, or family) to produce long-lasting change.

References

Adair, R., Bauchner, H., Philipp, B., et al. (1991). Night waking during infancy: role of parental presence at bedtime. *Pediatrics* 87(4):500–504.

Ainsworth, M. D. S., Blehar, M. C., Waters, E., and Wall, S. (1978). *Patterns of Attachment.* Hillsdale, NJ: Lawrence Erlbaum.

Anders, T. F., Halpern, L. F., and Hua, J. (1992). Sleeping through the night: a developmental perspective. *Pediatrics* 90(4):554–560.

Benoit, D., Zeanah, C. H., Boucher, C., and Minde, K. (1992). Sleep disorders in early childhood: association with insecure maternal attachment. *Journal of the American Academy of Child and Adolescent Psychiatry* 31:86–93.

Besana, R., Fiocchi, A., DeBartolomeis, L., et al. (1985). Comparison of niaprazine and placebo in pediatric behaviour and sleep disorders: double-blind clinical trial. *Current Therapeutic Research* 36(1):58–66.

Crowell, J., Keener, M., Ginsburg, N., and Anders, T. (1987). Sleep habits in toddlers 18 to 36 months old. *Journal of the American Academy of Child and Adolescent Psychiatry* 26:510–515.

Feinberg, I. (1969). Effects of age on human sleep patterns. In *Sleep, Physiology and Pathology: A Symposium,* ed. A. Kales, pp. 39–52. Philadelphia: Lippincott.

Ferber, R. (1985). Sleep, sleeplessness, and sleep disruptions in infants and young children. *Annals of Clinical Research* 17:227–234.

France, K. G., Blampied, N. M., and Wilkinson, P. (1991). Treatment of infant sleep disturbance by trimeprazine in combination with extinction. *Developmental and Behavioral Pediatrics* 12(5):308–314.

France, K. G., and Hudson, S. M. (1990). Behavioral management of infant sleep disturbance. *Journal of Applied Behavioral Analysis* 23(1):91–98.

Jenkins, S., Bax, M. and Hart, H. (1980). Behavior problems in preschool children. *Journal of Child Psychology and Psychiatry* 21:5–17.

Johnson, C. M. (1991). Infant and toddler sleep: a telephone survey of parents in one community. *Journal of Developmental and Behavioral Pediatrics* 12:108–114.

Johnson, M. C., and Lerner, M. (1985). Amelioration of infant sleep disturbances: effects of scheduled awakenings by compliant parents. *Infant Mental Health Journal* 6(1):21–30.

Kahn, E., Fisher, C., Edwards, A., and Davis, D. M. (1973). 24-hour sleep patterns. *Archives of General Psychiatry* 29:380–385.

Kataria, S., Swanson, M. S., and Trevathan, G. E. (1987). Persistence of sleep disturbances in preschool children. *The Journal of Pediatrics* 642–646.

Lawton, C., France, K., and Blampied, M. (1991). Treatment of infant sleep disturbance by graduated extinction. *Child and Family Behavior Therapy* 13(1):39–55.

Lozoff, B., Wolff, A. W., and Davis, N. S. (1985). Sleep problems in pediatric practice. *Pediatrics* 75:4777–4783.

Minde, K., Popiel, K., et al. (1993). The evaluation and treatment of sleep disturbances in young children. *Journal of Child Psychology and Psychiatry and Allied Disciplines* 34:512–533.

Ounsted, M. K. and Hendrick, A. M. (1977). The first-born child: patterns of development. *Developmental Medicine and Child Neurology* 19:446–453.

Piazza, C. C. and Fisher, W. W. (1991). A faded bedtime with response cost protocol for treatment of multiple sleep problems in children. *Journal of Applied Behavior Analysis* 24:129–140.

Ragins, N., and Schachter, J. (1971). A study of sleep behavior in two-year-old children. *Journal of the American Academy of Child Psychiatry* 10:464–480.

Richman, N. (1981). A community survey of characteristics of one- to two-year-olds with sleep disruptions. *Journal of the American Academy of Child Psychiatry* 20:281–291.

———— (1985). A double-blind drug trial of treatment in young children with waking problems. *Journal of Child Psychology and Psychiatry* 26(4):591–598.

Richman, N., Douglas, J., Hunt, H., et al. (1985). Behavioral methods in the treatment of sleep disorders—a pilot study. *Journal of Child Psychology and Psychiatry and Allied Disciplines* 26(4):581–590.

Rickert, V. I., and Johnson, M. (1988). Reducing nocturnal awakening and crying episodes in infants and young children: a comparison between scheduled awakenings and systematic ignoring. *Pediatrics* 81(2):203–212.

Roffwarg, H. P., Dement, W., and Fisher, C. (1964). Preliminary observations of the sleep dream pattern in neonates, infants, children, and adults. In *Monographs on Child Psychiatry*, ed. E. Harms, pp. 60–72. New York: Pergamon.

Russo, R. M., Gururaj, V. J. and Allen, J. E. (1976). The effectiveness of diphenhydramine HCl in pediatric sleep disorders. *The Journal of Clinical Pharmacology* 16:284–288.

Salzarulo, P., and Chevalier, A. (1983). Sleep problems in children and their relationship with early disturbances of the waking–sleeping rhythms. *Sleep* 6:47–51.

Schaefer, C. E. (1987). The efficacy of a multimodal treatment program for infant night waking. *Sleep Research* 16:442.

_____ (1990). Night waking and temperament in early childhood. *Psychological Reports* 67:192–194.

Scher, A., Epstein, R., Sadeh, A., et al. (1992). Toddlers' sleep and temperament: reporting bias or a valid link? *Journal of Child Psychology and Psychiatry* 33:1249–1254.

Thomas, A., and Chess, S. (1977). *Temperament and Development*. New York: Brunner/Mazel.

Weissbluth, M. (1984). Sleep duration, temperament, and Conners' ratings of three-year-old children. *Journal of Developmental and Behavioral Pediatrics* 5:120–123.

_____ (1987). *Healthy Sleep Habits, Happy Child*. New York: Ballantine.

Weitzman, E. D. (1981). Sleep and its disorders. *Annual Review of Neuroscience* 4:381–418.

# 6

# Night Terrors

Bryan Lask

## Introduction

Night terrors (pavor nocturnus) have been known since ancient times, and according to Kottek (1981) were, like epilepsy, ascribed to demons. One of the more detailed early descriptions was that of Rhazes, in the fifteenth century, quoted by Still (1931) and Kottek (1981). Rhazes described "a certain affliction that happens to children. . . . The sign of it is a great wailing or much fear during sleep." Still (1931) also quoted a German physician, Wittich, who described "night screaming or fearful dreams and terrors in children." Wittich believed this condition to have "a great affinity to the falling sickness" (i.e., epilepsy) (p. 169).

From the earliest times, there has been dispute as to exactly what are night terrors. Rhazes explained the condition as being due to "the taking of more milk than the child can digest. The child therefore is given the sixth part of a dram of dyapliris and diasmuscum with the milk daily" (Radbils 1971, p. 373). (This might actually be one of the earliest descriptions of milk intolerance!) Other popular explanations have included epilepsy and hysteria. Although we now know that neither of these conditions accounts for pavor nocturnus, the actual cause remains unclear.

## Definition and Presentation

Night terrors are nocturnal episodes of extreme dread and distress, intense vocalization including screaming, increased body movements, and marked autonomic arousal (Driver and Shapiro 1993, Fenwick 1986, Keener and Anders 1991, Lask 1988, Matthews and Oakey 1986, Schulz and Reynolds 1991). The body movements may be purposeless and uncoordinated, or complex, coordinated and purposeful, including sleepwalking in up to 70% of sufferers (Lowe and Scott 1991). There is marked autonomic arousal as manifested by tachycardia, palpitations, tachypnoea, dilated pupils, sweating, and piloerection.

The episodes tend to occur during the first few hours of sleep, and are of relatively short duration (one to twenty minutes). The first signs are those of autonomic arousal, such as restlessness, sweating, and tachycardia, but the parents usually do not become aware of the episode until the child suddenly starts screaming or becomes extremely restless. Children with night terrors are not readily awakened although often they seem to be awake, and it is not possible to console them. They appear to be confused and disoriented. They are unresponsive to their surroundings and seem rather to be responding to frightening mental images (Keener and Anders 1991). The episode usually remits with the child returning to normal sleep, and it is unusual for there to be more than one per night. There is no recall of the incident the next morning.

Onset of night terrors is usually between the ages of 4 and 12 (Lowe and Scott 1991), with an incidence of between 1 and 4% of children in this age group (Fenwick 1986, Schultz and Reynolds 1991). Boys are more commonly affected than girls and the problem usually resolves itself by early adolescence (Lowe and Scott 1991).

The frequency of episodes may vary from nightly to once every few months. There is divergence of opinion regarding regularity. Keener and Anders (1991) consider episodes to occur irregularly, whereas Lask (1988) has noted that in many cases parents report that the episodes are absolutely predictable, often occuring at the same time almost or even every night. With regard to triggering factors, Driver and Shapiro (1993) state that night terrors may occur in response to stress and anxiety and may be more common when sleep schedules are irregular. Lask (1988), in contrast, reports that stress seems not to be relevant and that change in routine diminishes or eliminates the episodes.

## Assessment and Differential Diagnosis

Developmental, medical, and family history are usually unremarkable, although Schultz and Reynolds (1991) have reported a greater incidence of night terrors than might be expected in the family history. Very rarely is there any evidence of psychiatric disorder in children with night terrors. Mental state examination is usually quite normal, and physical examination rarely reveals any abnormality.

Similarly, neurological investigations such as EEG (electroencephalogram) and CT (computerized tomography) scanning are within normal limits. Interestingly there is general consensus that late-onset night terrors (i.e., above the age of 12) are much more commonly associated with major life stress and more serious psychopathology than is reported in childhood (Crisp et al. 1990, Kales and Scharf 1973, Keener and Andrews 1991, Lowe and Scott 1991, Schulz and Reynolds 1991). Rarely will adults commit violent acts during a night terror (Fenwick 1986, Oswald and Evans 1985, Schatzman 1986).

The differential diagnosis includes nightmares and epileptiform disorders. Night terrors are easily distinguished from nightmares in that they occur in stage 3 to 4 non-REM sleep, usually between one and three hours after falling asleep. In contrast, nightmares occur in REM sleep between three and six hours after falling asleep. With night terrors there are usually loud vocalizations, including screaming, and vigorous movements, often of a defensive or evasive nature, and very marked autonomic arousal. With nightmares, vocalizations are less common and less intense; there is little movement, and less autonomic arousal. It is difficult and sometimes impossible to wake a child from a night terror, whereas a child having a nightmare is easily awakened. Children having night terrors cannot be consoled, while children having nightmares are usually fairly easily soothed. The next morning children who have had a night terror have no recall of the episode, but children with nightmares often have a vivid recall of the dream.

There should be no difficulty in distinguishing night terrors from epileptiform disturbances, given the characteristic features of the former. Convulsions are not normally accompanied by the intense and often piercing vocalizations associated with night terrors, while epileptiform movements are likely to be of a tonic and clonic type. When there is any doubt about the diagnosis an EEG should be performed.

## Pathogenesis

The cause of night terrors is not known. Given the frequency of a family history of either sleepwalking or night terrors, it is reasonable to assume a common genetically determined predisposition to these disorders (Kales et al. 1980). It has also been suggested that both these disorders represent an immaturity of the central nervous system in children (Driver and Shapiro 1993). Some such patients are reported to have a generalized, hypersynchronous symmetrical delta pattern on EEG before and during the episode (Driver and Shapiro 1993), while Kales and colleagues (1966) identified subsequent persistence of slow waves for a short while, which they suggested might also reflect cerebral immaturity. Broughton (1968) found the episodes to be associated with high-amplitude alpha rhythm, similar to that prompted in normal subjects wakened from deep sleep. He concluded that the patients were suffering from an arousal disorder.

It would appear, therefore, that night terrors occur at least to some extent in the context of cerebral immaturity, with some genetic contribution. It remains to be shown whether there is a different pathophysiology between childhood-onset and later-onset night terrors, given that the incidence of psychopathology differs. It is of course possible, however, that the psychopathology found in adults is primarily a secondary phenomenon.

## Management

Although night terrors are benign and usually resolve themselves with time, treatment is often necessary because of the distress and disruption that the episodes cause, and because of the potential dangers associated with the violent movements and any associated sleepwalking.

A wide range of approaches to management has been proposed, although few approaches have been tested empirically. It may also be that the treatment needs of children differ from those of adults. For example, Lowe and Scott (1991) have suggested that psychotherapy may be of value for later-onset night terrors, but not in childhood.

Suggested treatments in childhood may be categorized as pharmaco-logical, psychotherapeutic, and behavioral.

## Pharmacological Treatments

There is much controversy over the use of medication for childhood-onset night terrors. A number of reports have claimed the effectiveness of a variety of drugs including the benzodiazepines (Fisher et al. 1973, Kales and Scharf 1973, Keener and Anders 1991), Popoviciu and Corforiu 1986, Reimao and Lefevre 1982, Vela et al. 1982), the tricyclic antidepressants (Beitman and Carlin 1979, Keener and Anders 1991, Logan 1979, Pesikoff and Davies 1971), and phenobarbitone (Cornfield et al. 1979). Their suggested mode of action is the reduction of stage 3 and 4 slow wave sleep.

There is no convincing evidence to indicate that these medica-tions are more satisfactory than nonpharmacological treatment methods and they can have unpleasant side effects (Weisbluth 1984). It is probably wise to follow the recommendations of Lowe and Scott (1991) that medication should only be used in severe cases when other treatments have failed, and of Keener and Anders (1991) that medica-tion should only be used if the symptoms are particularly hazardous or disruptive to the family.

## Psychotherapeutic Treatments

The only authors to recommend the use of psychotherapy for night terrors in children are Driver and Shapiro (1993) who firmly state that psychotherapy and hypnosis are the treatments of choice, although they offer no rationale or evidence for their view. Maskey (1993) has pointed out that psychotherapy is expensive and often unavailable, while Lask (1993) has argued that both psychotherapy and hypnosis for young children are expensive, irrational, impractical, and of no ob-vious value.

## Behavioral Treatments

These are the least toxic and probably most effective techniques for the treatment of childhood night terrors. Lask (1988) has reported the value of what has become known as *the waking treatment*. Parents are asked to note on five successive nights at what time the episodes occur, and whether there are signs of autonomic arousal. They are then advised to fully wake their child ten to fifteen minutes before the night terror usually occurs, and to keep him or her awake for five minutes. If the terrors occur at different times, the parents are advised to observe for signs of autonomic arousal and then to immediately wake their child. This process should be repeated on five to seven successive nights.

This technique has now been used for over fifty children with night terrors. In about 80%, the episodes stopped within one week. A small proportion of children relapsed within six months; all but one of these children made a complete recovery after a repeat course of waking. It does seem that if the instructions are carried out correctly this treatment is usually effective.

The reason this treatment works is not clear but probably relates to interruption of faulty slow wave sleep patterns, with reversion to a normal sleep pattern and resolution of the disorder (Lask 1988). It is of interest that there have been anecdotal reports of resolution of night terrors following other less structured and intrusive changes to sleep patterns, such as going on holiday, moving home, changing bedrooms, or changing bedtimes. This treatment, and others for which claims of effectiveness are made, needs to be tested empirically against control and comparison interventions. A comparison of the waking treatment with relaxation is currently being conducted in Australia (James pers. com. 1994).

### Parental Counseling

This should be a sine qua non of the management of any childhood disorder. Parents need to have as full an understanding as possible of the etiology, course, treatment, and outcome of their child's problem. They should be encouraged to ask as many questions as they need, and where possible, be given written and even diagrammatic explanations and instructions. Such advice and support are not only usually reassuring, but in many conditions have a beneficial effect upon symptoms. With mild night terrors counseling may be sufficient for the parents to cope without the need for more complex treatments. When the terrors are more dramatic, parents are very much in need of the support and advice that should accompany any other treatment.

### Case Illustration

John, whose developmental and medical history had been unremarkable, developed night terrors at age 5. These occurred five to six times per week, usually within two hours of his falling asleep, and were characterized by his appearing to wake with a start, after which he would scream very loudly, thrash around in his bed, and then take what appeared to be evasive action, covering his head and cowering. He could not be awakened or consoled. The episodes lasted for about five minutes, after which he would seem to return to normal sleep. He never had any recall of the incident the next morning. Occasionally his parents would be in his room immediately prior to an episode and note restlessness and sweating.

There was no family history of similar episodes, but intermittently there had been considerable marital disharmony. Physical examination revealed no abnormality.

Treatment with diazepam reduced the frequency of the episodes for about three weeks but then seemed to lose any effect. Tricyclic antidepressants made no difference. John was referred for weekly play therapy, which was stopped after three months because of lack of any effect.

The episodes continued in a similar pattern for two years, at which point John was referred to a specialist center where he was admitted for two days for further investigations. The only abnormality was in the sleep electroencephalogram, which was reported as showing minor, nonspecific changes. No terrors occurred during the admission, but John did complain of sleeping poorly because of noise on the ward. When he returned home the episodes recurred. It was decided to readmit him to see if once again the episodes remitted, and this proved to be the case.

It was hypothesized that the remission in hospital could be due either to being away from home, and therefore away from the associated stresses, or to the alteration in the sleep pattern imposed by the noise on the ward. A decision was made to test the latter hypothesis, by waking him frequently in the early hours of his sleep at home. This was done at hourly intervals between 8:00 and 11:00 P.M. every night for one week, after which he had no more night terrors. Annual follow-up for five years revealed no relapse and no other significant problems.

John was the first child to be treated by waking. While it might be hypothesized that his recovery was a natural process, this seems unlikely, and would be a remarkable coincidence, in that it coincided with the institution of a new and previously untested treatment. The fact that so many other children seem to respond well to this approach suggests that there is something beneficial in artificially altering the sleep pattern.

Summary

Night terrors are a relatively benign but distressing condition affecting 1 to 4% of children between the ages of 4 and 12. The cause is unknown, but seems to be linked to an abnormality of slow wave sleep, which resolves with time in the majority of instances. There is rarely any evidence of individual psychopathology, and family pathology does not seem to occur any more commonly than in the general population. There are no abnormalities on physical examination or investigation. The most helpful treatment appears to be a combination of parental counseling and artificial waking in the early hours of sleep, and this is recommended when the terrors are particularly disruptive or distressing or threaten the child's safety.

## References

Beitman, B., and Carlin, A. (1979). Night terrors treated with Imimpramine. *American Journal of Psychiatry* 136:1087–1088.

Broughton, R. (1968). Sleep disorders: disorders of arousal. *Science* 159:1070–1078.

Cornfield, C., Chaplin, S., Doyle, A., et al. (1979). Side effects of Phenobarbital in toddlers: behavioural and cognitive aspects. *Journal of Paediatrics* 95:361–365.

Crisp, A., Matthews, B., Oakey, M., and Crutchfield, C.R.T.M. (1990). Sleep walking, night terrors and consciousness. *British Medical Journal* 300:360–362.

Driver, H., and Shapiro, C. (1993). Parasomnias. *British Medical Journal* 306:921–924.

Fenwick, P. (1986). Murdering while asleep. *British Medical Journal* 293:574–575.

Fisher, C., Khan, E., Edwards, A., et al. (1973). A psycho-physiological study of nightmares and night terrors. *Archives of General Psychiatry* 28:252–250.

James, L. (1994). Personal communication.

Kales, A., and Sharf, M. (1973). Sleep laboratory and clinical studies of the effects of Benzodiazapine on sleep. In *The Benzodiazapines*, ed. S. Garattini, E. Mussini, and L. Randall, pp. 577–598. New York: Roden Press.

Kales, J., Kales, A., Soldatos, C. et al. (1980). Night terrors: clinical characteristics and personality patterns. *Archives of General Psy-*

chiatry 37:1413–1417.

Kales, A., Jacobson, A., Paulson, N., et al. (1966). Somnambulism: psycho-physiological correlates. 1. All night EEG studies. *Archives of General Psychiatry* 14:586–594.

Keener, M., and Anders, T. (1991). New frontiers of sleep disorders medicine in infants, children and adolescents. In *Psychiatry*, ed. R. Mitchels, vol. 2, Philadelphia: J. Lippincott.

Kottek, S. (1981). "Matter Pueroum" a medieval naming for an enigmatic children's disease. *European Journal of Paediatrics* 137:75–79.

Lask, B. (1988). Novel and non toxic treatment for night terrors. *British Medical Journal* 297:592.

_____ (1993). "Waking Treatment" best for night terrors (correspondence). *British Medical Journal* 306:1477.

Logan, D. (1979). Antidepressant treatment of recurrent anxiety attacks and night terrors. *Ohio State Medical Journal* 75:653–655.

Lowe, T., and Scott, C. (1991). Elimination disorders and parasomnias in childhood. In *Psychiatry*, vol. 2, chapter 43:1–12, ed. R. Mitchels. Philadelphia: J. Lippincott.

Maskey, S. (1993). Simple treatment for night terrors (correspondence). *British Medical Journal* 306: 1477.

Matthews, B., and Oakey, M. (1986). Triumph over terror (correspondence). *British Medical Journal* 292:203.

Oswald, E., and Evans, J. (1985). On serious violence during sleepwalking. *British Journal of Psychiatry* 147:688–689.

Pesikoff, R., and Davies, P. (1971). Treatment of paver nocturnus and somnambulism in children. *American Journal of Psychiatry* 128:134–137.

Popoviciu, L. and Corforiu, O. (1986). Efficacy and safety of midazolam in the treatment of night terrors in children. *British Journal of Clinical Pharmacology* 16 (suppl. 1): 975–1025.

Radbils, J. (1971). The first treatise of paediatrics. *American Journal of Diseases of Children* 122:369–376.

Reimao, R., and Lefevre, A. (1982). Evaluation of Flurazepan and placebo in sleep disorders in childhood. *Arquivos de Neuro-Psiquiatria* 40:1–13.

Schatzman, M. (1986). To sleep, perchance to kill. *New Scientist* 110:60–62.

Schulz, S., and Reynolds, C. (1991). Sleep disorders. In *Psychiatry*, vol. 2, ed. R. Mitchels, chapter 105:1–18. Philadelphia: J. Lippincott.

Still, G. (1931). *The History of Paediatrics*. Oxford: Oxford University Press.

Vela, A., Dobidez, B., Rubio, M., et al. (1982). Action of Bormazepam on sleep in children with night terrors. 1. Sleep organisation and heart rate. *Pharmatherapuetica* 3:247–258.

Weisbluth, M. (1984). Is drug treatment of night terrors warranted (correspondence). *American Journal of Diseases of Childhood* 138:1086.

# 7

# Sleepwalking in Children and Adolescents

Kaan R. Özbayrak
Richard M. Berlin

## Introduction

Sleepwalking (somnambulism) is one of the clinical syndromes that are classified as *parasomnias*, a group of disturbances involving "an abnormal event occurring during sleep" (American Psychiatric Association, 1987, Diagnostic Classification Steering Committee, 1990). Though the clinical characteristics of sleepwalking have been recognized since the time of Hippocrates (Kales 1986), it is only recently that we have started to learn about its pathophysiological basis and possible etiologies.

Sleepwalking had long been considered either a purely psychological phenomenon (the acting out of a dream), a hysterical dissociative state (during which unconscious wishes are acted out), or an epileptic phenomenon (Narashima 1946, Teplitz 1958). The most important scientific findings about sleepwalking occurred after the development of all-night sleep laboratory studies in the 1950s and 1960s when it was discovered that sleepwalking is not the acting out of a dream. Sleepwalking is associated with slow-wave sleep rather than periods of rapid eye movement (REM) sleep, when dreaming occurs (Jacobson et al. 1965).

As the results of sleep laboratory studies have suggested, sleep-walking can best be defined as a disorder of impaired arousal (Broughton 1968), in which manifestations of sleep and wakefulness are combined (Berlin and Qayyum 1986). Episodes of impaired arousal usually take place when the child or adolescent shifts from deep, non-REM, stage 3 or 4 sleep to a lighter stage of sleep. Instead of proceeding with an episode of either another deep non-REM or REM sleep, a state of partial waking occurs, during which both sleep and waking processes occur together (Mahowald and Rosen 1990, Guille-minault 1987).

## Clinical Features

Episodes of sleepwalking take place during stage 3 or 4 sleep, which mainly occur during the first third of the night. Sleepwalking episodes usually last for fewer than fifteen minutes and rarely is there more than one episode per night. Typically, the child sits up, rises out of bed, and moves about in a slow, poorly coordinated, automatic manner. More complex activities that are clearly out of context and reflect the child's general lack of awareness sometimes take place, such as dressing, eating, or urinating. The child walks with a blank, staring look, and yet is able to move around objects without difficulty. The sleepwalker may mumble either spontaneously or in response to questions, but speech is often difficult to understand. Great effort is usually required to awaken the child, and conscious awareness returns only gradually. Usually the child has no memory or only a vague recollection of the episode (Berlin and Qayyum 1986, Guilleminault 1987, Thorpy and Glovinsky 1987).

Some authors tend to differentiate *quiet sleepwalking* from *agitated sleepwalking* (Ferber 1985, Mahowald and Rosen 1990). In quiet sleep-walking, the child appears calm and the clinical picture is similar to what was described above. In agitated sleepwalking, the child appears frightened or agitated, and may try to leave his room or the house. Trauma, injury, and even death may result because of loss of critical skills such as orientation, reactivity, motor skill, judgement, and relative lack of awareness of the surroundings. The child may walk through glass windows, jump out of windows, fall down stairs, or run outside (Ferber 1985, Guilleminault 1987, Kales 1986, Thorpy and Glovinsky 1987). In one unusual case, a child who lived near a railroad yard sleepwalked onto an open rail car and awakened the next morning on the train in another state.

Though the sleepwalker may become aggressive and attack other people, planned violence is rare (Thorpy and Glovinsky, 1987, Oswald and Evans 1985). Aggression is more likely to occur if an effort is made to force the child back to bed or when the parent tries to restrain the child. However, if gently escorted back to bed, the sleepwalker usually returns to sleep without ever completely waking.

All arousal disorders, such as confusional arousal (sleep drunkenness), sleepwalking, and sleep terror share some basic clinical features (Diagnostic Classification Steering Committee 1990, Guilleminault 1987, Mahowald and Rosen 1990). They tend to begin in stage 3 or 4 sleep, usually in the first third of the night and last between one and thirty minutes. Confusion, disorientation, and unresponsiveness are typical, and the child has no or only a vague, partial memory of the event in the morning. While confusional arousal is the mildest, sleep terror represents the most intense end of this continuum. Sleep terror is associated with panic, agitation, and signs of autonomic arousal (Diagnostic Classification Steering Committee 1990, Guilleminault 1987, Thorpy and Glovinsky 1987).

## Epidemiology

Sleepwalking is very common and occurs at least once in 15% to 30% of children (Clore and Hibel 1993, Thorpy and Glovinsky 1987, Vela-Bueno and Soldatos 1987). However, only 2 percent to 3 percent of children are estimated to have frequent episodes (Thorpy and Glovinsky 1987). Sleepwalking most commonly begins between ages 6 and 12 years, and usually subsides by age 15 (Kales 1986, Thorpy and Glovinsky 1987). In their survey of 1,695 children between ages 5 and 18, Fisher and Wilson (1987) found that 21% of children had sleepwalked at least once in the one-year period before the study, and 60% of them had had 1 to 3 episodes. In the same study, 49% of the children were reported to start sleepwalking between ages 4 and 7. In only 3% of them the onset was after 11 years of age (Fisher and Wilson 1987). Sleepwalking that was outgrown almost always began before age 10 (Kales et al. 1980a, Kales 1986).

The prevalence of sleepwalking in children does not appear to be influenced by socioeconomic status, academic performance, or chronic medical problems (Berlin and Qayyum 1986, Diagnostic Classification

Steering Committee 1990, Fisher and Wilson 1987, Thorpy and Glovinsky 1987). However, sleepwalking is associated with sleep terrors,
sleeptalking, enuresis, obstructive sleep apnea, sleep deprivation, febrile illness, migraine, Tourette's syndrome, and use of psychotropic
medications (Barabas and Matthews 1985, Berlin and Qayyum 1986,
Burd and Kerbeshian 1988, Charney et al. 1979 , Dorus 1979, Guilleminault 1987, Kales et al. 1979, Kales et al. 1980a, Murray 1991,
Thorpy and Glovinsky 1987). A knowledge of the nature of its relationship with each of these phenomena is necessary for a thorough
assessment and differential diagnosis, which will be discussed below.

Genetic factors play an important role in both the development
of sleepwalking and its association with sleep terrors, sleeptalking,
migraine, and Tourette's syndrome. As many as 80% of families of
those who sleepwalk include one or more other family members who
also were sleepwalkers (Berlin and Qayyum 1986, Kales et al. 1980b).
When a parent has a history of sleepwalking, the chances of a child
sleepwalking are six times as great as when neither parent sleepwalked
(Bakwin 1970, Berlin and Qayyum 1986). Monozygotic twins have
been reported to be concordant for sleepwalking six times as frequently
as dizygotic twins (Bakwin 1970, Berlin and Qayyum 1986). Children,
one or both of whose parents had sleepwalked during childhood, were
shown to be more likely to manifest sleepwalking and sleeptalking than
control children in a prospective study (Abe et al. 1984). Research
evidence supports the hypothesis that sleepwalking and sleep terrors
share a common genetic predisposition, but expression of the trait may
be influenced by environmental factors (Kales et al. 1980b). Children
with Tourette's syndrome and/or migraine headaches were found to
have a much higher incidence of arousal disorders than control children (Barabas and Matthews 1985, Burd and Kerbeshian 1988, Guilleminault 1987).

Standing the child up during slow-wave sleep, sleep deprivation,
febrile illness, distended bladder, environmental stimuli such as noise,
and a combination of lithium with neuroleptics, all have been reported
to precipitate sleepwalking in predisposed children and adolescents
(Charney et al. 1979, Dorus 1979, Kales et al. 1979, Mahowald and
Rosen 1990, Mindell 1993, Thorpy and Glovinsky 1987). Obstructive
sleep apnea may also trigger sleepwalking, which generally occurs
during the second part of the night (Guilleminault 1987).

Similarity of the clinical pictures and the episodic natures of
sleepwalking and nocturnal complex seizures have led researchers to

investigate the association between them. Although electrophysiological studies have shown that sleepwalking and sleep terror are not epileptic phenomena, daytime EEG (electroencephalogram) abnormalities are more frequent in affected children than normal controls (Amir et al. 1985, Guilleminault 1987). Moreover, epileptic children can have typical disorders of arousal not associated with epileptic discharges (Guilleminault 1987).

Children who sleepwalk were found to have more inhibited aggression and more pronounced anxiety-suppressing mechanisms than other children on the Rorschach test (Guilleminault 1987). Sleepwalking may also occur as a manifestation of post-traumatic stress disorder in children (Handford et al. 1991). However, psychopathology as measured by various psychological tests (e.g., pathologically elevated scores on the Mania, Psychopathic deviate, and Schizophrenia scales of the MMPI [Minnesota Multiphasic Personality Inventory]) and psychiatric interviews (e.g., higher prevalence of personality disorders) is less likely to be associated with sleepwalking if the episodes began before age 10 years as opposed to later onset sleepwalking, which usually continues through adult ages (Kales et al. 1980a). Sleepwalking in a child is rarely a manifestation of psychopathology if the onset is before 10 years of age, but it is more likely to be associated with psychological problems if it starts without any apparent reason in older children and adolescents.

## Pathophysiological Considerations

The pathophysiology of sleepwalking is not known. There appears to be a complex interplay of genetic, organic, psychological, and maturational factors. Mahowald and Schenck (1992) define three states of being: wakefulness, REM sleep, and non-REM sleep. They locate a wide array of clinical syndromes at the intersection areas of these states, describing them as intrusions of one state into another. Intrusions of wakefulness into non-REM sleep thus result in the disorders of arousal (Mahowald and Schenck 1992). However, the mechanism by which wakefulness intrudes into non-REM sleep is unknown.

Barabas and Matthews (1985) hypothesized a primary defect in serotonin metabolism in a subgroup of children with Tourette's syndrome who have a personal history or a family history of migraine headaches. They found that these children suffer from arousal disorders more often than other children with Tourette's syndrome who lack a personal or family history of migraine. Although this finding has brought the possibility of serotonergic dysfunction in arousal disorders into the fore, there is very little hard evidence even to support the connection between serotonergic mechanisms and the pathophysiology of Tourette's syndrome (Leckman and Cohen, 1991).

Amir and colleagues (1985) found variable and mixed interictal, waking EEG pathology in 47% of children with either sleep terrors or sleepwalking, as opposed to 10 to 15% of healthy children. They concluded that, at least in some children, arousal disorders may represent a nonconvulsive sleep manifestation of the electrophysiological dysrhythmia.

Since sleepwalking usually begins in childhood and terminates by late adolescence, immaturity of the central nervous system (CNS) has been suggested as playing a role in the etiology of sleepwalking (Vela-Bueno and Soldatos 1987, Handford et al. 1991). However, noting that most disorders related to delayed maturation are more common in boys than girls, Fisher and Wilson (1987) point out that the lack of an association with male sex in sleepwalking casts doubt on the CNS immaturity hypothesis.

In summary, it may be suggested that genetic, maturational, psychological, and organic factors render a group of children and adolescents susceptible to sleepwalking for a period of time. During this period of time, an episode of sleepwalking may occur either spontaneously, or under the influence of several different environmental (e.g., standing the child up, making noise, covering the child with a blanket), physiological (e.g., distended bladder, sleep deprivation, sleep apnea, febrile illness, medications), and psychological (e.g., a recent traumatic experience) events.

## Assessment and Differential Diagnosis

A complete history is the most important tool in the evaluation of a child or adolescent suspected of sleepwalking (Kales et al. 1983). The history should include a detailed description of the episodes; age of onset, timing, frequency, and duration of episodes; related stressful life events; family history for sleepwalking and sleep terror; daytime behavior, sleep–wake schedule, and other sleep problems; a complete developmental, psychiatric, and medical history, including any recent or past febrile illnesses and use of medications; and the attitudes of the child or adolescent and his family toward the symptom. Although in most cases this information is sufficient to make a differential diagnosis, in some cases a sleep laboratory study may be necessary (Mahowald and Rosen 1990, Vela-Bueno and Soldatos 1987).

The differential diagnosis of sleepwalking includes confusional arousals, sleep terrors, anxiety dreams, REM sleep behavior disorder, nocturnal seizures, and hysterical dissociative states (Kales et al. 1983, Vela-Bueno and Soldatos 1987).

*Confusional arousals* and *sleep terrors* are, like sleepwalking, disorders of arousal. Confusional arousals are the mildest among them, and are characterized by disorientation, decreased responsiveness, and inappropriate confusional behavior such as crying, sobbing, and bizarre, wild thrashing. Walking around is not usually seen in confusional arousals. Representing the most intense end of this continuum, sleep terrors start with a loud scream, which is usually followed by intense panic and fear, associated with excessive autonomic discharge, and sometimes with wild running (Ferber 1985, Kales et al. 1983, Mahowald and Rosen 1990). Confusional arousals and sleep terrors may occur together with sleepwalking (Berlin and Qayyum 1986, Kales et al. 1980a).

*Anxiety dreams*, or nightmares, being associated with REM sleep, usually occur during the second half of the night, when REM sleep is prominent. Motor behavior is limited. After an attack, the child usually is fully awake and able to recall the content of his dream (Mahowald and Rosen 1990).

*REM sleep behavior disorder* is typically a disorder of elderly men who usually have central nervous system disease. REM sleep behavior disorder is included here in the differential diagnosis, since it was reported in a 10-year-old girl (Thorpy and Glovinsky 1987). In REM sleep behavior disorder, the usual motor inhibition that occurs during REM sleep is lost, and the dreams of REM sleep are acted out with elaborate, purposeful, and sometimes violent behavior reflecting dream activity. It usually occurs in the middle or last third of the night, when REM sleep is prominent (Thorpy and Glovinsky 1987).

*Nocturnal seizures* are characterized by repetitive, stereotypical automatisms, which usually consist of chewing, swallowing, and salivation. These behaviors are rarely found in children with sleepwalking. Duration of the seizures is usually shorter than that of a sleepwalking episode. Children or adolescents with seizures do not typically return to their beds as sleepwalkers usually do (Mahowald and Rosen 1990, Thorpy and Glovinsky 1987, Vela-Bueno and Soldatos 1987). Despite these differences in their clinical pictures, it may sometimes be extremely difficult to differentiate sleepwalking from nocturnal seizures. Since the daytime EEG may be normal or pathological in both of them, its value in differentiation is limited, and an all-night sleep laboratory study may become necessary.

Hysterical dissociative states are usually associated with severe psychopathology and a detectable secondary gain. They last much longer than does a typical sleepwalking episode and are rare in children (Thorpy and Glovinsky 1987).

## Treatment

### General Considerations

A thorough assessment is the first step in the management of the sleepwalking child and his family. The clinician should be confident about the diagnosis and the circumstances that surround the problem event. If there are other sleep problems or a febrile illness that accompany sleepwalking, they should be addressed and treated first. Any medications that may be causative should be either discontinued or replaced by alternatives. Adequate sleep and a normal sleep–wake schedule should be ensured (Ferber 1985).

In children, sleepwalking is usually a benign, self-limited disorder. With childhood sleepwalkers in whom genetic and maturational factors are the primary causes, it is important to reassure the parents that the sleepwalking is usually not a reflection of serious emotional problems. Since genuine risk of physical injury exists during a sleepwalking episode, the parents should be instructed to provide a safe environment. For example, the child should sleep on the first floor. If possible, potentially dangerous objects should be removed from the room, windows and doors should be locked, and stairways should be gated. In general, parents should observe the child's sleepwalking behavior but intervene only if there appears to be a risk of injury (Berlin and Qayyum 1986).

### Pharmacotherapy

Two types of medication have been used to treat children and adolescents with sleepwalking: benzodiazepines and the tricyclic antidepressant imipramine (Berlin and Qayyum 1986, Kales et al. 1983). Pharma cotherapy is usually reserved for those few children with very intense, frequent episodes, or when the child is at high risk for self-injury (Berlin and Qayyum 1986, Ferber 1985). Benzodiazepines such as diazepam suppress sleep stages 3 and 4. Diazepam in doses of 5 to 20 mg/day may result in a marked decrease in frequency and intensity of episodes. The relapse rate, however, may be high when the drug is withdrawn (Berlin and Qayyum 1986, Kales et al. 1983).

Ten to 50 mg of imipramine at bedtime may be helpful in reducing the frequency of sleepwalking episodes. However, it has no pharmacologic effect on sleep stages 3 and 4. Its effectiveness may be related to drug-induced increases in wakefulness. The increased level of arousal may counteract the impaired arousal occurring in sleepwalking (Berlin and Qayyum 1986, Kales et al. 1983).

## Other Therapies

Sleepwalking that is associated with psychological difficulties may respond well to psychotherapy, hypnosis, and relaxation techniques (Guilleminault 1987). Conditioning procedures such as awakening the child fully either during (Clement 1970) or ten to thirty minutes before (Lask 1988, Tobin 1993) the sleepwalking episodes have been reported to be effective, if applied for at least five to seven consecutive days.

## Case Illustration

The parents of a 7-year-old white male child arranged a consultation at our Sleep Disorders Clinic after the child had a sleepwalking episode in which he walked into a glass storm door, broke the glass, and suffered numerous lacerations on his face, trunk, and arms.

The parents reported that their son had begun sleepwalking approximately three months before the consultation. Episodes occurred about once every week or two. Sleepwalking usually began one to two hours after their son went to sleep. They observed him walking aimlessly around the house. On one occasion he urinated in a garbage receptacle. After five or ten minutes, he would return to his room and go to sleep. In the morning, he had no memory of the sleepwalking episode. After he injured himself, the parents decided to seek professional consultation.

There was no history of sleepwalking occurring with a febrile illness, and there was no history of migraines, Tourette's syndrome, sleep apnea, enuresis, head trauma, seizures, or the use of any psychotropic medications. The child was doing well in school, socialized well, and was in good general health.

The mother reported that her parents had told her that she sleepwalked as a child. She had no memory of sleepwalking but was told that she outgrew the problem by the time she was 10. She recalled that her brother had terrible nightmares characterized by his screaming in fear.

Examination of the child revealed a healthy 7-year-old who showed no evidence of psychopathology and had no memory of the sleepwalking episodes.

Based on the history and examination of the child, we made the diagnosis of Sleepwalking Disorder. We explained to the parents that children usually outgrow this problem, it did not reflect an emotional problem in their child, and that sleepwalking often runs in families. We speculated that the mother's brother actually had night terrors rather than nightmares. We also explained that their son's amnesia for the episodes was normal. In addition, we told the parents that they needed to make the house safer for their son during his sleepwalking episodes. We suggested moving his bedroom to the first floor, putting a gate on the stairway, and locking the windows. They had already removed the glass storm door. We also predicted that their son (like his mother) would probably outgrow the problem. We cautioned them to take a low key approach in order not to stigmatize their son.

The parents asked if there was medication that might be helpful. We discussed the use of benzodiazepines and imipramine with them, but told them that we usually reserved the use of these medications for children who were sleepwalking much more frequently. However, we advised the parents that we would prescribe medication if the problem became more frequent or severe.

We followed this family with periodic phone calls and yearly visits. Two years after the initial consultation, the child was no longer sleepwalking.

## Summary

Sleepwalking is usually a benign, self-limited disorder of arousal which frequently occurs between ages 6 and 15. It is not the acting out of a dream, and it is not usually associated with psychopathology. However, sleepwalking may be associated with other sleep disorders, enuresis, and febrile illness. In children with sleepwalking disorder, family history is frequently positive for sleepwalking or night terrors. Sleepwalking is usually outgrown during adolescence. Reassurance of the parents and providing a safe environment for the sleepwalking child are the two basic elements in treatment, but both pharmacotherapeutic and psychotherapeutic approaches are available for more severe cases.

## References

Abe, K., Amatomi, M., and Oda, N. (1984). Sleepwalking and recurrent sleeptalking in children of sleepwalkers. *American Journal of Psychiatry* 141:800–801.

American Psychiatric Association. (1987). *Diagnostic and Statistical Manual of Mental Disorders*, 3rd ed. Revised. Washington, D. C.: American Psychiatric Association.

Amir, N., Navon, P., Silverberg, S., and Shalev, R. (1985). Interictal electroencephalography in night terrors and somnambulism. *Israeli Journal of Medical Sciences* 21:22–26.

Bakwin, H. (1970) Sleep-walking in twins. *Lancet* 11:446–447.

Barabas, G., and Matthews, W. S. (1985). Homogeneous clinical subgroups in children with Tourette syndrome. *Pediatrics* 75:73–75.

Berlin, R. M., and Qayyum, U. (1986). Sleepwalking: diagnosis and treatment through the life cycle. *Psychosomatics* 27:755–760.

Broughton, R. J. (1968). Sleep disorders: disorders of arousal? *Science* 159:1070–1078.

Burd, L., and Kerbeshian, J. (1988) Nocturnal coprolalia and phonic tics. *American Journal of Psychiatry* 145:132.

Charney, D. S., Kales, A., Soldatos, C. R. and Nelson, J. C. (1979). Somnambulistic-like episodes secondary to combined lithium-neuroleptic treatment. *British Journal of Psychiatry* 135:418–424.

Clement, P. C. (1970). Elimination of sleepwalking in a seven-year-old boy. *Journal of Consulting and Clinical Psychology* 34:22–26.

Clore, E. R., and Hibel, J. (1993). The parasomnias of childhood. *Journal of Pediatric Health Care* 7:12–16.

Diagnostic Classification Steering Committee. (1990). *International Classification of Sleep Disorders: Diagnostic and Coding Manual*. Rochester, MN: American Sleep Disorders Association.

Dorus, E. (1979). Sleepwalking and febrile illness. *American Journal of Psychiatry* 136:1620.

Ferber, R. (1985). *Solve Your Child's Sleep Problems.* New York: Simon & Schuster.

Fisher, B. E., and Wilson, A. E. (1987). Selected sleep disturbances in school children reported by parents: prevalence, interrelationships, behavioral correlates and parental attributions. *Perceptual and Motor Skills* 64:1147–1157.

Guilleminault, C. (1987) *Sleep and Its Disorders in Children.* New York: Raven.

Handford H. A., Mattison, R. E., and Kales, A. (1991). Sleep disturbances and disorders. In *Child and Adolescent Psychiatry,* ed. M. Lewis, pp. 715–725. Baltimore: Williams and Wilkins.

Jacobson, A., Kales, A., Lehmann, D., and Zweizig, J. R. (1965). Somnambulism: all-night electroencephalographic studies. *Science* 148:975–977.

Kales, A. (1986). Sleepwalking. In *Health & Medical Horizons.* New York: Macmillan Educational Company.

Kales, A., Soldatos, C. R., Bixler, E. O., et al. (1980b). Hereditary factors in sleepwalking and night terrors. *British Journal of Psychiatry* 137:111–118.

Kales, A., Soldatos, C. R., Caldwell, A. B., et al (1980a). Somnambulism: clinical characteristics and personality patterns. *Archives of General Psychiatry* 37:1406–1410.

Kales, J. D., Kales, A., Soldatos, C. R., et al. (1979). Sleepwalking and night terrors related to febrile illness. *American Journal of Psychiatry* 136:1214–1215.

Kales, J. D., Soldatos, C. R., and Vela-Bueno, A. (1983). Treatment of sleep disorders III: enuresis, sleepwalking, night terrors and nightmares. *Rational Drug Therapy* 17:1–7.

Lask, B. (1988). Novel and nontoxic treatment for night terrors. *British Medical Journal* 297:592.

Leckman, J. F., and Cohen, D. J. (1991). Tic disorders. *In Child and Adolescent Psychiatry,* ed. M. Lewis, pp. 613–621. Baltimore: Williams and Wilkins.

Mahowald, M. W., and Rosen, G. M. (1990). Parasomnias in children. *Pediatrician* 17:21–31.

Mahowald, M. W., and Schenck, C. H. (1992). Dissociated states of wakefulness and sleep. *Neurology* 42 (Suppl 6):44–52.

Mindell, J. A. (1993). Sleep disorders in children. *Health Psychology* 12:151–162.

Murray, J. B. (1991). Psychophysiological aspects of nightmares, night terrors, and sleepwalking. *Journal of General Psychology* 118:113–127.

Narashima, M. (1946). Sleep-walking and sleep activities. *Journal of Mental Science* 92:756–765.

Oswald, I., and Evans, J. (1985). On serious violence during sleepwalking. *British Journal of Psychiatry* 147:688–691.

Teplitz, Z. (1958) The ego and motility in sleepwalking. *Journal of the American Psychoanalytic Association* 6:95–110.

Thorpy, M. J., and Glovinsky, P. B. (1987). Parasomnias. *Psychiatric Clinics of North America* 10:623–639.

Tobin, J. D. (1993). Treatment of somnambulism with anticipatory awakening. *The Journal of Pediatrics* 122:426–427.

Vela-Bueno, A., and Soldatos, C. R. (1987). Episodic sleep disorders. *Seminars in Neurology* 7:269–275.

# 8

# Treating Nightmares in Children

Gordon Halliday

## Definitions

### Nightmares

The operational definition of *nightmares* for the purposes of this chapter is *a bad dream that awakens the dreamer*. Bad dreams that do not awaken the dreamer should be called *bad dreams* (Halliday 1987a). There are other definitions of nightmares in use besides the one given here, which explains some of the uncertainty over epidemiology, diagnostic issues, causes, and cures.

If a child awakens in distress, a nightmare is *confirmed* if the child is able to describe at least in part the contents of a visual story that reasonably can be expected to have awakened the child. Thus, we may suspect, but not be able to confirm, nightmares in very young children (ages 0 to 2 years) whose verbal skills are not yet well-developed enough to describe any dream that may have awakened them. Other sources of awakening in distress are possible, including sleep terror disorders, panic disorders, physical discomfort, and other conditions.

The word "nightmare" itself is a compound of "night" plus "mare," meaning "goblin" (see Jones 1951, for an enchanting discussion of the etymology of this word). In prescientific thought, a goblin was thought to cause bad dreams by sitting on a person's chest at night, or lying on him or her in a seductive manner. The physical weight of the goblin would explain the sense of suffocation many persons feel during a nightmare.

This sense of suffocation is integral to the older definition of nightmare that is frequently still encountered in the analytic literature. As formalized by Jones (1951) nightmares were distinguished from other upsetting dreams by the triad of (1) a feeling of an agonizing dread, (2) shortness of breath, and (3) the sensation of being paralyzed. This definition is evidently a distillation of older definitions of nightmares. For example, Buckley (1888), writing for the periodical *The Century Magazine*, stated, "In nightmare the mind is conscious of an impossibility of motion, speech, or respiration, with a dreadful sense of pressure across the chest, and an awful vision of impending danger" (p. 444).

This older, psychoanalytic definition of nightmares has fallen into disfavor with modern dream researchers, in part because it was thought to confuse night terror disorders with nightmares and in part because the operational definition of "a bad dream that awakens the dreamer" is so much simpler. It should be noted, however, that the frequency and the degree of association among the three elements of the psychoanalytic definition (fear, paralysis, suffocation) remain a very researchable question.

## Nightmare vs. Sleep Paralysis

Sleep paralysis is the sensation persons have of being awake (whether they are or not) and being unable to move. Sometimes this is accompanied by fearful cognitions, such as the thought that there is a burglar in the house. Persons often feel quite desperate and have the feeling that if they can move a toe, a finger, or shout, the spell of the paralysis will be broken.

A treatment that has been helpful to some people makes use of (1) a cognitive reframing, and (2) relaxation. The individual is reassured that relative paralysis during sleep is normal, and this inhibition of motor movement helps to keep most people from walking in their sleep. In sleep paralysis, there is a disruption of the normal arousal pattern — it does not mean that the person is losing his mind or suffering some other catastrophe.

Instead of further trying to awaken, the person is urged to relax. When he relaxes, muscles unlock and he can then move, or perhaps fall back to sleep and reawaken normally. The logic is similar to that seen with good hypnotic subjects who are unable to pull their hands apart when instructed to try to do so; instead, motor movement is restored and the hands fall apart when the hypnotic subject is told to relax the hands, stop trying, and let them fall. This general strategy is familiar to many clinicians under the category of *paradoxical intention*.

## Anxiety Dreams

*Anxiety Dreams* is an ambiguous term which may or may not refer to nightmares, as the term is used in this chapter. The term appears, in the psychoanalytic tradition, to indicate a type of dream that, although upsetting, did not meet the full criteria of the nightmare triad (fear, suffocation, paralysis). These dreams may be "unsettling, saddening, disturbing, or frightening" (Shapiro 1987, p. 158) but may or may not awaken the dreamer. Thus, the term has two inherent ambiguities for the current researcher or clinician: (1) lack of requirement for the dreamer to awaken and (2) the use of *anxiety* to cover other, non-anxious dream affects, such as aggression or depression, by at least some workers in the field, if not others.

Due to the inherent confusions in the use of this term, it is recommended that the term *anxiety dream* be dropped from further scientific usage. The use of the terms *nightmare* or *bad dreams*, as appropriate, is to be preferred.

## Self-Definitions of Nightmares

Researchers sometimes have subjects self-define nightmares, or give guidelines that do not require the nightmare to produce awakening (e.g., Bixler et al. 1979). Part of the value of self-definition may be the possible increase in ethnopsychological validity, insofar as the data collected are allowed to emerge out of the felt experience of the dreamer. Also, it is recognized that it is sometimes a judgment call as to whether a dream awakened the dreamer or if the dreamer just happened to awaken after the dream and so remembered it.

There are, however, some significant risks to reliability when nightmares are self-defined. Self-definitions of nightmares are sometimes idiosyncratic. For example, one adult patient of this author, who awoke from bad dreams, shaking and sweating, did *not* consider them nightmares because he was "just" caught in a burning building or similar themes, and was *not* chased by monsters. That is, many persons limit their use of "nightmare" to terrifying dreams of being chased or attacked by monsters (a definition endorsed by Hadfield 1954, p. 176). Other dreamers have their own definitions, which can include daytime flashbacks of experienced traumas.

## Traumatic Nightmares

*Traumatic nightmares* refer to nightmares that realistically reflect some very negative event the dreamer has actually experienced. For example, a person severely injured in a farming accident subsequently re-experienced the accident during frequent nightmares. Whereas patients may be puzzled by other dreams or nightmares and complain they "make no sense," traumatic nightmares appear striking in their realism; the nightmare is perceived "just like it happened." Such nightmares are often associated with post-traumatic stress disorder and can be one symptom of that condition.

Two important points concerning traumatic nightmares are that (1) other, more symbolic nightmares may nevertheless be *trauma driven*, and (2) elements of traumatic nightmares may still be symbolic and amenable to interpretation even when the nightmare as a whole appears to be based on an historical memory.

Concerning the first point, the clinician should be prepared (though certainly not be predisposed) to learn that a nightmare that initially presents with a fantastic story line may lead a patient to the recall and description of abuse or other traumas. Delaney (1990b) has illustrated, for example, how childhood incest may underlie the nightmares of adults even though the nightmares are not faithful copies of the original trauma. Belicki (1989) has also reported hidden traumas as driving the nightmares of some patients.

Concerning the second point, Lansky (1990, Lansky and Bley 1993) has commented on and illustrated how a close examination of a traumatic nightmare, which may initially be dismissed as the simple repetition of the traumatic event, may reveal fresh details that illustrate something of the dreamer's *current* life space. In my own caseload, for example, an adult patient had a recurrent traumatic nightmare of a work-related fall resulting in a back injury. Initially, he described all the nightmares as the same, and all were historically accurate. When questioned on specific elements of the dream, however, he discovered that one of the people in the nightmare was actually one of the officers from his disability hearing (not his co-worker, as he earlier implied), which certainly connected the nightmare to some realistic and current financial concerns.

## Prevalence

### Universality

Nightmares appear to be a universal (Davies 1987), or nearly universal, human experience. Nightmares are a transcultural experience, reported by dreamers from widely separated times and cultures. Nightmares are sufficiently common "that the clinician can expect to encounter them in the ordinary pursuit of his or her practice" (Halliday 1987a, p. 503). Further, the clinician can expect some children or their families to present for consultation with the specific request of getting rid of nightmares, or, occasionally, reassurance of the normality of the condition or the diagnosis of any significant problem of which the nightmare may be indicative.

### Threats to Reliability

Calculating estimates for nightmare frequencies is important not only in guiding diagnostic estimates of probability, but also in offering insights into vulnerable populations, risk factors, and ameliorative factors. Unfortunately, there are inherent difficulties to the reliable calculation of nightmare frequencies, for these frequencies are based on the coherent reports of memories of imaginary experiences that caused sufficient subjective distress to produce awakening. Very young children may be unable to verbalize coherent reports and so estimates of nightmare frequencies for very young children must be treated cautiously. Verbal fluency appears to influence length and coherence of nightmare descriptions. Garfield (1984) has reported that dream and nightmare descriptions by children age 3 to 5 are typically short, a sentence or two, although there are significant individual differences. She reports that a 4-year-old boy, for example, reported "I dreamed I was bitten by a poisonous snake" (p. 26).

Older children may be unable to resist the temptation to engage in fantasy play when asked for their nightmare report. For example, one boy about 6 years old initially described a nightmare of being attacked by turkeys, but then went on and on in an elaborate adventure which made me suspect he was making up the rest of the plot as he talked.

The problem of the recall of nightmares is an important one, as it is for the estimate of dream frequencies generally. Wood and Bootzin (1990) have argued that retrospective reports of nightmares significantly underestimate the frequencies of nightmares relative to reports obtained from daily dream diaries. Their daily log method yielded an estimate two and a half times greater than retrospective estimates of nightmare frequency for the past year by the same subjects. As a result, current research practice encourages the use of daily dream logs, where possible.

The issue of subjective distress from nightmares is an important one, and both Belicki (1992) and Wood and Bootzin (1990) have noted that subjective feelings of distress from nightmares have only moderate correlations with frequency of nightmares (i.e., $r = .38$ between distress and frequency as measured by two-week logs in Wood and Bootzin's study). Thus, survey questions that ask persons if they have a "problem" with "frightening dreams" (e.g., the interesting study of Bixler et. al. 1979) or nightmares as opposed to just asking nightmare frequency, introduce a complicating variable. That is, some persons can wake up from a nightmare, reassure themselves that "it was just a dream" and quickly return to sleep while other persons may fight sleep or be upset for days. Asking parents if their children "suffer" from nightmares may similarly underestimate nightmare frequency since many children do not cry out and do not seek out the parents when they awaken from a bad dream. It is therefore advisable to routinely inquire about dreams and nightmares as part of the child's mental status examination.

How nightmares are defined may have important effects on frequency estimates. Specifically, Halliday (1988) has noted that while "bad dreams" and "nightmare" frequencies are correlated ($r = .47$), "bad dreams" are reported by a higher percentage of adult dreamers (65% versus 38% for the prior month), a finding that would presumably apply to children as well. Surveys in which nightmares are self-defined without the specific requirement of awakening from the bad dream may therefore give higher estimates of nightmare frequency than surveys that specify the dreamer must be awakened.

Finally, the time period sampled has an effect on estimates of nightmare frequency. As previously noted, the presence of a nightmare anytime during childhood is near universal. Useful frequency break points include number of nightmares in the past year for personality research; in the past month for clinical outcome studies; and in the previous week for psychotherapy and for persons in significant distress or for the study of extreme groups.

## Frequency Estimates

The general consensus in the clinical literature and surveys of various quality is that young children have more nightmares than older children and adults. Frequencies are similar for boys and girls, and there may be an increase in nightmare frequency at adolescence (Galvin and Hartman 1990, Hartman 1984, Siegler 1987). Thus, adult nightmare frequencies may be useful estimates of minimal nightmare frequencies for children.

In the widely cited Bixler and colleagues (1979) study, for example, about 5% of a stratified sample of Los Angeles residents had a "current" complaint of nightmares, which may be used as a minimal estimate of children's nightmares. That study noted that 29% of the current nightmares began in the childhood-early adult ages of 0 to 20 years. This study is weakened, unfortunately, by limiting the survey question to "problems" (which confounds distress with frequency) with "frightening dreams" (which may fail to catch jealousy, anger, melancholy, or other strong affect dreams). Further, the frequency of nightmares (e.g., once per month versus once per night) was not addressed.

Table 8-1
Nightmare Frequencies

| Study | N | Ages | Frequency | Time Period |
|---|---|---|---|---|
| 1. Beltramini & Hertizig 1983 | 109 | longitudinal 1-5 | 5-39% 62% | ≥ 2 weeks |
| 2. Foster & Andeson 1936 | 79 | 1-4 | 43% | 1 week |
| | 217 | 5-8 | 39% | 1 week |
| | 221 | 9-12 | 22% | 1 week |
| 3. Yang et al. 1987 | 398 | 12-14 | 7% | 6 months |
| | 448 | 15-18 | 12% | 6 months |
| 4. Bixler et al. 1979 | 1,006 | 18-80 | 5% | $\bar{x}$ = 12.6 years |
| 5. Wood & Bootzin 1990 | 220 | $\bar{x}$ = 19 | 47% | 2 weeks |

Finally, it was not specified that the "frightening dream" awoke the dreamer. The excellently designed study of Wood and Bootzin (1990), that also defined a nightmare as "a dream that frightens the dreamer" (but did not specify that it must awaken the dreamer) yielded two-week diary reports of 47% of the undergraduates surveyed reporting nightmares.

Beltrami and Hertzig (1983) reported in a longitudinal study of children ages 1 to 5 that nighttime awakenings were fairly constant (57% to 65% awoke at least once per week), and the percentage reporting nightmares at least once every two weeks rose from 5% to 9% at age 1 and 2 to 28% to 39% for ages 3 to 5. Sixty-two percent reported nightmares at least once every two weeks over the life of the study. The effects of increasing language skills are clearly evident here. While this survey differentiates nightmares from night terrors (reporting 6% frequency of night terrors during the preschool period), no definition is given for nightmares.

In an interesting study, Foster and Anderson (1936) reported "unpleasant dreams" in children with a parental diary method over a one-week period. Unpleasant dreams (presumably nightmares) were scored as present if any one of three criteria was met: (1) child cried or moaned during night, (2) child came to adult at night showing fear, or (3) child reported a bad dream next morning when asked. Rates of 43% for children 1 to 4 years, 39% for 5 to 8 years, and 22% for children 9 to 12 years were reported.

While this study is strengthened by the use of the parental daily diary method and by a large (N = 517) sample, it does not differentiate bad dreams from nightmares, or, for the two behavioral criteria, nighttime distress from dream versus non-dream causes. Thus, it would be premature to say this study demonstrates that children aged 1 to 4 have more nightmares than children aged 5 to 8. The study's other conclusions, such as that children sleeping in a room alone have fewer bad dreams than children sharing a room with an adult or an adult and another child are intriguing and should be followed up in additional studies (e.g., perhaps sleeping alone facilitates good sleep, or children with nightmares elicit bedroom-sharing, or relative affluence drives both having one's own room and better sleep, and so on).

In a questionnaire survey of normal Chinese adolescents by Yang and colleagues (1987), the authors were puzzled to note a greater rate of nightmares for older adolescents than for younger ones (7%, rounded, for adolescents, aged 12 to 14, and 12% for adolescents age 15 to 18).

This referred to having at least two nightmares within the previous six months; nightmares themselves were evidently self-defined by respondents.

While a start has been made on estimating nightmare frequencies with children, more studies, better designed studies, and replications, with children of various ages and special populations are called for. The variation in absolute frequency of nightmares among different surveys is so great it is hard to be confident of developmental trends.

## Diagnosis

### Comparisons to Night Terror Disorders

Whereas nightmares are bad dreams that awaken the dreamer, night terrors (also called *sleep terror disorder* and *pavor nocturnus*) are now generally considered a partial or non-typical arousal from sleep with perhaps only a weak relation to dreams. The condition is thought to be more common but less pathological in children than in adults; the expectation is that most children outgrow the condition, just like most children outgrow wetting the bed at night.

Whereas nightmares are more likely to be recalled as occurring closer to the end of the sleep period, night terrors typically occur shortly after sleep onset, earlier in the night. Night terrors are typically announced with an ear-piercing scream. The child looks terrified, but is non-responsive to comforting (which is a major difference from nightmares). There may be perseverated motor movements, such as pulling a blanket up (if there are complex, coordinated movements, or intellectual activity, such as doing homework or carrying on a conversation, a dissociative disorder is suspected). The episode may last ten minutes or so, with the child then going back to sleep—although the parents may stay awake! Typically there is (partial) amnesia for the episode or for any associated dream content. Nightmares, in contrast (at least for older children), result in more elaborate dream stories.

Current thinking on night terror disorders considers this to be a disorder of arousal in children, in a class with bed wetting and sleeptalking (see Chapter 7, this book for a fuller discussion of night terrors, as well as Knapp [1987], who has a nice table contrasting night terror and anxiety dream characteristics).

This generally recognized dichotomy is compromised, somewhat, by traumatic nightmares. Given the supposition that night terrors in children are more physiologically than psychologically driven, if what appear to be night terror disorder behaviors occur after and appear dependent on the presence of a significant psychological stressor (such as a severe burn, accident, rape, or molestation), then the behaviors are classified as a nightmare, not a night terror.

## Pathology

Jones (1951) felt that nightmares were always the symptoms of mental disorder. This belief is no longer current. Instead, "the experiencing of nightmares alone is not sufficient to warrant a psychopathological diagnosis" (Davies 1987, p. 222). An analogy could be made to a child crying: the experience is universal, may or may not be pathological, and must be evaluated within the full life context and emotional status of the child. Nightmares may be a general indicator of the child's level of adjustment and may, like crying, covary with a variety of specific conditions or problems. Thus, prior to initiating treatment (or deciding no treatment is indicated) a full psychological diagnosis should be accomplished.

Clinical experience suggests a relative lack of concern for nightmare frequencies of less than once a month (keeping in mind that individual subjective distress levels will vary). When frequency increases, especially to two or three times a week, both humane considerations (reducing the suffering) and diagnostic suspicions of other disorders urge that the child's psychological situation be investigated most thoroughly, and, in general, treatment for ending the nightmares or their associated distress be offered.

The importance of diagnosis of associated conditions is illustrated by a child who presented with poor sleep and nightmares but who had a primary diagnosis of hyperkinetic syndrome. Nightmares are sometimes seen in the prodromal phase of schizophrenia. Drug and medication effects may be noted, for which consultation with the child's pediatrician may be particularly important. If nightmares appear as a result of fever, reassurance as to the commonness of this condition may be useful.

A particularly important factor to investigate is physical and sexual abuse. Abuse does appear to be a high base rate phenomenon, especially in clinical populations. Garfield (1986) has suggested that nightmares may be the primary indicator of abuse in small children, and second (behind sexual acting out) in adolescents. Under such circumstances, the safety of the child must be guaranteed by reporting this situation to the proper authorities before much headway can be expected in resolving the nightmares.

Significant family stressors may also be reflected in children's nightmares. As parental alcohol problems during childhood appear to predispose adults towards nightmares (Halliday 1992), it is probable that parental alcohol problems or other significant dysfunction predispose children toward nightmares, as well. For example, during the time of parental divorce, some children report dreams of their house burning down.

The diagnosis of additional psychological problems should not prevent one from treating the nightmares in their own right. Bishay (1987) has pointed out how chronic nightmares in adults may remain unchanged when just the concurrent problem of anxiety or depression is treated, but remit significantly once they are treated directly (through a rescripting approach). One would anticipate that this finding would hold for children as well.

## Theoretical Issues

### Causes

Our understanding of the causes of nightmares—and of the implications of this knowledge for therapy—is incomplete. Major themes suggested in the literature are (1) intrapsychic conflicts, (2) biological vulnerabilities, and (3) psychological stress or trauma. In keeping with other models of stress and adaptation (e.g., Hobfoll et al. 1991, Jones and Barlow 1990) I would suggest that nightmare frequency increases with trauma and stress and decreases with the activation of coping behaviors, including social supports. This adaptive model of nightmares avoids the Scylla of excessive intrapsychic determinism and the Charybdis of biological reductionism.

### Stress Emphasis

The adaptive approach suggests that if a child has good coping skills and is free of significant stress or trauma, he or she should also be relatively free of nightmares. The fact that even basically healthy children have nightmares is a reminder that death of family and friends, illness, and other stressors and tragedies are a normal part of living. Children should be more vulnerable to nightmares than adults both because their coping skills are less developed than those of adults and also because their small size and relative powerlessness may result in their being the realistic target of more frequent psychological insults. Younger children are easier to abuse than adolescents, as they are less likely to counterattack or run away. Incest and torture are all too frequent experiences of children. Cuddy and Belicki have noted both an increase in relative frequency of nightmares in college students abused as children (Cuddy and Belicki 1992) and differences in the kind of nightmares abuse survivors experience, with greater explicit violence and death of the dreamer (Cuddy and Belicki 1989).

Additionally, there are the "normal" traumas that happen to children that adults would never tolerate. These include being hit, bullied, teased, or ridiculed by family, teachers, and classmates. The sorts of experiences that lead to tears during the day could surely lead to nightmares at night! Thus, we should carefully look for real-life stresses behind children's nightmares. Rather than seeing nightmares as primarily the response to internal, psychological struggles, such as conflicts over aggression (Davies 1987, Kellerman 1987, Mack 1970, Siegler 1987), we should be alert for external, precipitating factors.

## Intrapsychic Emphasis

Mack (1970) and others certainly recognize external traumas as a source of nightmares but choose to place greater emphasis on intrapsychic conflicts. Davies (1987), for example, in his thoughtful article, suggests that *conflicts* over aggression cause nightmares rather than the hurts that lead to the aggressive feeling and the realistic risks associated with expressing aggression. Kales and colleagues (1980) emphasized neurophysiological changes in the developing brain of the child, and, in adults, unresolved anger in everyday life, although they also noticed 90% of their subjects reported that mental stress increased nightmare frequency.

The fact that children's coping skills are undeveloped helps explain why they often respond so quickly to educational approaches. There always has to be a first time for a dreamer to be told "it's just a dream" or "you're safe in your dreams, no matter what happens." These and other specific coping strategies may be brand new to a child, just like learning to read is new for the young child. Shapiro (1987) has outlined a developmental sequence for nightmare coping skills. He suggests that very young children (0 to 2 years) are primarily over-whelmed by nightmares and are relatively defenseless, but by age 2 to 3 years can get great reassurance from bedtime rituals. At early school age (6 to 8) children are often able to awaken themselves from a dream or to reassure themselves that "it's only a dream."

## Biological Emphasis

The search for biological correlates of nightmares is an interesting and useful one. The caution, however, is not to equate the biology of sleep and awakening with the psychology of dreams and nightmares. By analogy, our understanding of the physiology of tears and tear glands does not often advance our understanding of a 5-year-old's tearful distress. Moffit (1990) has strongly cautioned against biological reduc-tionism, and has noted, for example, that thirty years of research have shown that dreaming (and nightmares) occur throughout the night, not just in REM (rapid eye movement) stage sleep. Finally, as Jones (1951) noted: "When clerical belief ascribed nightmares to evil spirits and medical [belief] to bodily disturbances they both absolved the subject's personality for any share of bringing them about" (p. 7).

Hartman (1984) has reviewed and presented disconfirming evi-dence for some of the older but still popular biological theories of nightmares, such as lack of oxygen or eating particular foods. However, the association between nightmares and drug and alcohol use and withdrawal effects has been supported. Fevers may be associated with nightmares, as may be asthma (Wood et al. 1993). Genetic risk factors are also indicated in the group of lifelong nightmare sufferers studied by Hartman.

## Lifelong Nightmares

Lifelong nightmares may reflect multiple causes. In my own caseload, chronic trauma has been indicated. In one typical example, the dreamer had been beaten by her father, sexually molested by her stepfather, raped as an adult, and married for a while to an alcoholic and abusive husband. Her nightmares started in childhood and con-tinued about once or twice a week as an adult.

Lifelong nightmares may also develop out of a personality style driven by a genetic association to the schizophrenic illnesses. This is the group (Hartman 1984, Hartman et al. 1987) has referred to as having "thin boundaries" (1984, p. 136). His important studies have well documented a group of adult nightmare sufferers who had no obvious childhood traumas (Hartman 1984, Hartman et al. 1987) but did have high rates of psychopathology. This is the other half of the stress–coping skills perspective, the inefficient coping styles of some individuals increase their vulnerability to nightmares under even minimal or moderate stressors.

Gorton (1988) believed the lifelong nightmare sufferer he treated exemplified the concept of Hartman's "thin boundaries." While the patient experienced a near drowning and the death of a brother in childhood, there was no report of parental alcoholism, physical abuse, or sexual abuse.

Hartman (1984) has suggested that "frequent" (p. 108) nightmares in children past age 10 or so could be a prodromal sign of schizophrenic risk. He has also suggested that children with these "thin boundary" trait nightmares can be helped by having these traits channeled in poetry, writing, or other artistic modes, as well as by traditional psychological therapies. This suggestion is interesting and merits research investigation.

The base rate of lifelong nightmares that are driven by childhood trauma versus those that are driven by genetic personality predisposition without significant trauma remains open to empirical elucidation. The practicing clinician is urged to keep both possibilities in mind.

## Research Summary

Nine studies on therapy for children's (below age 18) nightmares were reviewed in Halliday (1987a); all but one (Wile 1934) were case studies or single-subject designs. While additional case studies have subsequently been published, no controlled experimental clinical outcome studies with children had been located by the time this chapter was written. Clinicians have been prolific and creative with their suggestions for reducing nightmares; controlled studies with children are now called for to better evaluate these suggestions.

Wile (1934) reported on twenty-five children (ages 6 to 14 years) in therapy, all of whom had frequent nightmares, up to nightly. Wile indicated the nightmares had negative behavioral consequences, in that they "inhibited normal activity during the day time and hampered normal restful sleep," (p. 449) which resulted in fatigue and fears of going to sleep.

Three interventions were utilized. The first group, comprising eleven children, was helped to think of positive dreams in place of the nightmares. For example, a girl frightened by her alcoholic father, who dreamed of a man without eyes, was encouraged to dream of graduating from school instead. A boy who dreamed of ghosts chasing him subsequent to hearing some ghost stories was encouraged to dream of heaven and resting spirits.

For the second group of eleven children, treatment primarily consisted of the therapist suggesting the child sleep well, e.g., "sleep is natural and normal", and "I shall sleep through the night without dreaming (p. 453)." The third group, comprising three children, was encouraged to engage in and reflect on dream-relevant coping tasks accomplished during the day. For example, a girl who had nightmares of black horses after seeing a dead black horse was taken to visit horses and encouraged to learn about them. The median time it took for the nightmares to disappear was three months for the first group, five months for the second group, and two months for the third group. Treatment benefits were reportedly maintained for five years.

Wile's (1934) study is very interesting but the study has a number of limitations and should be replicated. For example, nightmares are not explicitly defined, the method of assignment of subjects to treatment is not described, summary statistics are sketchy, no tests of statistical significance were used, length of time that children had the nightmares prior to therapy is unspecified, and a control group would have added power to the study. The small size (N = 3) of the third group is also a concern.

Erickson's (1980) complex intervention for his son's nightmares following a traffic accident is similar to Wile in emphasizing thoughts of healing in place of hurting. Handler's (1972) study followed the dream rescripting idea, with therapist and child ordering the dream monster to leave while the child was awake, but with subsequent positive carryover to the dream state.

Behavioral approaches for both children and adults have primarily followed classical, rather than operant, procedures and have emphasized desensitization to dream fear objects (Cavior and Deutsch 1975, Roberts and Gordon 1979), although Kellerman's (1979) case study did include a daily treat for good sleep once the child slept through the night without nightmares. There clearly is a need for more research (case studies as well as controlled experiments) that makes use of operant procedures.

Analytic therapies for children have also been described (Sperling 1958). It should be noted, however, that the traditional analytic belief that a properly interpreted nightmare will disappear (e.g., Jung 1974) has not held up in clinical practice, especially with traumatic nightmares. Analytically informed therapists have been very helpful, however, in suggesting possible interpretations for common nightmare themes. These interpretations can be offered to children when they are unable to provide them on their own. If accepted, the interpretation can reduce anxiety about the nightmares, offer validation of the dreamer's experience, and indicate the dreamer's problems are not unique. All of these could reduce anxiety and increase relaxation at sleep, which, in turn, could reduce nightmares. More research on the effects of analytic approaches to nightmare relief is called for.

"Face and conquer" techniques encourage the dreamer to face what he or she is afraid of and conquer or reconcile with it. These techniques may be rehearsed while the dreamer is awake and may also be applied while the dreamer is asleep. *Lucid* dreaming (being aware that one is dreaming during the dream itself) is a well-documented phenomenon (see Gackenbach and LaBerge 1988) that some children can use to their advantage to conquer nightmares. Kedziersky (1985), for example, when she was 6 or 7 got tired of her repetitive nightmares of being chased by a witch. She was aware she was dreaming and decided to no longer run from the witch. Once she did this, the nightmare disappeared and never returned.

Zadra (1990) reported a brief intervention with a 7-year-old boy who had a recurrent nightmare (about every two weeks) of being pecked by owls. The child was instructed to try flying with the owls. When the child attempted this three weeks later, the flying was only partially successful, with the boy taking twenty to twenty-five foot airborne leaps. Nevertheless, the dream owls evidently were responsive and flew around the child instead of tormenting him. Six months later, the boy remained free of nightmares. The case of an adult borderline patient treated by Brylowski (1990) reinforces the finding that lucid confrontation or rescripting can be helpful in nightmare reduction even when control is temporary or imperfect.

A controlled study by Kellner and colleagues (1992) indicated the value of having adult patients write down and rehearse positively changed versions of chronic nightmares. Nightmare frequency declined significantly, to a level equal to that obtained by a group who practiced desensitization with relaxation. These encouraging results give extra weight to the case studies in which children utilize rescripting techniques. It would be of value to repeat a similar study with children. This study is also of interest in that it demonstrated reductions in the two treatment groups in rated anxiety and depression, as well as in nightmares. This finding supports the conclusion from the review by Halliday (1987a) that there is no evidence for symptom substitution from treatment for nightmares and, in fact, improved adjustment in other areas of life often occurs as a result of nightmare treatment.

## Treatment Approaches

### Flexibility

The experience of nightmares is psychological, not physical, so the need for individualized treatment is emphasized. This implies the therapist will be flexible and have a variety of treatment options available, so that if one does not work or is distasteful to the patient, alternates are available. While some of my associates have been very enthusiastic about particular approaches, and insisted that they work without failure, my experience has been different.

For example, one associate stated that an imagery technique of filling monsters or attacking figures with white light transformed them and eliminated the nightmares—but this did not work with my own caseload. An adult patient in a motorcycle accident with traumatic nightmares refused to rescript his nightmares, because that would not be "honest." He was, however, willing to "continue the dream" and stay with it past the usual time of awakening—the accident itself—and (over a period of weeks) focused on his rescue, transportation to the hospital, and long period of recovery resulting in his triumphant ability to walk again. This patient-driven technique, to continue the dream, changed his attitude toward the nightmare (he now wanted *not* to wake up, so he could continue the dream), reduced his distress, and was more compatible with his personality style as a therapy approach.

### Sleep Hygiene

The conditions that promote good sleep hygiene may facilitate the treatment of nightmares as well. These include (1) a regular bedtime, within about the same hour every night or school night, to help build good sleep habits. The length of the sleep period should be appropriate to the child's age and needs. If there is chronic parental fighting or alcohol problems that keep the child awake, or awaken the child during the night, it would be hoped these problems could be addressed in ancillary therapy with the parents. If this is not possible, at least the child should be firmly reassured that the problem is the adult's, not the child's. Any realistic safety issues should also be addressed, including reminders as to when it is appropriate to call 911.

Sleep hygiene also includes (2) encouragement not to watch scary movies shortly before sleep (and, for some children and adults, this includes not watching television news as well), (3) avoidance of caffeine and alcohol in the hours before sleep (presumably this would be more of a risk for adolescents than for younger children), and (4) avoidance of vigorous exercise in the hour before sleep. Finally, (5) relaxation near bedtime is encouraged, and, in fact, relaxation in and of itself is a powerful way of eliminating much of the distress of nightmares (Miller and DiPalato 1983). Bedtime rituals, including story reading or prayers are often powerful stimuli for pleasant dreams and sleep (versus nightmares).

## *"Magical" Cures*

A nightmare that may appear as unbreakable as a diamond may "fracture" (dissipate) when tapped with a therapeutic hammer—when the dreamer is given some rationale for expecting change. That is, rather than being resistent to change, it is as if some nightmares have become functionally autonomous and, when some change is introduced, these nightmares fracture and dissipate. Particularly with playful elementary schoolaged children, "magical" cures are sometimes effective.

For example, some therapists and parents have wrapped a white piece of paper around an aerosol room freshener, printed "ghost spray" on it, and found that a few puffs of the spray in the bedroom at night and the nightmare ghosts are banished for the night! Another child was assured that if he ate a piece of cheese and one black olive at night, he would be free of nightmares (the technique was reportedly so effective that the child's father got back in touch with the therapist to find out what type of cheese would be the best for *his* dreams!). Magical or safety objects are often taken to bed by other children. For example, some children sleep with a Bible under their pillow.

The advantages of these magical techniques are that they are very quick (when they work) and are often fun for the child and therapist. Disadvantages include failure to promote recognition of nightmares as internal, psychological events, and placement of control outside the child, instead of within him- or herself.

## Rescripting

In rescripting techniques, children are taught they can create a new ending for their nightmares, or new dreams entirely. If this is done while the child is dreaming, distress from the nightmare is minimized. Some children merely have to be told that it is possible to control one's dreams and they are off and running with the technique with little further intervention. Garfield (1984) gives the example of an 11-year-old girl who heard her give a talk to the child's class about how one can fight back in dreams. When the child was subsequently chased in a dream by a monster, she stopped, turned around, and asked the monster why it was chasing her. "Because I'm a monster!" was the answer, which the child said was a stupid answer and demanded that the monster leave her alone (p. 296). The dream monster left and there was no recurrence of the dream.

Different types and levels of rescripting are possible. Color, movement, and unpleasantness appear to be independent visual imagery factors (White and Ashton 1977), so a failure to make a change in one aspect of a nightmare does not preclude attempting to make a change in other aspects. Rescripting possibilities include confronting and conquering monsters, escaping by flying or other means, calling on dream friends for help, changing some minor color detail of the dream, hitting the "pause control" to freeze the action and to allow the dreamer to escape, and shifting dream scenes entirely. Dialogue with dangerous or attacking figures in a dream (Tholey 1988) can be useful if the attacker represents a dissented (Piotrowski and Biele 1986) or unacknowledged part of the self, but may result in excessive anxiety if the attacker represents an actual person, as in traumatic nightmares of sexual or physical abuse. In such cases, scripts of escape or of alternate activities (such as swimming) may prove more beneficial.

## Reassurance and Education

Comforting a child who awakens from a nightmare, and allowing the child to talk about the dream, while the adult listens empathically, is generally a good first step. This comforting can admittedly sometimes backfire when high frequency nightmares (once per week or more) become maintained by social reinforcement (see Belicki and Belicki 1986), but this risk is less likely with ordinary, occasional nightmares.

A second important step, particularly with young children, is to help children recognize that certain experiences "are only a dream." This is not to disparage the child's subjective experience, but to recognize that confusions between awake and asleep experiences are relatively common, especially before about age 6. Even if a child is aware of this basic phenomenological distinction between dream and waking experience, the child often benefits from specific adult help to recognize that any experience during sleep is perfectly safe and harmless. Once a child recognizes and accepts, for example, that dream knives, bullets, or animals cannot actually harm one, it is much easier to consider the whole dream experience an adventure rather than a source of fear and to face adversity in dream life rather than to run from it.

Children can be encouraged to look for signs of strangeness that will alert them to the fact that they are dreaming, such as flying, talking to people they know are dead, or having conversations with animals. If the child is unable to accomplish this task while asleep, there can still be self-calming value to labeling these experiences correctly when awake, for example, "witches only exist in dreams, so it is safe to go back to sleep."

Education about dreams includes eliminating unhealthy super-stitions about them. Some persons believe that if they hit the ground in a falling dream, they will die (Halliday 1987b). Of course, this belief adds to anxiety and encourages the dreamer to awaken in fright "before it's too late." For children able to appreciate logic, a very quick way to dispel the superstition is to ask, if it were true, "how would anyone know?" That is, if someone actually died from hitting the ground in a dream, he or she would never be able to tell anyone about the dream experience. So this belief cannot be based on actual experience. And, in fact, many dreamers have hit the ground in their dreams. Some of my patients floated to the ground like a feather (after all, it is a dream), some landed hard, but all lived to tell about it.

Other persons have the belief that dreams foretell the future, especially if they dream something three times. If the child dreams about the death of a parent or other family members, this can be quite upsetting. Sometimes the simple reassurance that what we dream about does not always come true, spoken by a therapist or a parent, can give great reassurance. Adding that dreams are symbolic expressions of how we feel may further serve to reduce unhealthy superstitious attitudes, especially if the parent or therapist can illustrate this point with dreams from the child's own experience.

## Desensitization

Desensitization and related behavioral techniques have demonstrated efficiency for eliminating the fear associated with nightmares, thereby allowing persons to sleep quietly through the night (Halliday 1987a). The general technique is to encourage the person to relax (by progressive muscle relaxation exercises, hypnosis, deep breathing, or other means) while the fear object from the nightmare is visualized. This is often done in a graded manner so that, for example, a child might first be asked to relax while seeing a monster far away. When this is accomplished, the monster is gradually moved closer until it is at dream distance, while the patient is still relaxed. This relaxation then carries over to sleep. The technique is well researched and developed with realistic fears as well as imaginary ones, such as of surgical or other medical procedures that may drive nightmares. It has the advantage of reducing associated daytime fears as well as the nightmares.

## Writing, Drawing, and Collages

A number of therapists have found it useful to have the child write down his or her nightmare (if he or she is able to), draw it, or express it with paper collages. At a minimum, this helps to bring the nightmare "out there," where it can be more easily discussed. It can also be a first step toward recognizing and interpreting dream elements, and re-writing or drawing more healthy dream scripts. Garfield (1984) gives many helpful examples of rescripting.

## Interpretation

There are many different approaches to dream interpretation and the therapist is encouraged to read widely to develop a comfortable knowledge base in this area. Two approaches that appear to be especially helpful or influential include Delaney's (1988, 1991) *dream interview* method and the psychoanalytically informed approaches (including the Jungian approaches).

Delaney's method encourages the dreamer to define and describe dream elements in his or her own words, and then make connections to the dreamer's own life. For example, when a 9-year-old child was asked to describe the two dogs in her dream, one serious and one playful, the child was able to recognize her own conflicts over how she thought she should behave as she approached her teenage years (Delaney 1990a).

The analytic approaches have developed a corpus of hypotheses for certain dream and nightmare themes that can guide the therapist in discussion with the child. It is understood that dreams are very personal, and dream symbols just looked up in a dream dictionary result in procrustean interpretations. They can, however, offer starting points for dialogue. After realistic elements in a nightmare have been identified—and this is important, as illness, being chased, tornadoes, or fires in nightmares can represent actual past experiences or those likely to occur in the future—the remaining elements can be considered symbolic and so open to interpretation.

Themes of being chased or attacked are very common and may reflect the social or developmental threats the child is experiencing or the fact that they are "running from" their own emotions. Falling dreams may reflect the child's insecurities. Bullets and guns may reflect the dangerous aspects of male sexuality. Dreams of illness or death sometimes express the idea that the dreamer feels hurt. Specific images, such as having no hands, may reflect such ideas as feeling unable to "handle" things. Floods or fires destroying a child's house may reflect the child's devastation over the disintegration of the home life, due to divorce, domestic violence, or other conditions. Giants and witches may reflect aspects of parents the child finds unpleasant and controlling.

When the feelings and ideas behind these nightmares can be put into words, the child may experience relief. When indicated, they may also serve as a springboard for more extensive counseling.

### Case Example: Trading Nightmares for McDonald's

A young child (age 6) was seen at a mental health center at the suggestion of his pediatrician. Although healthy, the boy complained of stomachaches on mornings he had to go to school. This initial problem was soon solved, but his mother was also concerned by the fact that she often found the boy in her bed because of his nightmares.

This therapist took time to listen to the boy describe the nightmares, which the child seemed to enjoy. I then gave the child reassurance that he was safe in his dreams and that he was getting older and braver every day. Soon, sometime, he would be grown up, like his father. Soon he would sleep through the night, in his own bed. Wouldn't it be nice not to be bothered by scary dreams? Fortunately, the boy agreed!

Part of growing up, I told him, was having courage. If he could stay in bed all night, for five nights in a week, even if he was a little scared, maybe his mother would take him to McDonald's? Mother quickly agreed.

During the following week, the boy was more concerned with going to McDonald's than he was with his nightmares. He stayed in bed every night all week, evidently sleeping soundly, even when his mother forgot herself once or twice and called out at night, "Son, are you all right? Are you having a bad dream?"

The boy's natural health and courage asserted itself and he continued to sleep well and to go to school. He got to go to McDonald's. Other positive factors included a supportive and intact family and the absence of obvious traumas to which the dream may have related.

## Summary

Nightmares are bad dreams that awaken the dreamer. Most children probably have at least an occasional nightmare and for some it is a frequent and distressing occurrence. Potentiating factors for nightmares include psychological traumas or stresses, intrapsychic conflicts, certain illnesses, and biological vulnerabilities, while ameliorative factors include general health, social support, and effective coping strategies. Nightmares are not considered pathological, per se. Nightmares may reflect a child's overall level of adjustment, or the presence of specific traumas or conflicts, which require a thorough mental heath diagnosis to elucidate.

Treatment must be tailored to the individual and is usually brief (fewer than four therapy sessions is typical). While "magical" cures are sometimes effective, procedures that help the child recognize that dreams are internal fantasies over which he or she has some control are preferred. These procedures include rescripting, desensitization, and interpretive techniques. Reassurance that the child is always perfectly safe no matter how scary the nightmare, can also be helpful. With courage and good sleep habits the child can make the nightmares of yesterday fade into the wonderful dreams of tomorrow.

## References

Belicki, K. (1989). Limitations of lucid dreaming and dream control as techniques for treating nightmares. *Lucidity Letter* 8(1):95–98.

_____ (1992). The relationship of nightmare frequency to nightmare suffering with implications for treatment and research. *Dreaming* 2:143–148.

Belicki, K., and Belicki, D. (1986). A cognitive-behavioral strategy for reducing distress associated with nightmares. *Newsletter. Association for the Study of Dreams* 3(1):3–5.

Beltrami, A., and Hertzig, M. (1983). Sleep and bedtime behavior in preschool aged children. *Pediatrics* 71:153–158.

Bishay, N. (1987). Elimination of threat in nightmares: is it an essential therapy factor? *Newsletter. Association for the Study of Dreams* 4(2):8–9.

Bixler E., Kales, A., Soldatos, C., et al. (1979). Prevalence of sleep disorders in the Los Angeles metropolitan area. *American Journal of Psychiatry* 136:1257–1262.

Brylowski, A. (1990). Nightmares in crisis: clinical applications of lucid dreaming techniques. *Psychiatric Journal of the University of Ottawa* 15:79–84.

Buckley, J. (1888). Dreams, nightmares, and somnambulism. *The Century Magazine* 36:443–457.

Cavior, N., and Deutsch, A. (1975). Systematic desensitization to reduce dream induced anxiety. *The Journal of Nervous and Mental Disease* 161:433–435.

Cuddy, M., and Belicki, K. (1989). *Using nightmares to diagnose a history of sexual abuse.* Paper presented at the meeting of the Association for the Study of Dreams, London, England, July.

_____ (1992). Nightmare frequency and related sleep disturbances as indicators of a history of sexual abuse. *Dreaming* 2:15–22.

Davies, M. (1987). Nightmares and psychopathology. In *The Nightmare: Psychological and Biological Foundations*, ed. H. Kellerman, pp. 217–228. New York: Columbia University Press.

Delaney, G. (1988). *Living Your Dreams*, rev. ed. San Francisco: Harper & Row.

———— (1990a). *Dreams and the passionate life*. Paper presented at the meeting of the Association for the Study of Dreams, Chicago, June.

———— (1990b). Dreams and the recollection of incest. *Newsletter. Association for the Study of Dreams* 7(1):5–6.

———— (1991). *Break Through Dreaming*. New York: Bantam.

Erickson, M. (1980). Further clinical techniques of hypnosis: utilization techniques. In *The Collected Papers of Milton H. Erickson on Hypnosis. Volume I: The Nature of Hypnosis and Suggestion*, ed. E. Rossi, pp. 177–205. New York: Irvington.

Foster, J., and Anderson, J. (1936). Unpleasant dreams in childhood. *Child Development* 7:77–84.

Gackenbach, J., and LaBerge, S. eds. (1988). *Conscious Mind, Sleeping Brain: Perspectives on Lucid Dreaming*. New York: Plenum.

Galvin, F., and Hartman, E. (1990). Nightmares: terrors of the night. In *Dreamtime & Dreamwork: Decoding the Language of the Night*, ed. S. Krippner, pp. 233–243. Los Angeles: Tarcher.

Garfield, P. (1984). *Your Child's Dreams*. New York: Ballantine.

———— (1986). *Nightmares in sexually abused female teenagers*. Paper presented at the meeting of the Association for the Study of Dreams, Ottawa, Canada, June.

Gorton, G. (1988). Life-long nightmares: an eclectic treatment approach. *American Journal of Psychiatry* 42(4):610–618.

Hadfield, J. (1954). *Dreams and Nightmares*. Hammondsworth, England: Penguin.

Halliday, G. (1987a). Direct psychological therapies for nightmares: a review. *Clinical Psychology Review* 7:501–523.

———— (1987b). Therapy for prophecy nightmares. *Journal of Contemporary Psychotherapy* 17:217–224.

———— (1988). Relationship of spontaneous awakenings to dreams and nightmares. *Newsletter. Association for the Study of Dreams* 5:(6):4.

———— (1992). Developmental amnesia. *Journal of Contemporary Psychotherapy* 22:173–181.

Handler, L. (1972). The amelioration of nightmares in children. *Psychotherapy: Theory, Research, and Practice* 9:54–56.

Hartman, E. (1984). *The Nightmare*. New York: Basic Books.

Hartman, E., Russ, D., Oldfield, M., et al. (1987). Who has nightmares? The personality of the life-long nightmare sufferer. *Archives of*

*General Psychiatry* 44:49–56.

Hobfoll, S., Speilberger, C., Breznitz, S., et al. (1991). War-related stress: addressing the stress of war and other traumatic events. *American Psychologist* 46:848–855.

Jones, E. (1951). *On the Nightmare*. (New Ed.) New York: Liveright (First published 1931).

Jones, J., and Barlow, D. (1990). The etiology of posttraumatic stress disorder. *Clinical Psychology Review* 10:299–328.

Jung, C. (1974). *Dreams*. Princeton, NJ: Princeton University Press.

Kales, A., Soladatos, C., Caldwell, A., et al. (1980). Nightmares: clinical characteristics and personality patterns. *American Journal of Psychiatry* 137:1197–1201.

Kedzierski, B. (1985). *Personal exploration of lucid dreaming*. Meeting of the Association for the Study of Dreams, Charlottesville, VA, June.

Kellerman, H. ed. (1987). Epilogue. In *The Nightmare: Psychological and Biological Foundations*, pp. 361–363. New York: Columbia University Press.

Kellerman, J. (1979). Behavioral treatment of night terrors in a child with acute leukemia. *The Journal of Nervous and Mental Disease* 167:182–185.

Kellner, R., Neidhart, J., Krakow, B., and Pathak, D. (1992). Changes in chronic nightmares after one session of desensitization or rehearsal instructions. *American Journal of Psychiatry* 149:659–663.

Knapp, S. (1987). Night terrors in children and adults: emotional and biological factors. In *The Nightmare: Psychological and Biological Foundations*, ed. H. Kellerman, pp. 180–197. New York: Columbia University Press.

Lansky, M. (1990). The screening function of post-traumatic nightmares. *British Journal of Psychotherapy* 6:384–400.

Lansky, M., and Bley, C. (1993). Delayed onset of post-traumatic nightmares: case report and implications. *Dreaming* 3:21–31.

Mack, J. (1970). *Nightmares and Human Conflict*. Boston: Little, Brown.

Miller, W., and Dipilato, M. (1983). Treatment of nightmares via relaxation and desensitization: a controlled evaluation. *Journal of Consulting and Clinical Psychology* 51:870–877.

Moffit, A. (1990). *Presidential address: dreaming the outstanding issues*. Meeting of the Association for the Study of Dreams, Chicago, June.

Piotrowski, Z., and Biele, A. (1986). *Dreams: A Key to Self-Knowledge*. Hillsdale, N.J.: Lawrence Erlbaum.

Roberts, R., and Gordon, S., (1979). Reducing childhood nightmares subsequent to a burn trauma. *Child Behavior Therapy* 1:373–381.

Shapiro, R., (1987). Psychoanalytic perspectives on anxiety dreams in adults and children. In *The Nightmare: Psychological and Biological Foundations*, ed. H. Kellerman, pp. 157–179. New York: Columbia University Press.

Siegler, A. (1987). The nightmare and child development: some observations from a psychoanalytic perspective. In *The Nightmare: Psychological and Biological Foundations*, ed. H. Kellerman, pp. 198–214. New York: Columbia University Press.

Sperling, M. (1958). Pavor nocturnus. *Journal of the American Psychoanalytic Association* 6:79–94.

Tholey, P. (1988). A model for lucidity training as a means for self-healing and psychological growth. In *Conscious Mind, Sleeping Brain: Perspectives on Lucid Dreaming*, ed. J. Gackenbach and S. LaBerge, pp. 263–287. New York: Plenum.

White, K., and Ashton, R. (1977). Visual imagery control: one dimension or four? *Journal of Mental Imagery* 2:245–252.

Wile, I. (1934). Auto-suggested dreams as factor in therapy. *The American Journal of Orthopsychiatry* 4:449–463.

Wood, J., and Bootzin, R. (1990). The prevalence of nightmares and their independence from anxiety. *Journal of Abnormal Psychology* 99:64–68.

Wood, J., Bootzin, R., Quan, S., and Klink, M. (1993). Prevalence of nightmares among patients with asthma and chronic obstructive airway disease. *Dreaming* 3:231–241.

Yang, L., Zuo, C., and Eaton, L. (1987). Research note: sleep problems of normal Chinese adolescents. *Journal of Child Psychology and Psychiatry* 28:167–172.

Zadra, A. (1990). *Lucid dreaming, dream control, and the treatment of nightmares*. Paper presented at the meeting of the Association for the Study of Dreams, Chicago, June.

# 9

# Childhood Insomnia

Mark J. Chambers

As a clinical entity, insomnia is replete with contradictions. Relatively common and recognized for centuries, it is still poorly understood by sleep experts and the medical community at large. It is a seemingly simple disorder that is not a disorder at all, but rather a symptom with countless possible causes. Regarded by many as a malfunction of the most basic of physiological functions, it is most frequently assumed to result from psychological factors. And while insomniacs complain relentlessly of sleepiness and fatigue, they simultaneously insist that they are unable to sleep.

Insomnia is regarded largely as an adult problem, a fact reflected by the voluminous literature on the subject, which is oriented almost exclusively towards adults. Yet many adult insomniacs report that their sleep problems first appeared during childhood, suggesting that insomnia among children may be a significant clinical issue. In fact, the current nosology of the American Sleep Disorders Association (ASDA 1990) recognizes a subtype of insomnia, *idiopathic insomnia*, that is essentially defined as having childhood origins.

One reason that childhood insomniacs, especially those of school age, have been overlooked in the scientific literature may be that they are not often seen in the clinical setting. The infant or toddler whose sleep is disturbed will generally disturb the sleep of the parents as well. Such parents, desperate for more sleep themselves, readily seek clinical assistance. The adult insomniac, prompted by his or her own subjective distress, usually has the motivation and personal resources to obtain help. Adolescents and school-age children, on the other hand, may suffer with sleeplessness in silence, or they may find their sleep-related complaints met with insufficient concern by parents who do not fully understand or appreciate the problem.

## Definition and Prevalence

The actual prevalence of childhood insomnia is difficult to determine from the current literature. In a survey of mothers of children ranging in age from 5 to 18 years, Simonds and Parraga (1982) reported that 93.5% of the subject children "slept soundly" (p. 384), suggesting that the frequency of chronic sleeping difficulties among this group was relatively low. However, it is unclear what constituted sleeping "soundly" for these subjects. Moreover, because the survey was completed by mothers, the actual prevalence of sleeping problems among their children may have been underestimated if some insomniac children had never complained to their mothers of having difficulty sleeping. Lugaresi and colleagues (1983) have estimated the rate of chronic childhood insomnia to be only 1.6%; however, their study sample only consisted of children from San Marino and may not be representative of U.S. children.

Other studies have produced somewhat higher estimates of insomnia prevalence rates among children and adolescents. In a study conducted by Price and colleagues (1978), 12.6% of 15- to 18-year-olds were identified as "chronic poor sleepers" and an additional 37.6% were found to have occasional sleep problems. White and colleagues (1980) reported that 14% of the adolescents they surveyed complained of frequent difficulty falling asleep. However, a four-year longitudinal study (Strauch 1980) revealed that only 3.2% of a sample of children 10 years and older reported complaints of frequent insomnia at two or more points in time, suggesting that even many of the so-called "chronic" insomnia problems among older children and adolescents do not persist indefinitely.

Very little work concerning the prevalence of insomnia has focused exclusively on preadolescent children. In one of the few such studies, Dixon and colleagues (1981) found 14% of an outpatient pediatric population between the ages of 6 and 12 years to have insomnia, with a mean reported duration of over five years. However, given the multitude of medical problems that can disturb sleep, it can be assumed that the prevalence of insomnia among these patients is greater than that of the general population. Not surprisingly, insomnia was even more common among psychiatric patients, whose rate was nearly three times that of the pediatric outpatients.

Many of the inconsistencies in the data concerning insomnia prevalence can be attributed to varying definitions of insomnia among studies. The ASDA (1990) classification system describes insomnia as a complaint "of an insufficient amount of sleep, or not feeling rested after the habitual sleep episode" (p. 23) occurring on a nightly or almost nightly basis. This necessarily vague definition allows for the many guises under which insomnia may appear in its clinical presentation. The diagnostic criteria specifically avoid any stipulation of specific sleep parameters such as sleep latency or total sleep time, in recognition of the fact that these values may vary according to the sleep needs and habits of each individual. Instead, the emphasis is on insomnia as a *complaint* of inadequate sleep, even if this complaint cannot be objectively verified.

In contrast to the official definition of the ASDA, operational definitions of insomnia in clinical research typically include quantitative specifications for specific sleep variables. In the Price and colleagues (1978) study, for example, poor sleepers were labeled as such if they reported taking at least forty-five minutes to fall asleep and awakening for thirty minutes or more during the night at least three nights a week. It is interesting to note, however, that these "poor sleepers" were more likely than other subjects to report that they enjoyed staying up late at night, suggesting the possibility that for some of the adolescent survey respondents, the sleep patterns defined as insomnia were simply a reflection of poor sleep habits rather than an inability to sleep.

The adult sleep disorders literature has been similarly plagued by inconsistencies in operational definitions of insomnia. Many studies have excluded insomnia complainers who do not demonstrate objective evidence of sleep disturbance, with the result that the literature is often not fully representative of the insomniac population. In fact, there is evidence that those individuals who report insomnia in the absence of objective findings may have more impaired daytime functioning than do insomniacs with measurable sleep disturbance (Sugerman et al. 1985). It is also noteworthy that although several adult studies have estimated the prevalence of insomnia to be over 30% (Bixler et al. 1979, Mellinger et al. 1985, Welstein et al. 1983), fewer than 5% of subjects actually identify themselves as having insomnia (Welstein et al. 1983). Clearly, then, there is a need for greater clarification and standardization in the definition of insomnia.

## Assessment and Differential Diagnosis

The experienced clinician does not need to be reminded that successful treatment of any clinical problem depends on a thorough evaluation and accurate diagnosis. However, in the case of insomnia, this process can be complex and time-consuming, which may explain why many clinicians faced with an insomniac patient fail to obtain the information necessary to prescribe the appropriate treatment (Everitt et al. 1990).

Evaluating the insomnia complaints of children poses additional obstacles, particularly with younger children who may have difficulty articulating the details of their sleeping difficulties. Therefore, it is usually necessary to include at least one parent in the assessment. The parent can provide an independent perspective on the sleep problem and its impact and may have access to information (e.g., from observations of the sleeping child) not directly available to the patient. Still, the clinician must also interview the child so that the child's own thoughts and feelings regarding the problem can be ascertained.

There are five general areas that should be covered in any evaluation of a chronic insomnia complaint: (1) description of the complaint, (2) history of the complaint, (3) medical history and medications, (4) sleep hygiene and habits, and (5) cognitions or psychopathology that may be associated with the sleep complaint. Sleep logs can also be helpful to elucidate the precise nature of the sleep disturbance. Throughout the assessment the clinician must be mindful of the fact that the function of the information gleaned is to assist in the identification of potential causes of the sleep problem so that treatment can be tailored accordingly.

### Description of the Presenting Complaint

This includes the exact nature of the sleep disturbance as well as its apparent consequences. Does the child have difficulty initiating sleep, maintaining sleep, or both? A problem with falling asleep suggests anxiety at bedtime, negative conditioning, delayed sleep phase, or a bedtime that is simply too early. Awakenings during the night are more indicative of an organic sleep disorder (e.g., sleep apnea), particularly if they are brief and frequent. The child's total nightly sleep time should be compared against the appropriate age group norms, but it must also be noted that sleep needs may depend more on the child's maturational level than on his or her chronological age.

How the child is affected by the sleep disturbance is also important. Has performance in school been compromised? Is the child sleepy or lethargic during the day, or, alternatively, does he or she show signs of hyperactivity, inattentiveness, or disruptive behavior? Children with disordered sleep are often misdiagnosed with attention deficit hyperactivity disorder or learning disabilities because of the daytime functioning deficits associated with excessive sleepiness. On the other hand, if there is no evident sleepiness, daytime impairment or behavior disturbance, it is possible that the child may be obtaining adequate sleep despite the complaint of insomnia.

## History of Presenting Complaint

The origin and evolution of the insomnia often provide useful clues regarding its etiology. How and when did it first appear? What potential precipitating factors (e.g., family conflict, illness, change in sleeping arrangements) may have been temporally contiguous to the onset of the insomnia? How frequently does it occur, and under what circumstances? What previous attempts to solve the problem have been made, and what was the outcome? Information regarding failed treatment efforts may serve to rule out certain differential diagnoses. In some cases, however, an otherwise appropriate and effective treatment strategy may have failed because it was not fully understood or properly carried out. For this reason, the evaluation should include a detailed discussion of how previous treatment attempts were executed and for how long.

## Medical History and Medications

Because virtually any medical disorder has the potential to disrupt sleep or affect daytime functioning, a thorough medical history is arguably the most critical element of the insomnia evaluation. Conditions associated with pain or discomfort, such as middle ear disease or chronic headaches, should be ruled out, as should neurological disorders and gastrointestinal problems such as nocturnal reflux. Frequent awakenings to urinate may be symptomatic of diabetes. Respiratory dysfunction, childhood asthma in particular, may be exacerbated during sleep and result in insomnia. Sleep apnea should be considered in children who snore, are overweight, or have enlarged tonsils or adenoids. Failure to thrive or a slow growth rate may also be symptomatic of sleep-related respiratory obstruction.

Medications can also contribute to an insomnia problem. Antiasthmatic agents such as theophylline may disturb sleep by means of CNS (central nervous system) activation, especially if used close to bedtime. Methylphenidate (Ritalin) and other stimulants used to treat hyperactivity may similarly interfere with sleep initiation or maintenance. Among adolescents, possible use of over-the-counter diet pills or caffeine tablets should be considered. Medications with sedative effects—anticonvulsants and antihistamines, among others—might lead to an insomnia complaint if it is assumed that the associated daytime drowsiness is the result of a nocturnal sleep disturbance. Most important, chronic use of hypnotic medications can actually worsen sleep in some cases, with additional exacerbation during acute withdrawal.

### Sleep Hygiene and Habits

Many sleep problems can be traced to specific sleep-incompatible behaviors or habits. Does the child drink excessive quantities of caffeinated soft drinks? (For adolescents, alcohol and recreational drug use should also be assessed.) Is there vigorous, stimulating physical activity late in the evening? Does the timing of meals and snacks cause the child to be either starved or stuffed at bedtime? Is the child's daytime napping appropriate for his or her developmental level? Is the sleep schedule consistent from day to day, or are bedtimes and morning awakening times substantially later on weekends? Finally, is the sleeping environment quiet, dark, and comfortable?

### Cognitions and Psychopathology

In examining an insomnia complaint, the child's thoughts, fears, beliefs, and feelings, as well as those of the parents, should not be overlooked. Perhaps the child is afraid of the dark or even sleep itself because a family member was known to have died while sleeping.

Alternatively, he or she may fear *not* sleeping, having been told that lack of sleep may result in illness or death. In some cases, treatment may be sought out by parents with irrational fears or unrealistic expectations regarding their child's sleep. Other family dynamics, such as inadvertent parental reinforcement of the problem, may also be present. Obviously, overt psychopathology such as depression or generalized anxiety must be ruled out, but the clinician should not automatically assume that the presence of a psychiatric disorder wholly accounts for the insomnia.

## Sleep Logs

Because retrospective reports are not always accurate, a sleep log maintained for a two-week period can contribute substantially to understanding of the presenting sleep problem as well as supply a baseline against which treatment gains can be compared. The sleep log should be fashioned to furnish a daily record of the child's evening bedtime, morning awakening time, and any daytime naps. Estimates of the time to fall asleep, number of nocturnal awakenings, and total sleep time should also be included, although such estimates are often inaccurate, even among adults (Carskadon et al. 1976). If possible, relevant daytime variables (e.g., sleepiness, irritability, conduct problems) might also be recorded.

## Chronic Insomnia: Theory and Research

Some experts have postulated that the resemblance between childhood and adult insomnia increases with the age of the child. Sheldon and colleagues (1992), for example, suggested that sleep disturbance in infancy tends to be associated with neurological maturation or temperament, whereas sleep in older children and adolescents, as in adults, is more dependent on "mental and physical health status, environmental, and social factors" (p. 72). These authors also note that older children have more control over their environment and therefore they are less likely than infants and toddlers to be affected by specific sleep-onset associations. Consistent with this postulate, Klackenberg (1982) found that the presence of a sleep disturbances at age 4 has little relationship with similar sleep problems at a later age.

Still, there has been very little controlled research on the determinants of insomnia among school-age children. Some studies have examined psychological correlates of insomnia but have not been able to conclusively establish a causal role for such factors. Ferber and Boyle (1986), for example, reported that family dynamics and psychosocial issues are important factors among pediatric sleep disorder patients, but this observation was not elaborated. Price and colleagues (1978) and Strauch (1980) found a relationship between poor sleep and mood disturbance among a group of adolescents, but these authors could not rule out the possibility that the psychological problems noted were the result of the insomnia or even a third factor.

Because of the paucity of research on childhood insomnia, a theoretical perspective of this problem must borrow heavily from the adult insomnia literature. Most experts seem to agree that insomnia can result from a variety of medical and psychiatric disorders, as well as external factors such as drug use, poor sleep habits, or an inadequate sleeping environment. However, considerable attention has been devoted to understanding those variants of insomnia with no clear cause, collectively referred to as *primary insomnia*. Although the ASDA (1990) nosology further distinguishes two subtypes of primary insomnia, *psychophysiological insomnia* and *idiopathic insomnia*, the empirical validity of this distinction has been questioned (Reynolds et al. 1991). Furthermore, much of the theoretical research on primary insomnia has failed to differentiate between these two classifications.

A number of theoretical perspectives has been advanced to explain primary insomnia, perspectives that are not necessarily mutually exclusive. Physiological hyperarousal, cognitive activation, and psychological dysfunction have all been cited as potential culprits in chronic sleeplessness. The research relevant to these theories will be reviewed below. Recent work, however, has begun to question many assumptions regarding the basic nature of insomnia and in the process has cast doubt on the viability of a point of view that characterizes insomnia as a problem of inadequate nocturnal sleep.

### Physiological Hyperarousal

The postulate that primary insomnia is a manifestation of chronic physiological hyperarousal is one with considerable intuitive appeal. Most individuals have difficulty sleeping from time to time because of a transient source of physiological stimulation, whether it be excessive physical activity or a pharmacological substance such as caffeine. The first scientific evidence for this theory resulted from a study by Monroe

(1967), who found that subjects classified as poor sleepers exhibited higher rectal temperature, elevated phasic vasoconstriction, more body movements, and greater basal skin resistance than so-called good sleepers. Although Monroe himself stopped short of offering conclusions regarding causality, his data have often been cited in support of the hyperarousal hypothesis.

Unfortunately, subsequent work has been unable to replicate Monroe's findings. Adam and colleagues (1986) compared good and poor sleepers on nocturnal body temperature, pulse rate, muscle metabolism, urinary cortisol, and adrenaline excretion and found no significant differences. Johns and colleagues (1971) identified higher levels of adrenocortical activity among poor sleepers relative to controls but failed to detect differences in rectal temperature. In other studies, attempts to correlate sleep latency and muscle tension have been largely unsuccessful (Good 1975, Haynes et al. 1974).

Reports regarding the effectiveness of progressive relaxation and biofeedback in the treatment of insomnia have also fueled speculation that chronic physiological arousal may be responsible for persistent sleeping difficulties. On the whole, however, objective improvements in sleep from these techniques have been modest (Borkovec et al. 1979, Borkovec and Weerts 1976, Coursey et al. 1980, Freedman and Papsdorf 1976, Hauri 1981, Hauri et al. 1982). Moreover, most studies have not yielded significant correlations between changes in objective sleep variables and treatment-mediated physiological parameters (Borkovec and Fowles 1973, Borkovec et al. 1979, Coursey et al. 1980, Hauri 1981, Haynes et al. 1974, Lick and Heffler 1977).

## Cognitive Activation

Excessive mental activity at bedtime is a common complaint among chronic insomniacs, who often cite their inability to "turn off" their thoughts as a primary cause of their sleeplessness. Lichstein and Rosenthal (1980) verified this anecdotal observation through a survey that revealed insomniacs were more than twice as likely to attribute their disturbed sleep to cognitive arousal than to somatic factors. Other researchers (Nicassio et al. 1985) have established a significant relationship between reported cognitive activation and sleep latency. Also, insomniacs have been reported to demonstrate a style of thinking that is more negative and obsessional than that of good sleepers (Kuisk et al. 1989, Shealy 1979, Van Egeren et al. 1983).

A major drawback of these studies, however, is that they have relied on correlational analyses and therefore have not been able to establish a causal relationship between ruminative thoughts at bedtime and insomnia. In addition, research designed to examine the effects of experimentally induced mental activity on sleep has not produced strong evidence for the cognitive activation theory (Gross and Borkovec 1982, Haynes et al. 1981). In fact, Freedman and Sattler (1982) have speculated that the "racing mind" so often described by insomniacs may actually be the result, rather than the cause, of nocturnal sleeplessness.

## Psychological Dysfunction

Psychological factors have long been thought to have an important role in chronic insomnia. Clinical studies have repeatedly shown insomniacs to be more anxious and depressed than good sleepers (Adam et al. 1986, Ford and Kamerow 1989, Hauri and Fisher 1986, Kales et al. 1984, Mellinger et al. 1985, Morin and Gramling 1989, Vollrath et al. 1989, Zammit 1988) and to have more abnormal scale scores on the MMPI (Minnesota Multiphasic Personality Inventory) (Levin et al. 1984, Schneider-Helmert 1987, Shealy et al. 1980). Such findings have led some authorities to speculate that insomnia may be a manifestation of unresolved psychological conflicts or emotional arousal (Berlin 1985, Healey et al. 1981).

As with other theoretical perspectives, however, work on the relationship between psychological variables and insomnia has failed to explicate exact causal mechanisms. The possibility that insomnia may produce, rather than result from, emotional pathology has yet to be ruled out. Moreover, there are data to suggest that emotional disturbance may be characteristic only of those insomniacs who actually complain about their sleep. Stepanski and colleagues (1989) compared a group of clinical insomnia patients with a sample of subjects specifically recruited for the study who exhibited insomnia-like sleep patterns. Although the sleep of the two samples was virtually identical, the clinical patients displayed considerable evidence of psychopathology while the recruited group, who had never actively sought help for an insomnia problem, were found to have personality characteristics more resembling those of so-called "normal" sleepers.

Other work has introduced the notion that chronic insomnia may result from classical conditioning processes. Bootzin's (1972) stimulus control treatment presumes that wakefulness may become conditioned to the sleeping environment through sleep-incompatible behaviors such as reading, watching television, or worrying in bed. Anecdotal clinical observations and the success of the treatment itself have been taken as evidence for the theory. However, Haynes et al. (1982) were unable to detect a relationship between sleep-incompatible behaviors and sleep onset latency. Moreover, Zwart and Lisman (1979) demonstrated that insomniacs instructed to engage in a relaxing activity in bed when unable to sleep exhibit improvement equivalent to those treated with stimulus control. Such results prompted Espie et al. (1989) to suggest that the effectiveness of stimulus control treatment may rely on its instruction to get into bed only when sleepy, which functions as a "virtual guarantee" of reduced sleep onset latency (p. 87).

## Are Insomniacs Sleep Deprived?

Most clinical research on chronic primary insomnia unquestioningly accepts the basic premise that insomniacs are, in fact, sleep deprived. However, a review of the available empirical literature (see Chambers and Keller 1993) gives reason to challenge this assumption. Unlike experimentally sleep-deprived subjects or patients suffering from organic dyssomnias (e.g., obstructive sleep apnea), primary insomniacs are not abnormally sleepy during the day. Moreover, their daytime functioning, as measured by a wide variety of performance tasks, is comparable to that of noncomplaining controls. Of perhaps greatest importance, however, is the fact that the quality and quantity of the typical insomniac's sleep does not differ to any clinically significant degree from that of so-called good sleepers. Instead, insomniacs tend to overestimate the time it takes them to fall asleep and underestimate the total time they sleep at night (Carskadon et al. 1976, Coates et al. 1983, Hauri and Fisher 1986).

Some authorities have speculated that many primary insomniacs are simply naturally short sleepers who are unaware of their low sleep needs (Chambers and Keller 1993, Lichstein and Fisher, 1985). Insomnia complainers may also be more susceptible to anxiety and tension, causing them to worry when their nocturnal sleep patterns are not consistent with their preconceived notions of what constitutes a good night's sleep. By lying in bed for eight hours every night, these individuals, many of whom may require considerably fewer than eight hours of sleep, guarantee themselves lengthy episodes of sleeplessness in bed each night. This in turn may promote frustration and stress, which is then manifested in the daytime discomfort and fatigue reported by most insomnia patients (Chambers and Kim 1993).

## Insomnia Treatment: Techniques and Issues

As pointed out earlier in this chapter, insomnia may arise from a multitude of causes, and it cannot be assumed that a given case is the result of a single cause. Any medical or psychiatric conditions that may be responsible for the insomnia should be addressed directly. When behavioral or other psychological approaches are to be used, the clinician should attempt to tailor the treatment program to suit and accommodate the patient's special needs and circumstances. Potential compliance problems or other factors that might affect treatment outcome should also be identified and resolved early in the treatment process whenever possible. Regardless of the treatment approach chosen, however, the clinician must not lose sight of the fact that the ultimate goal of therapy is to improve the patient's waking functioning and comfort level, a goal that does not always require actual changes in nocturnal sleep.

### Sleep Hygiene Counseling

It should be self-evident that in a comprehensive insomnia treatment program, any patient behaviors or habits that are incompatible with sleep must be corrected. In many cases, however, improved sleep hygiene is a necessary but not sufficient element of successful treatment and thus by itself may not lead to a resolution of the complaint. Conversely, poor sleep hygiene does not always lead to disturbed nocturnal sleep. Therefore, the clinician should not insist on the elimination of a particular habit or practice unless it can be established that such a change actually results in improved sleep. Dogmatic demands of pristine sleep hygiene may promote patient dropout from treatment or resistance to further recommendations.

For children, alcohol and tobacco use are unlikely to be important sleep hygiene issues, although they should not be overlooked among adolescents. More common are problems with excessive caffeine consumption, particularly in the form of caffeinated soft drinks such as colas or iced tea. Although total abstinence from such beverages may not be necessary, some trial and error may be needed to establish the appropriate limits. The clinician must also ensure that the child's sleeping environment is conducive to sleep with respect to temperature, lighting, and noise. Co-sleeping with parents or other family members should be discouraged and alternative sleeping arrangements should be explored. Daytime naps may need to be shortened or eliminated. Finally, it is important that the child maintain a relatively consistent sleep schedule, with a morning awakening time that varies no more than an hour from day to day.

## Stimulus Control

Stimulus control treatment is predicated on the supposition that for some individuals, insomnia may be a manifestation of negative associations to the sleeping environment. This can occur, according to Bootzin (1972), when the insomniac repeatedly engages in sleep-incompatible activities in bed, such as reading, talking on the telephone, or solving problems. The goal of stimulus control, then, is to strengthen the bed as a cue for sleep. To accomplish this, the patient is instructed not to get into bed before he or she is sleepy and to use the bed only for sleep. The patient is also advised to remain in bed no longer than about ten minutes if unable to sleep.

Clinical studies have repeatedly demonstrated the effectiveness of stimulus control treatment for reducing sleep onset latency (Bootzin 1984, Espie et al. 1989, Lacks and Powlishta 1989, Lacks et al. 1983, Morin and Azrin 1987, Turner and Ascher 1982), although none of these studies has used polysomnography to verify objectively the subjectively reported improvements. In several studies this technique has proven superior to relaxation training (Bootzin 1984, Espie et al. 1989, Lacks et al. 1983), and at least two studies (Lacks et al. 1983, Schoicket et al. 1988) have indicated that stimulus control may also be efficacious in the treatment of sleep maintenance complaints.

The effectiveness of stimulus control may rely more on the reduction of anxiety-producing wake time in bed than on the formation of positive sleep associations. Therefore, the patient should be encouraged to pursue enjoyable but relaxing activities during out-of-bed episodes, rather than simply waiting (and hoping) for sleepiness to occur. It should be explained to patients that the stimulus control procedures are not expected to produce immediate or major increases in nocturnal sleep time but are instead intended to help them better manage wake time during the night to minimize the stress and discomfort that often accompany a chronic insomnia problem. Patients also benefit from the reassurance that with appropriate sleep habits, they will usually acquire the sleep that they need.

## Sleep Restriction

Similar to stimulus control, sleep restriction is a behavioral approach to treating insomnia that attempts to limit wake time spent in bed. The specific goal of sleep restriction therapy is to increase sleep efficiency (SE), which is the ratio of total sleep time (TST) to time in bed (TIB). The protocol for this procedure begins with two weeks of baseline sleep logs, which are used to determine the patient's mean TST. The patient is then instructed to modify his or her bedtime or morning awakening time so that TIB is equal to this mean TST value. Sleep logs are maintained throughout treatment as well, and if the mean SE for a five-day period exceeds .90, TIB is increased by fifteen minutes. If, on the other hand, SE is lower than .85, TIB is decreased to the mean TST during that period.

Subjective patient reports indicate that sleep restriction therapy produces significant improvement in SE, sleep latency, nocturnal wake time, sleep quality, and daytime fatigue (Edinger et al. 1990, Morin et al. 1989, Rubinstein et al. 1990, Schmidt-Nowara et al. 1991, Spielman et al. 1987). Sleep restriction has also yielded significantly better results than relaxation training in at least one study (Friedman et al. 1991). Studies employing polysomnography, however, have not documented substantial changes in nocturnal sleep parameters. Spielman and colleagues (1987) found a mean TST increase of only twenty-three minutes, and other studies have actually revealed decreases in TST resulting from sleep restriction therapy (Morin et al. 1989, Rubinstein et al. 1990).

Piazza and Fisher (1991a,b) have reported successful treatment of children with nocturnal sleeping difficulties using a variant of sleep restriction known as *bedtime fading*. In bedtime fading, the child's bedtime at the beginning of treatment is determined by adding thirty minutes to the average bedtime during a baseline period. From that point the child's bedtime is shifted earlier if he or she falls asleep in under fifteen minutes or later if sleep onset latency is longer than fifteen minutes. With this technique, the investigators significantly reduced inappropriate daytime sleep in addition to increasing appropriate nocturnal sleep.

## Hypnotic Pharmacotherapy

The use of hypnotic medications by insomniac children is generally discouraged by sleep experts (e.g., Sheldon et al. 1992, Ware and Orr 1983). Yet such treatment is not uncommon. Price and colleagues (1978) found that over 5% of their adolescent sample had begun to use medications to aid sleep, a figure comparable to that of the adult population. Unfortunately, there is little research on the effects of hypnotic use by children. Among adult insomniacs, however, sleeping pills increase mean TST by only thirty-five minutes (Gillin and Mendelson 1981) and tend to suppress REM and delta sleep (Borbély et al. 1991). Moreover, there is little if any evidence that the daytime functioning of insomniacs is improved by the nocturnal use of hypnotic medication (Johnson and Chernik 1982). Given the potential for abuse of and dependence on such medications, their use would not appear to be justified in most clinical circumstances.

## Cognitive Restructuring and Other Therapeutic Issues

In choosing a treatment approach and presenting it to the patient, the clinician must appreciate the unique characteristics of each patient and his or her condition. Because the literature provides few guidelines for the selection of specific treatment techniques, the tailoring of a treatment plan for an insomniac patient requires considerable clinical judgment. A foremost consideration in this process is patient compliance and execution of the treatment recommendations. Both patient and parents should clearly understand what they are to do and why the recommended program is expected to work. Douglas (1989) emphasizes the importance of involving the concerned parties in every aspect of the decision-making process and suggests that any anticipated resistance or other possible obstacles to adequate performance of the therapeutic regimen be resolved prior to the start of treatment.

The fears, expectations, and beliefs of patients and other family members can have a profound impact on the outcome of treatment. If the parents believe that poor sleep leads to serious health problems, for example, they may overstress the importance of sleep to the child, producing performance anxiety, which interferes with the child's ability to sleep. Perhaps there is concern that the child sleeps only seven hours a night, even though he or she functions normally during the day. Such instances demand education regarding the variability of sleep needs. In other cases, parents may mistakenly attribute a problem with daytime functioning to an imagined sleep problem, as did the mother described by Ware and Orr (1983) who believed that her daughter's poor swimming performance was the result of insufficient nocturnal sleep.

Secondary gain from the sleep problem, for either the child or parents, can perpetuate the problem and hinder treatment efforts. Extra attention or permission to sleep in the parents' bed may be inadvertent rewards of the insomnia. For the parents, the child's presence in the bed may serve as a convenient excuse to avoid intimacy. Alternatively, parental frustration and resentment toward the child and his or her sleep disturbance may create a stressful environment that is not conducive to sleep. Fear of the dark and separation anxiety should also be considered among the factors that may be contributing to the insomnia complaint.

### Case Illustration

The following is a composite of several cases seen at the Stanford University Sleep Disorders Clinic between 1988 and 1992.

### Description and History of Presenting Complaint

Cathy, a 10-year-old fourth-grade student, was brought by her mother to the sleep clinic for evaluation. The mother explained that Cathy had longstanding difficulties with sleep initiation, dating back to her preschool years. Left on her own, Cathy's mother stated, she would take up to two hours to fall asleep some nights. Cathy actually insisted that she was unable to fall asleep at all without her mother in bed with her. The mother admitted that she would often lie with Cathy until she fell asleep, explaining that she did this in part to assuage Cathy's vague fear about "something" being under the covers. Some problems with sleep maintenance were also reported, as Cathy would awaken frequently during the night and demand her mother's attention.

Despite the complaints of disturbed nocturnal sleep, Cathy's daytime functioning did not seem noticeably impaired. She was described as an active, energetic child, and neither mother nor child reported evidence of daytime sleepiness. She was an "A" student who enjoyed school and reportedly had not had any major disciplinary problems. Cathy spoke of one neighborhood friend with whom she often played, and Cathy's mother asserted that although Cathy was "bossy" at times, her social skills were, for the most part, quite adequate. With the exception of the typical childhood illnesses, Cathy was apparently a healthy child and was on no medications at the time of the evaluation.

## Sleep Habits and Hygiene

Cathy's scheduled bedtime, according to her mother, was 8:30 P.M., although it was often as late as 9:30 before she was ready to sleep, because of resistance at bedtime resulting from her purported fear of what might be under the covers. On school days she was usually awake by 7:00 A.M., although often not without a struggle. On weekends, however, she might sleep as late as 9:00 A.M. The patient reportedly had a healthy diet, although she was slightly overweight, and consumption of caffeinated beverages was limited to an occasional cola soft drink after school or on weekends.

## Recommendations

In formulating a treatment plan with Cathy and her mother, some discussion was devoted to the variability of sleep needs among children. It was explained that daytime functioning is usually the most reliable indicator of whether the physiological sleep requirement is being satisfied. In Cathy's case, there were no signs that she was suffering any ill effects from poor nocturnal sleep. When taken together with the fact that she would often take an hour or more to fall asleep at the beginning of the night, this suggested that her required total sleep time was less than the ten and a half hours she was expected to spend in bed each night.

As a result of this discussion, it was decided that Cathy's bedtime would initially be delayed until 9:30 P.M., but with instructions to move the bedtime thirty minutes later if she took longer than fifteen minutes to fall asleep on three consecutive nights. (Normally, sleep logs would be used to establish a working baseline, but Cathy's mother was insistent on beginning treatment immediately.) On the other hand, if she was falling asleep quickly on a consistent basis and showing signs of sleepiness or irritability during the day, her bedtime was to be moved earlier by thirty minutes. In addition, it was suggested that on the weekends Cathy avoid sleeping more than one hour past her usual weekday awakening time so that she might maintain a stable circadian cycle.

The subject of Cathy's fears was also raised, and her mother admitted that she suspected that Cathy's posturing might simply be a ploy to get her into bed with Cathy. After some consideration, it was agreed that the mother would no longer lie down with Cathy and instead would insist that Cathy fall asleep on her own, without the mother present. Similarly, should Cathy awaken during the night, the mother was to demand that she return to bed alone. Use of a star chart to reward Cathy when she remained in her own bed all night long was considered. It was also suggested that if the fears persisted, they could be addressed during the day, when bedtime was not an issue, by having Cathy explore under the bedcovers by herself.

## Results

Cathy and her mother returned to the sleep clinic two weeks after the start of treatment for a follow-up session. The mother reported that initially Cathy was intent on thwarting any attempts to change the status quo and threatened to stay awake all night if her mother did not lie down with her. Still, the mother persisted in carrying out the recommended procedures. One night after getting into bed, approximately one week into the program, Cathy loudly proclaimed, "Your plan has failed miserably!" then promptly fell asleep. At the two week follow-up, Cathy's mother indicated that the fears had all but disappeared and that Cathy was going to bed without a struggle at 9:30 and falling asleep easily. Because Cathy had continued to function adequately during the day with no evident sleepiness, no further intervention was deemed necessary.

## Summary

Although childhood insomnia has been largely neglected in the sleep disorders literature, the problem appears to represent a significant clinical issue. Still, there is considerable disagreement regarding the definition and etiology of insomnia. Innumerable medical disorders, environmental factors, and behavioral practices can disturb sleep, but in many cases, clear causes cannot be found. There is now evidence to suggest that such instances of primary insomnia may not be associated with clinically significant sleep deprivation, but instead may reflect unrealistic expectations or perceptual distortions on the part of the individual complaining of insomnia.

A number of techniques are available for the treatment of chronic insomnia. Sleep hygiene counseling attempts to modify the habits and behaviors that may be adversely affecting nocturnal sleep. Stimulus control and sleep restriction serve to reduce the patient's wake time in bed, possibly reducing the associated anxiety and stress as a result. In order to maximize the efficacy of such interventions, however, attention to patient cognitions and other therapeutic issues is also necessary. There are indications that behavioral techniques can be helpful for the vast majority of children with disturbed nocturnal sleep (Jones and Verduyn 1983, Richman et al. 1985), but future sleep disorders research must devote more attention to insomnia among children if understanding and management of this problem are to improve.

## Referencea

Adam, K., Tomeny, M., and Oswald, I. (1986). Physiological and psychological differences between good and poor sleepers. *Journal of Psychiatric Research* 20:301–316.

American Sleep Disorders Association (ASDA) (1990). *International Classification of Sleep Disorders: Diagnostic and Coding Manual.* Rochester, MN: ASDA.

Berlin, R. M. (1985). Psychotherapeutic treatment of chronic insomnia. *American Journal of Psychotherapy* 39:68–74.

Bixler, E. O., Kales, A., Soldatos, C. R., et al., (1979). Prevalence of sleep disorders in the Los Angeles metropolitan area. *American Journal of Psychiatry* 136:1257–1262.

Bootzin, R. R. (1972). A stimulus control treatment for insomnia. *Proceedings of the 80th Annual Convention of the American Psychological Association* 7:395–396.

────── (1984). Evaluation of stimulus control instructions, progressive relaxation, and sleep hygiene as treatments for insomnia. In *Sleep '84: Proceedings of the 7th European Congress on Sleep Research,* ed. W. P. Koella, E. Rüther, and H. Schulz, pp. 142–144. Stuttgart: Springer Verlag.

Borbély, A. A., Akerstedt, T., Benoit, O., et al. (1991). Hypnotics and sleep physiology: a consensus report. *European Archives of Psychiatry and Clinical Neuroscience* 241:13–21.

Borkovec, T. D., and Fowles, D. C. (1973). Controlled investigation of the effects of progressive and hypnotic relaxation on insomnia. *Journal of Abnormal Psychology* 82:153–158.

Borkovec, T. D., Grayson, J. B., O'Brien, G. T., and Weerts, T. C. (1979). Relaxation treatment of pseudoinsomnia and idiopathic insomnia: an electroencephalographic evaluation. *Journal of Applied Behavior Analysis* 12:37–54.

Borkovec, T. D., and Weerts, T. C. (1976). Effects of progressive relaxation on sleep disturbance: an electroencephalographic evaluation. *Psychosomatic Medicine* 38:173–180.

Carskadon, M. A., Dement, W. C., Mitler, M. M., et al. (1976). Self-reports versus sleep laboratory findings in 122 drug-free subjects with complaints of chronic insomnia. *American Journal of Psychiatry* 133:1382–1388.

Chambers, M. J., and Keller, B. (1993). Alert insomniacs: are they really sleep deprived? *Clinical Psychology Review* 13:649–666.

Chambers, M. J., and Kim, J. Y. (1993). The role of state-trait anxiety in insomnia and daytime restedness. *Behavioral Medicine* 19:42–46.

Coates, T. J., Killen, J. D., Silverman, S., et al. (1983). Cognitive activity, sleep disturbance, and stage specific differences between recorded and reported sleep. *Psychophysiology* 20:243–250.

Coursey, R. D., Frankel, B. L., Gaarder, K. R., and Mott, D. E. (1980). A comparison of relaxation techniques with electrosleep therapy for chronic, sleep-onset insomnia: a sleep-EEG study. *Biofeedback and Self-Regulation* 5:57–73.

Dixon, K. N., Monroe, L. J., and Jakim, S. (1981). Insomniac children. *Sleep* 4:313–318.

Douglas, J. (1989). Training parents to manage their child's sleep problem. In *Handbook of Parent Training: Parents as Co-Therapists for Children's Behavior Problems*, ed. C. E. Schaefer and J. M. Briesmeister, pp. 13–37. New York: John Wiley and Sons.

Edinger, J. D., Hoelscher, T. J., Marsh, G. R., et al. (1990). Treating sleep maintenance problems in older adults. *Sleep Research* 19:218.

Espie, C. A., Lindsay, W. R., Brooks, D. N., et al. (1989). A controlled comparative investigation of psychological treatments for chronic sleep-onset insomnia. *Behaviour Research and Therapy* 27:79–88.

Everitt, D. E., Avorn, J., and Baker, M. W. (1990). Clinical decision-making in the evaluation and treatment of insomnia. *The American Journal of Medicine* 89:357–362.

Ferber, R., and Boyle, M. P. (1986). Six year experience of a pediatric sleep disorders center. *Sleep Research* 15:120.

Ford, D. E., and Kamerow, D. B. (1989). Epidemiologic study of sleep disturbances and psychiatric disorders: an opportunity for prevention? *Journal of the American Medical Association* 262:1479–1484.

Freedman, R., and Papsdorf, J. D. (1976). Biofeedback and progressive relaxation treatment of sleep-onset insomnia: a controlled, allnight investigation. *Biofeedback and Self-Regulation* 1:253–271.

Freedman, R. R., and Sattler, H. L. (1982). Physiological and psychological factors in sleep-onset insomnia. *Journal of Abnormal Psychology* 91:380–389.

Friedman, L., Bliwise, D. L., Yesavage, J. A., and Salom, S. R. (1991). A preliminary study comparing sleep restriction and relaxation treatments for insomnia in older adults. *Journal of Gerontology* 46:P1–P8.

Gillin, J. C., and Mendelson, W. B. (1981). Sleeping pills: For whom? When? How long? In *Neuropharmacology of Central Nervous System and Behavioral Disorders*, ed. G. C. Palmer, pp. 285–316. New York: Academic Press.

Good, R. (1975). Frontalis muscle tension and sleep latency. *Psychophysiology* 12:465–467.

Gross, R. T., and Borkovec, T. D. (1982). Effects of a cognitive intrusion manipulation on the sleep-onset latency of good sleepers. *Behavior Therapy* 13:112–116.

Hauri, P. (1981). Treating psychophysiologic insomnia with biofeedback. *Archives of General Psychiatry* 38:752–758.

Hauri, P., and Fisher, J. (1986). Persistent psychophysiologic (learned) insomnia. *Sleep* 9:38–53.

Hauri, P. J., Percy, L., Hellekson, C., et al. (1982). The treatment of psychophysiologic insomnia with biofeedback: a replication study. *Biofeedback and Self-Regulation* 7:223–235.

Haynes, S. N., Adams, A., and Franzen, M. (1981). The effects of presleep stress on sleep-onset insomnia. *Journal of Abnormal Psychology* 90:601–606.

Haynes, S. N., Adams, A. E., West, S., et al. (1982). The stimulus control paradigm in sleep-onset insomnia: a multimethod assessment. *Journal of Psychosomatic Research* 26:333–339.

Haynes, S. N., Follingstad, D. R., and McGowan, W. T. (1974). Insomnia: sleep patterns and anxiety level. *Journal of Psychosomatic Research* 18:69–74.

Healey, E. S., Kales, A., Monroe, L. J., et al. (1981). Onset of insomnia: role of life-stress events. *Psychosomatic Medicine* 43:439–451.

Johns, M. W., Gay, T. J. A., Masterton, J. P., and Bruce, D. W. (1971). Relationship between sleep habits, adrenocortical activity and personality. *Psychosomatic Medicine* 33:499–508.

Johnson, L. C., and Chernik, D. A. (1982). Sedative-hypnotics and human performance. *Psychopharmacology* 76:101–113.

Jones, D. P. H., and Verduyn, C. M. (1983). Behavioural management of sleep problems. *Archives of Disease in Childhood* 58:442–444.

Kales, J. D., Kales, A., Bixler, E. O., et al. (1984). Biopsychobehavioral correlates of insomnia, V: clinical characteristics and behavioral correlates. *American Journal of Psychiatry* 141:1371–1376.

Klackenberg, G. (1982). Sleep behaviour studied longitudinally: data from 4–16 years on duration, night-awakening and bed-sharing. *Acta Paediatrica Scandinavica* 71:501–506.

Kuisk, L. A., Bertelson, A. D., and Walsh, J. K. (1989). Presleep cognitive hyperarousal and affect as factors in objective and subjective insomnia. *Perceptual and Motor Skills* 69:1219–1225.

Lacks, P., Bertelson, A. D., Gans, L., and Kunkel, J. (1983). The effectiveness of three behavioral treatments for different degrees of sleep onset insomnia. *Behavior Therapy* 14:593–605.

Lacks, P., and Powlishta, K. (1989). Improvement following behavioral treatment for insomnia: clinical significance, long-term maintenance, and predictors of outcome. *Behavior Therapy* 20:117–134.

Levin, D., Bertelson, A. D., and Lacks, P. (1984). MMPI differences among mild and severe insomniacs and good sleepers. *Journal of Personality Assessment* 48:126–129.

Lichstein, K. L., and Fischer, S. M. (1985). Insomnia. In *Handbook of Clinical Behavior Therapy with Adults*, ed. M. Hersen, and A. S. Bellack, pp. 319–352. New York: Plenum.

Lichstein, K. L., and Rosenthal, T. L. (1980). Insomniacs' perceptions of cognitive versus somatic determinants of sleep disturbance. *Journal of Abnormal Psychology* 89:105–107.

Lick, J. R., and Heffler, D. (1977). Relaxation training and attention placebo in the treatment of severe insomnia. *Journal of Consulting and Clinical Psychology* 45:153–161.

Lugaresi, E., Cirignotta, F., Zucconi, M., et al. (1983). Good and poor sleepers: an epidemiological survey of the San Marino population. In *Sleep/Wake Disorders: Natural History, Epidemiology, and Long-Term Evolution*, ed. C. Guilleminault, and E. Lugaresi, pp. 1–12. New York: Raven.

Mellinger, G. D., Balter, M. B., and Uhlenhuth, E. H. (1985). Insomnia and its treatment: prevalence and correlates. *Archives of General Psychiatry* 42:225–232.

Monroe, L. J. (1967). Psychological and physiological differences between good and poor sleepers. *Journal of Abnormal Psychology* 72:255–264.

Morin, C. M., and Azrin, N. H. (1987). Stimulus control and imagery training in treating sleep-maintenance insomnia. *Journal of Consulting and Clinical Psychology* 55:260–262.

Morin, C. M., and Gramling, S. E. (1989). Sleep patterns and aging: comparison of older adults with and without insomnia complaints. *Sleep and Aging* 4:290–294.

Morin, C. M., Kowatch, R. A., and Wade, J. B. (1989). Behavioral management of sleep disturbances secondary to chronic pain. *Journal of Behavior Therapy and Experimental Psychiatry* 20:295–302.

Nicassio, P. M., Mendlowitz, D. R., Fussell, J. J., and Petras, L. (1985). The phenomenology of the pre-sleep state: the development of the pre-sleep arousal scale. *Behaviour Research and Therapy* 23:263–271.

Piazza, C. C., and Fisher, W. W. (1991a). Bedtime fading in the treatment of pediatric insomnia. *Journal of Behavior Therapy and Experimental Psychiatry* 22:53–56.

_____ (1991b). A faded bedtime with response cost protocol for treatment of multiple sleep problems in children. *Journal of Applied Behavior Analysis* 24:129–140.

Price, V. A., Coates, T. J., Thoresen, C. E., and Grinstead, O. A. (1978). Prevalence and correlates of poor sleep among adolescents. *American Journal of Diseases in Children* 132:583–586.

Reynolds, C. F., Kupfer, D. J., Buysse, D. J., et al. (1991). Subtyping DSM-III-R primary insomnia: a literature review of the DSM-IV work group on sleep disorders. *American Journal of Psychiatry* 148:432–438.

Richman, N., Douglas, J., Hunt, H., et al. (1985). Behavioural methods in the treatment of sleep disorders – a pilot study. *Journal of Child Psychology and Psychiatry* 26:581–590.

Rubinstein, M. L., Rothenberg, S. A., Maheswaran, S., et al. (1990). Modified sleep restriction therapy in middle-aged and elderly chronic insomniacs. *Sleep Research* 19:276.

Schmidt-Nowara, W. W., Beck, A. A., and Jessop, C. A. (1991). An experimental evaluation of sleep restriction to treat chronic insomnia and reduce hypnotic use. *Sleep Research* 20:323.

Schneider-Helmert, D. (1987). Twenty-four-hour sleep-wake function and personality patterns in chronic insomniacs and healthy controls. *Sleep* 10:452–462.

Schoicket, S. L., Bertelson, A. D., and Lacks, P. (1988). Is sleep hygiene a sufficient treatment of sleep-maintenance insomnia? *Behavior Therapy* 19:183–190.

Shealy, R. C. (1979). The effectiveness of various treatment techniques on different degrees and durations of sleep-onset insomnia. *Behaviour Research and Therapy* 17:541–546.

Shealy, R. C., Lowe, J. D., and Ritzler, B. A. (1980). Sleep onset insomnia: personality characteristics and treatment outcome. *Journal of Consulting and Clinical Psychology* 48:659–661.

Sheldon, S. H., Spire, J. P., and Levy, H. B. (1992). Disorders of initiating and maintaining sleep. In *Pediatric Sleep Medicine*, pp. 69–90. Philadelphia: W. B. Saunders.

Simonds, J. F., and Parraga, H. (1982). Prevalence of sleep disorders and sleep behaviors in children and adolescents. *Journal of the American Academy of Child Psychiatry* 21:383–388.

Spielman, A. J., Saskin, P., and Thorpy, M. J. (1987). Treatment of chronic insomnia by restriction of time in bed. *Sleep* 10:45–56.

Stepanski, E., Koshorek, G., Zorick, F., et al. (1989). Characteristics of individuals who do or do not seek treatment for chronic insomnia. *Psychosomatics* 30:421–427.

Strauch, I. (1980). Developmental aspects of sleep disturbances in adolescents. *Sleep Research* 9:106.

Sugerman, J. L., Stern, J. A., and Walsh, J. K. (1985). Daytime alertness in subjective and objective insomnia: some preliminary findings. *Biological Psychiatry* 20:741–750.

Turner, R. M., and Ascher, L. M. (1982). Therapist factor in the treatment of insomnia. *Behaviour Research and Therapy* 20:33–40.

Van Egeren, L., Haynes, S. N., Franzen, M., and Hamilton, J. (1983). Presleep cognitions and attributions in sleep-onset insomnia. *Journal of Behavioral Medicine* 6:217–232.

Vollrath, M., Wicki, W., and Angst, J. (1989). The Zurich study. VIII.

Insomnia: association with depression, anxiety, somatic syndromes, and course of insomnia. *European Archives of Psychiatry and Neurological Sciences* 239:113–124.

Ware, J. C., and Orr, W. C. (1983). Sleep disorders in children. In *Handbook of Clinical Child Psychology*, ed. C. E. Walker, and M. C. Roberts, pp. 381–405. New York: John Wiley and Sons.

Welstein, L., Dement, W. C., Redington, D., et al. (1983). Insomnia in the San Francisco Bay Area: a telephone survey. In *Sleep/Wake Disorders: Natural History, Epidemiology, and Long-Term Evolution*, ed. C. Guilleminault and E. Lugaresi, pp. 73–85. New York: Raven.

White, L., Hahn, P. M., and Mitler, M. M. (1980). Sleep questionnaire in adolescents. *Sleep Research* 9:108.

Zammit, G. K. (1988). Subjective ratings of the characteristics and sequelae of good and poor sleep in normals. *Journal of Clinical Psychology* 44:123–130.

Zwart, C. A., and Lisman, S. A. (1979). An analysis of stimulus control treatment of sleep-onset insomnia. *Journal of Consulting and Clinical Psychology* 47:113–118.

# 10

# Nocturnal Bruxism in Children

Kenneth R. Lofland
Jeffrey E. Cassisi
Ronald S. Drabman

Many undesirable physiological events can occur during children's sleep. These often take the form of motor or autonomic nervous system changes associated with arousal (Mahowald and Rosen 1990). This chapter will focus on one category of such events, nocturnal bruxism. Bruxism is defined as nonfunctional tooth grinding, clenching, or gnashing (Nadler 1966).

Although earlier studies failed to differentiate nocturnal from diurnal bruxism, it is currently agreed that these are distinct problems, occurring in different stages of consciousness, with different etiologies and treatments (Glaros 1981, Reding et al. 1968a,b,Rugh and Harlan 1988). Nocturnal bruxism in adults has been extensively reviewed by health care professionals, most notably dentists and psychologists (Glaros and Rao 1977, McGlynn et al. 1985, Ramfjord and Ash 1983). While the focus of this chapter will be on nocturnal bruxism in children and adolescents, extensive reference will be made to the adult literature as comparatively little has been done with children.

Marie and Pietkiewicz (1907) were among the first dental researchers to describe bruxism, originally termed *bruxomania*. Shortly thereafter, bruxism was related to a variety of pathological dental conditions, including malocclusion and periodontitis (Ramfjord and Ash 1983). Although early studies focused on dental and systemic explanations for bruxism, others felt that bruxism was related to psychological states. Descriptions can be found throughout history associating human suffering and emotional distress with clenching and gnashing behaviors (Darwin 1872). Tishler (1928) was among the first to formally postulate that psychological factors were responsible for bruxism, calling bruxism *oral habit neurosis*. Thus, the most frequently invoked theories to explain bruxism are derived from dental and psychological models.

## Dental Theories of Bruxism

Dental, or local, theories hold that bruxism is caused by malocclusion. Occlusion is the dental term that describes the balance and alignment of the teeth. It is a guiding principle of dental treatment. When occlusion is disrupted (i.e., when dental alignment deviates), the masticatory system is less efficient. Interferences in occlusion are irritants that prompt bruxism (Ramfjord and Ash 1983).

Dental theorists speculate that bruxism originally had adaptive significance. Since the relationship between the upper and lower dentition changes over the life span due to tooth wear and tooth loss, bruxism evolved as a self-corrective mechanism to maintain occlusal harmony. From this perspective, bruxism is seen as a reflexive process that serves to reduce interferences in occlusion by grinding them down (Ramfjord 1961).

Following the logic of dental theories, children are particularly at risk for bruxism. While bruxism occurs throughout the life span, several periods of "normal" malocclusion occur during dental development. Childhood is marked by the rapid development of the periodontium. In the first two years of life, the primary teeth erupt one or two at a time, resulting in an unbalanced masticatory system. Between the ages of 5 and 10 years, the primary teeth are exfoliated by permanent teeth. This results in a period of mixed dentition that produces further disequilibrium in the masticatory system. Therefore, most dentists feel that bruxism increases during the mixed dentition stage and then decreases with age (Nilner 1981, Nilner and Kopp 1983, Reding 1966).

While this notion has intuitive appeal, dental theories of bruxism have received mixed support. In epidemiological studies based on dental examination and self-report using sample sizes ranging from 100 to 1,052, the incidence of bruxism in children has been found to range between seven to eighty-eight percent (Boyens 1940, Bungaard-Jorgenson 1950, Glaros 1981, Nilner 1981, Nilner and Kopp 1983). These findings are comparable to those of adults, with the incidence of bruxism ranging between fifteen and eighty-eight percent (Reding 1966, Scharer 1974). Thus, while increased bruxism is expected during periods of mixed dentition, epidemiological studies (Magnusson et al. 1993) do not support this notion (for a complete review see Cash 1988).

Experimental support for the dental theory of bruxism was originally obtained by Jankelson (1955). He temporarily produced bruxism by creating an occlusal interference with acrylic cement on the surfaces of the molars. He concluded that the resultant tooth-grinding was a subconscious effort to remove the interference in order to obtain maximal tooth contact.

Other researchers, however, failed to replicate these findings. Rugh and Robbins (1982) did not elicit nocturnal bruxism in patients after inserting crowns with defective contacts, even in patients with a past history of bruxism. They concluded that malocclusion itself does not elicit bruxism; rather, it is the patient's response to malocclusion. Thus, individual characteristics of the patient must be related to bruxism.

### Psychological Theories of Bruxism

Psychological theories originally focused on unconscious conflict, and more recently on stress, as causes of bruxism. Psychodynamic theorists view dreaming as a window to the unconscious. According to this model, primordial conflicts are defended from conscious experience by repression and other defense mechanisms. However, these defenses are less efficient during sleep and tensions rise to consciousness during dreaming. Freud postulated that dreams were camouflaged expressions of intolerable desires and fears. He asserted that the analysis of dreams can reveal the real causes of anxiety within an individual (Freud 1953). This is also why some have argued that unconscious conflicts lead to bruxism. As these themes are replayed during dreaming, anxiety levels rise. As anxiety rises, so do the oral manifestations of frustration and psychic pain in the form of bruxism.

The adult literature relating stress and emotional factors to bruxism has produced conflicting findings. While some studies found no relationship between psychogenic factors and bruxism, others have found compelling evidence for this relationship (Frisch et al. 1960, Reding et al. 1968a,b, Shapiro and Shannon 1965, Thaller 1967, Walsh 1965). Reding and colleagues (1968a) found no significant personality differences between subjects with nocturnal bruxism and controls based on histories of emotional disturbance or responses on the Minnesota Multiphasic Personality Inventory (MMPI) and the Cornell Medical Index. However, it may be that one's personality (the stable characteristics of an individual) has less to do with bruxism than do the transient day to day stressors that vary concomitantly with bruxism activity.

Several early studies found compelling evidence for a relationship between stress (anxiety, anger, frustration) and bruxism, but they were criticized for not differentiating between diurnal and nocturnal bruxism. However, later studies with improved methodology found evidence of this relationship as well. Nocturnal bruxism was reported to increase with the occurrence of naturally stressful life events (Rugh and Solberg 1975), as well as with increased levels of urinary catecholamines (Clark et al. 1980).

Emotional stress remains the most commonly reported precipitating factor of nocturnal bruxism (Lindqvist 1972, Rugh and Solberg 1975). Levels of bruxism during the sleep of adults have been found to be greater during periods of self-reported stress. Rugh and Harlan (1988) state that clinically, it is common to find that symptoms of bruxism appear during periods of difficult life situations (e.g., marital strife, school examinations, difficult work situations). Later, bruxism and accompanying symptoms often go into remission as life stressors are resolved (Rugh and Harlan 1988).

Other research has focused on the differentiation between actual stress and the anticipation of stress. Withey (1962) indicated that the anticipation of an event can be stressful. Support for this concept came from Birnbaum (1964), who found that a large portion of the physiological stress reaction occurs during an anticipation period.

Funch and Gale (1980) evaluated the relationship between bruxism and the anticipation of stress in a 27-year-old female graduate student. They found that bruxism resulted from the anticipation of stress, rather than from the stress itself. This distinction has important treatment implications since the therapist needs to know if bruxism is in response to, or in anticipation of, anxiety or stress. However, conclusions drawn from case studies must be made judiciously, due to limited generalizability.

The finding of a relationship between stress and bruxism has been replicated using children as subjects. Lindqvist (1972) examined 104 children, aged 12 years. Bruxism, as measured by atypical facets, was found to be significantly related to symptoms of stress and emotional disorders as assessed in a structured interview with each child's parents.

While there appears to be burgeoning evidence of a relationship between stress and bruxism, this relationship is far from proven. Although stress may be an exacerbating factor in bruxism, it is not clear to what degree stress is necessary or sufficient to bring about this behavior. In other words, further information is needed to explain occurrences of bruxism in nonstressed individuals, stressed individuals who do not engage in bruxism, and why stress can result in bruxism versus other physiological symptoms such as gastric distress or hypertension.

## Integrative Theories of Bruxism

An integrative theory offers a potential resolution for some of these issues. Many researchers now believe that bruxism is elicited by a combination of occlusal discrepancies and emotional stress (Forgione 1974, Lindqvist 1974a, Meklas 1971, Scharer 1974). Evidence for an integrative model may come from studies that examine the separate and combined effects of occlusal interference and transient stress on masseter activity. One such study has been attempted (McGlynn et al. 1989). Eight subjects viewed horrific and idyllic videotapes, with and without occlusal interferences fitted, while masseter electromyography (EMG) was recorded bilaterally. A clear increase in EMG was found during the videotape stressor. No effect was obtained with the occlusal interference alone. On first glance, this study seems to support a psychological model of bruxism over a dental model. However, as the authors themselves point out, this study was limited in that it used a small sample size and the fitted interferences were atypically large. Thus, definitive support for an integrative model awaits replication of this experiment with corrections.

In summary, the two primary models related to bruxism are dental and psychological (Leung and Robson 1991). To date, these models have not presented compelling evidence that either of them alone is sufficient to account for all bruxism activity. As a result, the most popular theories now combine mechanical and psychological factors (Ramfjord and Ash 1971, Robinson et al. 1969). A better understanding of the incidence of bruxism will clarify its significance to children and shed light on appropriate etiologic models. Therefore, additional epidemiological research is needed. The wide range of incidence reported in previous studies may reflect limited methodology. For example, both dental and psychological studies have inferred the presence of bruxism based on expert ratings made during a dental examination or the self-report of patients and significant others. This is problematic because the examination of tooth wear may reflect prior episodes of bruxism rather than current activity (Lindqvist 1973). In addition, self-report approaches may underestimate bruxism activity because patients are often unaware that they are engaging in bruxism and significant others generally respond only to audible bruxism (Leung and Robson 1991).

Future research must be sensitive to the potential interrelationships between differing levels of stress and access to dental care. Increased stress may be associated with lower socioeconomic status (SES), which in turn may be related to less frequent dental care (Syme 1984). Less frequent dental care could be associated with higher frequencies of malocclusion and other dental irritants. Larger-scaled epidemiological studies stratified by age, SES, race, and region, utilizing objective measurements of current bruxism behavior will address these issues.

### Sleep and Bruxism

Since nocturnal bruxism occurs during sleep, it is imperative to understand the relationship between sleep stages and bruxism. Support for the early psychological theories came from sleep lab studies, which concluded that bruxism occurred primarily during rapid eye movement (REM) sleep, when most dreaming and the resolution of daily stress are thought to occur (Powell 1965, Reding et al. 1964). However, many of the early studies were criticized due to methodological shortcomings that confounded their sample by including subjects with diurnal and nocturnal bruxism and often mistaking activities such as swallowing and natural tooth contacts for bruxism (Robinson et al. 1969).

Since then, much has been done to increase our understanding of the occurrence of bruxism during sleep. While bruxism occurs in all stages of sleep, there is a preponderance of activity in stage 2 sleep

(Reding et al. 1968b). In addition, most of the bruxism in other stages of sleep occurs during transitions from those stages into stage 2. The transitions between sleep stages are associated with an arousal, or lightening, of sleep, which is highly correlated with bruxism. This is supported by electroencephalograph (EEG) studies as well as by the monitoring of heart rate between sleep stages when bruxism occurs. Heart rate has been observed to increase significantly during sleep stage transitions and during bruxism activity.

Satoh and Harada (1973) found that bruxism is directly related to arousal. They monitored naturally occurring, spontaneous bruxism as well as artificially induced bruxism in order to gain insight into its central mechanism. They artificially aroused subjects during sleep by presenting sonic, photic, and tactile stimuli. In many instances, they were able to show that bruxism activity depended on sleep stage. Bruxism was observed during all background EEG patterns but seldom during deep, slow wave sleep (stage 4) and most often during light sleep (stages 1 and 2) which is in agreement with Reding et al. (1968b). In addition, Satoh and Harada (1973) identified several autonomic correlates of both spontaneous and artificially induced bruxism. Increased heart rate and phasic vasoconstriction of the fingertip were associated with bruxism in every case. Gross body movements were also correlated with bruxism, as were skin potential changes on the forearm and occasionally on the palm. It was concluded that bruxism "is triggered by an abrupt lightening of sleep and manifests itself during transition from sleep to wakefulness; that is, it appears as an arousal reaction" (p. 274).

Further understanding of the relationship between bruxism and sleep stages resulted from Ware and Rugh's (1988) identification of different subgroups of bruxism patients based on their level of symptom severity. They identified a destructive bruxism group who had severe oral symptoms (e.g., degenerative joint disease, excessive tooth mobility, temporomandibular joint [TMJ] pain) and compared it to a bruxism group without these severe symptoms. They determined that the sleep stage in which bruxism tended to occur was an important factor in differentiating these groups. Although the total amount of bruxism did not differ between the groups, the destructive group engaged in significantly more bruxism during REM sleep. This implies that the autonomic processes that minimize motor activity during REM sleep do not work in some individuals, allowing the full uninhibited forces of the masticatory system to do severe damage. From their data, they concluded that as little as one minute of REM sleep bruxism per night may contribute to severe oral symptoms.

Ware and Rugh's (1988) study also clarified earlier conflicting findings regarding bruxism and sleep stages. Previous studies had found mixed results, with some indicating that bruxism occurs during REM sleep and others finding that it does not (Reding et al. 1968b, Satoh and Harada 1973, Ware 1982). These results suggest that there are identifiable subgroups of bruxism patients who differ in the amount of REM bruxism exhibited. Thus, previously conflicting data may have been a consequence of selection techniques distributing a higher proportion of one or the other subgroup of bruxism patients. In addition to dividing bruxism patients into diurnal versus nocturnal groups and stress-related versus non-stress-related groups (Olkinuora 1969), it follows that bruxism patients should now be subdivided by the stage of sleep during which their bruxism occurs (Ware and Rugh 1988).

This information has potentially serious implications for children. Sleep research has found that the sleep patterns of children differ markedly from those of adults. The characteristic EEG picture of developed humans is not evident until 5 to 6 years of age. Early in development, humans sleep for much longer time periods, they can move directly from an awake state into REM sleep, and they spend as much as fifty percent of their sleep in REM, as opposed to adults who exhibit only fifteen to twenty percent REM sleep (Rosenzweig and Leiman 1982). The greater total sleep time and percent of time spent in REM sleep, combined with naturally occurring malocclusion, may mark childhood as a developmental period at the highest risk for destructive bruxism.

Thus, while the overall incidence of nocturnal bruxism may not differ between children and adults, these factors could make children vulnerable to more destructive forms of bruxism. Epidemiological studies have not yet reached the level of sophistication to evaluate the incidence of subgroups of bruxism patients. Evaluating the incidence of destructive bruxism in children is an area in need of further research.

To summarize, since nocturnal bruxism occurs during sleep, investigating its relationship to sleep activity is warranted. While earlier findings have been mixed, it appears that most bruxism results from arousal, or lightening, of sleep occurring in transitions between sleep stages and in sleep stages 1 and 2. Sleep arousal is also associated with increased heart rate, vasoconstriction, and body movements. A subgroup of individuals exhibits a particularly destructive form of bruxism during REM sleep. Identifying meaningful bruxism subgroups in order to clarify conflicting findings in the literature and to increase treatment efficacy appears to be a valuable area of continued effort. The emerging picture of bruxism and sleep predicts that children are a population at risk for destructive forms of bruxism; however, this prediction needs to be confirmed empirically.

## Systemic Theories of Bruxism

Sleep research also points to an alternate theory of the etiology of bruxism. This theory is based on systemic, or central nervous system, factors causing bruxism. In fact, Marie and Pietwiekwicz (1907) originally felt that bruxism was due to cortical lesions. Numerous potential systemic factors have been suggested, including genetic, gastrointestinal (GI), nutritional, and allergic.

McBride (1952) postulated that mouth breathing resulted in a dry mouth, which caused bruxism. Nocturnal bruxism has been reported to occur with increased frequency among allergic children with GI disturbances 300% over nonallergic children (Marks 1980). Magnesium deficiencies were thought to be of etiological significance by Lehvila (1974), who reported successfully treating bruxism with therapeutic doses of magnesium. Other studies found support for a genetic component with identical twins showing more similar wear facets on their teeth than dizygotic twins (Lindqvist 1974b). Another study found that nearly thirty percent of kindergarteners with bruxism had a member of their immediate family with a history of bruxism (Kuch et al. 1979).

Rett syndrome is a recently discovered, progressive neurological disorder that occurs primarily in young females (Buccino and Weddell 1989). It is a rare, often misdiagnosed disorder that is similar to autism, characterized by cognitive deterioration and severe repetitive and spastic motor behavior. Severe bruxism and perioral contractions are early symptoms of this syndrome. Therefore, while the incidence is extremely rare, the occurrence of severe bruxism in female children may be pathognomonic of Rett syndrome (Percy et al. 1988).

Many investigators currently subscribe to an integrative etiology that also includes systemic factors. Rugh and Harlan (1988) state that the current school of thought for the etiology of nocturnal bruxism is that it is a sleep disorder that is centrally mediated and precipitated by emotional stress.

## Assessment of Bruxism

The assessment of bruxism was advanced with the development of psychophysiological techniques such as EMG monitoring (Reding et al. 1968b). Electromyographic techniques measure the electrical activity produced by the masseter muscle during contraction. This is typically accomplished with surface sensors placed vertically over the belly of the masseter muscle, although fine wire needle electrodes are occasionally used. However, the measurement of nocturnal bruxism in children poses challenges. While the best controlled adult studies generally occur during all-night sleep studies in a laboratory, this approach is highly reactive with children due to the extreme stress of being separated from their parents.

Recently, the miniaturization of electronics has allowed for all-night masseter EMG recordings to be taken at home with the use of ambulatory monitors (Cassisi et al. 1987). This has proven to be a difficult approach with adults, and is untried with children. The prospect of having young children sleep with several electrodes attached to their face and wired to expensive monitors has no doubt limited the application of this technology.

Ultimately, there appears to be no satisfactory solution, as current assessment approaches are confounded by their inaccuracy, reactiveness, or invasiveness. Therefore, a series of studies is needed to establish the intercorrelations between the cost-effective procedures, such as the dental examination and self-report methods, with the more accurate but potentially reactive and expensive procedures, such as ambulatory EMG monitors. Once these interrelationships are established, true population estimates can be made using cost-effective approaches adjusting for error rates established across methods.

## Consequences of Bruxism

Ahmad (1986) states that the clinical symptoms or consequences of bruxism in children are essentially the same as in adults. In a review of the literature on bruxism in children, Cash (1988) listed the following symptoms of bruxism: attrition of teeth, faceting, pulpal exposure, hypertrophy of the muscles of mastication, muscle tenderness, injury to the periodontium, alteration of the bite, limited opening, loss of vertical dimension, TMJ disturbances, alveolar bone loss, hypermobility of teeth, hypersensitivity of teeth, gingival recession, inflammation of the gingiva, bulging facial muscles, spontaneous contraction of facial musculature, aching jaws on awakening, broken restorations, trismus, and headaches.

The most consistent dental finding of bruxism is attrition of the teeth and/or atypical faceting (shiny, uneven occlusal wear with sharp edges), observed in ninety percent of children with bruxism (Lindqvist 1971). In 6- to 12-year-olds, it was found that the abrasion from atypical faceting was most common on the incisal edges of the upper and lower incisors (Jankelson 1955, Lindqvist 1971). It has also been reported that the attrition of teeth increases significantly with age in all regions except the molars (Egermark-Eriksson 1983).

Another common symptom of bruxism is muscle pain and tenderness of the jaw muscles. Of the oral structures stressed by bruxism, pain is most easily elicited in the pterygoid and masseter muscles, and is typically experienced upon awakening. In one study, muscle tenderness was reported by thirty-three percent of 7-, 11-, and 15-year-old children with bruxism (Egermark-Eriksson 1983).

Bruxism can also result in TMJ symptoms (Ramfjord and Ash 1983). Both the joint and related muscles can be a source of pain. The pain is usually unilateral and associated with clicking in the joint, restricted movements, and limited ability to fully open the mouth. Nilner (1981) observed that seventy-seven percent of 749 children aged 7 to 14 years had from one to three of the following symptoms: TMJ sounds, decreased ability to open wide, and/or TMJ and muscle tenderness on palpation.

The relationship between bruxism and headache has been identified. In the general population, Nilner (1981) reported that fifteen percent of 7- to 14-year-olds suffered from recurrent headaches, which is comparable to the rate in adults (Nilner 1981). However, in a study of 366 children aged 6 to 16 years and diagnosed with bruxism, it was found that thirty-four percent had recurrent headaches (Ingerslev 1983). Egermark-Eriksson (1982) also found support for a relationship between dental wear and headaches, with the headaches often being of a muscle contraction type.

Although children are reported to have the same number of clinical signs and symptoms of bruxism as adults, the frequency of subjective complaints reported by children is lower (Egermark-Eriksson et al. 1981, Leung and Robson 1991). While this is poorly understood,

Moore (1956) postulated that this was due to the fact that "the child's maintenance and reparative processes are far superior to those of an adult" (p. 278).

## Treatment of Bruxism

Numerous therapeutic methods have been advocated for the treatment of severe bruxism. Since several physical disorders have been related to bruxism (e.g., TMJ, Rett syndrome), a complete dental evaluation should precede any intervention. Dental theory originally focused on restoring dental occlusion. At one time, occlusal adjustment was thought to be all that was necessary to eliminate bruxism (Tishler 1928). Several researchers found support for this view; one even reported 100% treatment effects (Ramfjord 1961). However, reliance on the subjective report of patients rather than objective data limited the reliability of these conclusions. In a more objective study, Rugh and Solberg (1976) found that six of nine patients showed no improvement after occlusal adjustment. Due to the permanency of this intervention and equivocal results, occlusal adjustment is of questionable utility in the treatment of bruxism.

Occlusal splints were first introduced by Karolyi (1906) and are frequently used to treat bruxism. Although different splints exist, one that offers full coverage of the mandibular or maxillary teeth is most often prescribed (Greene and Laskin 1972, Posselt 1962). It is constructed of acrylic after impressions and models are made. A carefully constructed splint may take several hours to make. Success rates of splint treatment, determined both clinically and electromyographically, have been estimated at seventy to ninety percent of patients (Fuchs 1969, Scharer 1974).

Several investigations have found that biteplane splints decrease bruxism activity and reduce the likelihood of permanent damage to the dentition (Cassisi et al. 1987, Clarke 1984, Rugh and Solberg 1976). Rugh and Solberg (1976) found that all of their patients reduced masseter muscle activity when wearing a splint, but this eventually returned to pretreatment levels when the splints were removed. Other researchers have found mixed results, with about half of patients reducing masseter activity but others remaining the same or actually increasing masseter activity (Clarke et al. 1984).

The mechanisms of action for biteplane splints are not fully understood. Current thought is that the carefully constructed splint not only prevents the surfaces of the upper and lower dentition from coming into contact, but also reduces muscle hyperactivity. Separating the teeth results in an inhibitory reflex that effectively shuts down the masticatory system. The splint also replaces disturbing occlusal interferences, allowing the mandible to close in a stable position. In addition, the splint discourages bruxism by removing the habitually used dysfunctional contact relations (Ramjford and Ash 1983). All splints need periodic adjustment. However, this is especially true with children, given the rapid changes in the periodontium that occur during the developmental period. This significantly increases the cost of this treatment.

The cost of splints is more likely to be justified in cases of headache resulting from bruxism. For example, Bennett and Mahan (1989) describe an 8½-year-old male who, after limited relief through traditional therapies for headache over a four-year period, was helped significantly with an occlusal splint. The child's headaches were actually a result of nocturnal bruxism that had been overlooked. This case illustrates the importance of consultation with dental and medical specialists in cases of recalcitrant headache.

Pharmacological interventions for bruxism have been limited to diagnostic and short-term uses in adults. Muscle relaxants that suppress arousal or motor activity, such as diazepam, have demonstrated good but temporary results (Montgomery et al. 1986, Rugh and Ohrbach 1988). Since destructive forms of nocturnal bruxism occur during REM sleep, antidepressants that suppress REM sleep may be used (Ware et al. 1982). However, the clinician should be conservative with these approaches due to the side effects of such treatments in children (Attanasio 1991).

Hypnosis was one early psychological treatment for nocturnal bruxism (Gelberd 1958). More recently, behavior therapy has been suggested to reduce stressors and other factors related to bruxism. Components of behavior therapy may include progressive muscle relaxation training, imagery, and/or breathing exercises. All of these procedures have been modified for application with children. However, there is insufficient information available to comment on the clinical effectiveness of diurnal psychological procedures on nocturnal bruxism. Generalization of treatment effects from waking states to sleeping states have not been established.

Nocturnal biofeedback or alarm procedures are based on principles of avoidance conditioning. This approach uses ambulatory EMG monitors attached to the masseter muscle. An EMG-defined threshold is set, beyond which a loud tone or alarm is emitted. This tone awakens the patient, thus interrupting the behavior. The application of this intervention to adults has been reviewed by Cassisi and colleagues (1987).

Alarm procedures have had mixed results in adults. Piccione et al. (1982) reported a rebound effect of increased bruxism after treatment using this technique in a single subject design. On the other hand, Moss and colleagues (1982) found this approach to be effective when combined with an arousal task in a single subject design. More recently, Cassisi and McGlynn (1988) studied nocturnal alarms with an effective arousal task in a group design. No rebound effects were obtained in this latter study.

Alarms are based on expensive ambulatory EMG monitors and they are difficult to implement consistently over long periods of time even with motivated adult patients. There are hidden costs of disposable electrodes and batteries that render this intervention somewhat impractical.

Ironically, early studies using nocturnal alarms borrowed heavily from the rationale of the bell and pad treatment of enuresis developed by Mowrer and Mowrer (1938). Although this intervention was originally extrapolated from a treatment for children, it has yet to be used for bruxism with this population. Again, the prospect of wiring children to a complicated and expensive apparatus may be too discouraging. The most promising applications of alarm therapy for adults or children are in those individuals for whom splint therapy seems to exacerbate bruxism, or in cases in which it is difficult to wean the patient from the splint.

There is no absolute cure for nocturnal bruxism in adults or children at this time. Cavalier adjustment of occlusal interferences is clearly not warranted due to equivocal efficacy and the permanency of the intervention. Of the alternatives, biteplane splints appear to be the treatment of choice for the management of bruxism symptoms, regardless of etiology (Zarb and Speck 1979). This intervention appears to be the most applicable to children and the most conservative. Even if splints do not reduce bruxism, they clearly redistribute the forces of grinding and clenching and offer protection to the dentition.

Lastly, it is prudent to consider the cost–benefit relationship of any treatment for bruxism. Magnusson and colleagues (1993) conducted a ten-year longitudinal study of the epidemiology of craniomandibular disorders (CMD) in children and adolescents. They found that subjective symptoms of general CMD were quite common, that they increase with age from childhood to young adulthood, and that they are typically occasional and mild in nature, rarely requiring extensive treatment. This is in agreement with the American Academy of Pediatric Dentistry (1990), which states that high prevalence figures do not necessarily represent the need for treatment. Therefore, only in severe cases is treatment of bruxism in children indicated at this time.

## References

Ahmad, R. (1986). Bruxism in children. *The Journal of Pedodontics* 10:105–127.

American Academy of Pediatric Dentistry (1990). Treatment of temporomandibular disorders in children: summary statements and recommendations. *Journal of the American Dental Association* 120:265–269.

Attanasio, R. (1991). Nocturnal bruxism and its clinical management. *Dental Clinics of North America* 35:245–252.

Bennett, C. G., and Mahan, P. E. (1989). Management of a preadolescent chronic headache patient with occlusal splint therapy: case report. *Pediatric Dentistry* 11:64–67.

Birnbaum, R. (1964). *Autonomic reaction to threat and confrontation conditions of psychological stress.* Unpublished doctoral dissertation, University of California, Berkeley.

Boyens, P. J. (1940). Value of autosuggestion in the therapy of "bruxism" and other biting habits. *Journal of the American Dental Association* 27:1773.

Buccino, M. A., and Weddell, J. A. (1989). Rett syndrome, a rare and often misdiagnosed syndrome: case report. *Pediatric Dentistry* 11:151–157.

Bungaard-Jorgenson, F. (1950). Rfslapingsouelser Som Led, behantzlingen af habituelle dysfunktioner i mastiketions apparatet. *Odontglogisk Tidskrift* 58:448.

Cash, R. C. (1988). Bruxism in children: review of the literature. *The Journal of Pedodontics* 12:107–127.

Cassisi, J. E., and McGlynn, F. D. (1988). Effects of EMG-activated alarms on nocturnal bruxism. *Behavior Therapy* 19:133–142.

Cassisi, J. E., McGlynn, F. D., and Belles, D. R. (1987). EMG-activated alarms for treatment of nocturnal bruxism: current status and future directions. *Biofeedback and Self-Regulation* 12:13–30.

Cassisi, J. E., McGlynn, F. D., and Mahan, P. E. (1987). Occlusal splint effects on nocturnal bruxing: an emerging paradigm and some early results. *The Journal of Craniomandibular Practice* 5:64–68.

Clark, G. T., Rugh, J. D., and Handelman, S. L. (1980). Nocturnal masseter muscle activity and urinary catecholamine levels in bruxers. *Journal of Dental Research* 59:1571–1576.

Clarke, N. G., Townsend, G. C., and Carey, S. E. (1984). Bruxing patterns in man during sleep. *Journal of Oral Rehabilitation* 11:123.

Darwin, C. R. (1872). *The Expression of Emotions in Man and Animals*. London: John Murray.

Egermark-Eriksson, I. (1982). Prevalence of headache in Swedish school children. A questionnaire survey. *Acta Paediatrica Scandinavica* 71:135–146.

———— (1983). Malocclusion and some functional recordings of the masticatory system in Swedish school children. *Swedish Dental Journal* 5:125–128.

Egermark-Eriksson, I., Carlsson, G. E., and Ingervall, B. (1981). Prevalence of mandibular dysfunction and orofacial parafunction in 7-, 11-, and 15-year old Swedish children. *European Journal of Orthodontics* 3:163–172.

Forgione, A. (1974). A simple but effective method of quantifying bruxism behavior. *Journal of Dental Research* 53:127.

Freud, S. (1953). *The Interpretation of Dreams: The Complete Psychological Works of Sigmund Freud*. London: Hogarth.

Frisch, J., Katz, L., and Ferreira, A. (1960). A study between bruxism and aggression. *Journal of Periodontology* 31:401.

Fuchs, P. (1969). Neue Untersuchungen uber die Kaumuskeltatigkiet des Nachtschlafes, *Deutsche Zahnarztliche Zeitschrift* 24:563.

Funch, D. P., and Gale, E. N. (1980). Factors associated with nocturnal bruxism and its treatment. *Journal of Behavioral Medicine* 3:385–397.

Gelberd, M. B. (1958). Treatment of bruxism. A case report. *Journal of Hypnosis and Psychology in Dentistry* 1:18.

Glaros, A. G. (1981). Incidence of diurnal and nocturnal bruxism. *Journal of Prosthetic Dentistry* 45:545–549.

Glaros, A. G., and Rao, S. M. (1977). Effects of bruxism, a review of the literature. *Journal of Prosthetics* 38:149–157.

Greene, C. S., and Laskin, D. M. (1972). Splint therapy for the myofacial pain-dysfunction (MPD) syndrome: a comparative study. *Journal of the American Dental Association* 84:624–628.

Ingerslev, H. (1983). Functional disturbances of the masticatory system in school children. *Journal of Dentistry for Children* 50:445–450.

Jankelson, B. (1955). Physiology of human dental occlusion. *Journal of the American Dental Association* 50:664.

Karolyi, M. (1906). Zur Therapie der Erkrankungen der Mundshleimhaut, Oesterr.-ungar Vrtljschr. *Zahnh* 22:226.

Kuch, E. V., Till, M. J., and Messer, L. B. (1979). Bruxing and non-bruxing children: a comparison of their personality traits. *Pediatric Dentistry* 1:182–187.

Lehvila, P. (1974). Bruxism and magnesium. Literature review and case reports. *Progressive Finnish Dental Society* 70:217–224.

Leung, A. K. C., and Robson, W. L. M. (1991). Bruxism: how to stop tooth grinding and clenching. *Postgraduate Medicine* 89:167–171.

Lindqvist, B. (1971). Bruxism in children. *Odontologia Revy* 22:413–423.

―――― (1972). Bruxism and emotional disturbances. *Odontologia Revy* 23:231–242.

―――― (1973). Occlusal interferences in children with bruxism. *Odontologia Revy* 23:231–242.

―――― (1974a). Bruxism in children. *Odontologia Revy* 22:413–424.

―――― (1974b). Bruxism in twins. *Acta Odontologica Scandinavica* 32:177–187.

Magnusson, T., Carlsson, G. E., and Egermark, I. (1993). Changes in subjective symptoms of craniomandibular disorders in children and adolescents during a 10-year period. *Journal of Orofacial Pain* 7:76–82.

Mahowald, M. W., and Rosen, G. M. (1990). Parasomnias in children. *Pediatrician* 17:21–31.

Marie, M. M., and Pietkiewicz, M. (1907). La bruxomanie. *Revue de Stomatologie et de Chirurgie Maxillo-Faciale* 14:107.

Marks, M. B. (1980). Bruxism in allergic children. *American Journal of Orthopaedics* 77:48–59.

McBride, W. (1952). *Juvenile Dentistry*, 5th ed. Philadelphia: Lea and Febiger.

McGlynn, F. D., Bichajian, C., Tira, D. E., et al. (1989). The effect of experimental stress and experimental occlusal interference on masseteric EMG activity. *Journal of Craniomandibular Disorders: Facial and Oral Pain* 3:87–92.

McGlynn, F. D., Cassisi, J. E., and Diamond, E. L. (1985). Diagnosis and treatment of bruxism: a behavioral dentistry perspective. In *Diagnosis and Intervention in Behavior Therapy and Behavioral Medicine*, vol 2, ed. R. J. Daitzman, pp. 28–87. New York: Springer-Verlag.

Meklas, J. F. (1971). Bruxism—diagnosis and treatment. *Journal of Academic and General Dentistry* 19:31–36.

Montgomery, M. T., Nishioka, G. J., Rugh, J. D., and Thrash, W. J. (1986). Effect of diazepam on nocturnal masticatory muscle activity. *Journal of Dental Research* 65: [Abstract 96].

Moore, D. S. (1956). Bruxism diagnosis and treatment. *Journal of Periodontology* 27:277–283.

Moss, R. A., Hammer, D., Adams, H. E., et al. (1982). A more efficient biofeedback procedure for the treatment of nocturnal bruxism. *Journal of Oral Rehabilitation* 9:125–131.

Mowrer, O. H., and Mowrer, W. (1938). Enuresis: a method for its study and treatment. *American Journal of Orthopsychiatry* 8:436–459.

Nadler, S. C. (1966). Detection and recognition of bruxism. *Journal of the American Dental Association* 61:472–479.

Nilner, M. (1981). Prevalence of functional disturbance and diseases of the stomatognathic system in 15–18 year olds. *Swedish Dental Journal* 5:189–197.

Nilner, M., and Kopp, S. (1983). Distribution by age and sex of functional disturbances and diseases of the stomatognatic system in 7–14 year olds. *Swedish Dental Journal* 7:191–198.

Olkinuora, M. (1969). A psychosomatic study of bruxism with emphasis on mental strain and familiar predisposition factors. *Proceedings of the Finnish Dental Society* 68:110.

Percy, A. K., Zoghbi, H. Y., Lewis, K. R., and Jankovic, J. (1988). Rett syndrome: qualitative and quantitative differentiation from autism. *Journal of Child Neurology* 3:S65–S67.

Piccione, A., Coates, T. J., George, J. M., (1982). Nocturnal biofeedback for nocturnal bruxism. *Biofeedback and Self-Regulation* 7:405–419.

Posselt, V. (1962). *Physiology of occlusion and rehabilitation*. Philadelphia: F. A. Davis.

Powell, R. N. (1965). Tooth contacts during sleep: association with other events. *Journal of Dental Research* 44:959–967.

Ramfjord, S. P. (1961). Bruxism, a clinical and electromyographic study. *Journal of the American Dental Association* 62:21–44.

Ramfjord, S. P., and Ash, M. M. (1971). *Occlusion*, 2nd ed. Philadelphia: Saunders.

——— (1983). *Occlusion* 3rd ed. Philadelphia: Saunders.

Reding, G. R. (1966). Incidence of bruxism. *Journal of Dental Research* 45:1198–1203.

Reding, G. R., Rubright, W. C., Rechtshaffen, A., and Daniels, R. S. (1964). Sleep pattern of tooth grinding: its relationship to dreaming. *Science* 145:725–726.

Reding, G. R., Zepelin, H., and Monroe, L. J. (1968a). Personality study of nocturnal teeth-grinders. *Perceptual Motor Skills* 26:523–531.

Reding, G. R., Zepelin, H., Robinson, J. E. Jr. et al. (1968b). Nocturnal teeth grinding: all night psychophysiological studies. *Journal of Dental Research* 47:786–797.

Robinson, J. E., Reding, G. R., Zepelin, H., et al. (1969). Nocturnal teeth-grinding: a reassessment for dentistry. *Journal of the American Dental Association* 78:1308–1311.

Rosenzweig, M. R., and Leiman, A. L. (1982). *Physiological Psychology*. Lexington, MA: D. C. Heath.

Rugh, J. D., and Harlan, J. (1988). Nocturnal bruxism and temporomandibular disorders. *Advances in Neurology* 49:329–341.

Rugh, J. D., and Ohrbach, R. (1988). Occlusal parafunction. *A Textbook of Occlusion*, ed. N. D. Mohl, G. A. Zarb, G. E. Carlsson, and J. D. Rugh, p. 249. Chicago: Quintessence.

Rugh, J. D., and Robbins, J. W. (1982). Oral habit disorders. In *Behavioral Aspects in Dentistry*, ed. B. Ingersoll, pp. 179–202. New York: Appleton-Century-Crofts.

Rugh, J. D., and Solberg, W. K. (1975). Electromyographic studies of bruxist behavior before and during treatment. *California Dental Association* 3:57.

——— (1976). Psychological implications in temporomandibular pain and dysfunction. *Oral Science Review* 7:3–30.

Satoh, T., and Harada, Y. (1973). Electrophysiological study on tooth-grinding during sleep. *Electroencephalography and Clinical Neurophysiology* 35:267–275.

Scharer, P. (1974). Bruxism. *Frontiers in Oral Physiology* 1:293–322.

Shapiro, S., and Shannon, J. (1965). Bruxism as an emotional reactive disturbance. *Psychosomatics* 6:427.

Syme, S. L. (1984). Sociocultural factors and disease etiology. In *Handbook of Behavioral Medicine*, ed. W. D. Gentry, pp. 13–37 New York: Guilford.

Thaller, J. L. (1967). Study of the relationship of frustration and anxiety to bruxism. *Journal of Periodontology* 38:193–197.

Tishler, B. (1928). Occlusal habit neuroses. *Dental Cosmos* 70:690.

Walsh, J. P. (1965). The psychogenesis of bruxism. *Journal of Periodontology* 36:417–420.

Ware, J. C., Pittard, J. T., Moorad, P. J., and Franklin, D. (1982). Reduction of sleep apnea, myoclonus and bruxism in Stage 4 sleep. *Sleep Research* 11:102.

Ware, J. C., and Rugh, J. D. (1988). Destructive bruxism: sleep stage relationship. *Sleep* 11:172–181.

Ware, J. C., Rugh, J. D., Brown, F. W., et al. (1982). Sleep related bruxism: differences in patients with dental sleep complaints. *Sleep Research* 11:182.

Withey, S. B. (1962). Reaction to uncertain threat. In *Man and Society in Disaster*, ed. G. W. Baker, and D. W. Chapman, p. 93–123. New York: Basic Books.

Zarb, G. A., and Speck, J. E. (1979). The treatment of mandibular dysfunction. In *Temporomandibular Joint: Function and Dysfunction*, ed. G. A. Zarb, and G. E. Carlson, pp. 373–396. Copenhagen: Munksgaard.

# 11

# Childhood
# Enuresis

Deborah R. Barclay
Arthur C. Houts

In keeping with the overall focus of this volume on sleep disorders in children, this chapter examines the problem of nocturnal enuresis or bed-wetting. Strictly speaking, enuresis is not a sleep disorder in the sense that we have reason to believe that the cause of bed-wetting is some abnormality of sleep. As we shall review below, most of the research relating bed-wetting to sleep EEG (electroencephalogram) indicates that children who wet the bed do not have abnormal sleep patterns. Contrary to the beliefs of most parents, enuretic children are not necessarily deeper sleepers than other children. However, some children who wet the bed are more difficult to arouse than others, and this is of particular concern because the most effective treatments for correcting bed-wetting require that children be awakened when they wet.

---
[1]Partial support for this research was provided by a Centers of Excellence grant from the State of Tennessee to the Department of Psychology at The University of Memphis and also by a National Institute of Health Grant (R01 HD21736) to Arthur C. Houts.

The Problem of Bed-Wetting

What to do to correct children's bed-wetting is a question that has perplexed professionals and parents since the earliest recorded histories of human society. The problem of bed-wetting is mentioned in the second oldest medical text, the *Ebers Papyrus* (1550 B.C., cited in Glicklich 1951), in which Egyptian professionals advocated treatment with a tonic of juniper berries, cypress, and beer. In the Middle Ages, medicinal prescriptions included pulverized pig bladder and ground rabbit cerebrum as well as dried comb of roosters, which was secretly sprinkled on the child's bed in the belief that it would assist the child in awakening. Throughout history, different cultures have devised "psychological" procedures for parents to use to correct the problem. Such folk wisdom has included tying a frog around the child's waist (Herskovits 1967), having the child stand naked over a burning bird's nest (Leighton and Kluckhon 1947), and simply beating the child. Today, children's bed-wetting continues to be a socially significant problem that affects large numbers of parents and professionals.

Currently defined as bed-wetting of at least twice per week for three months in a child 5 years of age or older (*DSM-IV* 1994), nocturnal enuresis is a problem in the social and emotional development of many elementary-school-aged children. Although epidemiological estimates of prevalence vary (see review by De Jonge 1973), even the most conservative indicate that about seven percent of all 8-year-old children wet their beds (Fergusson et al. 1986, Jarvelin et al. 1988). A useful rule of thumb for estimating the number of enuretic children in a population is one of every ten children age 6 to 18 years old. Thus, in a school system of 100,000 children, about 10,000 children wet the bed every night of the week.

Among children whose sole presenting problem is bed-wetting, only about ten percent have any organic complications of the urinary tract (American Academy of Pediatrics Committee on Radiology 1980, Jarvelin et al. 1990), so most are referred to as *functional enuretics*. Bed-wetting runs in families, and enuretic children show signs of delayed maturation of the nervous system (Jarvelin 1989). Approximately eighty percent of these children are called *primary* enuretics because they have never attained at least six months of continuous nighttime continence. Most of these children wet every night of the week, and about one of every five enuretic children wets multiple times in a single night. *Secondary* or onset enuresis affects a minority of enuretic children and has been associated with delayed acquisition of initial nighttime continence as well as a higher incidence of stressful life events (Fergusson et al. 1990). Up to the age of 11 years, more than twice as many males suffer from enuresis than do females. After this age, the number of males and females who continue bed-wetting is about equal.

Epidemiological surveys show that the prevalence of enuresis declines with age. This decline with age has led to a belief among some professionals and parents that bed-wetting is a problem children will simply outgrow (e.g., Haque et al. 1981, Novello and Novello 1987, Shelov et al. 1981). Although most children do eventually stop bed-wetting, cessation without treatment can take up to seven years. For example, Forsythe and Redmond (1974) found that only fifteen percent of 8-year-old children stop bed-wetting in any year if they are not treated, and the annual rate of remission among adolescents is only sixteen percent. What is even more troublesome is that as many as three percent of young adults may continue bed-wetting (Forsythe and Redmond 1974, Levine 1943).

Considering the social stigma and disruption to family life involved, it is not surprising that continued bed-wetting has been associated with problems of emotional and social adjustment among these children (Kaffman and Elizur 1977). In fact, experimental studies have demonstrated that enuretic children treated for bed-wetting improve more than untreated controls on measures of self-concept and peer relations (Baker 1969, Moffatt et al. 1987). Such evidence suggests that bed-wetting is more likely the cause of any associated emotional adjustment problems rather than the commonly held belief that bed-wetting is caused by emotional problems.

## Diagnosis and Assessment

As already indicated, the diagnosis of nocturnal enuresis is not complicated. Children who are wetting the bed regularly past the age of 5 years meet current diagnostic criteria. As a matter of practical consideration for treatment, children wetting beyond the age of 6 years should be considered candidates for some form of treatment. In our culture, this is about the age when children begin to experience some social impairment from having to keep their bed-wetting a secret. In addition, the most effective treatments, those using a urine alarm, require some level of maturity to be implemented. Most children are able to cooperate with the demands of treatment by the age of 6 years.

In presenting material on assessment, we have focused on assessment for urine alarm treatment because this is the treatment of choice for most enuretic children (Houts et al. 1994).

## Medical Assessment

Assessment of the bed-wetting child should begin with medical screening. Up to ten percent of nocturnal enuretics suffer from organic pathologies that can promote or prolong the problem. Therefore, all children need to have a basic physical exam that includes a urinalysis and, ideally, a sonogram of the bladder and kidneys. Children who have daytime wetting in addition to nighttime wetting are more likely to have organic complications. Among children who wet only at night, about three percent to five percent have diseases that may be responsible for poor bladder control. Nephritis and diabetes, for example, can cause incomplete processing of urine and result in excessive urination. Careful questioning about excessive fluid intake, dramatic changes in weight, and family history of diabetes or kidney problems can help determine if more extensive tests are needed.

All children with wetting problems need a basic urinalysis. Examination of the urine and reliable urine cultures can be performed quickly and inexpensively in most medical settings. As many as five percent of boys and ten percent of girls who wet the bed have urinary tract infections (Stansfeld 1973). Symptoms can include a painful burning sensation when the child urinates, but a child can have a urinary tract infection without any obvious symptoms. This is why there is no substitute for urinalysis as a necessary minimal screening. Among the small number of bed-wetting children who have urinary tract infections, roughly forty percent of those treated stop wetting the bed when the infection is cleared (Schmitt 1982). In most cases, however, urinary tract infections are more likely a result, rather than a cause, of enuresis (Shaffer 1985), and the bed-wetting will still have to be treated once the infection has been eliminated with antibiotic therapy.

The invention of portable ultrasonography has made it unnecessary to perform invasive medical examinations such as cystoscopy and intravenous pyelogram. In the absence of significant warning signs such as a history of disease, daytime wetting, and current signs of infection, medical researchers have generally agreed that bed-wetting alone is not sufficient reason to warrant the routine use of these invasive procedures (American Academy of Pediatrics Committee on Radiology 1980). Some investigators have used noninvasive medical procedures like uroflowmetric studies (Toguri et al. 1982) and renal sonography (Poston et al. 1983) to identify those children who may have medical problems associated with monosymptomatic bed-wetting. From a practical standpoint of ruling out structural abnormalities, bladder and renal ultrasound examination should be considered a necessary precaution before commencing treatment for bed-wetting.

## Psychological Assessment

For most children who wet only at night, the bed-wetting will not be complicated by medical problems. For these children, the treatment of choice is some type of urine alarm treatment. All versions of the urine alarm treatment require a substantial investment of time and energy from the entire family. An in-depth clinical interview with all family members is needed to determine if a family can implement the demanding treatment procedures. Information about the history of enuresis and previous treatment, parental attitudes and beliefs, family and home environment, behavioral problems, and the child's current wetting pattern is useful for deciding how to implement urine alarm treatment.

If a child has started bed-wetting after an extended period of continence (six months to one year), emotional factors may be involved in the resurgence of bed-wetting. For these secondary enuretic children, parents can be questioned about any kind of distress that may have coincided with the onset of wetting. Resolving the distress may be needed before commencing urine alarm treatment. Minimizing current stressful events before implementing treatment for bed-wetting is generally a good idea.

Behavioral, pharmacological, or even surgical interventions may have been tried with limited or no success. Parents and children can be educated about why these methods may have failed to correct the problem. For example, in the case of previous failure with the urine alarm, parents typically have not been properly instructed to awaken the child, and they did not understand that treatment typically takes up to sixteen weeks. Previous drug treatment failures are the norm rather than the exception, and parents can be reassured that their child's continued bed-wetting despite drug treatment was not due to some failure on their part such as inadequate parenting.

The family's attitudes and beliefs are important. Haque and colleagues' (1981) survey of parents indicated that thirty-five percent dealt with bed-wetting by punishing the child. Some parents are intolerant of bed-wetting, and believe that it is a problem that the child should be able to control. Butler and colleagues (1986) found that the more a mother perceived bed-wetting as a burden and the more she attributed the cause of enuresis to the child, the greater was parental intolerance. Less tolerant parents have been shown to drop out of treatment more often than more tolerant parents. Correcting false beliefs, changing hostile attributions, and eliminating punishment may be necessary first steps in correcting bed-wetting with urine alarm treatment.

A global assessment of stress, family disturbance, and the physical home environment is needed before implementing urine alarm treatment. Although family stresses may not cause bed-wetting, parents of children who seek help for enuresis are likely to experience more stress than those who do not seek treatment (Couchells et al. 1981). Morgan and Young (1975) reported that family disturbances and high levels of maternal anxiety characterized their group of slow responders. Dische and colleagues (1983) noted that family distress and discord were significant predictors of treatment failure and relapse. As a screening measure of family distress, we have found it useful to have parents complete the Locke-Wallace Marital Adjustment Test (MAT) (Locke and Wallace 1959).

Because some research has suggested that children with behavior problems are more likely to experience relapse after successful treatment (Dische et al. 1983, Sacks and DeLeon 1973), a careful assessment that includes parent and teacher self-report measures can identify children who need additional attention. We have found the Child Behavior Checklist (CBCL) (Achenbach and Edelbrook 1983) useful. In cases of extreme noncompliant behavior, treatment for bed-wetting may need to be postponed until parents first learn to manage oppositional behavior and noncompliance. Noncompliant children and children who are forced into treatment by their parents have the worst prognosis for remaining in urine alarm treatment.

A two-week baseline of wetting frequency should be established. As a rule, the more frequently a child wets, the longer it will take for the child to cease bed-wetting. In this regard, it is important to determine if a child wets more than once per night. Accurate assessment of this may have to wait until the child uses a urine alarm for one week. Multiple wetters typically take longer to reach a criterion of fourteen consecutive dry nights. Parents of multiple wetters need to be given realistic expectations about their child's progress to avoid discouragement and possible dropout from treatment.

We have also found it useful to assess a child's arousability to make a decision about whether or not it is necessary to disrupt the child's sleep in addition to routine use of the urine alarm. That assessment is described below in a case illustration and following a presentation of the rationale for considering the issue of arousability in the overall problem of nocturnal enuresis.

## Review of Theoretical Issues

The specific causes of nocturnal enuresis are still largely unknown, and several hypotheses have been proposed to explain the problem. Current investigators stress the importance of recognizing considerable heterogeneity among enuretic children (Geffken, Johnson, and Walker 1986, Whelan and Houts 1990) rather than assuming that enuretic children should be treated as a homogeneous group. As such, several of the hypothesized causes may combine to explain the problem for a particular child, while other hypothesized causes may in reality only be correlates of the problem for that child. Nevertheless, when factors that are significant correlates of enuresis are present, they may aid clinicians in identifying specific treatment components that may be warranted for some children.

Enuresis is most likely the result of complex interactions between genetically transmitted physiological factors and exposure to different environments during growth and development. The major etiological hypotheses that support such a conclusion include family history, delays in physical development, and ineffective learning history. In general, there is a trend for enuretic children to have a family history of the problem. In one of the most recent studies that considered family history, Fergusson and colleagues (1986) found that the strongest predictor of the age of attaining nocturnal bladder control was the number of first-order relatives having a known history of enuresis. In terms of risk for enuresis given a particular family history, of cases where both parents were enuretics, seventy-seven percent of children are enuretic, as opposed to forty-four percent when one parent was, and 15% if neither parent was (Bakwin 1973). What exactly is transmitted genetically is not clear, but family history findings point to delays in physical development as a likely cause of continued bedwetting (Jarvelin 1989).

The leading etiological hypotheses regarding delays in physical development are those focused on deficiencies in nocturnal antidiuretic hormone (ADH) secretion and on deficiencies in muscular responses needed to inhibit urination. The first of these is often referred to as the nocturnal polyuria hypothesis and was recently revived by Klauber in 1989 by reasoning backward from favorable outcomes of enuretic children who were treated with the synthetic ADH, DDAVP (desmopressin). According to this hypothesis, enuretic children continue bed-wetting because their kidneys do not adequately concentrate urine at night. Further, failure to concentrate urine produces excess nighttime urine that exceeds ordinary bladder capacity. This failure of the kidneys to concentrate urine is believed to be caused by a lack of normal cyclic increase in ADH during sleep (George et al. 1975). This hypothesis has been supported by research conducted by Norgaard and his colleagues (1985, 1989c).

This research group has also reported evidence that is important for the second physiological hypothesis regarding deficiencies in muscular responses needed to inhibit urination. Specifically, Norgaard (1989) observed that during artificial filling of the bladder while enuretic children were asleep, episodes of arousal to bladder filling were preceded by increased pelvic floor activity. In contrast, episodes of wetting without arousal were preceded by relaxation of the pelvic floor. In other words, when nighttime wetting was avoided, children appeared to be inhibiting detrusor contractions by spontaneously contracting the muscles of the pelvic floor. When nighttime wetting occurred, no such inhibitory responses were observed. Instead, the relatively relaxed pelvic floor was similar to that observed in normal daytime voiding.

Not inconsistent with these hypotheses about delays in physical development, learning theorists have hypothesized that inadequate experience of certain conditions is what causes children to continue bed-wetting. By reasoning backward from the success of conditioning treatments, behavioral psychologists have speculated that simple bedwetting is caused by children's failure to learn to attend and respond to the need to urinate while asleep (see review by Scott et al. 1990). If for any number of reasons (e.g., sleeping for long periods of time, becoming used to the discomfort of a wet bed) a child repeatedly fails to respond to the natural conditions of a wet bed, the child will fail to learn the responses necessary to avoid wetting the bed. Continued bed-wetting, then, is viewed as a failure to learn how to be dry from the naturally occurring conditions of development. We suspect that children who learn to be dry at night without any special assistance learn to inhibit wetting by making the inhibitory response in their sleep without waking. Almost all of these children will have acquired this inhibitory response during the day, and they are able to transfer this learning to the nighttime conditions because they have had the experience of wetting at night and being awakened. If children fail to be awakened by the wetting, they may instead learn to adapt to the discomfort of a wet bed and learn to sleep through the wetting. In this regard, the etiological hypothesis of ineffective learning history is complemented by hypotheses about delays in physical development. One recent investigation suggests that the delay in development may be at the level of the brain stem where signals from the bladder fail to be adequately processed during sleep (Ornitz et al. 1992). From this biobehavioral perspective, monosymptomatic nocturnal enuresis may be viewed as caused by an interaction between delays in physical development that are most likely genetically transmitted and behavioral experiences that further delay responses needed to stop bed-wetting (Houts 1991).

Other hypothesized causes of enuresis that in reality may only be correlates include psychological problems, functional bladder capacity, and most relevant to the present chapter, sleep and arousal difficulties. The hypothesis that bed-wetting is caused by emotional problems or psychic trauma was first proposed by Freud (1959), and is still commonly believed by parents and many health care professionals (Haque et al. 1981). Nevertheless, when compared to their nonenuretic peers, enuretic children do not exhibit more emotional problems. In the case of children who have stopped bed-wetting for a period of six months or more and then resumed bed-wetting (secondary enuretics) the resumption of bed-wetting may be precipitated by a traumatic event or other significant distress. In these instances, resolving the distress may be a priority. Otherwise, any emotional difficulties experienced by children with enuresis are most likely a result and not a cause of bed-wetting (see review by Scott et al. 1990). Thus, treating the enuresis may alleviate problems such as social anxiety and low self appraisal (Moffat 1989). At most, the child with emotional problems may only need extra support and encouragement during treatment.

Another hypothesized cause of enuresis, functional bladder capacity (FBC), is the volume of urine voided when a child has voluntarily postponed micturition for as long as possible after first experiencing the urge to urinate. FBC should not be confused with actual physical bladder capacity, which is a measure of bladder capacity derived from artificial filling of the bladder during catheterization. Although some investigators have reported that samples of enuretics have smaller FBCs than samples of nonenuretic controls (Esperanca and Gerrard 1969, Starfield 1967, Starfield and Mellits 1968, Zaleski et al. 1973), there are inconsistencies and problems with this hypothesis. For example, Rutter (1973) found considerable overlap in the FBCs of enuretics and nonenuretics of the same age, and Starfield's (1967) research suggests that bladder capacity may be a function of the child's voiding habits rather than the determinant of those habits. Further, hypotheses that have been offered to explain low FBCs have been highly speculative (Esperanca and Gerrard 1969), and treatment outcome research targeting methods of increasing FBC has found inconsistent results (Geffken et al. 1986, Starfield and Mellits 1968). Most likely, a low FBC is a correlate rather than a cause of bed-wetting, and if present for a given child, may indicate the need to add a treatment component directed toward increasing FBC.

Finally, parents and professionals have declared deep sleep as an important precipitating factor in enuresis, although research has never confidently confirmed this relationship (Friman 1986). Parents of enuretic children often report that their child is difficult to wake, cannot be awakened at night, or is a deep sleeper. Several researchers in the past have referred to enuresis as an arousal disorder (Finley 1971, Perlmutter 1976, Ritvo et al., 1969). Part of the problem has been due to confusion about the differentiation between depth of sleep and arousability. Depth of sleep has been operationalized in terms of sleep stages recorded on an electroencephalogram (EEG), whereas arousability refers to a behavioral measure of how easily a child can be awakened. These two measures of sleep are not, however, necessarily related (Graham 1973).

Although some of the first studies of sleep recordings in enuretic patients suggested that enuretic events occurred in deep sleep (Pierce et al. 1961), research has since shown that enuretic episodes may occur in any sleep stage. Thus, at least as measured by EEG, depth of sleep is not a reliable correlate of wetting episodes in enuretic children. Depth of sleep is therefore unlikely to be a major cause of bed-wetting. However, depth of sleep, or more specifically, ease of wakening, may have implications for treatments like the urine alarm that require the child to be awakened. Thus, if a child is difficult to arouse from sleep, specific treatment components designed to address this problem may be warranted for that child.

If we accept that children with enuresis are a heterogeneous group, any of these correlates may be important for a subset of these children. In keeping with the focus of this book on childhood sleep disorders, the empirical research on the sleep and arousability of enuretic children deserves careful discussion.

## Summary of Empirical Research

Nocturnal enuresis, by definition, occurs at night while the child is sleeping. Thus, it is often categorized as a sleep disorder. Nevertheless, empirical research in the area has evolved such that enuresis is not considered to be a true sleep disorder in the sense that it is caused by factors solely attributable to sleep and sleep patterns (Graham 1973, Mikkelson et al. 1980). Also, enuresis has not been found to relate to other sleep variables such as sleepwalking or nightmares (Fisher and Wilson 1987). On the other hand, research relating enuresis to depth of sleep and arousability does provide evidence suggesting that for some subgroup of children with enuresis, sleep habits may play an important role.

## Sleep Stage Research

The earliest studies to address the question of whether enuresis occurred in any particular phase of the sleep cycle reported that episodes occurred predominantly during "deep sleep" or stages 3 and 4 (Bental 1961, Ditman and Blinn 1955, Pierce 1963). Broughton (1968) proposed that enuresis was a disorder of arousal, suggesting that enuretic events occur during arousal from slow wave sleep. Ritvo and colleagues (1969), with a sample size of seven, defined *arousal* and *nonarousal* enuretic events, as they found enuretic episodes occurring in both lighter stages of sleep and stages 3 and 4. They formulated a somatopsychic model that related *arousal enuresis* to emotional disturbance. In essence, their study suggested two groups of enuretic children: one group comprising children who were psychiatrically disturbed and had normal arousal signals to which they did not respond versus the second group comprising children who were not disturbed and never generated arousal signals.

In 1977, Kales and colleagues provided evidence to dispute earlier contentions when they studied four severely enuretic children who did not have an associated psychiatric disorder. They found that the sleep patterns of the enuretic children did not differ from those of age-matched controls. Furthermore, they found that the frequency of bed-wetting accidents in any given stage is proportional to the amount of time spent in that stage (Kales et al. 1977). Mikkelsen and colleagues (1980), in a study of forty enuretic boys, again failed to find reliable differences in the sleep patterns of enuretic versus nonenuretic children once the relative proportion of time spent in various stages was taken into account.

More recently, Norgaard and colleagues (1989a,b), using EEG recordings, found that enuretic episodes were not related to any specific sleep stage and could be provoked at any sleep stage with artificial bladder filling. In general, it appears that wetting occurs in all four stages of sleep with the possible exception of REM sleep.

## Arousability Research

With regard to the data on arousability, most research has compared enuretics with nonenuretic controls, and the results of these comparisons have been contradictory (Doleys et al. 1981, Graham 1973). Bostock (1958), using a buzzer, reported that enuretic children took longer to arouse. The seven enuretic children took an average of 418 seconds to reach a waking state, while the twelve nonenuretic children took 319 seconds to wake. Unfortunately, this author failed to provide a statistical comparison of the arousal difference. In contrast, Boyd (1960) used calling the child's name and gentle shaking to wake the child. In her sample of 100 enuretic children aged 5 to 15 years and the same size matched control group, nonenuretics tended to take longer to arouse (20.5 seconds versus 16 seconds), but the difference was not statistically reliable. Recently, Bollard and Nettelbeck (1988) presented a brief description (without complete data) of an arousal study of enuretics where they reported significant between-subject variability with an alarm buzzer stimulus. Barclay (1990), also used an alarm buzzer stimulus in an objective assessment of arousability and found that children's arousability from sleep varied greatly. In general, these studies are not inconsistent with a hypothesis that arousal may be an issue in the treatment for some subgroup of enuretic children.

Finally, a recent study using overnight simultaneous monitoring of EEG and cystometry obtained results that led the researchers to propose a classification system of enuresis in which two of three proposed types are thought to be due to a disturbance in awakening (Wantanabe and Azuma 1989). The classification types Wantanabe and Azuma propose are based on the following findings from a sample of over 200 enuretic children.

1. *Type I (61% of cases).* The first bladder contraction was noticed on cystometrogram during stage 4 sleep when the bladder was full. Evidence of arousal in EEG appeared and EEG changed to a stage 1 or 2 sleep pattern; enuresis occurred without waking.
2. *Type IIa (11% of cases).* The first bladder contraction was again noticed in stage 4 sleep, but no EEG response was observed, and enuresis occurred.
3. *Type IIb (28% of cases).* Cystometry showed uninhibited contraction of the bladder only during sleep (not on awakening). There was no change in either first bladder contraction or EEG, but enuresis occurred.

The authors consider Type I to represent a mild disturbance in awakening and Type IIa a more serious grade of awakening problem. Type IIb is thought to be due to abnormal bladder function. The authors suggested that their Type I enuresis may correspond to the arousal enuretic events described by Ritvo and colleagues (1969). In their recent review of sleep research, Djurhuus and colleagues (1992) speculated that the work of Wantanabe and Azuma may point to some dysfunction in the pathway leading from the pontine micturition center to the cortex. This hypothesis is based on the fact that previous studies of nighttime voiding suggest that enuretic episodes reflect normal bladder function, and therefore are not the result of dysfunction between the bladder and spinal cord. This hypothesis is supported by the aforementioned findings of abnormal neurophysiology in the area of the brain stem near the pontime micturition center (Ornitz et al. 1992).

## Treatment Research and Sleep Variables

At varying stages in the history of the development of behavioral treatments based on the urine alarm, the hypothesized importance of arousal difficulties among enuretic children has sparked the introduction of several adjunctive components including: amphetamines, louder alarms, and the nightly waking schedule. Amphetamines were presumed to lower the threshold of arousal for internal and external stimulation (Blackwell and Currah 1973). When combined with urine-alarm training, stimulants have been found to accelerate conditioning. Unfortunately, the use of these medications has also been associated with increased relapse rates and undesirable side effects (Blackwell and Currah 1973, Kennedy and Sloop 1968). Finley and Wansley (1977) reported that for those children with arousability difficulties, treatment was facilitated by louder alarms. In contrast, Young and Morgan (1973) failed to find that treatment efficacy was related to the intensity of the urine alarm. As neither of these studies assessed children's arousability from sleep, outcome differences may have been due to sample differences on the variable of interest, arousability.

In developing their Dry Bed Training (DBT), Azrin and colleagues (1974) contended that arousability does affect response to treatment and that a scheduled waking of the child during the night could increase the child's arousability. Whelan and Houts (1990) added the nightly waking schedule to their multicomponent treatment package but could find no added utility from its addition. However, they concluded that the waking schedule may only be useful for children with a significant arousability problem.

Other early treatment studies have employed a waking schedule as the sole method of treatment. Young (1964) and Creer and Davis (1975) reported the successful use of a staggered-wakening procedure with institutionalized patients with enuresis. Young (1964) used a fixed schedule of wakening, whereas Creer and Davis (1975) used a variable-interval schedule. Similarly, Singh and colleagues (1976) reported a case study in which progressively earlier waking resulted in treatment success with a 13-year-old girl. These researchers did not speculate on the mechanism of this success as it may relate to sleep variables.

An important question in this area is whether effective treatments of enuresis act, in any way, by altering the quality or depth of sleep. The pharmacological agents amphetamine and imipramine, sometimes used to treat enuresis, are known to lighten sleep (Graham 1973). However, both of these medications are also known to have an effect on bladder function (Graham 1973). Both have been somewhat successful in the initial arrest of bed-wetting, but by which mechanism is not known. Further, the unprecedented success of the urine alarm in treating nocturnal enuresis is commonly accepted and supported by empirical research (Doleys 1977, Houts et al. 1994), and its use is based on theories of conditioning. Nevertheless, exactly what responses are being conditioned warrants further investigation.

In Graham's 1973 review of depth of sleep and treatment for enuresis, he speculated that the urine alarm's success may be explained by its effect on sleep pattern. He described an *expectancy arousal* phenomenon that produces lightening of sleep that may be conditioned by the alarm throughout the night rather than just at the time of bladder filling. Sireling and Crisp (1983) studied the effect of the *buzzer and pad* alarm on the sleep of healthy adult volunteers. They found that on the nights with the bed pad element of the alarm in place, there were significantly fewer shifts between stages, less restlessness, and a tendency towards less time spent awake, less time in light sleep, and a shorter sleep latency. They concluded that one therapeutic component of the alarm device could be its ability to alter sleep structure. Specifically, they concluded that the wire-mesh element may have helped produce deeper sleep. This was thought to be helpful to enuretics who wet in light sleep. They further contended that some other alarm component may influence enuresis occurring in deep sleep.

Such conclusions are highly speculative at best. It is just as likely that the urine alarm may affect the physiological variables of ADH release or detrusor muscle activity (Houts 1991). There is also the possibility that the urine alarm is successful for different reasons in different children. Future research needs to investigate the physiological changes that may occur during urine alarm treatment.

Although the majority of empirical research does not support the belief that enuresis is a disorder of sleep, this does not preclude the hypothesis that for some children, arousability is a problem that contributes to the maintenance of their enuresis. Thus, future research also needs to investigate successful treatments and the combination of urine alarm treatment with other components.

## Treatment Approach Based upon an Integration of Theory, Research, and Practice

Controlled outcome research has consistently shown that basic urine alarm treatment is the treatment of choice for monosymptomatic bed-wetting (Houts et al. 1994). Nevertheless, basic urine alarm treatment is difficult to implement. Because treatment may take several months for a child to cease bed-wetting, parents and children alike may become very discouraged and terminate treatment prematurely. Basic urine alarm treatments also result in considerable relapse. For these reasons, behavioral researchers have developed multicomponent treatments that include the basic urine alarm. The problem of relapse from basic urine alarm treatment has been minimized through use of over-learning and modifications to that basic relapse prevention component. The problem of speeding a child's response to urine alarm treatment so that families can maintain their enthusiasm for implementing a very demanding procedure has not been solved. This problem may only be solved by careful determination of what characteristics distinguish between groups of enuretic children. Continuing research on the physiological mechanisms underlying nocturnal enuresis as well as research examining interactions between child characteristics and treatment response should bring clinicians closer to individualizing treatment packages such that any child with enuresis, after careful assessment, could be successfully treated with minimum family distress.

The following section provides a description of two of the most thoroughly evaluated multicomponent treatments, Dry Bed Training (Azrin et al. 1974) and Full Spectrum Home Training (Houts and Liebert 1984). This discussion is followed by a case illustration demonstrating how a child with an observed arousal problem was successfully treated with the addition of a specific treatment component to a standard treatment package.

## Dry Bed Training

Dry Bed Training (DBT) was initially presented by Azrin and his colleagues in 1974, and it combines four major procedures. The first procedure, a nightly waking schedule, is started on the first night by a professional in the home and involves waking the child every hour. At each waking, the child is taken to the bathroom and asked to urinate, given fluids to drink, and then encouraged to postpone urinating for the next hour. On the second night, the child is awakened by parents three hours after going to bed. If the child has remained dry, then the next night, the parents wake the child 2 ½ hours after bedtime. The waking time is moved back toward the bedtime by half an hour each night following a dry bed and is stopped when the child is scheduled to be awakened one hour after bedtime. If the child wets twice in one week, the cycle of the nightly waking schedule begins again.

Positive practice, the second procedure, is a form of overcorrection. This component requires the child to lie in bed, count to fifty, and then get up and go to the bathroom and try to urinate. The process is repeated twenty times. These twenty trials of positive practice are to be done immediately after a wet bed and also before bedtime the next night. The third procedure is basic urine alarm treatment, which is introduced after the first night of waking the child every hour. When the alarm sounds, the child is awakened and reprimanded for wetting the bed. At this point, the fourth procedure—cleanliness training—is implemented. This requires the child to change wet clothes and bed linens. After completing the twenty trials of positive practice, the alarm is then reactivated and the child returns to bed.

The results of several outcome studies have demonstrated success rates of 80 to 100% (Azrin et al. 1979, Bollard and Nettelbeck 1981, 1982, Hunt and Adams 1989). Bollard and Nettelbeck (1981) reported that compared to basic urine alarm treatment, DBT was superior in terms of the proportion of children who ceased bed-wetting and the speed with which they did so. In a components breakdown evaluation of DBT, Bollard and Nettelbeck (1982) showed that the urine alarm could not be eliminated and that it was an essential ingredient for DBT to be effective. Further, they reported that children who received versions of the treatment that included the nightly waking schedule reached the success criterion more rapidly than children who received versions without the nightly waking schedule. The presence or absence of other components was not found to influence acquisition rate or treatment outcome. Relapse after DBT (thirty-nine percent) was virtually identical to that following basic urine alarm treatment (Bollard 1982).

## Full Spectrum Home Training

Full Spectrum Home Training (FSHT) was designed by Houts and Liebert (1984) and also has four components. Like DBT, two of these four components are basic urine alarm treatment and cleanliness training. In the basic urine alarm treatment, children must get out of bed and stand up before turning off the alarm. Parents are instructed never to turn off the alarm for the child. The steps involved in cleanliness training are provided for the child and parents in a convenient wall chart ("Daily Steps to a Dry Bed") that is placed in the child's room. This chart is also used for the child to record progress by coloring in either "wet" or "dry" for each day of the training program. Parents receive explicit instructions to make sure that their child is fully awake after a wetting episode and to have the child change the bed completely even if the sheets are not wet. This is important as newer alarm devices typically sound before the bed becomes completely wet. Parents may insure that their child is fully awake by asking questions that the child could only answer if awake (e.g., math problems, their phone number backwards).

The third component of FSHT is retention control training. This involves giving the child a monetary reward for postponing urination for increasing amounts of time in a step-by-step fashion up to a forty-five minute holding time. This training is carried out daily at a prearranged time. The child is given a large quantity of water and then informs the parent when the urge to urinate occurs. The parent instructs the child to withhold urination for increasing amounts of time (three-minute increments) during each daily trial. If the child succeeds in postponing urination, then he/she receives a prearranged monetary reward. If the child is not successful, the same time goal is repeated the next day. Once the child is able to delay urination for forty-five minutes, retention control training ends.

The fourth and final component of FSHT, overlearning, is included to reduce relapse and begins after the child attains fourteen consecutive dry nights. Houts and colleagues (1983) initially implemented overlearning by having the child drink sixteen ounces of water during the hour before bedtime. Following the methodology of Young and Morgan (1972), this nightly drinking continued until the child attained fourteen more consecutive dry nights while drinking the water. This has since been modified to graduated overlearning. The child begins by drinking four ounces of water during the last fifteen minutes before bedtime. The amount of water is increased in increments of two ounces for each two consecutive nights the child remains dry. For example, if the child remains dry for two nights while drinking the four-ounce amount, then the amount of water increases to six ounces. If he/she remains dry for two nights at the six-ounce amount, then the water is increased to eight ounces. The increases continue in this fashion until the child's maximum amount is reached. The maximum amount of water any child will drink is determined by the child's age plus two ounces, which is average normal bladder capacity (Berger et al. 1983). Thus, for a 6-year-old child, the maximum amount would be eight ounces. In the likely event that the child has an accident during overlearning, the child drinks the amount consumed before the night of the accident for five nights in a row. The amount consumed thereafter proceeds to increase in two-ounce increments until the maximum amount is reached. Drinking stops when the child has achieved fourteen consecutive dry nights during overlearning.

Outcome evaluations of FSHT have reliably resulted in initial arrest rates (fourteen consecutive dry nights) of seventy percent or greater (Houts et al. 1983, 1986, 1987, Whelan and Houts 1990). In addition, and perhaps most significant, these evaluations of FSHT have also indicated that the treatment package reliably produces one-year relapse rates that are approximately half that expected from basic urine alarm treatment (twenty percent vs. forty percent). Reduction in the percentage of children who relapse from FSHT has continued to improve with the graduated overlearning procedure such that the average relapse rate from FSHT is typically between ten percent and fifteen percent.

In an effort to combine the possible beneficial effects of the waking schedule of dry bed training with the relapse prevention benefits of FSHT, Whelan and Houts (1990) compared FSHT with and without the nightly waking schedule. They failed to detect any benefits from adding the waking schedule to the full spectrum package but concluded that further research using the nightly waking schedule may be particularly valuable for some subgroups of enuretics. Our ongoing research is attempting to identify this subgroup by objectively assessing children's arousability prior to treatment. We hypothesized that those children who were the most difficult to arouse would show more improvement with the addition of the waking schedule than with FSHT alone. Our preliminary results do not favor that hypothesis, but show instead that children who are more difficult to arouse have a poorer response to treatment regardless of whether or not they receive the nightly waking component. However, it appears that those children who are the most difficult to arouse are less likely to follow through with treatment, and despite nonsignificant statistical results, clinical practice has suggested that the addition of the nightly waking schedule may be beneficial for children who are very difficult to arouse. The following is an illustration of one such clinical case.

## Case Illustration

### History Information

Kelly was a 6-year-old white female. She lived with her parents and 10-year-old brother in an upper-middle-class neighborhood. Kelly had been wetting the bed regularly since infancy although she had attained daytime bladder control at age 3 ½ and bowel control at age 3. There was no history of daytime wetting accidents. Kelly's medical history was unremarkable with the exception of a family history of diabetes, and she suffered from no obvious psychological problems.

### Clinical Assessment

Kelly's parents were interviewed regarding her bed-wetting. Interestingly, there was a significant family history of bed-wetting with Kelly's mother and maternal aunt also having wet the bed on a regular basis as children. According to parental report, Kelly was wetting the bed every night at least two times each night. For a while, Kelly's parents had tried to wake her before they went to bed in an attempt to have her go to the bathroom. However, this had become very frustrating for them because they reported she would not get up, and they could not seem to wake her. Both parents agreed that Kelly was a deep sleeper.

Kelly's parents had sought the advice of their pediatrician who had suggested they restrict fluids at bedtime and wait for her to outgrow the problem. Approximately one year before attending our clinic, Kelly had been prescribed imipramine by her pediatrician. Her mother reported that Kelly only took this medication for a few days because the pills were bitter and she had trouble swallowing them. At the time they sought treatment from our clinic, Kelly's parents had become so discouraged that in an effort to avoid the time and trouble of wet sheets and a morning bath, they were putting Kelly in diapers at night. Kelly was also beginning to voice that she wanted to stop bed-wetting because she was worried about being invited to slumber parties with friends. She was embarrassed that they might find out she wore diapers at night, and she did not want to be with her mother when diapers were purchased for fear the cashier would know they were for her.

Kelly's parents completed the Enuresis Tolerance Scale (ETS) (Morgan and Young 1975), the Locke-Wallace Marital Adjustment Test (MAT) (Locke and Wallace 1959), and the Child Behavior Checklist (CBCL) (Achenbach and Edelbrock 1983). The ETS assesses parents' attitudes toward bed-wetting and has been shown to predict dropout from behavioral treatment. Kelly's parents' responses revealed that, despite their frustration, they were both relatively tolerant of Kelly's bed-wetting and did not hold any irrational beliefs regarding bed-wetting. Because the behavioral treatment of enuresis is a demanding process, parents need to be able to work together and support each other during treatment. For this reason, the MAT was given as a screening measure to determine if there might be any marital problems that would interfere with successful treatment. Kelly's mother and father were quite discrepant in their responses, with Kelly's mother reporting a significant degree of dissatisfaction with the marriage. These issues were subsequently discussed in a separate session with Kelly's parents and it was determined that the problems were not severe enough to contraindicate behavioral treatment. However, this situation was carefully monitored throughout treatment. Finally, the CBCL was given as a screening measure to determine if Kelly might be experiencing any significant psychological problems that would need to be addressed before undertaking treatment for her enuresis. Parental responses on this measure revealed no significant clinical problems.

## Arousal and Baseline Assessment

Because Kelly's parents reported such difficulty with waking Kelly at night, they were asked to perform an objective assessment of Kelly's arousability. The parents were asked to rate Kelly's arousability on a 9-point Likert scale with 1 being very easy to arouse and 9 being very difficult to arouse. Both rated Kelly as very difficult to arouse (9) prior to performing the arousability assessment. For the objective assessment, Kelly's parents were instructed to attempt to wake Kelly on alternate nights for one week using the urine alarm buzzer. On the nights Kelly was to be awakened, her parents went into her room two hours after she had gone to sleep and simultaneously rang the alarm next to her ear and started a stopwatch. They then measured the time (in seconds) it took for Kelly to rise and touch a stuffed animal located six feet from her bed. On one night, the parents were to wake Kelly by tapping her hand repeatedly; otherwise the procedure was the same. Before this began, Kelly was able to practice getting up and touching the stuffed animal. After each attempt to wake Kelly, the parents were asked to record the time she took to complete the task, and again rate Kelly on the 9-point Likert scale. The results of this assessment revealed that Kelly never woke to either the alarm or the tapping despite continued presentation for two minutes.

Prior to treatment, baseline records of wetting were obtained for two weeks. For the purpose of this assessment, Kelly did not wear diapers to bed. Baseline results revealed that Kelly wet every night. Because Kelly never woke up at night, it was not clear how many times she had wet, but on all but one night the amount of wetness was great enough to suggest that more than one wetting episode had occurred.

## Clinical Intervention

Kelly and her parents returned to the clinic together to learn how to implement the behavioral treatment package. Kelly was treated using the Full Spectrum Home Training Program with the addition of the nightly waking schedule borrowed from Dry Bed Training. The procedures were followed exactly as described in the previous section of this chapter with the exception that the first night of the nightly waking schedule was carried out by the parents rather than by a professional in the home.

The training session involved the completion of a behavioral contract and a didactic presentation of all treatment components. Each component was described and modeled as Kelly and her parents completed the related section of the contract that described the responsibilities of the parents and child for that component. In the contract, Kelly agreed to implement the procedures for each component and to record wet and dry nights on a wall chart placed in her bedroom. Her parents agreed to assist her in waking to the alarm when necessary, to give monetary rewards during the retention-control training, and to maintain records of wet and dry nights. They all agreed to carry out training for a minimum of sixteen weeks, to follow an agreed upon bedtime, and to enlist the cooperation of Kelly's brother as necessary. Both Kelly and her parents were asked to sign the contract and agreed to refer to it if clarification of responsibilities was needed. In addition, the parents were provided with a treatment manual, a wall chart, markers for the chart, a night light, and a urine alarm (Palco Wet Stop). Parents were also asked to refrain from restricting fluids and to refrain from the use of diapers.

Kelly's parents were contacted by telephone biweekly to discuss progress and any problems. On two occasions during the treatment period, Kelly and her parents returned to the clinic for problem-solving sessions due to frustration with setbacks and problems keeping Kelly motivated. The nightly waking schedule continued throughout the first six weeks of treatment, after which Kelly was successfully waking to the alarm on her own at all times. Kelly achieved fourteen consecutive dry nights after nine weeks in treatment. At this time, overlearning began and continued for six weeks. During this time, Kelly was achieving anywhere from nine to eleven consecutive dry nights. Seventeen weeks after the initiation of treatment, Kelly achieved her second fourteen consecutive dry nights on overlearning, and treatment was discontinued. Both parents reported being extremely satisfied with the program and that they felt Kelly's self-confidence had significantly improved. At three-month follow up, Kelly had no wetting episodes, and at six months posttreatment Kelly had two consecutive wetting episodes, which her mother attributed to Kelly's being sick at the time. She remained free of any bed-wetting a full year after the treatment ended and was accepting invitations from peers to attend sleepovers.

## Summary

Monosymptomatic nocturnal enuresis, or simple bed-wetting, is a problem that affects about one of every ten secondary-school-aged children and their families. Most of these children do not have associated medical problems, and their wetting occurs only at night during sleep. Despite the fact that most parents believe that depth of sleep is a major reason why their child wets the bed, three decades of research indicate that bed-wetting children do not have abnormal sleep patterns. Moreover, that research shows that for any given child, the wetting episodes are as likely to occur in the lighter stages of sleep as in the deeper stages of sleep as measured by EEG. In the sense that a sleep disorder is defined by some abnormal sleep pattern, nocturnal enuresis is not, strictly speaking, a sleep disorder.

However, the issue of sleep does enter into the matter of treating enuresis because the most effective treatment to date, the urine alarm, requires that a child be awakened at the time of a nighttime wetting episode. Arousability is a factor in the effective treatment of bedwetting. Treatment programs based on the urine alarm may be improved when additional efforts are made to change the child's sleep pattern through systematic awakening in addition to the routine of the urine alarm. Although the research evidence for improving on urine alarm treatment with waking schedules is mixed, this may be due to the heterogeneity of the samples with respect to arousability. Most investigators agree that there are individual differences of arousability within samples of enuretic children, and these differences need to be studied further. The relationship between arousability and possible developmental delay in the pontine micturition center deserves special attention.

## References

Achenbach, T. M., and Edelbrock, C. (1983). *Manual for the Child Behavior Checklist*. Burlington, VT: Department of Psychiatry, University of Vermont.

American Academy of Pediatrics Committee on Radiology (1980). Excretory urography for evaluation of enuresis. *Pediatrics* 65:644–655.

Azrin, N. H., Sneed, T. J., and Foxx, R. M. (1974). Dry-bed training: rapid elimination of childhood enuresis. *Behaviour Research and Therapy* 12:147–156.

Azrin, N. H., Thienes-Hontos, P., and Besalel-Azrin, V. (1979). Elimination of enuresis without a conditioning apparatus: an extension by office instruction of the child and parents. *Behavior Therapy* 10:14–19.

Baker, B. L. (1969). Symptom treatment and symptom substitution in enuresis. *Journal of Abnormal Psychology* 74:42–49.

Bakwin, H. (1973). The genetics of enuresis. In *Bladder Control and Enuresis* ed. I. Kolvin, R. C. MacKeith, and S. R. Meadow, pp. 73–77. London: William Heinemann.

Barclay, D. R. (1990). *Effects of a waking schedule as a function of children's arousability in the treatment of primary enuresis*. Unpublished master's thesis, Memphis State University, Memphis, TN.

Bental, E. (1961). Dissociation of behavioral and electroencephalographic sleep in two brothers with enuresis nocturna. *Journal of Psychosomatic Research* 5:116–119.

Berger, R. M., Maizels, M., Moran, G. C., et al. (1983). Bladder capacity (ounces) equals age (years) plus 2 predicts normal bladder capacity and aids in diagnosis of abnormal voiding patterns. *The Journal of Urology* 129:347–349.

Blackwell, B., and Currah, J. (1973). The psychopharmacology of nocturnal enuresis. In *Bladder Control and Enuresis* ed. I. Kolvin, R. C. MacKeith, and S. R. Meadow, pp. 231–257. London: William Heinemann.

Bollard, J. (1982). A 2-year follow-up of bedwetters treated with dry-bed training and standard conditioning. *Behaviour Research and Therapy* 20:571–580.

Bollard, J., and Nettelbeck, T. (1981). A comparison of dry-bed training and standard urine alarm conditioning treatment of childhood bedwetting. *Behaviour Research and Therapy* 19:215–226.

———— (1982). A component analysis of dry-bed training for treatment for bedwetting. *Behaviour Research and Therapy* 20:383–390.

———— (1988). *Bedwetting: A Treatment Manual for Professional Staff.* Unpublished manuscript, Adelaide Children's Hospital, Adelaide, South Australia.

Bostock, J. (1958). Exterior gestation, primitive sleep, enuresis and asthma: a study in aetiology. *Medical Journal of Australia* 149:185.

Boyd, M. M. (1960). The depth of sleep in enuretic school children and in non-enuretic controls. *Journal of Psychosomatic Research* 4:274–281.

Broughton, R. J. (1968). Sleep disorders: disorders of arousal? *Science* 159:1070–1078.

Butler, R. J., Brewin, C. R., and Forsythe, W. I. (1986). Maternal attributions and tolerance for nocturnal enuresis. *Behaviour Research and Therapy* 24:307–312.

Couchells, S. M., Johnson, S. B., Carter, R., and Walker, D. (1981). Behavioral and environmental characteristics of treated and untreated enuretic children and matched nonenuretic controls. *The Journal of Pediatrics* 99:812–816.

Creer, T. L., and Davis, M. H. (1975). Using a staggered-wakening procedure with enuretic children in an institutional setting. *Journal of Behavior Therapy and Experimental Psychiatry* 6:23–25.

De Jonge, G. A. (1973). Epidemiology of enuresis: a survey of the literature. In *Bladder Control and Enuresis* ed. I. Kolvin, R. C. MacKeith, and S. R. Meadow, pp. 39–46. London: William Heinemann.

*Diagnostic and Statistical Manual of Mental Disorders* (1987). (4th ed.). Washington, DC: American Psychiatric Association.

Dische, S., Yule, W., Corbett, J., and Hand, D. (1983). Childhood nocturnal enuresis: factors associated with outcome of treatment with an enuresis alarm. *Developmental Medicine and Neurology* 25:67–80.

Ditman, K. S., and Blinn, K. A. (1955). Sleep levels in enuresis. *American Journal of Psychiatry* 111:913–920.

Djurhuus, J. C., Norgaard, J. P., and Rittig, S. (1992). Monosymptomatic bedwetting. *Scandinavian Journal of Urology and Nephrology Supplementum* 141:7–19.

Doleys, D. M. (1977). Behavioral treatments for nocturnal enuresis in children: a review of the recent literature. *Psychological Bulletin* 84:30–54.

Doleys, D. M., Schwartz, M. S., and Ciminero, A. R. (1981). Elimination problems: enuresis and encopresis. In *Behavioral Assessment of Childhood Disorders* ed. E. J. Mash, and L. G. Terdal, pp. 679–710. New York: Guilford.

Esperanca, M., and Gerrard, J. W. (1969). Nocturnal enuresis: comparison of the effect of imipramine and dietary restriction on bladder capacity. *Canadian Medical Association Journal* 101:65–68.

Fergusson, D. M., Horwood, L. J., and Shannon, F. T. (1986). Factors related to the age of attainment of nocturnal bladder control: an 8-year longitudinal study. *Pediatrics* 78:884–890.

_____ (1990). Secondary enuresis in a birth cohort of New Zealand children. *Paediatric and Perinatal Epidemiology* 4:53–63.

Finley, W. W. (1971). An EEG study of the sleep of enuretics at three age levels. *Clinical Electroencephalography* 2:35–39.

Finley, W. W., and Wansley, R. A. (1977). Auditory intensity as a variable in the conditioning treatment of enuresis nocturna. *Behaviour Research and Therapy* 15:181–185.

Fisher, B. E., and Wilson, A. E. (1987). Selected sleep disturbances in school children reported by parents: prevalence, interrelationships, behavioral correlates and parental attributions. *Perceptual and Motor Skills* 64:1147–1157.

Forsythe, W. I., and Redmond, A. (1974). Enuresis and spontaneous cure rate: study of 1129 enuretics. *Archives of Disease in Childhood* 49:259–263.

Freud, S. (1959). Fragment of an analysis of a case of hysteria. In *Sigmund Freud: Collected Papers* ed. A. Strachey, and J. Strachey, pp. 13–146. New York: Basic Books.

Friman, P. C. (1986). A preventive context for enuresis. *Pediatric Clinics of North America* 33(4):871–886.

Geffken, G., Johnson, S. B., and Walker, D. (1986). Behavioral interventions for childhood nocturnal enuresis: the differential effect of bladder capacity on treatment progress and outcome. *Health Psychology* 5:261–272.

George, C. P. L., Messerli, F. H., Genest, J., et al. (1975). Diurnal variation of plasma vasopressin in man. *Journal of Clinical Endocrinology and Metabolism* 41:332–338.

Glicklich, L. B. (1951). An historical account of enuresis. *Pediatrics* 8:859–876.

Graham, P. (1973). Depth of sleep and enuresis: a critical review. In *Bladder Control and Enuresis*, ed. I. Kolvin, R. C. MacKeith, and S. R. Meadow, pp. 78–83. London: William Heinemann.

Haque, M., Ellerstein, N. S., Gundy, J. H., et al. (1981). Parental perceptions of enuresis: a collaborative study. *American Journal of Diseases of Childhood* 135:809–811.

Herskovits, M. J. (1967). *Dahomey: An Ancient West African Kingdom.* Vol. 1. Evanston, IL: Northwestern University Press.

Houts, A. C. (1991). Nocturnal enuresis as a biobehavioral problem. *Behavior Therapy* 22:133–151.

Houts, A. C., Berman, J. S., and Abramson, H. A. (1994). The effectiveness of psychological and pharmacological treatments for nocturnal enuresis. *Journal of Consulting and Clinical Psychology* 62:737–745.

Houts, A. C., and Liebert, R. M. (1984). *Bedwetting: A Guide for Parents and Children.* Springfield, IL: Charles C Thomas.

Houts, A. C., Liebert, R. M., and Padawer, W. (1983). A delivery system for the treatment of primary enuresis. *Journal of Abnormal Child Psychology* 11:513–519.

Houts, A. C., Peterson, J. K., and Whelan, J. P. (1986). Prevention of relapse in full-spectrum home training for primary enuresis: a components analysis. *Behavior Therapy* 17:462–469.

Houts, A. C., Whelan, J. P., and Peterson, J. K. (1987). Filmed vs. live delivery of full-spectrum home training for primary enuresis: presenting the information is not enough. *Journal of Consulting and Clinical Psychology* 55:902–906.

Hunt, S., and Adams, M. (1989). Bibliotherapy-based dry bed training: a pilot study. *Behavioral Psychotherapy* 17:290–302.

Jarvelin, M. R. (1989). Developmental history and neurological findings in enuretic children. *Developmental Medicine and Child Neurology* 31:728–736.

Jarvelin, M. R., Huttunen, N., Seppanen, J., et al. (1990). Screening of urinary tract abnormalities among day and nightwetting children. *Scandinavian Journal of Urology and Nephrology* 24:181–189.

Jarvelin, M. R., Vikevainen-Tervonen, L., Moilanen, I., and Huttunen, N. P. (1988). Enuresis in seven-year-old children. *Acta Paediatrica Scandinavica* 77:148–153.

Kaffman, M., and Elizur, E. (1977). Infants who become enuretics: a longitudinal study of 161 kibbutz children. *Monographs of the Society for Research in Child Development* 42 (2, serial no. 170):1–54.

Kales, A., Kales, J. D., Jacobson, A., et al. (1977). Effects of imipramine on enuretic frequency and sleep stages. *Pediatrics* 60:431–436.

Kennedy, W. A., and Sloop, E. W. (1968). Methedrine as an adjunct to conditioning treatment of nocturnal enuresis in normal and institutionalized retarded subjects. *Psychological Reports* 22:997–1000.

Klauber, G. T. (1989). Clinical efficacy and safety of desmopressin in the treatment of nocturnal enuresis. *Pediatrics*, 114:719–722.

Leighton, D., and Kluckhohn, C. (1947). *Children of the People*. Cambridge, MA: Harvard University Press.

Levine, A. (1943). Enuresis in the navy. *American Journal of Psychiatry* 100:320–325.

Locke, H. J. and Wallace, K. M. (1959). Short marital adjustment and prediction tests: their reliability and validity. *Marriage and Family Living* 21:251–255.

Mikkelsen, E. J., Rapoport, J. L., Nee, L., et al. (1980). Childhood enuresis I: sleep patterns and psychopathology. *Archives of General Psychiatry* 37:1139–1144.

Moffatt, M. E. K. (1989). Nocturnal enuresis: psychologic implications of treatment and nontreatment. *The Journal of Pediatrics* 114(4, pt. 2):697–704.

Moffatt, M. E. K., Kato, C., and Pless, I. B. (1987). Improvements in self-concept after treatment of nocturnal enuresis: a randomized clinical trial. *The Journal of Pediatrics* 110:647–652.

Morgan, R. T. T., and Young, G. C. (1975). Parental attitudes and the conditioning treatment of childhood enuresis. *Behaviour Research and Therapy* 13:197–199.

Norgaard, J. P. (1989). Urodynamics in enuretics II: a pressure/flow study. *Neurourology and Urodynamics* 8:213–217.

Norgaard, J. P., Hansen, J. H., Neilsen, J. B., et al. (1989a). Nocturnal studies in enuretics. A polygraphic study of sleep-egg and bladder activity. *Scandinavian Journal of Urology and Nephrology Supplementum* 125:73-78.

Norgaard, J. P., Hansen, J. H., Wildschiotz, G., et al. (1989b). Sleep cystometries in children with nocturnal enuresis. *The Journal of Urology* 141:1156-1159.

Norgaard, J. P., Pedersen, E. B., and Djurhuus, J. C. (1985). Diurnal anti-diuretic-hormone levels in enuretics. *The Journal of Urology* 134:1029-1031.

Norgaard, J. P., Rittig, S., and Djurhuus, J. C. (1989c). Nocturnal enuresis: an approach to treatment based on pathogenesis. *Pediatrics* 14:705-710.

Novello, A. C., and Novello, J. R. (1987). Enuresis. *Pediatric Clinics of North America* 34:719-733.

Ornitz, E. M., Hanna, G. L., and de Traversay, J. (1992). Prestimulation-induced startle modulation in attention-deficit hyperactivity disorder and nocturnal enuresis. *Psychophysiology* 29:437-450.

Perlmutter, A. D. (1976). Enuresis. In *Clinical Pediatric Urology*, ed. P. Kelalis, and L. King, pp. 2116-2124. Philadelphia: W. B. Saunders.

Pierce, C. M. (1963). Dream studies in enuresis research. *Canadian Psychiatric Association Journal* 8:415.

Pierce, C. M., Whitman, R. M., Mass, T. W., and Gay, M. L. (1961). Enuresis and dreaming: experimental studies. *Archives of General Psychiatry* 4:166-170.

Poston, G. J., Joseph, A. E. A., and Riddle P. R. (1983). The accuracy of ultrasound in the measurement of changes in bladder volume. *British Journal of Urology* 55:361-363.

Ritvo, E. R., Ornitz, E. M., Gottlieb, F., et al. (1969). Arousal and non-arousal enuretic events. *American Journal of Psychiatry* 126(1):115-122.

Rutter, M. (1973). Indications for research: III. In *Bladder Control and Enuresis*, ed. I. Kolvin, R. C. MacKeith, and S. R. Meadow, pp. 292-300. London: William Heinemann.

Sacks, S., and DeLeon, G. (1973). Case histories and shorter communications: conditioning of two types of enuretics. *Behaviour Research and Therapy* 11:653-654.

Schmitt, B. D. (1982). Nocturnal enuresis: an update on treatment. *Pediatric Clinics of North America* 29:21-37.

Scott, M. A., Barclay, D. R., and Houts, A. C. (1990). Childhood enuresis: etiology, assessment, and current behavioral treatment.

In *Progress in behavior modification*, ed. M. Hersen, R. M. Eisler, and P. M. Miller, pp. 83-117. Beverly Hills, CA: Sage.

Shaffer, D. (1985). Enuresis. In *Child and Adolescent Psychiatry: Modern Approaches*, ed. M. Rutter, and L. Hersov, pp. 465-481. Oxford: Blackwell Scientific.

Shelov, S. P., Gundy, J., Weiss, J. C., et al. (1981). Enuresis: a contrast of attitudes of parents and physicians. *Pediatrics* 67:707-710.

Singh, R., Phillips, D., and Fischer, S. C. (1976). The treatment of enuresis by progressively earlier waking. *Journal of Behavior Therapy and Experimental Psychiatry* 7:277-278.

Sireling, L. I., and Crisp, A. H. (1983). Sleep and the enuresis alarm device. *Journal of the Royal Society of Medicine* 76:131-133.

Stansfeld, J. M. (1973). Enuresis and urinary tract infection. In *Bladder Control and Enuresis*, ed. I. Kolvin, R. C. MacKeith and S. R. Meadow, pp. 102-103. London: William Heinemann.

Starfield, B. (1967). Functional bladder capacity in enuretic and non-enuretic children. *Pediatrics* 70:777-781.

Starfield, B., and Mellits, E. D. (1968). Increase in functional bladder capacity and improvements in enuresis. *Pediatrics* 72:483-487.

Toguri, A. G., Uchida, T, and Bee, D. E. (1982). Pediatric uroflow rate nomograms. *The Journal of Urology* 127:727-731.

Wantanabe, H., and Azuma, Y. (1989). A proposal for a classification system of enuresis based on overnight simultaneous monitoring of electroencephalography and cystometry. *Sleep* 12:257-264.

Whelan, J. P., and Houts, A. C. (1990). Effects of a waking schedule on the outcome of primary enuretic children treated with Full-Spectrum Home Training. *Health Psychology* 9:164-176.

Young, G. C. (1964, March 6). A "staggered-wakening" procedure in the treatment of enuresis. *The Medical Officer* 142-143.

Young, G. C., and Morgan, R. T. T. (1972). Overlearning in the conditioning treatment of enuresis: a long-term follow-up study. *Behaviour Research and Therapy* 10:419-420.

—— (1973). Conditioning treatment of enuresis: auditory intensity. *Behaviour Research and Therapy* 11:411-416.

Zaleski, A., Gerrard, J. W., and Shokeir, M. K. K. (1973). Nocturnal enuresis: the importance of a small bladder capacity. In *Bladder Control and Enuresis*, ed. I. Kolvin, R. C. MacKeith, and S. R. Meadow, pp. 95-101. London: William Heinemann.

# 12

# Managing the Child with Obstructive Sleep Apnea

Sandra Palasti
William P. Potsic

## Introduction

### Historical Perspective

Obstructive sleep apnea was described in the classic work of Charles Dickens, *The Posthumous Papers of the Pickwick Club* (Dickens 1837), well before its appearance in the medical literature. Over fifty years later in 1889, William Hill pinpointed nasal obstruction as the cause of the behavior of the "stupid-looking lazy child who frequently suffers from headaches at school, breathes through his mouth instead of his nose, snores and is restless at night, and wakes up with a dry mouth in the morning." The term *pickwickian* was coined by Sir William Osler in 1912 to describe these children.

In the late 1950s, the association between obesity, excessive sleepiness, and heart failure was described by Burwell (1956). His work was the first to link hypoventilation with the symptoms outlined above. In 1965, Menashe, Cox, and their respective colleagues discovered enlarged tonsils and adenoids as the cause of heart failure in some patients. During the same year, the term obstructive sleep apnea (OSA) was developed to describe the syndrome of snoring, daytime sleepiness, and right heart failure (Schafer 1982).

Guilleminault and colleagues (1976a) were the first investigators to use polysomnography to diagnose OSA in children. They linked the apneic events of the evening with daytime hypersomnolence. Removal of the tonsils and adenoids (adenotonsillectomy) was curative in many of these patients. Obstructive sleep apnea has replaced chronic infection as the primary indication for most of the adenotonsillectomies done in the United States today.

## Definitions

Obstructive sleep apnea is defined as a cessation of airflow at the nose and mouth of at least a ten-second duration that occurs a minimum of thirty times in a seven-hour sleep period (Guilleminault et al. 1976b). These are the accepted standards for adults; pathologic standards for children are more difficult to identify. The pediatric population tends to exhibit shorter and more frequent periods of interrupted airflow than adults.

Some authors suggest that the most common pattern of upper airway obstruction during sleep in children is one of repetitive partially obstructive hypoventilation. This has been termed *obstructive sleep dyspnea* or the *sleep hypopnea syndrome* (Gould et al. 1988, Rosen et al. 1992). Characterized by loud snoring, restless sleep patterns, decreases in oxygenation, and increases in carbon dioxide, this syndrome is not included under the umbrella term of OSA. Obstructive sleep apnea syndrome refers to the nocturnal symptoms along with signs of right heart failure known as cor pulmonale.

There are other types of apnea that will not be covered in this chapter: apparent life-threatening events (previously called near-miss SIDS), apnea of prematurity, and congenital hypoventilation syndrome.

OSA and its related syndromes are probably more common than is currently realized. Physicians in diverse fields such as pediatrics, neonatology, pulmonary medicine, otolaryngology, and allergy may all apply widely differing criteria to their patients. Well-defined standards have yet to be established in children. Also, parents may not feel it necessary to report snoring to their primary care physician. Often this is the only presenting symptom of chronic airway obstruction in the pediatric population.

## Causes and Contributing Factors

Enlargement of the tonsils and adenoids is by far the most common cause of OSA in children over the age of 6 weeks. Prior to this age, obstructive apnea is usually due to blockage of the nostrils with thick secretions during upper respiratory infection (Roloff and Aldrich 1990).

Adenotonsillar enlargement is normal in childhood, affecting most children between the ages of 4 and 6 (Crepeau et al. 1982). The mean age for patients undergoing adenotonsillectomy for obstruction ranges from 4.8 to 5.8 years (Brodsky et al. 1989, Laurikainen et al. 1987, Lind and Lundell 1988, Potsic et al. 1986). It is not clear why certain children are more susceptible to the deleterious effects of tonsillar enlargement than others. Although the figures vary, most agree that obstruction is replacing recurrent infection as the primary indication for adenotonsillectomy in the United States and Europe (Check 1982, Grundfast and Wittich 1982, Lind and Lundell 1988). At Children's Hospital of Philadelphia, that figure approaches eighty percent (Handler et al. 1986).

The tonsils and adenoids need not be exceedingly large to cause significant obstruction. The additive effect of even moderate tonsil enlargement with collapse of the airway during sleep has been proven to result in obstructive apnea. During sleep, the normal tone of the airway muscles is decreased. This is especially true during periods of rapid eye movements (REM) and dream stages when muscle tone is diminished, with the exception of the diaphragm (Mark and Brooks 1984). When activity of the diaphragm exceeds that of the airway muscles, collapse of the upper airway ensues (Brouillette and Thach 1980). This collapse, coupled with any anatomic barriers that are present in the upper airway, can lead to complete obstruction.

Whereas the palatine tonsils are visible when the patient opens his/her mouth (Figure 12–1), the lingual tonsils are deep in the throat. Along with the palatine tonsils, the lingual tonsils have also been implicated as a cause of severe airway obstruction. This has been noted to occur primarily in patients who have undergone subsequent tonsillectomy. It is unclear whether this represents a compensatory growth or a generalized predisposition to overgrowth of lymph tissue (Guarisco et al. 1990).

Many of the craniofacial syndromes are associated with OSA. These include Pierre-Robin, Apert, Crouzon, and Treacher-Collins syndromes. Certain series of patients report up to one third of children

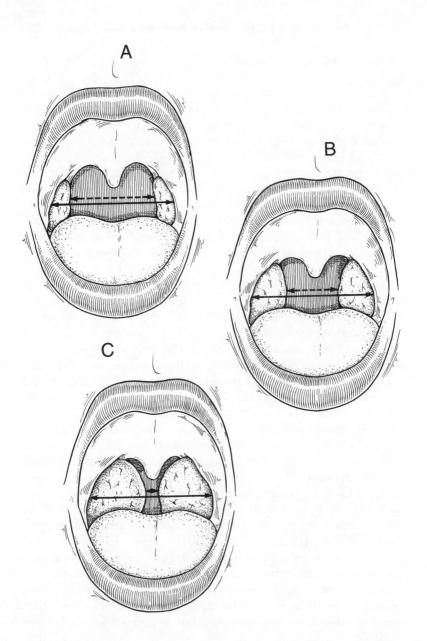

Figure 12–1: Evaluation of tonsil size. Drawing by S. Shapiro Brenman. Adapted from "Modern Assessment of Tonsils and Adenoids" by L. Brodsky, in *Pediatric Clinics of North America*. Copyright © 1989 by W. B. Saunders and used by permission.

with documented OSA as having an underlying facial dysmorphia (Brouillette et al. 1982, Guilleminault et al. 1981). The anatomic basis of obstruction is usually due to an undersized jaw. OSA may occur at any time during the child's development and is often aggravated by adenotonsillar enlargement. A marginal airway is vulnerable to obstruction by relatively minor enlargement. Removal of a normal volume of adenoids can restore adequate function in some congenitally compromised airways.

Children with Down's syndrome commonly snore and suffer from OSA. The cause of the obstruction is an enlarged tongue and an undersized mouth and nose. Altered airway muscular composition may play a role as well. Studies have found that the skeletal muscle of Down's patients is more susceptible to fatigue than normal muscle (van Lunteren 1993).

Children with cerebral palsy or other neuromuscular disorders frequently develop upper airway obstruction. Poor muscular tone combined with enlargement of the tonsils and adenoids lead to further airway compromise. It is often unclear what degree of the obstruction is related to enlargement of the tonsils and adenoids and what degree is related to impaired control of the airway muscles.

Gastroesophageal reflux (GER) is the abnormal flow of the acidic contents of the stomach up the esophagus and into the throat and airway. Controversy exists over whether GER plays an important role in the pathogenesis of OSA. Recent studies in rabbits have shown a definite correlation between GER and obstructive, central, and mixed apnea, and a possible correlation with sudden infant death syndrome (Wetmore 1993). Other factors contributing to OSA include tumors of the nose and mouth, deviated nasal septum, and nasal polyps.

## Complications of Obstructive Sleep Apnea

The symptoms of OSA in children are very different from those of adults. Whereas daytime hypersomnolence is practically universal in the adult population, children are more likely to manifest morning crankiness and headaches, hyperactivity, or aggressive behavior. Poor school performance is commonly reported, perhaps due to impairment of memory and concentration (Guilleminault et al. 1976a, Findley et al. 1986). The literature suggests that OSA may result in developmental delay secondary to repeated bouts of low blood oxygen, but these have yet to be substantiated (Brouillette et al. 1982, Kravath et al. 1977, Lind and Lundell 1988).

Most adults presenting with OSA are obese, whereas children are more likely to demonstrate failure to thrive (Brouillette et al. 1982, Grundfast and Wittich 1982, Guilleminault et al. 1981, Kravath et al. 1977, Lind and Lundell 1988, Williams et al. 1991). The exact cause of this has yet to be elucidated; however, difficulty swallowing is a common denominator. These children are slow and methodical eaters. They dislike swallowing as it is uncomfortable and may find food unappealing if they are unable to detect food odors secondary to nasal obstruction. Abnormally low secretion of growth hormone due to chronic sleep disturbance may be a factor as well (Lind and Lundell 1988, Schiffman et al. 1985, Singer and Saenger 1990).

Behavior during sleep is varied among children with OSA. Some children will have only snoring as their presenting symptom. Others, however, may exhibit thrashing movements, kicking and head extensions in attempts to find a comfortable sleep position. Enuresis is fairly common, as is sleepwalking (Guilleminault et al. 1976a, Weider and Hauri 1985). These symptoms usually resolve after relief of the obstruction.

By far the most serious of all complications are the adverse effects on the cardiovascular system. Decreased ventilation leads to accumulation of carbon dioxide and loss of oxygen. The right side of the heart soon begins to enlarge and will eventually fail—this is what is referred to as cor pulmonale.

Chronic hypoxemia has many secondary effects: life-threatening cardiac arrhythmia (Tilkian et al. 1977) and decreased cognition (Findley et al. 1986) are but a few. Fortunately, all but the most chronic changes are promptly reversed by correction of the obstruction.

## Diagnostic Studies

Children deserve special considerations when physicians attempt to diagnose OSA. They may be unwilling to submit to invasive, uncomfortable, and unfamiliar tests. Since apneic events occur mostly in the home and are rarely observed by health care personnel, the history from the parents and the physical exam are extremely important in establishing a diagnosis of OSA. Parents typically describe loud snoring, sleep pauses, unusual sleep positions, and behavioral disturbances. Two independent studies have shown that parental responses to

questions about these difficulties clearly differentiate obstructed from non-obstructed children (Brouillette et al. 1984, Potsic et al. 1986). The size of the adenoid tissue can be determined by x-ray with a lateral neck film. However, size has not been shown to correlate with degree of obstruction (Crepeau et al. 1982, Laurikainen et al. 1987, Mahboubi et al. 1985). A static radiograph cannot adequately represent the dynamic process of obstruction. Dynamic radiographic studies that photograph the airway during breathing are useful in the rare occurrence when the etiology of the obstruction is obscure.

When the diagnosis of OSA remains questionable, home monitoring in the form of sleep sonography is very useful. Sleep sonography, described by Marsh and colleagues (1983), is a method of recording breath sounds and analyzing respiratory patterns that is less expensive and invasive than polysomnography.

Sleep sonography uses a stethoscope attached to the child's neck. This is connected to a tape recorder and two one-hour samples are recorded. The tape is subjected to analog and digital processing to identify periods of snoring, irregular breathing and apnea (see Figure 12-2). Potsic (1987) has shown a high degree of correlation between sleep sonography and polysomnography (PSG) in predicting the amount of obstruction in patients with adenotonsillar hypertrophy.

There are definite advantages of sleep sonography over PSG. Low cost, ease of administration, and avoidance of hospitalization are obvious. In addition, if the obstruction is variable from night to night, the parents are able to tape when the child's difficulties are at their peak.

Sleep sonography cannot differentiate between central and obstructive apnea. If central apnea is suspected, then PSG is indicated. In fact, there are certain instances when PSG is the evaluation of choice, such as in the evaluation of children with neuromuscular disorders, craniofacial anomalies, neonates, and in patients with complex medical histories. PSG is also used to study the post-operative patient who has failed to show improvement (Potsic 1987).

The monitors used in PSG in children are similar to those that are used in adults. The three essential pieces of information gathered from this study are the assessment of sleep, the assessment of breathing, and the cardiovascular response. The first parameter is evaluated with the standard montage for determining sleep versus wakefulness and stage of sleep: electroencephalogram (EEG), electrooculogram (EOG), and submental electromyogram (EMG). EOG determines the stage of

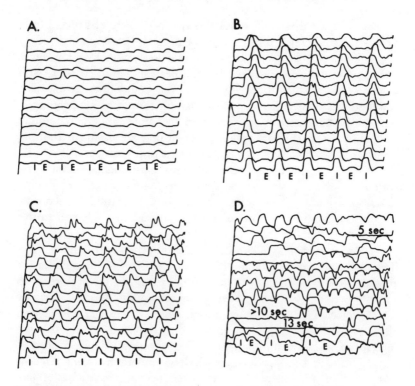

Figure 12–2: Sleep sonograms: computer-generated displays of breathing sounds recorded during sleep. (A) Normal breathing pattern. (B) Effort is elevated, but rate is stable. (C) There is variation in rate and wave form noting difficulty in breathing. (D) Severe breathing difficulty with two apneic periods of greater than ten seconds. Reprinted from "Relief of Upper Airway Obstruction by Adenotonsillectorny," by W. P. Potsic, P. S. Pasquariello, and C. C. Baranak, et al., in *Otolaryngology Head and Neck Surgery*. Copyright © 1986 by Mosby-Year Book, Inc. and used by permission.

rapid eye movement (REM) sleep, when apneic episodes tend to occur. Submental EMG measures the tone of the pharyngeal muscles, which tends to diminish during REM sleep.

Breathing is evaluated by means of nasal and oral thermistors and chest strain gauges. The thermistors detect airflow by means of heat sensors and/or carbon dioxide analyzers. Cardiovascular response is monitored by electrocardiogram (ECG). Pulse oximetry supplies a continuous monitoring of oxygen levels. Finally, if gastroesophageal reflux is suspected, an esophageal pH probe may be placed to correlate periods of apnea with reflux.

Interpretation of PSG in children differs from that in adults.

Although there are children who develop complete obstructive apnea, the majority of children have continuous partial obstructions (Brouillette et al. 1984, Rosen et al. 1992). Brouillette et al. have suggested that the duration of these partial obstructions and their associated hypoxia and hypercapnea are just as clinically significant as the complete obstructions found in adults (Brouillette et al. 1982). PSG does not measure these partial obstructions.

Despite the wealth of data that can be obtained, PSG has its limitations. First, in infants, there is no universal agreement on definitive standards for normal and abnormal respiration in different sleep stages. Second, the procedure is expensive, and if more than one night of recording is required to make a diagnosis the cost may become prohibitive. Third, because some children may not sleep well in the sleep laboratory, a disorder brought on by deep sleep and poor arousal could be missed (Roloff and Aldrich 1990).

Fiberoptic nasopharyngoscopy permits visualization of the entire upper airway and aids in determining the site of obstruction. Its limitation lies in the fact that the scope is not well tolerated by most children and that sleep stages are difficult to reproduce under sedation or general anesthesia. Sher et al. (1986) examined children with OSA secondary to craniofacial anomalies with the nasopharyngoscope to determine the exact site of obstruction. They found the site of obstruction to be variable between, as well as within, syndromes. Therefore, an approach that is successful in one patient may be inadequate for another. Children with complicated airways such as these require a thorough upper airway examination in order to formulate a treatment plan.

## Treatment

The efficacy of adenotonsillectomy in the relief of OSA in children is well established. Lymphoid hyperplasia is the cause of pediatric OSA in the vast majority of cases and removal of the obstructing tissue will improve the child's ability to breath normally during sleep. Richardson et al. (1980) report a reduction in the number of obstructive and central apneas after adenotonsillectomy; why central apnea is affected is not clear. Some patients note immediate relief following adenotonsillectomy, although most require several days to weeks for complete resolution of swelling at the operative sites to achieve an optimal airway.

Adenotonsillectomy is usually accomplished as a day surgery or overnight procedure. However, patients with severe OSA require close observation for post-operative respiratory difficulties (Brown et al. 1988, McColley et al. 1992). The combined effects of post-operative tissue swelling, residual anesthetic effects, and an impaired breathing may lead to respiratory obstruction and pulmonary edema. Children 3 years of age and younger are more likely to have post-operative complications and require extended care. Observation in a pediatric intensive care unit (PICU) for twenty-four to forty-eight hours in some patients is needed to avoid potentially lethal complications.

Children with neuromuscular disorders may benefit from uvulo-palatopharyngoplasty (UPPP), a procedure that removes the uvula, tonsils, and a portion of the soft palate (Handler et al. 1986, Hulcrantz et al. 1988, Reilly 1988). These patients lack rigidity of their upper airway. A competent airway is provided by excising this soft tissue, which may avoid the need of a tracheotomy.

Artificial airways, such as nasopharyngeal tubes and nasal continuous positive airway pressure (CPAP), are alternatives in treating the child with OSA. Since they are usually poorly tolerated by children, they are not suitable as long-term solutions. CPAP and nasal airways are frequently relied upon in children whose medical conditions are too unstable to undergo surgery or in instances when surgery is deferred by the parents.

If all other methods fail to control the obstruction, a tracheotomy must be considered. A tracheotomy bypasses the entire upper airway and is a very effective means of treating OSA. Children with craniofacial syndromes and neuromuscular disorders may require this procedure after attempts to relieve OSA by means of adenotonsillectomy and UPPP fail.

**Case Illustration**

J.P. is a 6-year-old female whose parents complain of loud snoring, nasal discharge, and mouth breathing. Further questioning of the parents elicits a history of sleep pauses lasting from five to ten seconds and finicky eating habits. The child has difficulty with arousal in the morning, but does not seem excessively sleepy during the daytime. She is an excellent student.

The child has von Willebrand's disease, an inherited disorder of the coagulation system, which was discovered when she had prolonged bleeding during dental cleaning. She is otherwise healthy and has never undergone a surgical procedure.

On physical exam, the child appears slightly small for her age. She breathes mainly through her mouth and has clear nasal secretions. Oral exam reveals enlarged tonsils. The rest of the exam is within normal limits. A lateral neck radiograph is obtained, which displays enlarged and obstructing adenoids.

Because of her bleeding disorder, sleep somnography is ordered to more adequately assess the degree of obstruction that may accompany the child's snoring. The study reveals multiple apneas ranging from ten to thirty seconds.

Due to the severity of the obstruction, an adenotonsillectomy is performed after correction of the bleeding disorder. The surgery and post-operative recovery period are uneventful. The parents note marked improvement in the child's obstructive signs and symptoms one month following surgery.

## Summary

OSA is a common disorder in children. The causes are many, although hypertrophic tonsils and adenoids are usually a large component of the obstruction. Children display a variety of symptoms including loud snoring, poor school performance, and failure to thrive. Left untreated, OSA can have serious cardiovascular sequelae.

The diagnosis can usually be made by a thorough history and physical exam. Sleep sonography and polysomnography are reserved for cases that pose diagnostic dilemmas. The simplicity and economy of sleep sonography is noteworthy. Adenotonsillectomy is often necessary to relieve the obstruction. UPPP and tracheotomy are reserved for those patients who are refractory to conventional treatment.

## References

Brodsky, L., Adler, E., and Stanievich, J. F. (1989). Naso- and oropharyngeal dimensions in children with obstructive sleep apnea. International Journal of Pediatric Otorhinolaryngology 17:1–11.

Brouillette, R. T., Fernbach, S. K., and Hunt, C. E. (1982). Obstructive sleep apnea in infants and children. Journal of Pediatrics 100:31–40.

Brouillette, R., Hanson, D., David, R., et al. (1984). A diagnostic approach to suspected obstructive sleep apnea in children. Journal of Pediatrics 105:10–14.

Brouillette, R. T., and Thach, B. T. (1980). Control of the genioglossus inspiratory activity. Journal of Applied Physiology 49:801–806.

Brown, O. E., Manning, S. C., and Ridenour, B., (1988). Cor pulmonale secondary to tonsillar and adenoidal hypertrophy: management considerations. *International Journal of Pediatric Otorhinolaryngology* 16:131–139.

Burwell, C., Robin, E. D., Whaley, R. D., and Sharrar, W. G. (1956). Extreme obesity associated with alveolar hypoventilation: a pickwickian syndrome. *American Journal of Medicine* 21:811–818.

Check, W. A. (1982). Medical news: does drop in T and A's pose new issue of adenotonsillar hypertrophy? *Journal of the American Medical Association* 247:1229–1230.

Cox, M. A., Schiebler, G. L., Taylor, W. J., et al. (1965). Reversal of pulmonary hypertension in a child with respiratory obstruction and cor pulmonale. *Journal of Pediatrics* 67:192.

Crepeau, J., Patriquin, H. B., Poliquin, J. F., and Tetreault, L. (1982). Radiographic evaluation of the symptom-producing adenoid. *Otolaryngology Head and Neck Surgery* 90:548–554.

Dickens, C. (1837). *The Posthumous Papers of the Pickwick Club*. London: Chapman and Hall.

Findley, L. J., Barth, J. T., Powers, D. C., et al. (1986). Cognitive impairment in patients with obstructive sleep apnea and associated hypoxemia. *Chest* 90:686–690.

Gould, G. A., Whyte, K. F., Rhind, G. B., et al. (1988). The sleep hypopnea syndrome. *American Review of Respiratory Disease* 137:895–898.

Grundfast, K. M., and Wittich, D. J. (1982). Adenotonsillar hypertrophy and upper airway obstruction in evolutionary perspective. *Laryngoscope* 92:650–660.

Guarisco, J. L., Littlewood, S. C., and Butcher, R. B. (1990). Severe upper airway obstruction in children secondary to lingual tonsil hypertrophy. *Annals of Otology Rhinology and Laryngology* 99:621–624.

Guilleminault, C., Eldridge, F. L., Simmons, F. B., and Dement, W. C. (1976a). Sleep apnea in eight children. *Pediatrics* 58:23–30.

Guilleminault, C., Korobkin, R., and Winkle, R., (1981). A review of 50 children with obstructive sleep apnea syndrome. *Lung* 159:275–1287.

Guilleminault, C., Tilkian, A., and Dement, W. C. (1976b). The sleep apnea syndromes. *Annual Review of Medicine* 27:465–484.

Handler, S. D., Miller, L., Richmond, K. H., and Baranak, C. C. (1986). Post-tonsillectomy hemorrhage: incidence, prevention and management. *Laryngoscope* 96:1243–1247.

Hill, W. (1889). On some causes of backwardness and stupidity in children. *British Medical Journal* 2:711–712.

Hulcrantz, E., Svanholm, H., and Ahlqvist-Rastad, J. (1988). Sleep apnea in children without hypertrophy of the tonsils. *Clinical Pediatrics* 27:350–352.

Kravath, R. E., Pollack, C. P., and Boroweiki, B. (1977). Hypoventilation during sleep in children who have lymphoid airway obstruction treated by nasopharyngeal tube and T and A. *Pediatrics* 59:865–871.

Laurikainen, E., Erkinjuntti, M., Alihanka, J., et al. (1987). Radiological parameters of the bony nasopharynx and the adenotonsillar size compared with sleep apnea episodes in children. *International Journal of Pediatric Otorhinolaryngology* 12:303–310.

Lind, M. G., and Lundell, B. P. W. (1988). Tonsillar hyperplasia in children: a cause of obstructive sleep apnea, $CO_2$ retention, and retarded growth. *Archives of Otolaryngology* 16:39–44.

Mahboubi, S., Marsh, R. R., Potsic, W. P., and Pasquariello, P. S. (1985). The lateral neck radiograph in adenotonsillar hyperplasia. *International Journal of Pediatric Otorhinolaryngology* 10:67–73.

Mark, J. D., and Brooks, J. G. (1984). Sleep associated airway problems in children. *Pediatric Clinics of North America* 31:907–1003.

Marsh, R. R., Potsic, W. P., and Pasquariello, C. (1983). Recorder for assessment of upper airway disorders. *Otolaryngology Head and Neck Surgery* 91:584–585.

McColley, S. A., April, M. M., Carroll, J. L., et al. (1992). Respiratory compromise after adenotonsillectomy in children with obstructive sleep apnea. *Archives of Otolaryngology Head and Neck Surgery* 118:940–943.

Menashe, V. D., Farrehi, C., Miller, M., et al. (1965). Hypoventilation and cor pulmonale due to chronic airway obstruction. *Journal of Pediatrics* 67:198–263.

Osler, W. (1912). *The Principles and Practice of Medicine*. East Norwalk, CT: Appleton and Lange.

Potsic, W. P. (1987). Comparison of polysomnography and sonography for assessing regularity of respiration during sleep in adenotonsillar hypertrophy. *Laryngoscope* 97:1430–1437.

Potsic, W. P., Pasquariello, P. S., Baranak, C. C., et al. (1986). Relief of upper airway obstruction by adenotonsillectomy. *Otolaryngology Head and Neck Surgery* 94:476–480.

Reilly, J. S. (1988). Tonsillar and adenoid airway obstruction: modes of treatment in children. *International Anesthesiology Clinics* 26:54–57.

Richardson, M. A., Seid, A. B., Cotton, R. T., et al. (1980). Evaluation of tonsils and adenoids in sleep apnea syndrome. *Laryngoscope* 90:1106–1110.

Roloff, D. W., and Aldrich, M. S. (1990). Sleep disorders and airway obstruction in newborns and infants. *Otolaryngologic Clinics of North America* 23:639–650.

Rosen, C. L., D'Andrea, L., and Haddad, G. G. (1992). Adult criteria of obstructive sleep apnea do not identify children with serious obstruction. *American Review of Respiratory Disease* 146:1231–1234.

Schafer, M. E. (1982). Upper-airway obstruction and sleep disorders in children with obstructive sleep apnea syndrome. *Clinics of Plastic Surgery* 9:555–567.

Schiffmann, R., Faber, J., and Eidelman, A. I. (1985). Obstructive hypertrophic adenoids and tonsils as a cause of infantile failure to thrive: reversed by tonsillectomy and adenoidectomy. *International Journal of Pediatric Otorhinolaryngology* 9:183–187.

Sher, A. E., Shprintzen, R. J., and Thorpy, M. J. (1986). Endoscopic observations of obstructive sleep apnea in children with anomalous upper airways: predictive and therapeutic value. *International Journal of Pediatric Otorhinolaryngology* 11:135–146.

Singer, L. P., and Saenger, P., (1990). Complications of pediatric obstructive sleep apnea. *Otolaryngologic Clinics of North America* 23:665–676.

Tilkian, A. G., Guilleminault, C., Schroeder, J. S., et al. (1977). Sleep-induced apnea syndrome: prevalence of cardiac arrhythmias and their reversal after tracheotomy. *Americal Journal of Medicine* 63:348–357.

van Lunteren, E., (1993). Muscles of the pharynx: structural and contractile properties. *Ear, Nose, and Throat Journal* 72:27–30.

Weider, D. J., and Hauri, P. J. (1985). Nocturnal enuresis in children with upper airway obstruction. *International Journal of Pediatric Otorhinolaryngology* 9:173–182.

Wetmore, R. F. (1993). Effects of acid on the larynx of the maturing rabbit and their possible significance to the sudden infant death syndrome. *Laryngoscope* 103:1242–1254.

Williams, E. F. III, Woo, P., Miller, R., and Kellman, R. M. (1991). The effects of adenotonsillectomy on growth in young children. *Otolaryngology Head and Neck Surgery* 104:509–516.

# 13

# Narcolepsy in Children

Vincent P. Gibbons
Suresh Kotagal

## Introduction

A discussion of narcolepsy should take place with reference to the larger number of causes of excessive daytime sleepiness in children. Narcolepsy is a chronic, life-long disorder that is characterized by a tetrad of symptoms: irresistible daytime sleepiness, cataplexy, sleep paralysis, and hypnagogic hallucinations (Yoss and Daly 1957). The first descriptions of narcolepsy date back to 1880, when Gelineau, a French psychiatrist, described it as a "rare, little known neurosis characterized by an imperative need to sleep of a sudden onset and short duration, recurring at more or less close intervals" (Gelineau 1880, p. 623). Little attention was paid to narcolepsy in the early twentieth century, perhaps because it had been labeled as a rare disorder. Narcolepsy is neither psychogenic, nor a form of epilepsy. Interest in narcolepsy as a neurological disorder evolved gradually following the discovery by Aserinsky and Kleitman (1953) of "regularly occurring periods of eye motility and concomitant phenomena during sleep" (p. 273), now called rapid eye movement (REM) sleep. This paved the way for the discovery of sleep-onset REM periods in patients with narcolepsy (Rechtschaffen and Dement 1967). A broad overview of narcolepsy with special emphasis on its pediatric manifestations and its recognition in children is presented in this chapter.

Despite the initial onset of symptoms in the first two decades of life, the disorder may remain undiagnosed until the third or fourth decades. Its prevalence has been estimated at one in 500,000 in Israel (Lavie and Peled 1987), one in 600 in Japan (Honda 1988), and between one in 1,000 to one in 10,000 in the United States (Dement et al. 1973). It is equally prevalent in both sexes.

## Clinical Features

*Excessive daytime sleepiness* and cataplexy are the two most important features of narcolepsy. Retrospective studies date the onset of sleepiness to before the age of 20 years in sixty percent of patients, and before the age of 10 years in eighteen percent (Kales et al. 1982). The symptom of excessive daytime sleepiness does not initially cause great concern amongst parents and health professionals. Children may deny the symptom or minimize its adverse effects (Allsopp and Zaiwalla 1992). This may lead to an under-diagnosis of narcolepsy in children. The attacks of irresistible daytime sleepiness are most likely to occur when the patient is carrying out sedentary activities. The narcoleptic child may fall asleep in the classroom, while being driven in an automobile, while watching television, or even while talking. Onset of excessive daytime sleepiness due to narcolepsy has been documented as early as 6 years of age (Lenn 1986). Lenn's patient would fall asleep five to ten times a day. This phenomenon would occur at various times, including during meals. The child also experienced visual and auditory hallucinations, including hearing voices telling him to do "bad things," and seeing strangers, a movie personality, gorillas, and other animals at sleep onset. Wittig et al. (1983a) described a 7 year, 5-month-old boy with narcolepsy who would fall asleep while watching television for longer than one half hour, while sitting at the dinner table, and in his mother's arms while at a physician's office. This sleepiness occurred despite ten hours of regular night sleep and two regular daily naps of one to one and a half hours. The frequency of the daytime naps in children with narcolepsy may vary from two to three per day. These naps tend to be longer in duration than those in adults with narcolepsy, and may last sixty to ninety minutes. They may or may not be followed by a refreshed feeling (Kotagal et al. 1990). Narcoleptics do not need to sleep longer over a twenty-four-hour period than non-narcoleptic, control subjects, but they do need to nap more often. Although planned daytime nap opportunities help the narcoleptic subject feel refreshed, extending the duration of the naps beyond twenty to thirty minutes does not further enhance the level of alertness. The daytime hypersomnolence may impair attention, memory, and learning (Broughton and Ghanem 1976, Guilleminault and Dement 1977, Rogers and Rosenberg 1990), or predispose to accidents. School-teachers may notice inattentiveness and a decline in the child's academic performance. Irritability and emotional lability may also be noticed.

*Cataplexy*, the second major feature of narcolepsy, is present in fifty to seventy percent of narcoleptics. It is characterized by episodes of sudden muscular weakness and atonia generally brought on by emotions like fear, laughter, or rage. Cataplexy can, however, occur even in the absence of emotional trigger factors. The patient may complain of his jaw sagging open, a "rubbery" feeling in his legs, having to lean momentarily against a wall for support, or actually falling to the floor. Although extraocular muscles are supposedly not involved, patients may occasionally complain of blurring of vision. Speech may become of soft volume. There may be irregular breathing due to transient respiratory muscle weakness, but prolonged apnea has not been observed. Consciousness is fully maintained during these episodes, which may last from a few seconds to thirty minutes. Although daytime sleepiness usually begins several months before the onset of cataplexy, six to ten percent of patients have cataplexy as the initial manifestation. In ten to fifteen percent of patients, cataplexy may develop ten or more years after onset of the sleepiness (Passouant and Billiard 1976).

*Sleep paralysis* is characterized by an inability to move the body for a few seconds at sleep onset, or upon awakening from sleep. It is usually of the flaccid type. Consciousness is fully preserved during these events, which can be terrifying to the patient. They can be terminated by calling the name of the patient or touching him.

*Hallucinations* at sleep onset (*hypnagogic*) or upon awakening from sleep (*hypnopompic*) may accompany sleep paralysis. They have a vivid, dream-like, frightening quality, and can be either auditory or visual in nature. The affective response is related to the inappropriateness of the situation in which the hallucinations occur (Zarcone 1973).

*Disturbed nighttime sleep*, with frequent awakenings, is also an important feature. An increased incidence of periodic leg movements in sleep was found in the series of children with narcolepsy described by

Young and colleagues (1988), being present in five-eighths (sixty-three percent) of their subjects. *Periodic leg movements* are defined as series of rhythmic electromyographic bursts of activity, of 0.5 to 5 seconds' duration, with an interburst interval of 5 to 120 seconds, occurring in series of three or more. Some of these discharges are known to coincide with electroencephalographic evidence of arousal and sleep disruption. Adults with narcolepsy may also have an increased incidence of sleep apnea, but such an association has not been established in children with narcolepsy.

*Neuropsychological impairments* as a consequence of daytime hypersomnolence are receiving increasing attention. Rogers and Rosenberg (1990) evaluated thirty adults with narcolepsy and thirty controls using the Wechsler Memory Scale (WMS), the Rey Auditory Verbal Learning Test, the Rey Complex Figure Test, Strub and Black's List of Letters and the Symbol Digits Modalities Test (SDMT). In addition, the Profile of Mood States was used to detect variation in performance due to anxiety or fatigue. Continuous polygraphic recordings were obtained during the testing to detect any changes in the level of alertness. Subjects with narcolepsy experienced more difficulty in maintaining attention than controls, as evidenced by more perseveration errors (p < 0.01) on Strub and Black's List of Letters. Despite differences in their ability to sustain attention, there was no difference between the two groups on measures of concentration (digit span from the WMS and SDMT). Whether these findings can be extrapolated to children with narcolepsy still needs to be determined.

Henry and colleagues (1993) studied body temperature, vigilance, memory, information processing, and motor function in ten unmedicated narcoleptics and ten age-matched controls at four different times of the day. Time of day and body temperature were not related to performance. Narcoleptics displayed selective cognitive deficits in response latency, word recall, and estimation of frequency. Narcoleptics did not differ from controls in motor speed, vigilance, information processing speed, or decision-making accuracy. These researchers propose that a perceptual encoding deficit underlies the problems in memory and complex reaction time in patients with narcolepsy.

Children with narcolepsy initially are most likely to manifest excessive daytime sleepiness and cataplexy. Hypnagogic hallucinations and sleep paralysis may be infrequent at the onset, but become apparent over the next few months (Kotagal et al. 1990). One important characteristic of pediatric narcolepsy is that the complete tetrad of symptoms becomes apparent within a short period, whereas in adult-onset narcolepsy it may take many years to evolve (Young et al. 1988).

## Pathophysiology

Cataplexy, sleep paralysis, and hypnagogic hallucinations are all rapid eye movement (REM) sleep phenomena, representing an intrusion of fragments of REM sleep onto wakefulness. REM sleep is normally characterized by skeletal muscle atonia, which is also very typical of cataplexy and sleep paralysis. Cataplectic behavior can be induced in cats after micro-injection of carbachol into the pontine reticular formation (Mitler and Dement 1974), thus suggesting a cholinergic basis for this REM sleep phenomenon. Cholinergic and monoaminergic systems have opposite effects in the regulation of cataplexy. It also appears that uptake inhibitors that enhance norepinephrine, such as desipramine and protryptiline, are more potent in controlling cataplexy than drugs that selectively enhance serotonergic activity, such as amitryptiline or imipramine. This suggests that norepinephrine is more important than serotonin in regulating the control of cataplexy (Foutz et al. 1981). Cataplexy is also associated with an inhibition of the monosynaptic H-reflex and of the multisynaptic tendon reflexes (Guilleminault 1989). REM sleep is also abnormal in narcolepsy with regard to its temporal relationship to wakefulness. Upon sleep onset, adults and normal children older than 3 months initially enter non-REM sleep, with the appearance of REM sleep sixty to ninety minutes later. Patients with narcolepsy, however, frequently go directly from wakefulness into REM sleep. The development of symptoms around adolescence perhaps also suggests a hormonal influence (Zarcone 1973).

Well-documented, *symptomatic narcolepsy* (secondary to identifiable brain lesions) is a rare entity. Aldrich and Naylor (1989) have, however, reported three patients who fulfilled clinical and polysomnographic criteria for the diagnosis of narcolepsy. Their brain lesions consisted of a craniopharyngoma, a hypothalamic syndrome of unknown etiology, and obstructive hydrocephalus associated with a sarcoid granuloma in the region of the third ventricle. Two of the three patients possessed the HLA-DR2 antigen. This study suggests that diencephalic lesions can be associated with symptoms and signs that are indistinguishable from idiopathic narcolepsy, and that the HLA-DR2 is not required in all cases of narcolepsy.

Montplaisir and colleagues (1982) measured serum and cerebrospinal fluid concentrations of several biogenic amines (dopamine, norepinephrine, epinephrine, and serotonin) and some of their metabolites (homovanillic acid, 5-hydroxyindoleacetic acid, and indoleacetic acid) in narcoleptics, patients with idiopathic hypersomnia, and normal controls. Both groups of patients with hypersomnia demonstrated significantly decreased cerebrospinal fluid concentrations of dopamine and indoleacetic acid, a metabolite of tryptamine. Normally, the corpus striatum has high concentrations of dopamine and tryptamine, which are probably involved in the genesis of hypersomnia. Stimulants used in the treatment of hypersomnia, such as amphetamines, are known to enhance dopamine release from pre-synaptic terminals.

*Abnormal monoaminergic function* has also been confirmed on post-mortem neurochemical analysis of the brains of three patients with narcolepsy (Mamelak 1992). The salient findings were an increase in noradrenergic and serotonergic neuronal activity, as well as a decrease in dopaminergic neuronal activity. In two of the three brains, there was also a decrease in the number of alpha-1-noradrenergic receptors in the frontal cortex and the amygdala. Mamelak (1991) suggests that the locus ceruleus neurons and raphe nucleus serotonergic neurons are overactive in narcolepsy. This increased neurochemical activity depresses the activity of cholinergic pedunculopontine (PP) REM sleep effector neurons. PP neurons in turn project to and stimulate the dopaminergic neurons of the substantia nigra. Decreased PP activity in narcolepsy thus could lead to pontine cholinergic supersensitivity, and consequently, cataplexy. The low cortical noradrenergic activity could lead to decreased cortical arousal and consequently, hypersomnia.

### Genetics

*Familial narcolepsy* has been described in fifteen breeds of dogs, cats, miniature horses, quarter horses, and Brahman bulls (Knecht et al. 1984, Richardson et al. 1990 Strain et al. 1984). Between one-third and one-half of patients with narcolepsy also have a first-degree relative with the condition (Baraitser and Parkes 1978, Yoss and Daly 1957). Narcolepsy has been found to be inherited in a single gene, recessive pattern in three different strains of Doberman pinschers (Foutz et al. 1979).

In humans, however, narcolepsy is not inherited in an autosomal recessive pattern. Certain histocompatibility antigens (HLA), that is,

DRw15 (previously termed DR2) and DQw6 (previously DQw1) are present in close to 100 percent of patients with narcolepsy, whereas their prevalence in the general population is between twenty and forty percent (Billiard et al. 1986, Langdon et al. 1986). This association with HLA antigens suggests a genetic and immunologic basis for narcolepsy, but at this time there is little information about the mechanism(s) that may form the basis of this relationship. The HLA encoding region is located on the short arm of chromosome 6. It is possible that the gene for susceptibility to narcolepsy is the same as the HLA gene itself, or located very close to it. The total size of this area on chromosome 6 has been estimated to be about 500 kilobases. Honda and colleagues (1989) suggest a multifactorial mode of developing human narcolepsy, with two thresholds—first, a genetic threshold, and second, an acquired, or environmental, threshold. Both these thresholds would need to be exceeded before a patient becomes clinically symptomatic. They point out that this hypothesis might explain the instances of patients developing post-traumatic narcolepsy, and that perhaps these individuals were already genetically predisposed to develop narcolepsy.

Ditta and colleagues (1992) studied restriction fragment length polymorphism associated with human leukocyte antigen gene-specific probes in two Caucasian families, each with two confirmed narcoleptic siblings. In one family, one of the siblings was DRw15 positive, while in the second family, both siblings were DRw15 negative. These results suggest that at least in DRw15 negative narcolepsy, the DNA patterns are not informative with regard to diagnosing or predicting the presence of narcolepsy. Such results also argue for genetic heterogeneity in human narcolepsy, and that the role of DRw15 in the development of narcolepsy can best be viewed as contributory, but not essential.

*Idiopathic narcoleptics* may at times be HLA-DR2 negative. Douglass and colleagues (1989) studied a pair of monozygotic twins who were concordant for narcolepsy. Monozygosity was assessed by HLA antigens and blood groups. In contrast to most narcoleptics, they were HLA-DQ1 positive instead of HLA-DR2.

### Diagnosis

The diagnosis of narcolepsy in children is based on the presence of the characteristic clinical features (at a minimum, excessive daytime sleepiness and cataplexy) combined with typical findings on the nocturnal polysomnogram and the multiple sleep latency test. (See Table 13–1 on page 274.)

Table 13-1
Characteristics of Narcolepsy

---

**CLINICAL**
excessive daytime sleepiness
cataplexy
hypnagogic hallucinations
sleep paralysis
**IMMUNOLOGIC**
histocompatibility antigens DRw15 or DQw6
**NEUROPHYSIOLOGIC**
1. POLYSOMNOGRAPHIC
   sleep-onset REM periods (SOREMPs)
   frequent nocturnal awakenings
   increased stage 1 sleep
   increased periodic leg movements
   increased wake time after sleep onset
2. MSLT
   average sleep onset fewer than 5 minutes
   sleep-onset REM periods (SOREMPs)

---

The electroencephalogram, eye movements, chin and leg electromyogram, respiratory effort, oral and nasal airflow, and oxygen saturation should be monitored during the *nocturnal polysomnogram*. The data can be recorded on a standard paper polygraph or an automated recording and analysis system. The test is important in excluding other types of sleep pathology, such as obstructive sleep apnea, that may mimic narcolepsy by causing excessive daytime sleepiness. Children with narcolepsy may demonstrate REM sleep at the very onset of night sleep. The sleep of most narcoleptics is also disturbed, with presence of frequent nocturnal awakenings, increased wake time after sleep onset, increased time spent in Stage 1 non-REM sleep, increased prevalence of periodic leg movements, and central sleep apnea (Wittig et al. 1983b). These changes may lead to impaired sleep efficiency, and contribute to the excessive daytime sleepiness.

The nocturnal polysomnogram should be followed the next morning by the *Multiple Sleep Latency Test* (MSLT) (Carskadon et al. 1986). This test measures the speed with which an individual falls asleep, as well as electrophysiologic events at the sleep–wake interface. It consists of the provision of a series of four nap opportunities at two hourly intervals (usually at 10:00 A.M., 12:00 P.M., 2:00 P.M., and 4:00 P.M.) in a darkened, quiet room. The electroencephalogram, eye movements, and chin electromyogram are simultaneously recorded. For each nap, the time from "lights out" to the onset of electroencephalographic sleep onset constitutes the sleep latency. In normal children, the average latency to sleep varies as a function of sexual maturation, from approximately eighteen minutes in the preadolescent to closer to fourteen minutes later in pubescence (Carskadon and Dement 1987). In patients with pathologic daytime sleepiness, the mean sleep latency derived from the four naps is generally less than ten minutes. In order to make a definitive diagnosis, patients with narcolepsy are also re-quired to have two or more naps with REM-onset sleep. The charac-teristic polygraphic findings of decreased sleep latency and two or more REM-onset sleep periods may not be present initially, however, in every child with narcolepsy. Serial polysomnographic studies may be necessary for the definitive ascertaining of these features (Kotagal et al. 1990). One disadvantage of the MSLT is that it measures the tendency for sleepiness in an environment that is most conducive to sleep, and this may not be representative of the environment in which the patient normally functions.

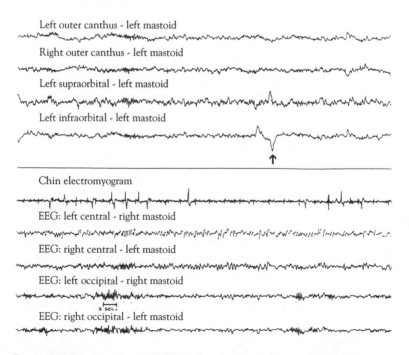

Left outer canthus - left mastoid

Right outer canthus - left mastoid

Left supraorbital - left mastoid

Left infraorbital - left mastoid

Chin electromyogram

EEG: left central - right mastoid

EEG: right central - left mastoid

EEG: left occipital - right mastoid

EEG: right occipital - left mastoid

Figure 13-1: Transition from wakefulness directly into rapid eye movement (REM) sleep during a multiple sleep latency test in a 15-year-old with narcolepsy. The arrow denotes an eye movement at the onset of REM sleep.

The *Maintenance of Wakefulness Test* is another test that has been used for quantifying the level of sleepiness in adults with daytime hypersomnolence (Mitler et al. 1982). It is similar to the MSLT, except that the subject is asked to resist sleep. It requires the subject to sit in a darkened room and stay awake for forty minutes. The test, however, has not received validation in children. Studies of the blood for HLA antigens DR2 and DQW1 are also helpful in establishing the diagnosis.

*Cortical evoked potentials*, which measure the latency and amplitude of the positive cortical wave form recorded from the scalp, derived approximately 350 milliseconds after auditory tone burst stimulation (*P350 paradigm*) have also been used to study information processing at the cortical level in patients with narcolepsy (Broughton and Aguirre 1984). The subject listens to a train of stimuli of which 10 percent are randomly interspersed at a different frequency. These are tones to which the individual is expected to respond by counting and pressing a button. The P350 is about half the amplitude in narcoleptics as compared to controls, suggesting impaired cortical function.

## Differential Diagnosis

Pediatricians, neurologists, primary care providers, psychologists, and psychiatrists will encounter children with narcolepsy either among those with excessive daytime sleepiness or those with a short attention span, increased distractibility, and poor school performance. The differential diagnosis of childhood narcolepsy includes hypersomnia due to obstructive sleep apnea, obesity-hypoventilation syndrome, depression, drug abuse, the delayed phase syndrome, idiopathic hypersomnia, poor sleep hygiene, Kleine-Levin syndrome, and the primary disorder of vigilance. Narcolepsy is more likely to be the reason for excessive daytime sleepiness in a teenager than in a preadolescent. A two- to three-week log of sleep–wake habits, psychological assessment, urine drug screen, combined with the nocturnal polysomnogram and MSLT will help in distinguishing these other disorders from narcolepsy. Psychological evaluation is also very helpful in assessing for depression, and determining the overall level of intellectual functioning. It should include projective tests, intelligence tests, measures of attentiveness (e.g., a continuous performance task) and tests of classroom achievement. (See Figure 13–2.)

It is not unusual for children with narcolepsy to be overweight (as

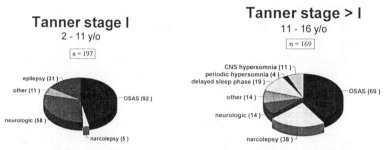

Figure 13-2: Relative incidence of diagnoses leading to excessive daytime sleepiness in pre-pubertal and pubertal children. OSAS = obstructive sleep apnea syndrome. Adapted from "Disorders of Excessive Daytime Sleepiness," pp. 178, 179, in *Sleep and its Disorders*, ed. C. Guilleminault. Copyright © 1987 by Raven Press and used by permission of C. Guilleminault and Raven Press.

were three of four children in the Kotagal et al. 1990 series). This was possibly related to their adopting more sedentary habits on account of sleepiness, but initially gave the impression of an underlying obstructive sleep apnea syndrome. While sleep apnea may occur concurrently in adults with narcolepsy, such an association is relatively infrequent in childhood narcolepsy. If there is polysomnographic evidence of a severe *obstructive sleep apnea* syndrome in a sleepy child, it is quite likely that the respiratory disturbance in itself, rather than narcolepsy, is the primary cause of daytime hypersomnolence. Obstructive sleep apnea in children is most commonly related to adeno-tonsillar enlargement, cranio-facial anomalies like the Pierre Robin syndrome, Crouzon's disease, and neuromuscular disorders like the muscular dystrophies. There is a history of habitual nocturnal snoring that is punctuated by silent periods (apnea). These silent periods are very often terminated by snorting noises. There may also be a history of the child sleeping with the mouth open (due to nasal obstruction) and nocturnal enuresis. Sleep is restless, with frequent tossing and turning. The nocturnal sleep disruption is due to frequent episodes of oxygen desaturation, which lead to arousals from sleep. The patient's daytime sleepiness, inattentiveness, and hyperactive behavior are secondary to the disrupted nocturnal sleep. Surgical correction of the upper airway obstruction, such as by tonsillectomy and/or adenoidectomy, use of continuous positive pressure ventilation, or weight loss can relieve the symptoms.

Patients with a *primary disorder of vigilance* are visibly sleepy and distractible, and show a preference for shifting activities that allow random changes in schedule. Their temperament is characteristically and prominently caring, compassionate, and affectionate (Weinberg and Brumback 1990).

*Idiopathic hypersomnia* is a disorder of presumed central nervous system origin in which the patients have a complaint of constant or recurrent hypersomnia (International Classification of Sleep Disorders 1990). Typically, the sleep episodes last longer than in most narcoleptics (one to two hours), and are composed of non-REM sleep. Polysomnographic monitoring usually demonstrates normal quality and quantity of night sleep. The multiple sleep latency test demonstrates pathological daytime sleepiness, with a mean sleep latency of fewer than ten minutes. Sleep-onset REM periods characteristic of narcolepsy, however, are not seen. HLA studies of the blood may also be helpful. Whereas most narcoleptics carry the HLA DQw15 (DR2) marker, only the HLA Cw2 incidence is elevated in individuals with idiopathic hypersomnia (Poirier et al. 1986).

The *Kleine-Levin syndrome* (recurrent hypersomnia/periodic hypersomnia) should also be ruled out in the investigation for narcolepsy. It is characterized by recurrent episodes of hypersomnia that tend to occur weeks to months apart, usually with onset around adolescence, and a male predominance (International Classification of Sleep Disorders 1990). The periods of sleepiness may be associated with a voracious appetite, increase in body weight during these periods of sleepiness, and hypersexual behavior. Nocturnal polysomnographic monitoring during the symptomatic periods shows normal sleep efficiency, reduced stages 3 and 4 of non-REM sleep, reduced sleep latency, and REM latency. The MSLT may also show a reduced mean sleep latency of fewer than ten minutes.

## Management

Narcolepsy is a life-long disorder. It is critical, therefore, that there be unequivocal clinical and electrophysiologic evidence to support the diagnosis. The pharmacological mainstay for management of narcolepsy is a combination of stimulants (for counteracting the daytime sleepiness) and a tricyclic agent (for counteracting cataplexy).

*Central nervous system stimulants* used to relieve daytime sleepiness include pemoline sodium (Cylert, 2–3 tablets per day of 37.5 mg each on an empty stomach), methylphenidate (Ritalin, 20–60 mg per day in two to three divided doses), and dextroamphetamine (Dexedrine spansules, 15–30 mg per day). These agents enhance the release of catecholamines from the presynaptic terminals, but are only modestly effective in controlling sleepiness in childhood narcolepsy (Kotagal 1990). Increasing the dose above the recommended limits rarely leads to further improvement in the level of alertness. Side effects are infrequent, but may include anorexia, difficulty in initiating night sleep, and an occasional tendency to provoke tics in patients who are genetically susceptible to developing Tourette's syndrome. Tolerance can develop to any of the stimulants, and usually requires a two- three-week drug holiday for the child, typically during the summer vacation. Modafinil (an alpha adrenergic agent), and mazindol (an imidazole derivative) may also improve daytime sleepiness, but are not as effective as amphetamines. Propranolol, L-tyrosine, and codeine have not been found to be effective in controlled clinical trials (Aldrich 1990).

Cataplexy may be relatively mild or infrequent in the early stages of childhood narcolepsy and therefore not require drug therapy. As and when it becomes more bothersome, it can be counteracted with *tricyclic agents*, which act mainly by inhibiting the reuptake of norepinephrine and serotonin rather than by cholinergic blockade. Protryptiline (Vivactil) in a dose of 2.5-5 mg per day and imipramine in a dose of 25-75 mg per day are the most commonly used medications. Specific inhibitors of serotonin reuptake, such as fluoxetine, or of norepinephrine, such as viloxazine, may be just as effective as tricyclic agents, with fewer side effects. Abrupt discontinuation of tricyclics should be avoided as it may lead to a rebound increase in cataplexy. Sleep paralysis is also generally treated with tricyclic agents.

In patients with significant nocturnal sleep disruption, Thorpy and colleagues (1992) have attempted a trial of night-time *triazolam*, a short-acting benzodiazepine. They found that it improved nocturnal sleep efficiency and the overall quality of night sleep. The degree of daytime sleepiness, however, was not altered. *Gamma hydroxybutyric acid* has also been used to enhance sleep continuity and slow wave sleep during the night. While there have been reports of some subjects having fewer daytime sleep attacks, there has been no clear objective documentation of improvement (Aldrich 1990).

*Sleep hygiene measures* that are beneficial to the narcoleptic child usually include the provision of planned daytime nap opportunities. One to two naps per day, such as upon return from school, with nap length of fifteen to twenty minutes is recommended. This helps the patient feel more alert and refreshed. Teenagers should be told to avoid alcohol and sedative drugs and to limit driving. The patient should exercise regularly, go to bed at night, and awaken from sleep in the morning at about the same time every day (Richardson 1990).

Emotional and behavioral problems are common, stemming in part from difficulties in interaction with peers as well as from impaired academic performance. Teenagers may require long-term *supportive psychotherapy*. Those with narcolepsy should be discouraged from driving because of the risk of accidents. They should be encouraged to participate in recreational physical activities. Vocational counseling efforts should direct them towards professions in which they do not place themselves or others at risk of injury, and where there is sufficient flexibility for the individual to take daytime naps. For example, a self-employed narcoleptic working as a computer specialist should be able to function quite well in society. At least two national organizations, the American Narcolepsy Association and the Narcolepsy Network provide emotional support and educational and advocacy assistance to patients with narcolepsy.

### Case Illustration

An 8-year-old girl was evaluated because of a three-month history of falling asleep while riding in a car, reading books, and talking. The naps were 60 to 120 minutes long, and were followed by her feeling tired and unrefreshed. Whenever she laughed suddenly or became excited, she would fall to the floor. If seated at a table, she would strike her head on it. She remained conscious during these events. Hypnagogic hallucinations and sleep paralysis were absent. She also snored at night. She was moderately obese (122 pounds, above the ninety-fifth percentile). The daytime sleepiness was not altered by tonsillectomy and adenoidectomy carried out a few days after the first set of sleep studies. The results of the nocturnal polysomnogram and multiple sleep latencies tests are presented in Table 13–2.

A human leukocyte antigen assay was positive for the DR2 antigen. While the initial battery of sleep studies did not provide sufficient data for the diagnosis of narcolepsy, the second battery of studies was diagnostic. The daytime sleepiness was well controlled initially with 150 milligrams per day of pemoline (Cylert). After nine

Table 13-2
Diagnostic Test Data

| | STUDY 1 | STUDY 2 |
|---|---|---|
| Nocturnal polysomnogram: | | |
| Total recording time (minutes) | 647.5 | 611 |
| Total sleep time (TST, minutes) | 524.5 | 559 |
| Sleep latency (minutes) | 18.5 | 5 |
| Latency to REM sleep (minutes) | 154.0 | 3.5 |
| Sleep efficiency (%)[2] | 81.0 | 91.5 |
| Sleep stages (as % of TST) | | |
| Stage 1 | 19.7 | 18.6 |
| Stage 2 | 23.4 | 30.1 |
| Stages 3 + 4 | 23.8 | 23.6 |
| Stage REM | 16.5 | 20.0 |
| Multiple Sleep Latency Test: | | |
| Mean sleep latency (minutes) | 10.2 | 0.4 |
| Number of REM-onset sleep periods | 0/4 | 4/4 |

Note:  1. Time interval between study 1 and study 2 was three months
2. Sleep efficiency = total sleep time/total recording time × 100

months, however, the medicine became ineffective. She was therefore switched to dexidrine spansules (fifteen milligrams each) and currently takes one capsule twice a day. While she does not fall asleep at school, she still finds herself struggling to stay awake. She takes a two-hour nap upon returning home at 3.30 P.M. Her school performance is average. There are times when she appears depressed, and starts crying without provocation. She has few friends.

## References

Aldrich, M. S. (1990). Narcolepsy. *New England Journal of Medicine* 323:389-394.

Aldrich, M. S., and Naylor M. W. (1989). Narcolepsy associated with lesions of the diencephalon. *Neurology* 39:1505-1508.

Allsopp, M. R., and Zaiwalla, Z. (1992). Narcolepsy. *Archives of Disease in Childhood* 67:302-306.

Aserinsky, E., and Kleitman, N. (1953). Regularly occurring periods of eye motility and concomitant phenomena during sleep. *Science* 118:273-274.

Baraitser, M., and Parkes, J. O. (1978). Genetic study of narcoleptic syndrome. *Journal of Medical Genetics* 15:254-259.

Billiard, M., Seignalet, J., Besset, A., and Cadilhac, J. (1986). HLA-DR2 and narcolepsy. *Sleep* 9:149–152.

Broughton, R., and Aguirre, M. (1984). Evidence for qualitatively different types of excessive daytime sleepiness. In *Sleep '84*, ed. W. P. Koella, E. Ruther, and H. Schultz, pp. 86–87. Stuttgart: Fischer Verlag.

Broughton, R., and Ghanem, Q. (1976). The impact of compound narcolepsy on the life of the patient. In *Narcolepsy:Advances in Sleep Research*, vol. 3, ed. C. Guilleminault, W. C. Dement, and P. Passouant, pp. 201–220. New York: Spectrum.

Carskadon, M. A., and Dement, W. C. (1987). Sleepiness in the normal adolescent. In *Sleep and its Disorders in Children*, ed. C. Guilleminault, pp. 53–66. New York: Raven.

Carskadon, M. A., Dement, W. C., Mitler, M. M., et al. (1986). Guidelines for the multiple sleep latency test (MSLT): a standard measure of sleepiness. *Sleep* 9:519–524.

Dement, W. C., Carskadon, M., and Ley, R. (1973). The prevalence of narcolepsy. *Sleep Res* 2:147.

Ditta, S. D., George, C. F. P., and Singh, S. M. (1992). HLA-D-region genomic DNA restriction fragments in DRw15 (DR2) familial narcolepsy. *Sleep* 15:48–57.

Douglass, A. B, Harris, L., and Pazderka, F. (1989). Monozygotic twins concordant for narcolepsy. *Neurology* 39:140–141.

Foutz, A. S., Delashaw, J. B., Guilleminault, C., and Dement, W. C. (1981). Monoaminergic mechanisms and experimental cataplexy. *Annals of Neurology* 10:369–376.

Foutz, A. S, Mitler, M. M., Cavalli-Sforza, L. L., and Dement, W. C. (1979). Genetic factors in canine narcolepsy. *Sleep* 1:413–421.

Gelineau E., (1880). De la narcolepsie. *Gaz. Hosp. Paris* 55:623

Guilleminault, C., ed. (1987). Disorders of excessive daytime sleepiness. In *Sleep and its Disorders in Children*. New York: Raven.

_____ (1989) Narcolepsy syndrome. In *Principles and Practice of Sleep Medicine*, ed. M. H. Kryger, T. Roth, and W. C. Dement, p. 339. Philadelphia: W. B. Saunders.

Guilleminault C., and Dement W. C. (1977). Amnesia and disorders of excessive daytime sleepiness. In *Neurobiology of Sleep and Memory*, ed. R. R. Drucker-Colin, and J. L. McGaugh, pp. 439–456. New York: Academic Press.

Henry, G. K., Satz, P., and Heilbronner, R. L. (1993). Evidence of a perceptual-encoding deficit in narcolepsy? *Sleep* 16:123–127.

Honda, Y. (1988). Clinical features of narcolepsy: Japanese experiences. In HLA in Narcolepsy, ed. Y. Honda, and T. Juji, pp. 24–57. Berlin: Springer-Verlag.

Honda, Y., Matsuki, K., Juji, T., and Inoka, H., (1989). Recent progress in HLA studies and a genetic model for the development of narcolepsy. Proceedings of the Third International Symposium on Narcolepsy, pp. 27–33.

International Classification of Sleep Disorders: Diagnostic and Coding Manual. (1990). Diagnostic Classification Steering Committee. Rochester, MN: American Sleep Disorders Association.

Kales, A., Cadieux, R. T., Soldatos, C. R., et al. (1982). Narcolepsy-cataplexy. I. Clinical and electrophysiologic characteristics. Archives of Neurology 39:164.

Knecht, C. D, Oliver, J. E., Redding, R., et al. (1984). Narcolepsy in a dog and a cat. Journal of the American Veterinary Medical Association 162:1052–1053.

Kotagal, S., Hartse, K. M., and Walsh, J. K. (1990). Characteristics of narcolepsy in preteenaged children. Pediatrics 85:205–209.

Langdon, N., Lock, C., Welsh, K., et al. (1986). Immune factors in narcolepsy. Sleep 9:143–148.

Lavie, P., and Peled, R., (1987). Narcolepsy is a rare disease in Israel. Sleep 10:608–609.

Lenn, N. J. (1986). HLA-DR2 in childhood narcolepsy. Pediatric Neurology 2:314–315.

Mamelak, M. (1991). A model for narcolepsy. Canadian Journal of Psychology 45:194–220.

────── (1992). A perspective on narcolepsy. Encephale 18:347–351.

Mitler, M. M., and Dement, W. C. (1974). Cataplectic-like behavior in cats after micro-injections of carbachol in pontine reticular formation. Brain Research 68:335–343

Mitler, M. M., Gujavarty, K. S., and Browman, C. P. (1982). Maintenance of wakefulness test: a polysomnographic technique for evaluating treatment efficacy in patients with excessive somnolence. Electroencephalography and Clinical Neurophysiology 53:658–661.

Montplaisir, J., de Champlain, J., Young, S. N., et al. (1982). Narcolepsy and idiopathic hypersomnia: biogenic amines and related compounds in CSF. Neurology 32:1299–1302.

Passouant, P., and Billiard, M., (1976). The evolution of narcolepsy with age. In Narcolepsy, ed. C. Guilleminault, W. C. Dement, and

P. Passouant, pp. 179–196. New York: Spectrum.

Poirier, G., Montplaisir, J., Lebrun, A., and Decary, F. (1986). HLA antigens in narcolepsy and idiopathic hypersomnolence. *Sleep* 9:153–158.

Rechtschaffen, A., and Dement, W. C. (1967). Studies on the relation of narcolepsy, cataplexy, and sleep with low voltage random EEG activity. *Research Publications—Association for Research in Nervous and Mental Disease* 45:488–505.

Richardson, J. W., Fredrickson, P. A., and Lin, S. C. (1990). Narcolepsy update. *Mayo Clinic Proceedings* 65:991–998.

Rogers, A. E, and Rosenberg, R. S. (1990). Tests of memory in narcoleptics. *Sleep* 13:42–52.

Strain, G. M., Olcott, B. M., Archer, R. M., McClintock, B. K. (1984). Narcolepsy in a Brahman bull. *Journal of the American Veterinary Medical Association* 185:538–541.

Thorpy, M. J., Snyder, M., Aloe, F. S., et al. (1992). Short-term triazolam improves nocturnal sleep of narcoleptics. *Sleep* 15:212–216.

Weinberg, W. A., and Brumback, R. A. (1990). Primary disorder of vigilance: a novel explanation of inattentiveness, daydreaming, boredom, restlessness, and sleepiness. *Journal of Pediatrics* 116:720–725.

Wittig, R., Zorick, F., Piccione, P., et al. (1983b). Narcolepsy and disturbed nocturnal sleep. *Clinical Electroencephalography* 14:130–134.

Wittig, R., Zorick, F., Roehrs, T., et al. (1983a). Narcolepsy in a 7-year-old child. *Journal of Pediatrics* 102:725–727.

Yoss, R. E., and Daly, D. D. (1957). Criteria for the diagnosis of the narcoleptic syndrome. *Mayo Clinic Proceedings* 32:320–328.

Young, D., Zorick, F., Wittig, R., et al. (1988). Narcolepsy in a pediatric population. *AJDC* 142:210–213.

Zarcone, V. (1973). Narcolepsy. *New England Journal of Medicine* 288:1156–1166.

# 14

# The Relationship of Sleep Disturbances to Childhood Panic Disorder

E. Jane Garland

## Childhood Anxiety Disorders and Disturbed Sleep

Children with anxiety disorders frequently have disturbances of initiating and maintaining sleep. Specific problems include initial insomnia, poor sleep quality with frequent wakenings, excessive movement in sleep, sleep panic attacks, and an association with night terrors and other parasomnias. Furthermore, poor sleep quality and sleep deprivation will exacerbate anxiety symptoms and increase the occurrence of panic attacks. Anxious children may develop sleep avoidance and an exaggerated concern about their inability to sleep well or the occurrence of nightmares and sleep panic attacks. Parents of anxious children often report that the sleep difficulties disrupt the whole family, and lead to angry parental responses, which then increase the child's distress.

Children assessed at psychiatric clinics are found to have a particularly high rate of sleep disorders, including restless sleep (43%), night waking (47%), and a high incidence of night terrors (19%) (Simonds and Parraga 1984). Although studies have not yet reported the rates of psychiatric disorder in children assessed in sleep clinics, adult studies report a high rate of depression and anxiety disorders in individuals assessed for sleep disturbance, especially night terrors (Kales et al. 1980, Llorente et al. 1992).

Recent research has clarified the nature of sleep disorders in anxious individuals using sleep laboratory investigations (Mellman and Uhde 1990). A variety of consistent sleep disturbances has been confirmed in studies of adult individuals who suffer panic attacks and associated anxiety symptoms, supporting the reports of anxious children and their parents regarding poor sleep quality. In addition, an unexpectedly high rate of sleep panic attacks has been recognized. The significant role of panic disorder in contributing to sleep problems has led to the coding of panic disorder separately from other anxiety disorders among the specific medical and psychiatric conditions associated with sleep disorders (Diagnostic Classification Steering Committee 1990).

Anxiety disorders are among the most common psychiatric disorders found in epidemiological surveys of both adults and children. The overall rate of anxiety disorder in childhood populations has been found to be 8.9% (Costello 1989), and as high as 12.6% in adolescent studies (McGee et al. 1990). The two most common specific anxiety disorders are separation anxiety and overanxious disorder, each with population rates ranging from three to six percent in various studies (Anderson et al. 1987, Bernstein and Borchardt 1991). Rates of panic disorder were not specifically recorded in earlier epidemiological studies of children, but are presumed to be included among the other anxiety disorders, especially the separation anxiety sample.

Anxiety disorders tend to be chronic, although one disorder may evolve into another over a child's history, reflecting different manifestations of trait anxiety at different developmental stages. The most dramatic, acute, and disabling of these disorders is panic disorder, which is likely to come to the attention of health professionals due to the impairment of function that results. Furthermore, various researchers have proposed that panic episodes underlie most other anxiety disorders as a trigger for anticipatory anxiety and associated avoidant behaviors (Gorman et al. 1989).

Panic disorder refers to the occurrence of spontaneous panic attacks at least four times in four weeks, or one panic attack followed by avoidant behavior that has persisted for a month (DSM-III-R 1987). Panic attacks are defined as acute, spontaneous episodes of severe anxiety of abrupt onset and rapidly reaching a peak severity of symptoms. At least four of the following symptoms are present: shortness of breath or smothering sensations; dizziness or faintness; palpitations or accelerated heart rate; trembling or shaking; sweating; choking; nausea or abdominal distress; depersonalization or derealization; numbness or tingling sensations; flushes or chills; chest pain or discomfort; fear of dying; and fear of going crazy or doing something uncontrolled. These attacks must not occur only in situations of exposure to specific phobic stimuli or only under social scrutiny, as in social phobia.

Occurrence of panic disorder in children was not recognized until the past decade (Van Winter and Stickler 1984). As children did not spontaneously report the classical panic attack symptoms, their clinical presentations have been in the form of separation anxiety, avoidant symptoms including agoraphobia and school refusal (Ballenger et al. 1989, Vitiello et al. 1987), complicating depression (Alessi and Magen 1988, Alessi et al. 1987), neurological symptoms that may mimic temporal lobe epilepsy (Herskowitz 1986), hyperventilation syndrome (Herman et al. 1981) and other somatic complaints (Garland and Smith 1990). The evidence for the importance of panic disorder in producing disability in children is mounting, and is stimulating more systematic research (Moreau and Weissman 1992). The propensity to develop recurrent panic attacks is a lifelong risk, and twenty percent of adult patients with panic disorder report onset in adolescence or earlier (Sheehan et al. 1981).

While the full syndrome of panic disorder is relatively uncommon, estimated as occurring in fewer than one percent of the childhood population, the high prevalence of isolated panic attacks is noted in community surveys, ranging from a low of 11.6% in ninth graders, (Hayward et al. 1989) to a high of 42.9% in one self-report study of adolescents (King et al. 1993). This finding parallels the contrast between the estimated higher rate of occasional night terrors (Kahn et al. 1989) compared to the documented rate of persistent disorder, which is estimated around three percent (Gordon 1992, Demario and Emery 1987) and tends to improve with developmental maturation. It appears that episodes of inappropriate autonomic arousal in both awake and sleep states may be within the spectrum of incidental physiological events that become pathological disorders due to frequency and severity of occurrence, as well as associated impairment of function.

Anxiety disorders in children are commonly presented to health professionals by their parents as problems of poor sleep, particularly initial insomnia associated with worrying. Bedtime worrying produces a chronic sleep disturbance in children with overanxious disorder. Panic disorder is particularly likely to produce acute symptoms of sleep disturbance due to separation anxiety and high levels of anticipatory anxiety. Furthermore, panic disorder may be complicated by sleep panic attacks, which are at the most dramatic end of the spectrum of anxiety symptoms that may disturb sleep. Sleep panic attacks provide a challenging clinical diagnostic situation as the associated symptoms may resemble those of dream anxiety disorder, of the parasomnias such as night terrors, and of the more rare disorders such as paroxysmal nocturnal dystonia or seizures occurring during sleep. The traumatizing effect of panic attacks is likely to make other sleep-related behavioral problems more pernicious.

Current research on sleep disturbances in children with panic disorder is providing an opportunity to elucidate the pathophysiology of panic attacks as well as other arousal disorders such as night terrors. The clarification of mechanisms of sleep disturbances in anxious children is leading to specific effective treatment interventions.

## Assessment and Differential Diagnosis of Sleep Problems in Anxious Children

Chronically anxious children and adolescents will usually give a history of chronic initial insomnia related to worrying. In children who also have panic attacks, more complex sleep problems are common. Even when acute panic attacks are relatively infrequent, the child is left with anticipatory anxiety, which is often associated with difficulty settling to bed and initial insomnia, as well as frequent wakings. In addition, if sleep panic attacks or night terrors occur, further disruption and sleep avoidance may develop.

The kinds of sleep disturbances seen in anxious children can span the night and the sleep stages. Effective intervention requires a careful delineation of the specific difficulties faced by these children.

### Difficulty Settling to Bed

In anxious children, this is often related to a reluctance to be left alone in bed as this is a time of worrying. Furthermore, separation anxiety frequently accompanies panic disorder in both children and adults. The high familial occurrence of panic disorder may result in an anxious parent who is having difficulties separating from, or setting limits for, an anxious child, which compounds the problem. Because children experience the anxiety as intense, physical, and very real, they may become irrationally oppositional and even violent in their efforts to avoid separation that feels life-threatening to them. Bedtime crises, often concluding with physical punishment of the child, will then reinforce everyone's dread of future bedtimes.

## Difficulty Initiating Sleep

The high arousal level of anxious children, and the tendency to obsessive worrying about past and future events, leads to difficulty falling asleep. The child's catastrophic worries about imagined failures or future disasters lead to self-arousing worry, with initial insomnia that may last hours. Frequent calling out to the parents may reinforce this wakefulness as frustrated parents come in repeatedly to try to settle the child.

## Frequent Wakings

Poorer quality of sleep, with frequent sleep movements and wakings, is well documented in individuals with panic disorder (Mellman and Uhde 1990). The complication of worrying and continued arousal after night waking may lead to middle insomnia.

## Dream Anxiety Disorder

There is no specific evidence for an increased risk of dream anxiety disorder in anxious individuals, but children with high trait anxiety are likely to have more difficulty resettling after an unpleasant dream experience.

## Sleep Panic Attacks

These are distinguished by fully waking the child from sleep with the physiological and psychological features of a panic attack, which the parents and child will recognize as similar to daytime episodes. The terrifying occurrence of these nighttime attacks may lead to sleep avoidance just as the child avoids daytime situations in which it is feared an uncontrollable panic attack may occur.

## Night Terrors and Somnambulism

Discussed in detail in Chapter 6 in this volume, night terrors, also referred to as sleep terrors or pavor nocturnus, are dramatic, acute, partial arousals from delta sleep. In a night terror, the child abruptly appears to awaken, usually in the first third of the night, with a scream or cry, and appears terrified, with signs of autonomic arousal including sweating, flushing, accelerated heart rate and respiration, confused mental state, and an affect of extreme fear or terror. The episode lasts a few minutes, with the child settling to sleep again usually within fifteen minutes. Usually the child is only partially aroused, is difficult to make contact with, and fights the parents. Recall is often absent, although fragmentary, frightening images of animals or being pursued may be remembered by the child. The child is usually inconsolable, and these events are quite frightening for parents. When these symptoms occur in anxious children, they are often interpreted as due to the anxiety. Parents become worried that the anxious child is profoundly disturbed when these events occur in addition to the daytime dysfunction. The parents' concern may further fuel the child's worry and sleep avoidance. However, the child's general lack of recall of sleepwalking and classical night terrors should distinguish these clinically from dream anxiety or nighttime panic attacks. As noted below, these distinctions may be less clear than we have assumed, and treatment interventions may overlap with those of panic disorder.

## Nocturnal Seizures

Nocturnal seizures, reviewed elsewhere in this volume, should be considered when children are having acute night wakings with behavioral disturbance. There are several reports (Schenck et al. 1989, Montagna et al. 1990, Staufenberg 1993) of apparent pavor nocturnus arising from an epileptic focus. A high percentage of children with underlying seizure disorder will also have documented nocturnal seizures, and this differentiation is complicated by the high rate of various electroencephalographic (EEG) abnormalities reported in cases of night terrors (Shouse 1987). In addition, the uncommon syndrome of paroxysmal nocturnal dystonia (Stoudemire et al. 1987, Lugaresi and Cirignotta 1981, Borrow et al. 1993) has been noted to resemble clinically both night terrors and panic attacks. While scalp EEG is normal, a presumed deeper seizure focus has been proposed, based on resemblance to frontal lobe partial complex seizures, and the response to carbamazepine. The co-occurrence of daytime panic attacks and paroxysmal nocturnal dystonia in individual patients has complicated our perceptions of the presumed distinctions (Stoudemire et al. 1987).

Distinguishing among these causes of sleep difficulty in anxious children requires a careful documentation of the timing and phenomenology of the sleep problem. Sleep problems will fall into two general categories, and the clinician will need to address key questions with the parents and child in ascertaining the cause of the sleep disturbance. The following specific issues need to be addressed with the child and his or her caretakers in order to clarify the origin of the sleep disturbance, and to determine appropriate treatment intervention.

## Difficulty Getting to Sleep

Is the difficulty getting to sleep due to avoidance of settling to bed, reinforced by lack of parental limit-setting and bedtime routines, or is this a true initial insomnia due to the child's continuous worrying? Generalized anxiety or overanxious disorder in children is characterized by initial insomnia that is due to the constant worry about future and past events. Is there separation anxiety or phobic avoidance of the dark? Has this anxious child developed the complication of a depressive episode, which typically has insomnia as a persistent symptom?

## Wakings During the Night

If sleep problems arise during the night, do these represent the more frequent wakings common in anxious children, or are these true parasomnias? Is the child having a normal number of wakings, but secondarily responds with overanxious worrying, separation anxiety, or fears of the dark? Is this waking tendency then reinforced behaviorally by parental contact? Finally, is this child having sleep panic attacks due to uncontrolled panic disorder?

Further understanding of the relationship between anxiety and sleep disorders in children requires a review of the theoretical issues and the laboratory documentation of the nature of sleep disturbances in anxious individuals. Recent research has provided a meaningful theoretical and empirical basis for treatment protocols.

## Theoretical Issues in the Relationship between Panic Disorder and Sleep Disorders in Children

Panic attacks are increasingly viewed as the physiological substrate for many anxiety disorders, including panic disorder, separation anxiety disorder, agoraphobia, and specific phobias (see Gorman et al. 1989 for review). Generalized anxiety in some individuals may represent a residual anxiety state triggered by panic attacks. Current theories regarding the origin of panic attacks focus on the failure of regulation of the locus ceruleus, the location of the alarm or "fight or flight" noradrenergic system in the brainstem. Related areas theoretically involved in this alarm response include the medullary respiratory chemoreceptors, and regulatory serotonergic neurons in the dorsal raphe nucleus. Inappropriate activation of the acute panic response may occur due to excessive sensitivity or poor regulation of these brainstem reflexes and control centers.

The trait anxiety that may underlie the tendency to panic attacks is found in the constitutional temperamental construct *behavioral inhibition to the unfamiliar* (see Biederman et al. 1993 for review). Children with this tendency, noted from birth, have a high risk of developing various childhood anxiety disorders, and show a chronically high arousal level as manifested by high baseline heart rate, tonically larger pupils, and higher salivary cortisol levels, (Kagan et al. 1990). A role for overactive noradrenergic systems has been proposed in this temperamental pattern (Kagan et al. 1988).

It is of interest that the area of the brain involved in panic disorder is also responsible for regulation of sleep and arousal. This includes the noradrenergic locus ceruleus, which needs to be inhibited for sleep to occur, and which is activated in arousal, and the serotonergic dorsal raphe nucleus in the brainstem, which when activated, promotes sleep (Jacobs 1985, Sheldon et al. 1992). Specific sleep disorders involving problems with the initiation and maintenance of sleep likely reflect poor regulation of these brainstem mechanisms. A case of night terrors arising from a brainstem tumor (Mendez 1992) supports the anatomical relationship postulated here. Parasomnias such as night terrors and somnambulism are characterized by acute partial arousal from slow wave sleep, and are proposed to be fundamentally disorders of arousal (Broughton 1968). Sleep panic attacks, occurring in individuals with high baseline arousal levels, involve an abrupt sympathetic discharge that leads to waking from slow wave sleep with symptoms similar to those noted in night terrors.

In theory, the close clinical resemblance between panic attacks and night terrors, the similarity in underlying physiological mechanisms, and the co-occurrence of these events in some patients, will lead to a better understanding of the pathophysiology of both disorders. In practical terms, the theoretical similarities have already led to the development of additional treatment strategies for children with anxiety and sleep disorders.

## Empirical Evidence Relating Panic Disorder and Sleep Disorders

The propensity to develop disabling panic attacks is a lifelong disturbance with many adults reporting childhood or adolescent onset (Sheehan et al. 1981). Once established, panic disorder has a high relapse rate and high incidence of complicating disorders such as secondary depression (Lesser et al. 1988). Evidence for the physiological basis for this vulnerability to develop panic attacks is provided by genetic twin studies, which demonstrate a strong heritability, suggestive of an autosomal dominant inheritance (Torgersen 1990). This is similar to the multigenerational occurrence of parasomnias such as night terrors and somnambulism involving disordered regulation of arousal (DiMario and Emery 1987, Hallstrom 1972, Llorente et al. 1992).

The crucial role of brainstem monoaminergic systems in the genesis of panic disorder is supported by extensive research. Panic attacks are physiological phenomena that may occur in the complete absence of triggering worries, traumas, or psychological stresses. They can be specifically provoked in vulnerable individuals by administering chemical agents that stimulate the sympathetic nervous system, such as caffeine or isoprotenerenol, by inhaling carbon dioxide, or by having an infusion of lactate (see Gorman et al. 1989 for review). These data support the presumed sensitivity of noradrenergic regulatory systems in the brainstem area, leading to a tendency for the alarm or fight-or-flight sympathetic system to discharge inappropriately. This may be associated with a sensitive medullary chemoreceptor for carbon dioxide that makes patients sensitive to small changes in respiratory physiology. Such minor fluctuations in respiratory control during the sleep cycle have been postulated to account for sleep panic attacks (Craske and Barlow 1989). This dysregulation also appears to involve serotonergic neurons in the dorsal raphe nucleus that interact with the locus ceruleus. Modulation by limbic lobe and pre-frontal cortical projections is suggested by positron emission tomography (PET) studies of panic attack sufferers, and by animal research. Finally, a role for panic attacks in "kindling" future spontaneous discharges of the locus ceruleus has been proposed, similar to the repetitive neuronal discharges in a seizure disorder. While this tendency to noradrenergic dysregulation appears to be strongly inherited (Kagan et al. 1990), the role of stressors and psychological mechanisms in determining the time of onset of the disorder itself has also received attention (Bradley and Hood 1993, Hayward et al. 1989).

The specific phenomenology and physiology of sleep panic attacks have recently been studied systematically in sleep laboratories. Nocturnal panic attacks have been reported in over 100 patients with daytime panic disorder (Craske and Barlow 1989, Krystal et al. 1991). The rate of sleep panic attacks in patients with daytime panic disorder is as high as forty percent, with more severely affected daytime panickers more likely to have nighttime episodes as well. The phenomenon of nocturnal panic attacks had received little documentation or attention until these recent studies. Other documentation of sleep panic attacks has arisen indirectly out of sleep research on panic disorder in general, with nighttime panic attacks recorded incidently (Hauri et al. 1989, Mellman and Uhde 1989b). However, the consideration of sleep panic attacks as a potential differential diagnosis is still often absent in evaluation of patients presenting primarily with a sleep disorder (Fisher et al. 1973, Schenck et al. 1989). This parallels the history of panic disorder in general, as various specialities described the phenomenology as *irritable heart*, *hyperventilation syndrome*, or neurological in origin, before recognizing that these were all manifestations of the core panic disorder, leading to the disappearance of many of these earlier terms. The now well-documented occurrence of sleep panic attacks provides a challenging diagnostic situation because of the strong resemblance to other acute parasomnias, particularly night terrors. These attacks also provide an opportunity to study panic attacks in "pure" physiological form without apparent situational stimuli.

Sleep panic attacks are clearly distinguished from dream anxiety disorder in that sleep panic consistently arises only out of slow wave, non-REM (rapid eye movement) sleep (Hauri et al. 1989, Mellman and Uhde 1989a,b,) This evidence has confirmed the theoretical construct of panic attacks as primarily physiological rather than psychological events. Furthermore, the prominent physiological symptoms rather than psychic distress in nocturnal panic attacks compared to daytime attacks in the same individual, confirms the probability that the awake individual has more cognitive and attributional elaboration on the initial physiological event of the panic attack (Craske and Barlow 1989, Hauri et al. 1989).

Clinically, sleep panic attacks greatly resemble night terrors in the appearance of terror and the physiological arousal with prominent tachycardia, sweating, and increased respiratory rate (Hauri et al. 1989). The primary distinction is the classically described lack of recall and lack of a fully awake state in night terrors. Because of the observed similarity, researchers are continuing to try to establish the distinction between sleep panic attacks and night terrors. One caution to observe in interpreting the results of this research is a potential artifact created by the method of patient selection for research protocols. Patients in research studies of *sleep panic attacks* are selected by the concurrent presence of daytime panic attacks (Craske and Barlow 1989, Hauri et al. 1989, Mellman and Uhde 1989a,b), while *night terror* patients are selected by their presentation primarily with parasomnias to sleep disorder clinics (Fisher et al. 1973, Kales et al. 1980, Llorente et al. 1992, Schenck et al. 1989). Notably, a high rate of lifetime psychiatric disturbance, particularly anxiety and depression, has been reported in the night terror cases. The most consistent clinical difference between sleep panic attacks and night terrors emphasized in these reports has been the confusional partial arousal, motor restlessness, and amnesia seen in the night terror events, compared to the sudden arousal to a fully alert state described for sleep panic attacks. It must be noted, however, that none of these studies has reported directly comparing these two groups of patients under the same laboratory conditions. The most significant polysomnographic finding reported is a distinction between night terrors and sleep panic attacks in terms of the stage of slow wave sleep in which these events are most likely to occur.

Distinguishing between these events through polysomnography has been challenging. It is clear that both sleep panic attacks and night terrors consistently occur during non-REM, slow wave sleep. It has been reported that sleep panic attacks occur more commonly during stage 2 or stage 3 or during the transition between stages of slow wave sleep (Hauri et al., 1989 Mellman and Uhde 1989a), while night terrors arise primarily in stage 3 and 4 sleep (Broughton 1968, Fisher et al.

1973). However, detailed review of these reports indicates that the sleep stage distinction between nocturnal panic attacks and night terrors has been much less consistent than researchers had hoped. In several studies, patients with well-documented daytime panic attacks have been shown to have nighttime panic attacks arising specifically out of stage 3 to 4 sleep, similar to night terrors (Lesser et al. 1985, Mellman and Uhde 1989a). Furthermore, almost seventy percent of the cases in one large series of "night terrors" were arising in multiple stages of non-REM sleep including stages 2 to 3 rather than specifically in stages 3 to 4 (Schenck et al. 1989). In addition, there was a high rate of partial recall of the "night terror" episodes, reported as well in other studies (Fisher et al. 1973).

These research observations increasingly render suspect the categorical distinctions between sleep panic attacks and night terrors. Based on the clinical, polysomnographic, and physiological similarities, further research is likely to confirm that these events are pathophysiologically related. An important question to answer will be why some individuals present only with sleep related autonomic discharges, rather than associated daytime episodes. This difference may lie in other aspects of the regulatory process, such as serotonergic modulation.

Systematic sleep studies on adult panic disorder patients have confirmed the patients' subjective impressions of poorer quality of sleep on several measures. These include increased latency to sleep onset, more frequent wakings, and more middle insomnia. In addition, increased movements during sleep and a decreased total sleep time have been noted (Grunhaus et al. 1986, Hauri et al. 1989, Mellman and Uhde 1990). Studies in anxious children have relied on parental reports of similar symptoms (Kahn 1989, Simonds and Parraga 1984), and need to be confirmed with sleep laboratory evaluation.

The clinical overlap between childhood panic disorder and night terrors has been little researched to date. Children with panic disorder may present a history of classical night terrors and somnambulism. A familial tendency to persistent night terrors has been documented (DiMario and Emery 1987, Hallstrom 1972), similar to the strong familial pattern for panic disorder. Case reports of the co-occurrence of panic disorder and night terrors in children (Garland and Smith 1991) suggest that this relationship merits further systematic documentation in both sleep clinics and childhood anxiety disorder clinics. The observed overlap between the clinical presentations and sleep physiology of night terrors and panic attacks is supported by the overlap in effective treatment strategies for both disorders (Kohen et al. 1992, Lugaresi and Cirignotta 1981, Pesikoff and Davis 1971, Stoudemire et al. 1987).

## Treatment of Sleep Disorders in Anxious Children

Treatment of sleep disturbances in anxious children requires a careful evaluation for the presence of specific components of the sleep disturbance, particularly the presence of nighttime panic attacks or the presence of daytime anxiety symptoms.

### Education of Parents

Explaining to parents the benign nature of night awakenings, especially night terrors, may be the only treatment required in some cases (Guilleminault 1987), and the reader is referred to Chapter 6 in this volume for details of the educational approach recommended. A similar approach is taken with infrequent panic attacks. In most situations, however, anxious children are enmeshed with anxious parents, and there are many parental behaviors that are reinforcing the child's difficulty settling to bed or prolonging awakenings during the night. Because of the familial occurrence of anxiety disorders, there is more risk of mutually reinforcing worry and behavioral avoidance in these families. An understanding of these reinforcement patterns is essential when eliciting parental cooperation with other recommendations.

Parents need to take into account the effect of prolonged sleep latency on total sleep time. An earlier settling time may be essential to enable an anxious child to gradually unwind and fall asleep. Sleep deprivation reduces coping ability, increases emotional instability, impairs cognitive function, and increases the risk of a subsequent daytime panic attack, thus setting up a vicious cycle that exacerbates the level of anxiety in the child and parents.

In anxious children, the global anxiety and stress level needs to be considered. There needs to be adequate daytime exercise, a calming evening routine, and care not to overburden the child with excessive extracurricular activities and high performance expectations. These tend to be children who are perfectionistic and put tremendous pressures on themselves. Worrying about performance and competence in all spheres keeps them awake at night. Consideration of strategies to promote effective problem solving, self-esteem, and stress management are part of the comprehensive treatment approach. Specific contributors to performance anxiety, such as unrecognized learning disabilities, should be considered in the overall evaluation of such a child.

## Behavior Management Strategies

Effective behavioral strategies are essential for creating bedtime routines that will reduce worry in anxious children. It should be noted that anxious children with separation anxiety may become very oppositional in their efforts to maintain the parent close by, and parents will need to be firm in order to avoid intermittent reinforcement of this behavior. The use of positive reinforcement techniques for cooperative settling at the expected time is coupled with ignoring excessive calls for parental contact, allowing extinction of the dependence on frequent parental reassurance. Star charts and prizes are dramatically effective in providing reinforcement. Charts also remind parents to reward appropriate behaviors consistently, rather than giving attention for inappropriate nighttime behaviors. Parents can be taught these skills rapidly, and they can be reinforced through parenting courses or parenting books.

## Relaxation, Self-Hypnosis, and Cognitive Strategies

The general treatment of anxious children includes teaching relaxation and self-control or self-hypnosis strategies. There are several reports of the efficacy of self-hypnosis combined with educational strategies (Kramer 1989) and with pharmacological interventions (Kohen et al. 1992) for reducing the frequency of night terrors. This approach should also be helpful in increasing the sense of self-control and reducing the baseline anxiety level in children with sleep panic attacks.

In anxious children, it is often necessary to provide extra reassurances such as night lights and a quiet radio or soft music tape to distract from worries. The use of relaxation strategies, including relaxation tapes for children or simple self-hypnosis techniques, is also helpful to distract children from their self-reinforcing worry habits. If the child wakes during the night, the parent can encourage use of the tape or relaxation strategies to facilitate resettling independent of parental contact. Reinforcement, in the form of a prize in the morning,

a star on a chart, or accumulated points, can be given for staying in the bedroom all night. The reader is referred to other chapters in this volume on bedtime resistance behavior, night frights, and anxiety dreams for details on behavioral and reassurance strategies that parents can use in these situations.

In older children, a cognitive approach can be taken to the tendency to worry and to elaborate on potential catastrophic outcomes. Children are often quite interested in exploring how worrying is further reinforced by the physical anxiety, or how their bodies react to their thoughts. It can be effective to reframe the tendency to worry as a "talent" for a creative imagination. The children are then encouraged to use their talent for problem solving, imagining more positive outcomes, or distracting themselves through active fantasy while lying in bed. An attitude of encouraging experimentation with cognitive strategies is helpful to overcome the likelihood that these children will try something once and then pessimistically conclude that it does not work, thus confirming to themselves that things cannot possibly get better. Other cognitive strategies that may be used by the child include examining and challenging these automatic negative thoughts through logic, humor, and systematic experimentation. The cognitive approach increases the sense of self-control, and counters the learned helplessness that worsens physiological anxiety and imagined catastrophic outcomes. Research has confirmed the effectiveness of cognitive behavioral therapy in adult panic and anxiety disorders (Barlow et al. 1989, Beck et al. 1992) and in reducing childhood anxiety symptoms (Kendall et al. 1988).

## Pharmacological Interventions

Antihistaminic or other sedative hypnotic agents such as chloral hydrate have been used with anxious children (Bernstein and Borchardt 1991) as well as for children with sleep disturbances (Dahl 1992). Benzodiazepines have been used to suppress night terrors in adults (Fisher et al. 1973, Schenck et al. 1989) and in young people (Popoviciu and Corfariu 1983) with some response in most patients. There is the disadvantage of daytime sleepiness and paradoxical reactions, as well as disruption of sleep architecture, with the potential for REM rebound on discontinuation.

The observation of the similarity between night terrors and panic attacks supports the earlier reported use of imipramine in children with night terrors (Pesikoff and Davis 1971). This effectiveness has been confirmed in more recent case reports (Garland and Smith 1991, Kohen et al. 1992). This is the most logical pharmacotherapy if the child also has daytime anxiety and panic attacks (Ambrosini et al. 1993, Bernstein and Borchardt 1991). Imipramine in most children will function also as a sedative hypnotic, assisting sleep onset in anxious children with initial insomnia. Daytime functioning is not impaired, and in fact imipramine is well documented to be effective in improving behavior, attention, and cognitive function in children with attention deficit hyperactivity disorder (Ambrosini et al. 1993). It has the added advantage of targeting nocturnal enuresis. Imipramine is known to have specific effects on noradrenergic activity in the locus ceruleus, but also has serotonergic effects and antihistaminic effects that promote sleep.

At imipramine doses of twenty-five to seventy-five milligrams in most school-age children, marked improvement will be seen in panic attacks, night terrors, and initial insomnia. Response is prompt, improving within a week and resolving within two to three weeks (Garland and Smith 1991, Kohen et al. 1992) An earlier study in much younger children reported the rapid benefit of doses ranging from ten to twenty-five milligrams in preschool children with night terrors (Pesikoff and Davis 1971). Generally, when the anxious child is treated with imipramine, parents will report a better quality of sleep, fewer wakenings, rapid resettling, resolution of night terrors or sleep panic attacks, and easier waking in the morning. Medication is usually continued for two to three months, tapered by dose reduction, and eventually discontinued as long as the child does not relapse. The value of low dose imipramine in "breaking the cycle" of sleep disturbances has been suggested (Dahl 1992) while other interventions of a behavioral or educational nature are being undertaken.

In children with features of obsessive compulsive disorder, often accompanied by panic attacks and initial insomnia, a more specific treatment to consider is clomipramine or agents of other antidepressant classes that have a primarily serotonergic effect (Ambrosini et al. 1993).

Finally, if there is evidence of an epileptic focus, carbamazepine is the most effective pharmacological intervention for paroxysmal nocturnal awakenings and parasomnias. This medication has also been found helpful, however, when *paroxysmal nocturnal dystonia* occurs in the absence of documented scalp EEG-supported epileptic activity even when other anticonvulsants such as valproate and benzodiazepines are ineffective (Montagna et al. 1990). There are also case reports of nonepileptic nocturnal wanderings responsive to carbamazepine (Schenk et al. 1989). The overlap between daytime panic and these paroxysmal nocturnal events (Stoudemire et al. 1987) is notable in some cases, with an equivalent response to both imipramine and carbamazepine documented. Several other researchers have found an equivalent response to imipramine and carbamazepine in acute arousals resembling night terrors (Lugaresi and Cirignotta 1981). This efficacy of carbamazepine may reflect its pharmacological similarity to the tricyclic antidepressant imipramine, rather than its anticonvulsant properties.

## Comprehensive Approach to Anxious Children with Sleep Problems

Many anxious children have strong inborn trait anxiety, manifested from infancy in the pattern of behavioral inhibition to the unfamiliar. This pattern is associated with heightened baseline arousal level, difficulties adapting to change, and a high propensity to develop anxiety disorders over a lifetime. Hence the strategies used in these children need to be viewed not only as treatment for the acute presenting disorder, but also as prevention for future sleep behavioral disturbances and sleep disorders. The comprehensive approach to these vulnerable children focuses on education of the parents, equipping parents with skills in behavior management, and empowering the child with coping strategies that will improve his or her adaptive capacity.

### Case Illustration

The following case illustrates the typical sleep disturbances of anxious children seen in a psychiatric setting and the comprehensive treatment approach required.

A 9-year-old girl was referred to a teaching hospital child psychiatric outpatient clinic with symptoms of anxiety, sleep disturbance, and intermittent "bizarre" episodes that puzzled her family doctor and worried the parents and teachers.

This child had been a colicky, difficult to soothe infant who remained fussy and fastidious throughout her childhood. She had a temperament characterized by behavioral inhibition to the unfamiliar, resulting in a cautious approach to new situations. She had a history of anxiety symptoms in the form of excessive separation anxiety from her mother, insect and animal phobias, and overanxious worries about all aspects of her life. Of her various symptoms, however, the parents found her sleep disturbances to be most disruptive to the family and most provoking of angry parental responses.

This child had been a poor sleeper throughout life. As an infant she slept for brief periods, startling and waking with the slightest noise, usually waking fussy and upset. From toddlerhood, she resisted settling to bed, and ended up sleeping with the parents many nights as her mother was too exhausted to fight with her or to tolerate her crying. As a preschooler she had several dramatic night terrors that frightened her mother and increased the amount of co-sleeping. At age 5 years, she began a period of six months of once or twice weekly episodes of somnambulism that worried the parents, as she wandered around the house and they feared for her safety. For the two years prior to assessment, she had improved in her ability to stay in her own bed at night, but lay awake worrying for several hours before falling off to sleep. She worried about problems with peers, upcoming tests and projects at school, the health and the safety of family members and herself, and the potential for a spider bite, an earthquake, or a fire to occur during the night while she was asleep. Since the age of 8, her anxiety had been exacerbated by acute episodes of physical symptoms typical of full-symptom panic attacks, including feeling scared, dizzy, and as if she were going to die or pass out, accompanied by abdominal pain, nausea, palpitations, shortness of breath, tingling of her hands and feet, numbness of her mouth, and a sense that things around her sounded and looked blurry and distorted. Her dramatic descriptions of these episodes to the parents and family doctor led them at various points to suspect a seizure disorder or even psychotic symptoms. Physical examination had been normal despite her frequent worries that she was developing some serious illness. Her only physical disorder had been migraine headaches.

At the time of referral for assessment, she continued to have bedtime resistance behaviors with severe temper tantrums and even physical fights with her mother who would then become angry and at times physically abusive. When she was finally put to bed, very late, she had prolonged latency to onset of sleep while she worried about past and potential future catastrophic events. Once asleep, she would wake frequently after one or two hours, and might try to join her parents or older sister in bed because she was "frightened." She would then want all the lights on in the room, and repeatedly check for insects, burglars, and fires in the house. On several occasions, she woke with nighttime episodes of panic similar to her daytime experiences. The net result of all of this sleep disruption was that she was only achieving a few hours of fragmented sleep, night after night, and other family members were also sleep-deprived because of her nighttime behaviors. Daytime problems of irritability, fatigue, and poor concentration, as well as crying at school, were occurring.

The family history was significant for anxiety, depression, and parasomnias as well as developmental problems. Her mother had panic disorder and secondary depression, as did the maternal grandmother. The father had intermittently abused alcohol. There was a history of alcohol abuse and depression in his parents. One of the patient's brothers had somnambulism and both brothers had learning disabilities and enuresis.

There were significant family problems that had both contributed to, and been exacerbated by, this child's problems. This child was the second of four children. The parents had chronic marital conflict for which they had received marital and parental counseling. There was inconsistent limit setting by the parents, alternating from unstructured and overly permissive, to angry and physically abusive. Maternal abusive behavior was primarily directed at this child in situations of opposition to settling at night, when the mother was exhausted, anxious, and overwhelmed herself. At the same time, the mother's own anxiety led her to be overly protective of the symptomatic child, thus reinforcing avoidant, attention-seeking, and co-sleeping behaviors.

The primary psychiatric diagnosis for this child was Overanxious Disorder with concurrent panic attacks meeting criteria for Panic Disorder. While some depressive features were present, they did not meet diagnostic criteria for a depressive disorder. The past history of separation anxiety disorder and some continued features of panic-induced separation anxiety were noted. Sleep problems were subsumed under the primary anxiety disorders, in the category of "Sleep Disorders Associated with Medical/Psychiatric Disorders"

(Diagnostic Classification Steering Committee 1990). She did have features of other sleep disorders including psychophysiological insomnia, and had a history of sleep terrors. The presenting sleep disturbances included a problem of bedtime resistance behavior that represented a combination of separation anxiety and sleep avoidance due to distressing night wakings. In addition, sleep latency appeared to reflect the overanxious worrying and high autonomic arousal characteristic of this child's temperament. Night wakings were consistent with the frequent wakings of anxious individuals, and were then prolonged by her secondary worrying once awake. There was a clear history of parasomnias, including night terrors and somnambulism earlier in life, and a current problem of occasional sleep panic attacks. There was a significant role of concurrent maternal anxiety in contributing to the level of this child's anxiety, and in providing reinforcement of avoidant and oppositional behavior. The lack of parental limit setting, physical abuse, and chaotic family structure further exacerbated the child's anxiety.

Treatment first involved educating the parents regarding the anxiety symptoms and associated sleep problems. Parent training was then provided in behavior management strategies including establishing predictable routines, consistency particularly around bedtime routines, and a specific reward system employing positive reinforcement for behaviors such as going to the bedroom at a specified time and staying in the room all night.

The child was taught several relaxation and self-soothing strategies including a brief self-hypnosis routine. A night-light and quiet classical music in her room were set up. Her tendency to excessive worry was reframed as a capacity for creative imagination, and she was encouraged to use this in a positive way to control her own worry. For example, she was instructed to set aside a specific "worry time" for fifteen minutes each evening, and thereafter to place any leftover worries that came up in her mind into a mental treasure chest that she could close and lock to keep these worries safe. Over several sessions, she was also coached in the more elaborate active imagination of a "special place" she could imagine herself in to create a feeling of calm and comfort.

The child's symptoms greatly improved over four to six weeks with these parental and individual interventions. Maternal anger and physical abuse completely resolved. Additional marital counseling was recommended regarding the serious marital problems.

Although bedtime resistance and separation anxiety during the night were largely resolved, there was persistent sleep latency of several hours associated with worrying, and daytime panic attacks up to once a week as well as classical migraines at intervals of every few weeks. At this point, twenty-five milligrams of imipramine were added an hour before bedtime, increasing to fifty milligrams after a week. Initial insomnia was reduced to half an hour, panic attacks resolved completely, and migraine frequency decreased to once every few months. This medication reduced worrying at bedtime, reduced sleep latency, and reduced night wakening. Daytime coping at school improved as well. While she remained rigid and perfectionistic, she was a much easier child to parent. Medication was continued for six months, and then tapered and discontinued with sustained gains, although migraine frequency increased again.

The subsequent course of this child's symptoms is notable. Two years later, at age 11, she presented with a major depressive episode. This was associated with initial insomnia as well as early morning awakening of several hours' duration, and an increase in obsessive compulsive features. Intervention included cognitive therapy and imipramine at a higher dose of 100 milligrams daily. However, persistent panic attack episodes and disabling obsessions regarding her risk of contracting various diseases did not fully remit until the medication was changed to clomipramine. Full remission of all symptoms occurred within two months. The parents and teachers also noted that she seemed generally more flexible and less of a perfectionist in all activities after clomipramine therapy was initiated. Medication was continued for nine months and then reduced to a low maintenance dose.

This case illustrates the multiple sleep problems that anxious children may present. The typical family history and constitution of the anxious child are illustrated, as well as the role of concurrent parental anxiety in exacerbating the symptoms. Sleep disturbances, as in this case, may be damaging to family function and relationships, and may also be symptomatic of a primary psychiatric disorder. This child's symptoms illustrate the chronic poor sleep quality, the temperamental features, the associated episodes of panic disorder, and the parasomnia history of many anxious children. Treatment combined educational, behavioral, cognitive, and pharmacological interventions. The high risk of recurrent or additional anxiety and mood disorders is also demonstrated in this case.

## Summary

Anxious children have a high rate of complex sleep disturbances, often involving difficulty settling, frequent waking, and nighttime behavioral problems associated with sleep resistance and separation anxiety. Because of the chronicity of anxiety disorders and the frequent co-occurrence of an anxiety disorder in the parents, these sleep disturbances may be tenacious and chronic. Anxiety-associated sleep disturbances will respond to the educational and behavioral interventions for other sleep-associated behavior problems, but may require the adjunctive use of pharmacotherapy.

Recent research has examined the specific occurrence of sleep panic attacks and the associated occurrence of parasomnias such as night terrors and somnambulism in anxious children. The theoretical pathophysiological relationships between panic attacks and night terrors are being evaluated in current research. Our understanding of the shared noradrenergic dysregulation in panic disorder and night terrors is being applied in the development of alternative pharmacological interventions for night terrors.

## References

Alessi, N. E., and Magen, J. (1988). Panic disorder in psychiatrically hospitalized children. *American Journal of Psychiatry* 145:1450-1452.

Alessi, N. E., Robbins, D. R., and Dilsaver, S. C. (1987). Panic and depressive disorders among psychiatrically hospitalized adolescents. *Psychiatry Research* 20:275-283.

Ambrosini, P. J., Bianchi, M. D., Rabinovich, H., and Elia, J. (1993). Antidepressant treatments in children and adolescents II: anxiety, physical and behavioral disorders. *Journal of the American Academy of Child and Adolescent Psychiatry* 32:483-493.

Anderson, J. C., Williams, S., McGee, R., and Silva, P. A. (1987). DSM-III disorders in preadolescent children. *Archives of General Psychiatry* 44:69-76.

Ballenger, J. C., Carek, D. J., Steele, J. J., and Cornish-McTighe, D. (1989). Three cases of panic disorder with agoraphobia in children. *American Journal of Psychiatry* 146:922-924.

Barlow, D. H., Craske, M. G., Cerny, J. A., and Klosko, J. S. (1989). Behavioral treatment of panic disorder. *Behavior Therapy* 20:261-282.

Beck, A. T., Sokol, L., Clark, D. A., et al. (1992). A crossover study of focused cognitive therapy for panic disorder. *American Journal of Psychiatry* 149:778-783.

Bernstein, G. A., and Borchardt, C. M. (1991). Anxiety disorders of childhood and adolescence: a critical review. *Journal of the American Academy of Child and Adolescent Psychiatry* 30:519-532.

Biederman, J., Rosenbaum, J. F., Bolduc-Murphy, E. A., et al. (1993). Behavioral inhibition as a temperamental risk factor for anxiety disorders. *Child and Adolescent Psychiatric Clinics of North America* 2:667-683.

Borrow, S., Hartman, D., Sedgwick, P., et al. (1993) Consider paroxysmal nocturnal dystonia. *British Medical Journal* 306:1476-1477.

Bradley, S. J., and Hood, J. (1993). Psychiatrically referred adolescents with panic attacks: presenting symptoms, stressors and comorbidity. *Journal of the American Academy of Child and Adolescent Psychiatry* 32:826-829.

Broughton, R. J. (1968). Sleep disorders: disorders of arousal? *Science* 159:1070-1078.

Costello, E. J. (1989). Child psychiatric disorders and their correlates: a primary care pediatric sample. *Journal of the American Academy of Child and Adolescent Psychiatry* 28:851-855.

Craske, M. G., and Barlow, D. H. (1989). Nocturnal panic. *Journal of Nervous and Mental Disorders* 177:160-167.

Dahl, R. E. (1992). The pharmacological treatment of sleep disorders. *Psychiatric Clinics of North America* 15:161-178.

DiMario, F. J., and Emery, E. S. (1987). The natural history of night terrors. *Clinical Pediatrics* 26:505-511.

Diagnostic Classification Steering Committee (1990). *The International Classification of Sleep Disorders: Diagnostic and Coding Manual*, Rochester, MN: American Sleep Disorders Association.

*Diagnostic and Statistical Manual for Mental Disorders* (1987). 3rd. ed. Revised. Washington, D.C.: American Psychiatric Association.

Fisher, C., Kahn, E., Edwards, A., and Davis, D. M. (1973). A psychophysiological study of nightmares and night terrors. *Archives of General Psychiatry* 28:252-259.

Garland, E. J., and Smith, D. H. (1990). Panic disorder on a child psychiatric consultation service. *Journal of the American Academy of Child and Adolescent Psychiatry* 29:785-788.

_____ (1991). Simultaneous prepubertal onset of panic disorder, night terrors and somnambulism. *Journal of the American Academy of Child and Adolescent Psychiatry* 30:553-555.

Gordon, N. (1992). The more unusual sleep disturbances of childhood. *Brain Development* 14:182-184.

Gorman, J. M., Liebowitz, M. R., Fyer, A. J., and Stein, J. (1989). A neuroanatomical hypothesis for panic disorder. *American Journal of Psychiatry* 146:148-161.

Grunhaus, L., Rabin, D., Harel, Y., et al. (1986). Simultaneous panic and depressive disorders: clinical and sleep EEG correlates. *Psychiatry Research* 17:251-259.

Guilleminault, C., ed. (1987). Disorders of arousal in children: somnambulism and night terrors. In *Sleep and its Disorders in Children*, pp. 243-252. New York: Raven.

Hallstrom, T. (1972). Night terror in adults through three generations. *Acta Psychiatrica Scandinavica* 48:350-352.

Hauri, P. J., Friedman, M., and Ravis, C. L. (1989). Sleep in patients with spontaneous panic attacks. *Sleep* 12:323-337.

Hayward, C., Killen, J. D., and Taylor, C. B. (1989). Panic attacks in young adolescents. *American Journal of Psychiatry* 146:1061-1062.

Herman, S. P., Stickler, G. B., and Lucas, A. R. (1981). Hyperventilation syndrome in children and adolescents: long term follow-up study. *Pediatrics* 76:183-187.

Herskowitz, J. (1986). Neurological presentations of panic disorder in childhood and adolescence. *Developmental Medicine and Child Neurology* 28:617-623.

Jacobs, B. L. (1985). Overview of the activity of brain monoaminergic neurons across the sleep–wake cycle. In *Sleep: Neurotransmitters and Neuromodulators*, ed. A. Wauquier, J. M. Gaillard, J. M. Monti, and M. Radulovacki, pp. 1-14. New York: Raven.

Kagan, J., Reznick, J. S., and Snidman, N. (1988). Childhood derivatives of inhibition and lack of inhibition to the unfamiliar. *Child Development* 59:1580-1589.

Kagan, J., Reznick, J. S., Snidman, N., et al. (1990). Origins of Panic Disorder. In *Frontiers of Clinical Neuroscience, Volume 8: Neurobiology of Panic Disorder*, ed. J. C. Ballenger, pp. 71-87. New York: Wiley-Liss.

Kahn, A., Van de Merckt, C., Rebuffat, E., et al. (1989). Sleep problems in healthy preadolescents. *Pediatrics* 84:542-546.

Kales, J. D., Kales, A., Soldatos, C. R., et al. (1980). Night terrors:

clinical characteristics and personality patterns. *Archives of General Psychiatry* 37:1413-1417.

Kendall, P. C., Howard, B. L., and Epps, J. (1988). The anxious child: cognitive-behavioral treatment strategies. *Behavior Modification* 12:281-310.

King, N. J., Gullone, E., Tonge, B. J., and Ollendeck, T. H. (1993). Self-reports of panic attacks and manifest anxiety in adolescents. *Behavior Research and Therapy* 31:111-116.

Kohen, D. P., Mahowald, M. W., and Rosen, G. M. (1992). Sleep terror disorder in children: the role of self-hypnosis in management. *American Journal of Clinical Hypnosis* 34:233-244.

Kramer, R. L. (1989). The treatment of childhood onset night terrors through the use of hypnosis—a case study. *International Journal of Clinical and Experimental Hypnosis* 37:283-284.

Krystal, J. H., Woods, S. W., Hill, C. L., and Charney, D. S. (1991). Characteristics of panic attack subtypes: assessment of spontaneous panic, situational panic, sleep panic and limited symptom attacks. *Comprehensive Psychiatry* 32:474-480.

Lesser, I. M., Poland, R. E., Holcomb, C., and Rose, D. E. (1985). Electroencephalographic study of nighttime panic attacks. *Journal of Nervous and Mental Disease* 173:744-746.

Lesser I. M., Rubin, R. T., Pecknold, J. C., et al. (1988). Secondary depression in panic disorder and agoraphobia. *Archives of General Psychiatry* 45:437-443.

Llorente, M. D., Currier, M. B., Norman, S. E., and Mellman, T. A. (1992). Night terrors in adults: phenomenology and relationship to psychopathology. *Journal of Clinical Psychiatry* 53:392-394.

Lugaresi, E., and Cirignotta, F. (1981). Hypnogenic paroxysmal dystonia: epileptic seizure or a new syndrome? *Sleep* 4:129-138.

McGee, R., Feehan, M., Williams, S., et al. (1990). DSM-III disorders in a large sample of adolescents. *Journal of the American Academy of Child and Adolescent Psychiatry* 29:611-619.

Mellman, T. A. and Uhde, T. W. (1989a). Electroencephalographic sleep in panic disorder. *Archives of General Psychiatry* 46:178-184.

_____ (1989b). Sleep panic attacks: new clinical findings and theoretical implications. *American Journal of Psychiatry* 146:1204-1207.

_____ (1990). Sleep in panic and generalized anxiety disorders. In *Frontiers of Clinical Neuroscience, Volume 8: Neurobiology of Panic Disorder*, ed. J. C. Ballenger, pp. 365-376. New York:Wiley-Liss.

Mendez, M. F. (1992). Pavor nocturnus from a brainstem glioma.

Journal of Neurology Neurosurgery and Psychiatry 55:860.

Montagna, P., Sforza, E., Tinuper, P., et al. (1990). Paroxysmal arousals during sleep. Neurology 40:1063–1066.

Moreau, D., and Weissman, M. (1992). Panic disorder in children and adolescents: a review. American Journal of Psychiatry 149:1306–1314.

Pesikoff, R. B., and Davis, P. C. (1971). Treatment of pavor nocturnus and somnambulism in children. American Journal of Psychiatry 128:778–781.

Popoviciu, L., and Corfariu, O. (1983). Efficacy and safety of midazolam in the treatment of night terrors in children. British Journal of Clinical Pharmacology 16:975–1025.

Schenck, C. H., Milner, D. M., Hurwitz, T. D., et al. (1989). A polysomnographic and clinical report on sleep-related injury in 100 adult patients. American Journal of Psychiatry 146:1166–1173.

Sheehan, D. V., Sheehan, K. E., and Minchiello, W. E. (1981). Age of onset of phobic disorders: a re-evaluation. Comprehensive Psychiatry 22:544–553.

Sheldon, S. H., Spire, J.-P., and Levy, H. B. (1992). Anatomy of sleep. In Pediatric Sleep Medicine, pp. 37–45. Philadelphia: W. B. Saunders.

Shouse, M. N. (1987). Sleep, sleep disorders and epilepsy in children. In Sleep and Its Disorders in Children, ed. C. Guilleminault, pp. 291–307. New York: Raven.

Simonds, J. F. and Parraga, H. (1984). Sleep behaviors and disorders in children and adolescents evaluated at psychiatric clinics. Developmental and Behavioral Pediatrics 5:6–10.

Staufenberg, E. F. A. (1993). Sleep disorders: epilepsy a differential diagnosis in children. British Medical Journal 306:1476.

Stoudemire, A., Ninan, P. T., and Wooten, V. (1987). Hypnogenic paroxysmal dystonia with panic attacks responsive to drug therapy. Psychosomatics 28:280–281.

Torgersen, S. (1990). Twin studies in panic disorder. In Frontiers of Clinical Neuroscience Volume 8: Neurobiology of Panic Disorder, ed. J. C. Ballenger, pp. 51–58. New York: Wiley-Liss.

Van Winter, J. T., and Stickler, G. B. (1984). Panic attack syndrome. Journal of Pediatrics 105:661–665.

Vitiello, B., Behar, D., Wolfson, S., and Delaney, M. A. (1987). Panic disorder in prepubertal children. American Journal of Psychiatry 144:525–526.

# 15

# Treatment of Multiple Sleep Disorders in Children

V. Mark Durand
Jodi Mindell
Eileen Mapstone
Peter Gernert-Dott

Children often display more than one type of sleep-related problem. It is common for a clinician to be confronted by a child who will not go to sleep at bedtime, who wakes crying frequently throughout the night, and who may have other problems surrounding sleep (e.g., bruxism, nightmares, sleep terrors). This chapter highlights the issues and unique problems that accompany attempts to treat children who have multiple sleep problems. As we discuss, providing treatment to children who have more than one sleep problem involves more than just the application of multiple interventions. Coordinating treatment efforts requires a knowledge of the biological and behavioral influences that affect sleep, as well as the social and cultural factors that impact on intervention strategies.

Throughout this chapter we use the *International Classification of Sleep Disorders* (ICSD) (American Sleep Disorders Association 1990) to refer to the specific disorders. Of these disorders, children will display most of the same sleep problems experienced by adults—including insomnia, narcolepsy, sleepwalking, and confusional arousals. In addition, several problems are specific to children and should be considered when evaluating each case. *Limit-setting sleep disorder*, for example, is primarily a sleep problem observed among children and is characterized by stalling or refusing to go to bed. It is assumed that the cause of this problem is extrinsic to the child, and involves a failure on the part of the parent or caretaker to enforce bedtime. Another disorder that is primarily (but not exclusively) a sleep disorder in childhood is referred to as *sleep-onset association disorder*. Here sleep onset is impaired when certain objects or circumstances that are usually associated with bedtime are changed or absent. The unavailability of a favorite toy or the absence of a parent can disrupt initial sleep onset and can result in excessive night waking. *Nocturnal eating (drinking) syndrome* involves recurrent awakenings and the inability to return to sleep without eating or drinking. Among young children, this problem usually arises when an association is made between bedtime and nursing and when large amounts of food/drink are consumed during wakings.

### Prevalence

Sleep disturbances are highly prevalent among children, with overall estimates placed at at least 25% of all children (Mindell 1993). There appears to be a great deal of overlap in the prevalence of the various sleep disorders, suggesting that most children exhibit two or more sleep disturbances. For example, Salzarulo and Chevalier (1983) report the following percentages of sleep problems among a group of children age 2 to 15: sleep talking (32%), nightmares (31%), night waking (28%), bedtime problems (23%), and sleep terrors (7%). In a second study, an overall estimate of parasomnias was approximately 29%, with sleep walking estimated at 5%, and nighttime fears at 15% (Kahn et al. 1989).

### Assessment and Differential Diagnosis

A thorough evaluation of multiple sleep disorders is similar in nature to the assessment of a single sleep disorder. As we have noted, the majority of individuals has more than one sleep problem. It is rare, for example, that a person has just apnea or just periodic limb movements. Therefore, clinicians are advised to approach an assessment expecting to find multiple sleep problems rather than taking the tack of searching for a single disorder. The latter approach may lead to missed diagnoses as once one problem is identified no further assessment takes place. A brief outline of the steps of a comprehensive sleep assessment is supplied, although more detailed information about each sleep disorder can be found in pertinent chapters elsewhere in this book.

First, a complete sleep history should be conducted. All aspects of the sleep–wake cycle need to be reviewed. Areas that need to be addressed include evening activities such as television watching, intake of caffeinated beverages, bedtime, and bedtime routines. Areas to be evaluated during the night include latency to sleep onset, the number and duration of nighttime awakenings, and behaviors during the night. Details about abnormal nighttime events should be collected, such as night terrors, confusional arousals, respiratory disturbances, seizures, and enuresis. In the morning, the time of awakening, sleepiness, and initial behaviors upon arising should be evaluated. During the day, sleepiness, naps, and behavior problems should be assessed. A review of psychological symptoms during the day is also important. Symptoms of anxiety and depression can be the result of lack of sleep, as can fatigue, irritability, and sluggishness. Medication intake should also be reviewed as many drugs affect sleep.

The second step in the evaluation of sleep problems is the keeping of sleep diaries. Sleep diaries typically include information on bedtime, latency to sleep onset, number and duration of night wakings, time awake in the morning, total sleep time, and time and duration of naps. Two weeks of baseline data are the most useful so that sleep patterns can be clearly evaluated. Clinicians are cautioned, however, when relying solely on reports from parents for sleep problems. Recent data suggest that parents, whether through fatigue or other factors, may underreport the sleep problems of their children (Sadeh 1994).

In cases in which there is a concern about a specific underlying physiological problem such as with sleep apnea, narcolepsy, epilepsy, or periodic limb movements, a polysomnogram (PSG) is an essential component of assessment. Even in some cases in which the child does not report any physiological symptoms it may be important to evaluate completely the person's sleep. For example, many parents are unaware of their child's snore arousals or sleep apnea which may be interrupting sleep and resulting in complaints of insomnia, frequent night wakings, and daytime sleepiness. Polysomnography typically consists of an overnight sleep study in which recordings of oxygen saturation, nasal and oral airflow, thoracic and abdominal respiratory movements, limb muscle activity, and electroencephalogram (EEG) are taken. As an adjunct to a PSG, a multiple sleep latency test (MSLT), which evaluates the child's level of daytime sleepiness, may be conducted. The MSLT consists of four twenty-minute nap opportunities given at two-hour intervals throughout the day following the overnight study. Measures of latency to sleep onset are obtained as an index of sleepiness. Most PSGs and MSLTs are conducted at accredited sleep disorders centers.

Another important aspect of assessment of sleep disorders is a thorough evaluation of daytime functioning and other psychological problems. Behavioral or psychological problems may be contributing factors to a sleep disorder. For example, significant life stressors may be related to acute sleep problems. Failure in school, death in the family, or a recent move can all contribute to a sleep problem that resembles insomnia. A thorough evaluation should include questioning about school performance, social functioning, and family functioning. A recent change in a family's financial status can result in sleep problems among children even if the parents do not believe that the child is aware of such problems. Often children, and especially adolescents, are much more aware of tensions in a family than are the parents. It is important, therefore, that a complete assessment of all aspects of sleep and daytime functioning be conducted.

Regarding differential diagnosis, the presenting complaints for many of the sleep disorders are similar. For example, excessive daytime sleepiness may be the result of insomnia, sleep apnea, or narcolepsy. Night wakings may be a sleep onset association disorder, or result from sleep apnea, periodic limb movements in sleep, or night terrors. It is clear, then, that a focus on differential diagnosis in the area of sleep disorders is essential.

Differentiation between a sleep disorder and other medical or psychological problems is also important. A child with what looks like night terrors may actually be having seizures during sleep. In other cases, difficulties at bedtime may be symptomatic of more general problems with noncompliance. Nighttime fears may be just one symptom of a child with extensive fears. Furthermore, delayed sleep phase syndrome should always be assessed before a diagnosis of school refusal is made. Given the similar characteristics of each disorder, it is likely that delayed sleep phase disorder may present as school refusal, especially among adolescents, who constitute the majority of individuals with this sleep disorder.

Finally, a brief review of parental expectations of their child's sleep is also important. The "sleep culture" of the family—beliefs about appropriate bedtimes, where the child will sleep (alone, in bed with the parent), the appropriateness of naps—will often impact on the sleep problem itself as well as the outcome of treatment approaches. Sometimes minor problems can be resolved by educating parents about the range of sleep needs among children (i.e., not all children need eight or more hours of sleep) and about options for nighttime routines, appropriate bedtimes, naps, and so on.

## An Integrated Multidimensional Model of Sleep Disorders

As our science progresses, along with our understanding of multiple influences on children's sleep problems, a complex picture of these disorders begins to develop. It is clear from our discussion of assessment issues that biology—the physiological mechanisms that underlie the sleep problems—interacts with cognitive, behavioral/interpersonal, developmental, and even cultural dimensions to create the sleep problem that is presented to the clinician (Anders et al. 1992, Blampied and France 1993). This multidimensional view of sleep problems mirrors recent work with other disorders, such as depression, substance abuse, and anxiety, and reflects our growing understanding of how biology and other factors interact (Barlow and Durand in press).

This integrated multidimensional view of sleep disorders has several assumptions. The first assumption is that at some level, *both biological and non-biological factors will be present* in most cases of sleep problems. For example, a child who has frequent night waking may have a disruption in her sleep cycles such that she is likely to have full instead of partial waking during the night (Anders 1979, Ferber and Boyle 1983). At the same time, parental interactions surrounding bedtime and this waking will also affect this pattern. For example, a recent study found that children of parents who were present when the children fell asleep were more likely to wake during the night (Adair et al. 1991).

A second assumption held by this model is that these multiple factors are *reciprocally related*. One example of this reciprocal relationship can be seen in the study we just described on parental presence at bedtime. Adair and colleagues observed that parents were more likely to be present at the bedtime of children who had frequent night waking (Adair et al. 1991). However, they also noted that child temperament may have played a role in this relationship. It was found that children with more difficult temperaments were more likely to have their parents present at bedtime—presumably to attend to sleep initiation difficulties. One explanation of these findings is that parental presence at bedtime does influence night waking, but that this will more likely occur among infants with difficult temperaments. In other words, sleep difficulties, parental reaction to these difficulties, and personality characteristics of the child (e.g., difficult temperament) interact in a reciprocal manner to produce and maintain these sleep problems. An adequate explanation of sleep disorders must account for all of these findings.

To help illustrate this model in a preliminary way, we present a schematic in Figure 15–1. The diagram shows how children are biologically vulnerable to having disturbed sleep patterns. This vulnerability differs from child to child and can range from mild to more severe disturbances. For example, a child may be easily aroused at night, more commonly known as being a light sleeper. Or, he or she may have a family history of insomnia, narcolepsy, or obstructed breathing or may be of an age more vulnerable to sleep problems, such as among some infants. All of these factors can make a child vulnerable to sleeping problems. These influences have been referred to by others as *predisposing conditions* (Spielman and Glovinsky 1991), and they may not, by themselves, always cause sleep problems, but may combine with other factors to interfere with sleep.

Interacting with this biological vulnerability is the occurrence of what we refer to as *sleep stress*. Sleep stress includes a number of events that can negatively impact on sleep. For example, many of the children we work with have no usual bedtime routine and engage in many of the poor "sleep hygiene" habits that we know interfere with the initiation of sleep (Hauri 1991). In addition, a number of the parents of children who are referred for sleep problems often have unusual sleep habits themselves. It is common for some of these parents to work late into the evening (e.g., working night shifts at a restaurant) or to be up very early in the morning (e.g., working on a farm). This may indicate a familial pattern of disturbed sleep that leads adults into these occupations, but it also appears to serve as an additional stress on the child's sleep, which can be impacted negatively by the coming and going of people during expected sleep time for the child.

Cultural influences will also impact on sleep patterns. For example, the predominant culture in the United States appears to expect infants to sleep on their own, in a separate bed and, if available, in a separate room. However, other cultures as diverse as those from rural Guatemala to urban Japan expect the young child to spend the first few years of life in the same room and sometimes in the same bed as the mother (Morelli et al. 1992). As a result, families in these cultures

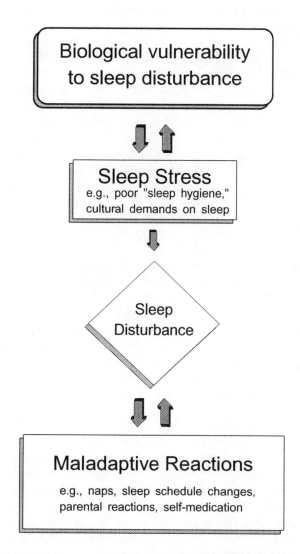

Figure 15-1: Integrative Multidimensional Model of Sleep Disturbance.

infrequently report bedtime problems such as limit-setting sleep disorder.

In a recent study, for example, researchers questioned fourteen mothers from a Mayan village and eighteen middle-class mothers from the United States, each of whom had a young child (Morelli et al. 1992). In contrast to the U.S. mothers, the Mayan mothers had their infants and toddlers sleep with them for several years. They reported that this sleeping arrangement helped them to create a close bond with their children, and usually resulted in few bedtime problems. Similarly, a recent study in Korea found that 98% of Korean mothers had their infants sleep with them (Lee 1992). The study also found that out of 218 mothers questioned, only one said that she ignored the cries of her child. This is in stark contrast to parents in the U.S., where most pediatricians recommend that parents ignore the cries of their infants at night (Ferber 1985). One view of this type of research is that sleep problems can be negatively impacted by cultural demands, such as in the United States. These sleep demands can serve as an additional sleep stress that will affect the ultimate sleep outcome of children.

It is important to point out that biological vulnerability and sleep stress influence each other reciprocally (as noted by the double arrows in Figure 15-1). Although it may be most intuitive to think of biological factors coming first, extrinsic influences such as poor sleep hygiene also impact on the physiology of sleep. One of the most striking examples of this phenomenon is jet lag, in which the act of flying across different time zones can seriously disrupt sleep patterns. Among children, sleep stress such as vacations (during which sleep schedules are significantly modified) or visits from relatives can disturb previously normal sleep habits.

The combination of biological vulnerability and sleep stress may create one or more sleep disturbances. However, whether or not these disturbances continue or become more severe may depend on how they are managed. For example, many people will react to disrupted sleep by taking over-the-counter sleeping pills. Unfortunately, most people are not aware of the *rebound effect* that occurs after they stop taking these medications. Once these medications are stopped, many people will experience an exacerbation in sleep disruption above baseline levels that is caused by the withdrawal of the medication. This rebound leads people to think they still have a sleep problem, re-administer the medicine, and go through this vicious cycle over and over again. In other words, taking sleep aids can be a perpetuating factor in sleep problems.

Other ways people react to poor sleep can also prolong these problems. For example, if a child hasn't had enough sleep, it seems reasonable that he or she make up for this loss of sleep by taking naps during the day. Unfortunately, this may make the child feel rested that day, but it will also disrupt sleep the next night. Anxious thoughts can help to extend this problem. Lying in bed worrying about school, about family problems, or even about not being able to sleep will interfere with sleep (Morin 1993). For children, the behavior of their parents can also help to maintain these problems. Giving children a great deal of positive attention at night when they wake up can cause them to wake up during the night more often (Durand and Mindell 1990). These maladaptive reactions, when combined with sleep stress (e.g., disrupted sleep schedule) and a biological predisposition for sleep problems may explain why children have continuing problems with their sleep (Morin 1993, Spielman and Glovinsky 1991). Following a brief review of the research on treatment, we return to this model as we discuss treatment approaches to multiple sleep problems.

## Treatment Research

There is an increasing number of both biological and behavioral strategies used to intervene with children's sleep problems. We next briefly review the more widely used of these interventions and their effects on a variety of sleep problems experienced by children.

## Medical Interventions

The most widely used treatment strategy for sleep problems is medical. For example, Ounsted and Hendrick (1977) report that by 18 months, 25% of first-born children have been prescribed sedatives. An extensive literature exists concerning the pharmacological treatment of sleep disorders in adults, yet few studies have involved treating children with drugs affecting sleep. Many sources (e.g., American Academy of Child and Adolescent Psychiatry 1991, Kales et al. 1987, McDaniel 1986) recommend drug therapy as an adjunctive effort to behavioral treatments only when sleep problems are extreme and chronic.

The sedating effect of the antihistamine diphenhydramine has been used to reduce sleep onset latency. In a sample of fifty 2- to 12-year-old children, Russo and colleagues (1976) found that diphenhydramine reduced sleep latency significantly more than placebo and in only 4% of the sample was it associated with minimal side effects. In addition, treatment with diphenhydramine was associated with a significant reduction in the number of night wakings in children with this sleep difficulty (Russo et al. 1976). Diphenhydramine has also been suggested for treating nightmares and night terrors in children (Herskowitz and Rosman 1982). However, evidence exists that it does not significantly reduce the frequency of these disturbances when compared to placebo (Russo et al. 1976). Hollister (1978) cautions that, while diphenhydramine may be an effective hypnotic, it is associated with some unpleasant anticholinergic side effects and is difficult to manage in the event of an overdose. In many cases, benzodiazepines may be more appropriate.

The primary use of benzodiazepines with children has been in the treatment of night terrors. These drugs tend to suppress stage 4 non-REM sleep, the stage when night terrors most often occur (Herskowitz and Rosman 1982). In a placebo-controlled study of fifteen hospitalized 6- to 15-year-olds, Popoviciu and Corfariu (1983) suppressed night terrors in all but one of their subjects using midazolam. The authors also noted an overall decrease in the frequency of nocturnal arousals and no reported side effects. Unfortunately, follow-up data were not available. Effective reduction of night terrors has also been associated with alprazolam (Cameron and Thyer 1985) and diazepam (Fisher et al. 1973, Glick et al. 1971). Noting relatively few side effects, McDaniel (1986) considers diazepam to be "the drug of first choice" (p. 71) in the pharmacological treatment of night terrors.

However, the use of benzodiazepines has several drawbacks. Discontinuation of drug treatment is often associated with a recurrence of sleep disturbances (American Academy of Child and Adolescent Psychiatry 1991, Fisher et al. 1973, Glick et al. 1971, Kales et al. 1974). Adverse side effects including daytime sedation, cognitive and performance deficits, abuse, or dependence may occur in children treated with benzodiazepines (Coffey 1993). In adult samples, rebound effects have been reported following drug discontinuation (Kales et al. 1979). Suppression of REM sleep increases with intermediate and long-term use of benzodiazepines although the REM duration eventually returns to baseline levels after discontinuation (Kales et al. 1974). In light of the generally short duration of therapeutic effects and the potential side effects, the efficacy of benzodiazepine treatment remains controversial. The tricyclic antidepressant imipramine has been used to treat sleep terrors in children. The mechanism by which imipramine works for this disorder is not known but, unlike the benzodiazepines, there is no reduction of stage 4 sleep. Imipramine treatment has been associated with a temporary reduction of sleep terrors in children (Pesikoff and Davis 1971). However, this evidence was weakened by the lack of a control group in the study. Reduction of sleep terrors was also reported using a combined treatment with imipramine, relaxation, and self-hypnosis (Kohen et al. 1992). However, the authors noted similar success when imipramine was excluded from the treatment protocol. Pesikoff and Davis (1971) warned that the risk of overdosage with imipramine is considerable and must be considered carefully before prescribing the drug.

The hypnotic, trimeprazine tartrate, has been used as a treatment for sleep disturbances in children. France and colleagues (1991) reported an abrupt decrease in sleep disturbances for children receiving a combination of drug treatment and behavioral extinction. Children receiving extinction with placebo or extinction alone did not respond as quickly but reached the same low frequency of nightly disturbance as the drug group. Trimeprazine tartrate alone was shown to be superior to placebo in reducing the frequency of night wakings in a sample of 1- to 3-year-old children (Simonoff and Stores 1987). In a double-blind study of children treated with this drug, Richman (1985) reported a significant but "not clinically striking" (p. 596) decrease in the number of night wakings in 66% of her subjects. One third showed no improvement and a six-month follow-up of all subjects revealed no significant decreases in night waking from baseline. Richman went on to suggest that hypnotic drugs are of limited usefulness and should only be used in short-term (two to three weeks), carefully monitored treatments.

Many other drugs have been suggested in the treatment of sleep disorders. Unfortunately, research regarding their efficacy with children is sparse. The studies reviewed above highlight the controversial nature of drug treatment in childhood sleep disorders. It is clear, however, that certain medications may provide short-duration symptom relief. In certain situations, a combination of medication and behavioral methods (to be reviewed next) may be the optimal solution for intractable sleep problems.

*Behavioral Interventions*

Extinction procedures (e.g., ignoring the cries of the child) are often recommended as a first effort at treating bedtime disturbances or disruptive night waking. In a classic extinction study (Williams 1959), these procedures were used to effectively eliminate the bedtime disturbances of a 4-year-old boy. The treatment involved the withdrawal of parental attention during nighttime tantrums. The tantrums were successfully eliminated until the boy's grandmother attended to his disruptive behavior. The tantrums were subsequently reduced after parental attention was again withdrawn. Unfortunately, an obstacle encountered when using extinction is that caretakers frequently find it difficult to ignore the cries of children for an extended period of time (Milan et al. 1981, Rolider and Van Houten 1984).

An alternative to extinction that is often recommended for bedtime disturbances is graduated extinction (Ferber 1985). In a study by Rolider and Van Houten (1984) parents were trained to use a graduated extinction procedure to decrease crying at bedtime. The procedure consisted of delaying parental attention when the child cried for a specified amount of time and then briefly attending to the child. The duration of time spent ignoring their child increased by five minutes in each subsequent interval, but the parents were allowed to attend to their child after waiting the specified amount of time. This graduated extinction procedure resulted in a decrease in the children's crying. In addition, it enabled the parents to attend to their children without reinforcing the crying. Similar graduated extinction procedures have also been used effectively to reduce night waking in children (Durand and Mindell 1990, Mindell and Durand 1993, Rolider and Van Houten 1984).

Scheduled awakenings have also been used successfully to reduce night wakings in children (Johnson et al. 1981, Johnson and Lerner 1985, Rickert and Johnson 1988). Scheduled awakenings entail having the parents wake the child fifteen to sixty minutes before a spontaneous awakening and doing what they normally do when the child wakes them (e.g., give backrubs, hugs, bottles, and so forth). As the frequency of spontaneous wakings decreases, the scheduled wakings are eliminated.

Other behavioral interventions that have been used to treat sleep disorders include time-out and social reinforcement (Ronen 1991), the establishment of stable bedtime and wake-up routines (Weissbluth

1982), relaxation training (Anderson 1979), and shaping of an earlier bedtime (Piazza and Fisher 1991). Adams and Rickert (1989) found that graduated extinction and positive bedtime routines were equally effective in reducing bedtime disturbances in a group of thirty-six young children.

Treatment of multiple sleep disorders frequently combines many of the previously mentioned interventions. In one study (Ronen 1991), a 4-year-old girl with bedtime disturbances and night wakings was treated using extinction, time-out, social reinforcement, and immediate rewards. Durand and Mindell (1990) used graduated extinction successfully to treat both night wakings and bedtime disturbances in a 14-month-old girl. Richman and colleagues (1985) used graduated extinction, positive reinforcement, shaping (making a gradually earlier bedtime), and establishing a stable bedtime routine successfully to treat night wakings and bedtime disturbances.

The treatment literature on multiple sleep disorders has usually focused on one disorder at a time (Durand and Mindell 1990, Ronen 1991). However, in one recent exception we have found that intervention designed to help one problem may effectively resolve other sleep problems. We examined the multiple sleep problems displayed by six young children whose average age at intervention was approximately 3 years (Mindell and Durand 1993). Each of these children exhibited bedtime disturbances characterized by tantrums and other efforts to resist going to sleep. The children also displayed frequent instances of night waking, averaging one and a half per night. A combination of interventions was used to improve the bedtime problems, including establishing bedtime routines and using graduated extinction (gradually fading attention to tantrums). This package of treatments was successful in reducing the bedtime disturbances of all of the children, and importantly, also resulted in a near elimination of night waking for five of the six children. Although night waking was not specifically targeted, the improvement of bedtime disturbances appeared to lead to improvements in this second sleep disturbance.

Several explanations may account for the success of this intervention for multiple sleep disturbances. It is possible, for example, that the establishment of bedtime routines and the reduction of behavior problems helped normalize sleep patterns in the children. At the same time, although parents reported no change in their handling of the children during night waking, the training given to them surrounding bedtime problems may have influenced how they reacted to the children waking at night. It should be noted that it may be premature to speculate too much on the mechanisms involved in this finding. Future treatment research should address how interventions affect sleep-related behavior across a spectrum of problem areas.

## Treatment Approach

Given the often complex nature of sleep problems exhibited by children, a single approach or set of approaches is usually not appropriate for treating multiple sleep problems (see Mindell and Durand 1993 for a possible exception). Intervention often takes place on multiple aspects of the problem simultaneously. Therefore, a clinician must be familiar with the range of approaches used to intervene specifically on sleep problems as well as on the associated issues that surround the sleep problems (e.g., unrealistic expectations by parents, cultural differences in sleeping arrangements, anxiety-related concerns). We have found the integrative multidimensional model alluded to previously helpful in guiding these intervention activities. What follows are two case descriptions that illustrate this model and describe our efforts to treat multiple sleep disorders using a range of approaches.

### Case 1: Paul

Paul, a 16-year-old boy, had a chief complaint of excessive daytime sleepiness. Paul reported that for at least the past two years he fell asleep at inappropriate times such as while at church or during school. In addition, he had difficulty functioning in the morning. Paul generally went to sleep between 1:00 and 1:30 A.M. and was out of bed at approximately 7:30 A.M. on weekdays. On weekends, Paul's schedule was similar. He rarely slept in on weekdays or weekends; however, if he was able to he would sleep until at least 12:00 noon. Paul's mother had to wake him in the morning and typically it took one hour until he was finally out of bed. Upon awakening, he described feeling groggy and unable to function as well as he would like. He was frequently late to school because of this problem. Throughout the day Paul often dozed off when sitting quietly, such as while reading or riding a bus. However, he denied sleepiness while driving or watching television or movies. Furthermore, Paul napped two to four times per week after school from approximately 6:00 P.M. to 9:00 P.M. He often missed dinner because of his sleepiness. Even after getting a good night's sleep Paul still felt sleepy upon awakening in the morning. He described that he could fall asleep at almost anytime. Paul denied awareness of snoring or awakening with a snore or shortness of breath. On occasion, he had early morning headaches. There was no history of cataplexy; however, Paul had experienced sleep paralysis and hypnagogic hallucinations several times.

Paul's schedule and excessive daytime sleepiness appeared to be consistent with inadequate total sleep nightly, that is, sleep deprivation. However, there was the possibility of an underlying sleep disrupter such as sleep apnea or narcolepsy that needed to be considered. In order to fully characterize his sleep disorder an all night sleep recording and multiple sleep latency test were done. Paul was instructed to maintain a regular sleep schedule with a bedtime of 11:00 P.M. and wake time of 7:00 A.M. prior to the sleep study.

His PSG results were significant for snore arousals, mild sleep apnea, and prior sleep deprivation. In addition, his multiple sleep latency test results indicated a severe degree of daytime sleepiness and he experienced REM sleep during two of his four naps. His snore arousals and mild sleep apnea alone did not account for these results. However, as Paul continued his prior sleep schedule of going to bed between 1:00 and 1:30 A.M. and awakening between 6:00 and 6:30 A.M., and thus was extremely sleep deprived, it was difficult to assess if he also had diagnosable narcolepsy as insufficient sleep could lead to these findings.

It was recommended that Paul be evaluated by an ear, nose, and throat specialist for a possible tonsillectomy and adenoidectomy to treat his problems with snoring and mild sleep apnea. It was further recommended that Paul maintain a very regular sleep schedule to alleviate his problems with sleep deprivation. He was to have a bedtime of between 10:00 and 10:30 P.M. with a wake time between 6:30 and 7:00 A.M. In addition, Paul's weekend schedule was discussed with the potential of rearranging his activities so he might sleep later on weekends. He was asked to keep daily logs and return in eight weeks for follow-up. At that time, if Paul had maintained a regular sleep schedule, an all-night sleep recording and multiple sleep latency test would be repeated in order to fully characterize his sleep disorder. At follow-up, Paul had undergone a tonsillectomy and adenoidectomy that significantly reduced his snoring and alleviated his problems with sleep apnea and was maintaining a regular sleep schedule. A repeat PSG and MSLT were conducted to further assess his potential narcolepsy. On the follow-up testing, Paul again had REM sleep on two of his four naps and was excessively sleepy. It was concluded that in addition to being sleep deprived in the past and having a history of sleep apnea Paul had diagnosable narcolepsy. His narcolepsy was then treated with a combination of medication and sleep scheduling.

This case is an excellent illustration of multiple sleep problems. Paul had a two-year history of being sleepy throughout the day. His final diagnoses were primary snoring, obstructive sleep apnea, narcolepsy, and insufficient sleep. All four sleep problems required treatment. Without the thorough evaluation that was conducted he would probably have continued to have sleep problems since the diagnosis of narcolepsy would have been missed. This case highlights the importance of conducting a comprehensive sleep assessment that evaluates all major sleep disorders.

## Case 2: Nick

Nick was 12 years old at the time of our first contact, and had received a diagnosis of autism. He lived at home with his natural father, stepmother and half sister, attending an integrated sixth grade class at the local public school. Nick exhibited frequent self-injurious behavior (primarily poking his own eyes). He also engaged daily in disruptive behavior at home and at school (e.g., throwing objects, breaking windows). In addition to Nick's disability and challenging behaviors, he exhibited multiple sleep disorders. Nick experienced difficulties initiating sleep, and it was common for him to be awake four or five hours after his parents had put him to bed. During this time he would engage in very destructive and disturbing behaviors (e.g., screaming, yelling, throwing things, banging on the walls). Nick's bedtime disturbances were very frequent, occurring almost nightly.

Occasionally Nick also experienced difficulties maintaining sleep. After sleeping for a few hours he would awaken in the middle of the night and be unable to fall back to sleep. During these night wakings he would engage in many of the same problematic behaviors. These night wakings occurred once or twice a month. Two or three nights per month Nick did not sleep at all, remaining awake all night engaging in disruptive behaviors. Sometimes sleepless nights were consecutive; one extreme instance lasted for five nights.

Nick's parents were quite concerned about his sleeping and behavioral difficulties at bedtime. He was frequently tired during the school day. His parents were also concerned about the effect his sleep disorders were having on them. During Nick's awake times at night he was very loud and frequently destructive, a situation which was very stressful for his tired parents. His loud activities commonly woke his sister as well.

Nick had been seen by a neurologist for his sleep disorders. Several trials of medication had been tried in an effort to increase the amount of time Nick slept. Benadryl was administered initially, but Nick reacted paradoxically, becoming more agitated and staying up later. He was switched to Inderal temporarily, but it had no effect on his sleep. Mellaril was then prescribed with some success. Nick received Mellaril every night shortly before bedtime. His parents reported that Nick would fall asleep much more easily (i.e., within twenty to thirty minutes), and without as many disruptions. Unfortunately, the Mellaril had some undesirable side effects. Nick gained forty pounds in four months while on the drug. On one occasion he also managed to drink a large quantity of the Mellaril, which precipitated emergency treatment. As a result of the problems with Mellaril, his parents were anxious to try nonmedical treatments to intervene with Nick's sleep problems.

Of primary concern to his parents was the disruptive behavior at bedtime and the subsequent inability to fall asleep. Nick had a relatively stable bedtime routine. Data were collected to get a baseline on Nick's sleep disorders. During baseline, Nick received Mellaril an average of every other night. It took Nick an average of two hours to fall asleep after being placed in his bed and told to go to sleep (range: fifty minutes to not falling asleep at all). He exhibited several occurrences of night waking and several sleepless nights during baseline.

Following this baseline period, the treatment plan was developed. It was suggested to the parents that Nick could benefit from a later bedtime. Eight o'clock was early for someone of Nick's chronological age. Nick's parents were reluctant to change his bedtime because they valued their time alone in the evening. However, they did agree to allow Nick to remain awake and playing in his room until 10:00.

The treatment plan consisted of the following. Nick participated in the established routine at 8:00 but was allowed to play
quietly in his room until 10:00. His parents would only attend to
Nick during this period if it sounded as though he were in danger of
injuring himself. At 10:00 an alarm would sound. His parents would
enter Nick's room and tell him it was time to go to sleep. They would
sit on the bed with him and spend some quiet time with him (i.e.,
rubbing his back, talking quietly). After fifteen minutes of this quiet
time they would tell him it was time to go to sleep, turn off the light,
and leave the room.

If Nick got out of bed, his parents employed a graduated
extinction procedure. They were instructed to delay their attention
to Nick and to keep all interactions with him neutral. When Nick
got out of bed they waited five minutes and then entered his room.
Nick's parents would tell him to get in bed and go to sleep. If
necessary, they would assist Nick to bed with minimal physical
contact. If he got out of bed again they would wait five minutes
longer and repeat the same procedure. Each subsequent time Nick
got out of bed they waited five additional minutes. Each time they
entered the room they kept their attention to a minimum and
avoided physical contact. When Nick experienced night wakings his
parents would use the same graduated extinction procedure.

After treatment began Nick was falling asleep an average of
forty-five minutes after he was told to go to sleep. This was an
improvement over the average of two hours to initiate sleep during
baseline. During baseline Nick stayed up all night at least once a
month. During treatment and at two follow-up points, there were
no sleepless nights. The number of night wakings did not decrease
significantly with treatment, but the amount of time he was awake
during these night wakings did decrease. In addition, Nick received
Mellaril less frequently during treatment, receiving it only a few
times a month by the end of the treatment phase. It is interesting to
note that on nights when he did not receive the medication his
parents gave him a placebo that tasted very similar to the Mellaril.
They felt it was important to Nick to believe he was receiving
Mellaril every night. He seemed to enjoy taking the Mellaril and
looked forward to it as part of his bedtime routine.

Nick's parents reported being very happy using the graduated
extinction procedures. They felt they were able to take some control
over Nick's seemingly uncontrollable sleep disorders. It was neces-

sary to work closely with the family and set realistic goals for them. Ideally, Nick's parents would have liked him to be asleep by 8:00, but they eventually realized that was probably not an attainable goal. The role of the clinician in this case was to help the parents develop an intervention they felt comfortable using and to provide support and encouragement for their efforts to intervene with their son's sleep disorder. The graduated extinction procedure and later bedtime were effective in reducing the amount of time it took Nick to fall asleep at night.

## Summary

Significant advances have been made in our understanding and treatment of children's sleep disturbances. What is unfolding from this improved knowledge of sleep problems is an appreciation of the dynamic nature of the interplay between biology and the environment in these disorders. We suggest that only by addressing all aspects of these problems will a satisfactory resolution be forthcoming for these children. The integrative multidimensional model of sleep disturbances presented in this chapter provides a guideline for identifying the varied influences contributing to sleep disturbances among children. Especially when multiple sleep problems are present, it is important to assess and possibly intervene in a number of different aspects of the child and family's life. We stress the integration of both biological and psychological intervention efforts to fully address the multifaceted problems surrounding sleep disturbances. Clearly, more work is needed to develop our model and its implications for treatment. However, it is anticipated that through this work improved care for children with sleep problems is at hand.

## References

Adair, R., Bauchner, H., Philipp, B., et al. (1991). Night waking during infancy: role of parent presence at bedtime. *Pediatrics* 87:500–504.

Adams, L. A., and Rickert, V. I. (1989). Reducing bedtime tantrums: comparison between positive routines and graduated extinction. *Pediatrics* 84:756–761.

American Academy of Child and Adolescent Psychiatry (1991). *Textbook of Child and Adolescent Psychiatry*, ed. J. M. Weiner. Washington, D.C.: American Psychiatric Press.

American Sleep Disorders Association (1990). *The International Classification of Sleep Disorders: Diagnostic and Coding Manual.* Rochester, MN: Author.

Anders, T. F. (1979). Night waking in infants in their first year of life. *Pediatrics* 63:860–864.

Anders, T. F., Halpern, L. F., and Hua, J. (1992). Sleeping through the night: a developmental perspective. *Pediatrics* 90:554–560.

Anderson, D. (1979). Treatment of insomnia in a 13-year-old boy by relaxation training and reduction of parental attention. *Journal of Behavior Therapy and Experimental Psychiatry* 10:263–265.

Barlow, D. H., and Durand, V. M. (in press). *Abnormal Psychology: An Integrative Approach.* Pacific Grove, CA: Brooks/Cole.

Blampied, N. M., and France, K. G. (1993). A behavioral model of infant sleep disturbance. *Journal of Applied Behavior Analysis* 26:477–492.

Cameron, O. G. and Thyer, B. A. (1985). Treatment of pavor nocturnus with alprazolam. *Journal of Clinical Psychiatry* 46:504.

Coffey, B. J. (1993). Review and update: benzodiazepines in childhood and adolescence. *Psychiatric Annals* 23:332–339.

Durand, V. M., and Mindell, J. A. (1990). Behavioral treatment of multiple childhood sleep disorders. *Behavior Modification* 14:37–49.

Ferber, R. (1985). *Solve your child's sleep problems.* New York: Simon and Schuster.

Ferber, R., and Boyle, M. P. (1983). Sleeplessness in infants and toddlers: sleep initiation difficulty masquerading as sleep maintenance insomnia. *Sleep Research* 12:240.

Fisher, C., Kahn, E., Edwards, A., and Davis, D. M. (1973). A psychophysiological study of nightmares and night terrors: the suppression of stage 4 night terrors with diazepam. *Archives of General Psychiatry* 28:252–259.

France, K. G., Blampied, N. M., and Wilkinson, P. (1991). Treatment of infant sleep disturbance by trimeprazine in combination with extinction. *Journal of Developmental and Behavioral Pediatrics* 12:308–314.

Glick, B. S., Schulman, D., and Turecki, S. (1971). Diazepam (Valium) treatment in childhood sleep disorders: a preliminary investigation. *Diseases of the Nervous System* 32:565–566.

Hauri, P. J. (1991). Sleep hygiene, relaxation therapy, and cognitive

interventions. In *Case Studies in Insomnia*, ed. P. J. Hauri, pp. 65–84. New York: Plenum Medical Books.

Herskowitz, J. and Rosman, N. P. (1982). *Pediatrics, Neurology, and Psychiatry: Common Ground.* New York: Macmillan.

Hollister, L. E. (1978). *Clinical pharmacology of psychotherapeutic drugs.* New York: Churchill Livingstone.

Johnson, C. M., Bradley-Johnson, S., and Stack, J. M. (1981). Decreasing the frequency of infant's nocturnal crying with the use of scheduled awakenings. *Family Practice Research Journal* 1:98–104.

Johnson, C. M., and Lerner, M. (1985). Amelioration of infants' sleep disturbances: II. Effects of scheduled awakenings by compliant parents. *Infant Mental Health Journal* 6:21–30.

Kahn, A., Van de Merckt, C., Rebuffat, E., et al. (1989). Sleep problems in healthy preadolescents. *Pediatrics* 84:542–546.

Kales, A., Bixler, E. O., Tan, T. L., et al. (1974). Chronic hypnotic drug use: ineffectiveness, drug withdrawal insomnia, and dependence. *Journal of the American Medical Association* 5:573–577.

Kales, A., Scharf, M. B., Kales, J. D., and Soldatos, C. R. (1979). Rebound insomnia: a potential hazard following withdrawal of certain benzodiazepines. *Journal of the American Medical Association* 241:1691–1695.

Kales, A., Soldatos, C. R., and Kales, J. D. (1987). Sleep disorders: insomnia, sleepwalking, night terrors, nightmares, and enuresis. *Annals of Internal Medicine* 106:582–592.

Kohen, D. P., Mahowald, M. W., and Rosen, G. M. (1992). Sleep-terror disorder in children: the role of self-hypnosis in management. *American Journal of Clinical Hypnosis* 34:232–244.

Lee, K. (1992). Pattern of night waking and crying of Korean infants from 3 months to 2 years old and its relation with various factors. *Journal of Developmental & Behavioral Pediatrics* 13:326–330.

McDaniel, K. D. (1986). Pharmacologic treatment of psychiatric and neurodevelopmental disorders in children and adolescents (Part 1). *Clinical Pediatrics* 25:65–71.

Milan, M. A., Mitchell, Z. P., Berger, M. I., and Pierson, D. F. (1981). Positive routines: a rapid alternative to extinction for elimination of bedtime tantrum behavior. *Child Behavior Therapy* 3:13–25.

Mindell, J. A. (1993). Sleep disorders in children. *Health Psychology* 12:151–162.

Mindell, J. A., and Durand, V. M. (1993). Treatment of childhood sleep disorders: generalization across disorders and effects on family members. *Journal of Pediatric Psychology* 18:731–750.

Morelli, G. A., Rogoff, B., Oppenheim, D., and Goldsmith, D. (1992). Cultural variation in infants' sleeping arrangements: questions of independence. *Developmental Psychology* 28:604–613.

Morin, C. M. (1993). *Insomnia: Psychological Assessment and Management.* New York: Guilford.

Ounstead, M. K., and Hendrick, A. M. (1977). The first-born child: patterns of development. *Developmental Medicine and Child Neurology* 19:446–453.

Pesikoff, R. B., and Davis, P. C. (1971). Treatment of pavor nocturnus and somnambulism in children. *American Journal of Psychiatry* 129:134–137.

Piazza, C. C., and Fisher, W. W. (1991). A faded bedtime with response cost protocol for treatment of multiple sleep problems in children. *Journal of Applied Behavior Analysis* 24:129–140.

Popoviciu, L., and Corfariu, O. (1983). Efficacy and safety of midazolam in the treatment of night terrors in children. *British Journal of Clinical Pharmacology* 16:97–102.

Richman, N. (1985). A double-blind drug trial of treatment in young children with waking problems. *Journal of Child Psychology and Psychiatry* 26:591–598.

Richman, N., Douglas, J., Hunt, H., et al. (1985). Behavioural methods in the treatment of sleep disorders: a pilot study. *Journal of Child Psychology and Psychiatry* 26:581–590.

Rickert, V. I., and Johnson, C. M. (1988). Reducing nocturnal awakening and crying episodes in infants and young children: a comparison between scheduled awakenings and systematic ignoring. *Pediatrics* 81:203–212.

Rolider, A., and Van Houten, R. (1984). Training parents to use extinction to eliminate nighttime crying by gradually increasing the criteria for ignoring crying. *Education and Treatment of Children* 7:119–124.

Ronen, T. (1991). Intervention package for treating sleep disorders in a four-year-old girl. *Journal of Behavior Therapy and Experimental Psychiatry* 22:141–148.

Russo, R., Gururaj, V., and Allen, J. (1976). The effectiveness of diphenhydramine HCl in paediatric sleep disorders. *Journal of Clinical Pharmacology* 16:284–288.

Sadeh, A. (1994). Assessment of intervention for infant night waking:

parental reports and activity-based home monitoring. *Journal of Consulting and Clinical Psychology* 62:63–68.

Salzarulo, P., and Chevalier, A. (1983). Sleep problems in children and their relationships with early disturbances of the waking–sleeping rhythms. *Sleep* 6:47–51.

Simonoff, E. A., and Stores, G. (1987). Controlled trial of trimeprazine tartrate for night waking. *Archives of Disease in Childhood* 62:253–257.

Spielman, A. J., and Glovinsky, P. (1991). The varied nature of insomnia. In *Case Studies in Insomnia*, ed. P. J. Hauri pp. 1–15. New York: Plenum.

Weissbluth, M. (1982). Modification of sleep schedule with reduction of night waking: a case report. *Sleep* 5:262–266.

Williams, C. D. (1959). The elimination of tantrum behavior by extinction procedures. *Journal of Abnormal Social Psychology* 59:269–273.

# Index

Abuse. *See* Child abuse
Adenoids, obstructive sleep
    apnea, 255–257
Adenotonsillectomy, obstructive
    sleep apnea, 261–262
Adolescence, sleep in, 10–11
Adults, sleep in, 11–13
Aggression, sleepwalking and,
    139
Alarm procedures
    nocturnal bruxism, 215–216
    urine alarm treatment,
    enuresis, 227, 228,
    236–237
Alcoholism, nightmares, 159
American Sleep Disorders
    Association (ASDA), 177,
    179, 311
Anxiety
    fears and, 74–75
    nighttime fear treatment, 72

sleepwalking and, 139
Anxiety disorders, childhood
    panic disorder, 285–288.
    *See also* Childhood panic
    disorder
Anxiety dreams
    definitions, 151
    sleepwalking, assessment and
    differential diagnosis,
    141
Apnea. *See* Obstructive sleep
    apnea; Sleep apnea
    syndrome
Apparent Life Threatening
    Events (ALTE), 18
Arousal, enuresis, 233–235
Art, nightmare treatment, 169
Artificial airways, obstructive
    sleep apnea, 262
Association of Sleep Disorders
    Centers (ASDC), 1, 3

Attachment issues, toddler sleep
   problems, 109–110
Attention, narcolepsy and, 270

Bedtime fading, toddler sleep
   problem treatment, 113
Bed-wetting. See Enuresis
Behavior
   enuresis and, 228
   sleep disorders and, xi
Behavioral interventions,
   childhood panic disorder
   treatment, 298
   enuresis, 227
   infant night waking, 55–65.
      See also Infant night
      waking: behavioral
      interventions
   multiple sleep disorders,
      322–324
   nightmares, 163
   nightmare treatment, 169
   night terror management,
      129–130
   toddler sleep problem
      treatment, 112–115
Biofeedback, nocturnal bruxism,
   215–216
Biological factors
   multiple sleep disorders,
      315–319
   nightmares, 161
Biteplane splints, nocturnal
   bruxism, 214–215
Botulism, sudden infant death
   syndrome (SIDS), 23–24
Brain
   hypothalamus, narcolepsy,
      271
Brain lesion, narcolepsy, 271

Brainstem, sudden infant death
   syndrome (SIDS), 21
Brainstem monoaminergic
   system, childhood panic
   disorder, 293–294
Bruxism. See Nocturnal bruxism

Cardiac arrhythmia, sudden
   infant death syndrome
   (SIDS), 23
Cardiorespiratory home
   monitor, SIDS treatment,
   33–35
Cardiovascular system,
   obstructive sleep apnea, 258
Cataplexy, 268, 269. See also
   Narcolepsy
Causal analysis, nighttime fear
   treatment, 78–80
Causation, nightmares, 159
Central nervous system
   immaturity of, sleepwalking
      and, 140
   nocturnal bruxism, 211
Cerebral palsy, obstructive sleep
   apnea, 257
Child abuse
   lifelong nightmare, 161–162
   nightmares, 158–159
Childhood
   nighttime fears, 76
   sleep in, 10
Childhood insomnia. See
   Insomnia
Childhood panic disorder,
   285–310
   anxiety disorders, 285–288
   assessment and differential
      diagnosis, 288–291
   dream anxiety disorder, 289

frequent wakings, 289, 291
generally, 288
night terrors and
  somnambulism, 290
nocturnal seizures, 290–291
settling to bed difficulty,
  288–289
sleep initiation difficulty, 289,
  291
sleep panic attacks, 289
case illustration, 301–306
empirical evidence and,
  293–297
epidemiology, 286
theoretical issues, 292–293
treatment, 297–301
  behavior management
    strategies, 298
  comprehensive approaches,
    301
  parent education, 297–298
  pharmacotherapy, 299–301
  relaxation, self-hypnosis,
    and cognitive
    strategies, 298–299
Circadian rhythm, sudden infant
  death syndrome (SIDS), 23
Cognition
  insomnia, assessment and
    differential diagnosis,
    182–183
  narcolepsy and, 270
Cognitive activation, insomnia,
  theory and research,
  185–186
Cognitive-developmental
  approach, nighttime fear
  treatment, 76–81
Cognitive reframing
  insomnia treatment, 191–192

nighttime fear treatment,
  87–88
sleep paralysis, 150
Cognitive strategies, childhood
  panic disorder treatment,
  298–299
Collages, nightmare treatment,
  169
Comorbidity, nighttime fear
  treatment, 72
Computerized tomography (CT),
  night terrors, 127
Conditioning procedures,
  sleepwalking, 143
Confusional arousal,
  sleepwalking, assessment
  and differential diagnosis,
  141
Continuous positive airway
  pressure (CPAP)
  obstructive sleep apnea, 262
  sleep apnea syndrome, 6
Cortical evoked potentials,
  narcolepsy, 276
Cot death. See Sudden infant
  death syndrome (SIDS)
Crib-bed shift, toddler sleep
  problems, 105–106
Crib death. See Sudden infant
  death syndrome (SIDS)
Culture
  infant night waking, 53
  multiple sleep disorders, 316,
    318

Delayed sleep phase syndrome,
  described, 3–5
Dental theories, of nocturnal
  bruxism, 203–204

Depression, nighttime fear
    treatment, 72
Desensitization
    nightmare treatment, 169
    nighttime fear treatment, 82
Developmental factors, 9–13
    adolescence, 10–11
    childhood, 10
    enuresis, 225–226
    infancy, 9–10
    night terrors, 126–127
    nighttime fears, 69–70, 75–76
    obstructive sleep apnea, 255,
        257
    sudden infant death syndrome
        (SIDS), 20
    toddler sleep problems,
        103–124. See also Toddler
        sleep problems
    young adult, 11–13
Diabetes, enuresis, 226
Diagnostic and Statistical
    Manual-III-R (DSM-III-R)
    enuresis, 224
    panic disorder, 286
Diphtheria-tetanus-pertussis
    (DPT) immunization,
    sudden infant death
    syndrome, 31
Disturbed nighttime sleep,
    narcolepsy and, 269–270
Down's syndrome, obstructive
    sleep apnea, 257
Drawing, nightmare treatment,
    169
Dream anxiety disorder,
    childhood panic disorder,
    differential diagnosis, 289,
    294–295
Dream interpretation, nightmare
    treatment, 169–170

Dream rescripting, nightmare
    treatment, 163, 167
Dry Bed Training, 236, 238–239
Dysphagia, obstructive sleep
    apnea, 258

Education
    nightmare treatment, 167–169
    parent, childhood panic
        disorder treatment,
        297–298
Electroencephalography (EEG)
    childhood panic disorder, 290
    enuresis, 223, 232, 234
    multiple sleep disorders, 313
    narcolepsy, 274–275
    night terrors, 127, 128
    nocturnal bruxism, 209, 210
    obstructive sleep apnea,
        259–260
    sleep studies, 2, 7
    sleepwalking and, 139, 140
Electromyography (EMG)
    narcolepsy, 274–275
    nocturnal bruxism, 212,
        215–216
    obstructive sleep apnea,
        259–260
    periodic leg movements,
        narcolepsy and, 270
    sleep studies, 2, 7
Electrooculogram (EOG)
    obstructive sleep apnea,
        259–260
    sleep research, 7
Enuresis, 223–252
    case illustration, 242–245
    diagnosis and assessment,
        225–229
    generally, 225–226
    medical, 226–227

psychological, 227–229
epidemiology, 225
overview of, 223
problem of, 224–225
research summary, 233–237
    arousability research,
        234–235
    generally, 233
    sleep stage research, 233–234
    treatment research, 235–237
theoretical issues, 229–233
treatment, 237–241
    Dry Bed Training, 238–239
    Full Spectrum Home
        Training, 239–241
    generally, 237–238
Environment, fears and, 73–74,
    80, 91–92
Enzymology, sudden infant
    death syndrome (SIDS),
    20–21
Epilepsy, childhood panic
    disorder treatment, 300–301
Ethnicity, infant night waking,
    53
Evoked potentials, cortical,
    narcolepsy, 276
Extinction
    gradual
        infant night waking, 57–59
        toddler sleep problem
            treatment, 112
    infant night waking, 56–57
    toddler sleep problem
        treatment, 112
Eye movements, sleep and, 1–2

Face and conquer techniques,
    nightmares, 164
Failure to thrive, obstructive
    sleep apnea, 258

Family dynamics. See also
    Parents
    enuresis, 228
    nightmares, 159
Fears. See Night terrors;
    Nighttime fear treatment
Fiberoptic nasopharyngoscopy,
    obstructive sleep apnea, 261
Full Spectrum Home Training,
    enuresis treatment, 239–241
Functional bladder capacity,
    enuresis, 232

Gastroesophageal reflux,
    obstructive sleep apnea, 257
Genetics
    enuresis, 229–230
    lifelong nightmare, 161–162
    narcolepsy, 272–273
    nightmares, 161
    night terrors, 128
    sleepwalking, 138
Gradual extinction. See also
    Extinction
    infant night waking, 57–59
    toddler sleep problem
        treatment, 112

Hallucination, narcolepsy and,
    268, 269
Heart
    cardiorespiratory home
        monitor, SIDS treatment,
        33–35
    obstructive sleep apnea, 258
    sudden infant death syndrome
        (SIDS), 23
Hydrocephalus, narcolepsy, 271
Hyperarousal, insomnia theory
    and research, 184–185

Hypersomnia, narcolepsy,
    differential diagnosis,
    277–278
Hypnosis
    nocturnal bruxism, 215
    self-hypnosis, childhood panic
        disorder treatment,
        298–299
    sleepwalking, 143
Hypothalamus, narcolepsy, 271
Hypoxemia, obstructive sleep
    apnea, 258

Idiopathic hypersomnia,
    narcolepsy, differential
    diagnosis, 278
Infancy
    infant–parent interaction,
        infant night waking,
        52–53
    nighttime fears, 75–76
    sleep in, 9–10
Infant night waking, 49–68
    behavioral interventions,
        55–65
        extinction, 56–57
        generally, 55–56
        gradual extinction, 57–59
        quick-check method, 59–65
            case examples, 62–65
            described, 59–62
    causes of, 51–52
    frequency, 49
    infant–parent interaction,
        52–53
    pharmacotherapy, 53–55
    sleep patterns and, 50–51
Insomnia, 177–201
    assessment and differential
        diagnosis, 180–183
        cognitions and

        psychopathology,
            182–183
        generally, 180
        history of presenting
            complaint, 181
        medical history and
            medications, 181–182
        presenting complaint
            description, 180–181
        sleep hygiene and habits,
            182
        sleep logs, 183
    case illustration, 192–194
    definition and prevalence,
        178–180
    overview of, 177–178
    theory and research, 183–188
        cognitive activation,
            185–186
        generally, 183–184
        hyperarousal, 184–185
        psychological dysfunction,
            186–187
        sleep deprivation, 187–188
    treatment, 188–192
        cognitive restructuring,
            191–192
        generally, 188
        pharmacotherapy, 191
        sleep hygiene counseling,
            188–189
        sleep restriction, 190
        stimulus control, 189–190
Interpretation. See Dream
    interpretation
Intrapsychic factors, nightmares,
    160–161

Klein-Levin syndrome,
    narcolepsy, differential
    diagnosis, 278

Leg movements, narcolepsy and, 269–270
Lifelong nightmare, theoretical issues, 161–162

Magical cures, nightmare treatment, 166–167
Media
    fears and, 73
    nighttime fear treatment, 91–92
Medical history, insomnia assessment and differential diagnosis, 181–182
Medical illness. *See also* Psychopathology; Surgical management
    enuresis, 226–227
    infant night waking, 52
    insomnia assessment and differential diagnosis, 181–182
    narcolepsy, 271–272
    nocturnal bruxism, 211
    obstructive sleep apnea, 257, 258
    sleepwalking, 139–140
Medications, insomnia assessment and differential diagnosis, 181–182. *See also* Pharmacotherapy
Migraine, sleepwalking and, 140
Modeling, fears and, 73
Monoaminergic system
    childhood panic disorder, 293–294
    narcolepsy, 272
Multiple sleep disorders, 311–333
    assessment and differential diagnosis, 312–315
    case illustrations, 324–329

integrated multidimensional model of, 315–319
    overview of, 311–312
    prevalence of, 312
    treatment research, 319–324
        behavioral interventions, 322–324
        medical interventions, 319–321
Multiple sleep latency test
    multiple sleep disorders, 313–314
    sleep research, 8–9

Narcolepsy, 267–284
    case illustration, 280–281
    clinical features of, 268–271
    diagnosis, 273–276
    differential diagnosis, 276–278
    genetics, 272–273
    management of, 278–280
    overview of, 267–268
    pathophysiology, 271–272
Nasopharyngoscopy, obstructive sleep apnea, 261
Nephritis, enuresis, 226
Neurochemistry
    enuresis, 230
    narcolepsy, 271–272
    sudden infant death syndrome (SIDS), 21–23
Neurological disorder, nocturnal bruxism, 211
Neuromuscular disorder, obstructive sleep apnea, 257, 262
Neuropsychology, narcolepsy and, 270
Neurotransmitter, sudden infant death syndrome (SIDS), 23

Nightmares, 149–175
case example, 170–171
definitions, 149–153
anxiety dreams, 151
nightmares, 149–150
self-definitions, 151–152
sleep paralysis versus
nightmares, 150–151
traumatic nightmares,
152–153
diagnosis, 157–159
night terror disorder
compared, 157–158
pathology, 158–159
prevalence, 153–157
frequency, 155–157
reliability, 153–155
universality, 153
research summary, 162–165
theoretical issues, 159–162
biological emphasis, 161
causation, 159
intrapsychic emphasis,
160–161
lifelong nightmare, 161–162
stress, 159–160
treatment, 165–170
desensitization, 169
dream rescripting, 167
flexibility in, 165
interpretation, 169–170
magical cures, 166–167
reassurance and education,
167–169
sleep hygiene, 165–166
writing, drawing, and
collages, 169
Night terrors, 125–134
assessment and differential
diagnosis, 127–128

case example, 130–131
childhood panic disorder and,
290, 295–297
definition and presentation,
126–127
management of, 128–130
behavioral treatments,
129–130
generally, 128–129
parental counseling, 130
pharmacotherapy, 129
psychotherapeutic
treatments, 129
nightmare and, 150, 157–158
overview of, 125
pathogenesis of, 128
sleepwalking, assessment and
differential diagnosis, 141
Nighttime fear treatment,
69–102
assessment and differential
diagnosis, 70–72
case example, 89–96
integrative approach, 85–89
overview of, 69–70
research summary, 81–85
theoretical issues, 72–81
cognitive-developmental
approach, 76–81
developmental factors, 75–76
single-factor theories, 72–75
Night waking. See Infant night
waking
Nocturnal bruxism, 203–222
assessment, 212
consequences of, 212–214
overview of, 203–204
sleep and, 208–211
theories of
dental, 203–204

integrative theories,
207–208
psychological, 204–207
systemic theories, 211
treatment, 214–217
Nocturnal seizures
childhood panic disorder and,
290–291
sleepwalking and, 138–139,
141–142
Non-rapid eye movement
(NREM) sleep. *See also*
Rapid eye movement (REM)
sleep; Sleep–wake cycle
childhood panic disorder
contrasted, 295–296
described, 1–3, 17
developmental effects, 9–13
narcolepsy, 271
night terrors, 127
sleepwalking, 135–136, 137
sudden infant death
syndrome, 25, 28, 30, 37
Noradrenaline, sudden infant
death syndrome (SIDS),
21–23


Obesity, obstructive sleep apnea,
258
Obstructive sleep apnea,
253–266. *See also* Sleep
apnea syndrome
case illustration, 262–263
causes and contributing
factors, 255–257
complications of, 257–258
definitions, 254
diagnostic studies, 258–261
epidemiology, 254

historical perspective on,
253–254
treatment, 261–262

Panic disorder. *See* Childhood
panic disorder
Parents. *See also* Family
dynamics
counseling of, night terror
management, 130
education of, childhood panic
disorder treatment,
297–298
enuresis, 228
infant–parent interaction,
infant night waking,
52–53
relationship with child,
toddler sleep problems,
109–110
toddler sleep problem
treatment, 115–116
Pathophysiology, narcolepsy,
271–272. *See also* Medical
illness
Pavor nocturnus. *See* Night
terrors
Periodic leg movements,
narcolepsy and, 269–270
Pharmacotherapy
childhood panic disorder
treatment, 299–301
enuresis, 227, 236
infant night waking, 53–55
insomnia treatment, 191
multiple sleep disorders,
319–321
narcolepsy, 278–279
night terror management, 129
nocturnal bruxism, 214–215

Pharmacotherapy (*continued*)
    toddler sleep problem
        treatment, 111–112
Phobias. *See* Night terrors;
    Nighttime fear treatment
Physical illness. *See* Medical
    illness
Physiological hyperarousal,
    insomnia theory and
    research, 184–185
Polysomnography
    childhood panic disorder
        contrasted, 295–296
    multiple sleep disorders, 313
    narcolepsy, 274
    obstructive sleep apnea, 259
    sleep research, 7–8
Position, sudden infant death
    syndrome (SIDS), 24
Positive reinforcement, toddler
    sleep problem treatment,
    113–114
Positron emission tomography,
    childhood panic disorder,
    294
Premature infant, sudden infant
    death syndrome and, 19–20
Primary disorder of vigilance,
    narcolepsy, differential
    diagnosis, 277–278
Prototype emotion theory,
    nighttime fear treatment, 77
Psychoanalysis, nightmares, 164
Psychopathology. *See also*
    Medical illness
    insomnia
        assessment and differential
            diagnosis, 182–183
        theory and research,
            186–187
    lifelong nightmare, 161–162

nightmares, 158–159
Psychopharmacology. *See*
    Pharmacotherapy
Psychotherapy
    night terror management, 129
    sleepwalking, 143

Rapid eye movement (REM)
    sleep. *See also* Non-rapid eye
        movement (NREM) sleep;
        Sleep–wake cycle
    described, 1–3, 17
    developmental effects, 9–13
    enuresis, 234
    narcolepsy, 267, 271, 272, 274,
        275, 278
    nightmares, 161
    night terrors, 127
    nocturnal bruxism, 209–211
    obstructive sleep apnea, 255,
        260
    sleepwalking, 135–136, 139
    sudden infant death
        syndrome, 25, 28, 30, 37
Rapid eye movement (REM)
    sleep behavior disorder,
    sleepwalking, assessment
    and differential diagnosis,
    141
Reassurance, nightmare
    treatment, 167–169
Reframing. *See* Cognitive
    reframing
Reinforcement practice method,
    nighttime fear treatment,
    81–82
Relaxation techniques
    childhood panic disorder
        treatment, 298–299
    sleep paralysis, 150–151
    sleepwalking, 143

Rescripting. *See* Dream
rescripting
Rett syndrome, nocturnal
bruxism, 211
Scheduled awakening, toddler
sleep problem treatment,
112–113
Schizophrenia, lifelong
nightmare, 161–162
School, nighttime fear
treatment, 91
Secondary gains, insomnia
treatment, cognitive
restructuring, 192
Seizures (nocturnal)
childhood panic disorder,
290–291
sleepwalking and, 138–139,
141–142
Self-definitions, nightmares,
151–152
Self-hypnosis, childhood panic
disorder treatment, 298–299
Sleep
bruxism and, 208–211
developmental factors, 9–13
adolescence, 10–11
childhood, 10
infancy, 9–10
young adult, 11–13
physiology of, 1–3
Sleep apnea syndrome. *See also*
Obstructive sleep apnea
described, 5–7
sudden infant death syndrome
and, 18
Sleep deprivation, insomnia,
theory and research,
187–188
Sleep disorders. *See also entries*
*under specific disorders*

behavior and, xi
childhood panic disorder and,
285–310. *See also*
Childhood panic disorder
classification of, 3–7
delayed sleep phase
syndrome, 3–5
generally, 3
sleep apnea syndrome, 5–7
frequency, xi
Sleep hygiene
insomnia
assessment and differential
diagnosis, 182
treatment of, 188–189, 193
narcolepsy, 279–280
nightmare treatment, 165–166
Sleep logs, insomnia, assessment
and differential diagnosis,
183
Sleep paralysis
narcolepsy and, 269
nightmares versus, definitions,
150–151
Sleep position, sudden infant
death syndrome (SIDS), 24
Sleep research, 7–9
multiple sleep latency test, 8–9
polysomnographic studies, 7–8
Sleep restriction, insomnia
treatment, 190
Sleep terrors, sleepwalking,
assessment and differential
diagnosis, 141. *See also*
Night terrors
Sleep–wake cycle. *See also*
Non-rapid eye movement
(NREM) sleep; Rapid eye
movement (REM) sleep
infant night waking and,
50–51

Sleep–wake cycle (*continued*)
  multiple sleep disorders, 313
  toddler sleep problems,
    104–106
Sleepwalking, 135–147
  assessment and differential
    diagnosis, 140–142
  case illustration, 143–144
  childhood panic disorder, 290
  clinical features of, 136–137
  epidemiology of, 137–139
  overview of, 135–136
  pathophysiological
    considerations, 139–140
  treatment, 142–143
    generally, 142
    pharmacotherapy, 142–143
    suggested, 143
Snoring, obstructive sleep apnea,
  258
Somnambulism. *See*
  Sleepwalking
Sonography. *See*
  Ultrasonography
Stimulus control, insomnia
  treatment, 189–190
Stress
  multiple sleep disorders, 316
  nightmares, 159–160
  nocturnal bruxism, 206–207
Sudden A-Ventilatory Event
  (S.A.V.E.), 18, 27, 32, 37
Sudden infant death syndrome
  (SIDS), 15–47
  assessment and differential
    diagnosis, 17–20
  case presentation, 35–37
  defined, 15
  epidemiology, 16
  generally, 16–17

incidence, 16
  research summary, 25–32
  sleep apnea syndrome, 5
  theoretical issues, 20–24
  treatment of, 32–35
Suffocation, nightmare, 150
Suggestion, nightmare, 163
Surgical management. *See also*
  Medical illness
  enuresis, 227
  obstructive sleep apnea,
    261–262
Swallowing, obstructive sleep
  apnea, 258
Symbolic displacement, fears
  and, 73

Temporal displacement, fears
  and, 73
Toddler sleep problems,
  103–124
  assessment, 110
  case examples, 116–121
  definition and incidence,
    106–107
  intervention, 110
  overview of, 103–104
  predictors and correlates of,
    107–110
  sleep patterns, 104–106
  treatment, 111–116
    adjunctive treatment,
      115–116
    behavioral approaches,
      112–115
    pharmacotherapy, 111–112
Tonsils, obstructive sleep apnea,
  255–257
Tourette's syndrome,
  sleepwalking and, 139–140

Toxins, sudden infant death
    syndrome (SIDS), 23-24
Tracheotomy, obstructive sleep
    apnea, 262
Trauma
    enuresis, 231
    lifelong nightmare, 161-162
    nightmares, 159-160
    nighttime fear treatment, 78
Traumatic nightmares,
    definitions, 152-153

Ultrasonography
    enuresis, 226-227
    obstructive sleep apnea, 259
Universality, nightmares, 153

Upper respiratory infection
    (URI), sudden infant death
    syndrome and, 17-18
Urine alarm treatment,
    enuresis, 227, 228, 236-237
Uvulopalatopharyngoplasty,
    obstructive sleep apnea,
    262

Verbal mediation self-control
    approach, nighttime fear
    treatment, 82-85

Writing, nightmare treatment,
    169

Young adults, sleep in, 11-13